LABOR AND EMPLOYMENT

RELATIONS ASSOCIATION SERIES

The Ethics of Human Resources and Industrial Relations

EDITED BY

John W. Budd and James G. Scoville

First Edition

ISBN 0-913447-90-0

Price: $29.95

LABOR AND EMPLOYMENT RELATIONS ASSOCIATION SERIES
Proceedings of the Annual Meeting
Annual Research Volume
LERA 2002 Membership Directory (published every four years)
LERA Newsletter (published quarterly)
Perspectives on Work (published biannually)

Inquiries and other communications regarding membership, meetings, publications, and general affairs of the Association, as well as notice of address changes, should be addressed to the LERA National Office.

LABOR AND EMPLOYMENT RELATIONS ASSOCIATION
University of Illinois at Urbana-Champaign
121 Labor & Industrial Relations Bldg.
504 East Armory Ave.
Champaign, IL 61820
Telephone: 217/333-0072   Fax: 217/265-5130
Internet: www.irra.uiuc.edu   E-mail: irra@uiuc.edu

CONTENTS

Preface and Overview

In fixing wages, as in other actions, there are men who will not hesitate to gain their ends by deliberate dishonesty and extortion. Others ignore the moral side of the wage-contract merely because it does not attract their attention. The greater number, however, of those who strive to make the best possible bargain, regardless of any formal ethical standard of wages, seem to think that the contract is fair, inasmuch as it is free and made under rule of competition.

—John A. Ryan, *A Living Wage:
Its Ethical and Economic Aspects,* 1912

I'd keep making and selling the product. My job as a businessman is to be a profit center and to maximize return to the shareholders. It is the government's job to step in if a product is dangerous.

—Jeffrey Skilling, former CEO of Enron,
when asked what he would do if his company
was producing a dangerous product

The motivation for this edited volume is simple—ethics are important but almost always absent beyond hollow rhetoric in both the scholarship and practice of human resources and industrial relations (HRIR). National and international business leaders, policymakers, advocates, and critics frequently employ the rhetoric of ethics. There are calls for more ethical business practices, a more ethical global economy, and more ethics training for managers. In the business and economic spheres, many of the most pressing ethical issues involve the employment relationship, such as the rights of employees versus shareholders, employee privacy and monitoring, whistle blowing, pay equity, discrimination, employee safety, anti-union campaigns, and minimum labor standards. At the same time, there is vibrant scholarship in the field of business ethics in which ethical theories and moral philosophy are applied to business issues, but with just a few exceptions, traditional HRIR scholars are unaware of business ethics scholarship. The subject of ethics is clearly an underanalyzed area in HRIR. Since HRIR is ultimately about people and quality of life, there is a pressing need to develop the positive (analytical) and normative (prescriptive) applications of business ethics for the employment relationship in the context of research, practice, and teaching.

We therefore sought out a diverse set of authors to provide a comprehensive examination of major ethical theories and their application to important and wide-ranging HRIR issues. We are extremely proud of the group of contributors we were able to bring together in this volume. Some of the authors are familiar to traditional HRIR scholars, but we explicitly also included scholars from other fields such as business ethics and computer science to underscore the wide-ranging impact of ethical issues in HRIR and to demonstrate the vibrant possibilities for HRIR scholars to reach out to like-minded researchers in other disciplines. We also cast our net widely across what we define as the full spectrum of human resources and industrial relations—including not only traditional industrial relations topics such as labor–management relations, labor unions, and government regulation, but also human resource management topics such as selection, training, and compensation.

Against this backdrop of a diverse set of scholars and an inclusive vision of the broad domain of human resources and industrial relations, we organized this volume around four objectives:

1. To demonstrate the importance and power of using rigorous theoretical frameworks when addressing ethical issues in the employment relationship in research, practice, and teaching.

2. To reveal the broad nature of HRIR applications that are relevant to ethical issues.

3. To present both labor and management case studies to blend practitioner issues with the theories and applications.

4. To present all of the material in a fashion accessible to scholars, practitioners, and students who are not familiar with research in ethics.

The result is a balanced, accessible analysis of ethics in the employment relationship that includes both theory and application, supportive and critical views, and labor and management perspectives.

Overview of the Volume

We owe it to our readers to provide a quick guide to the subjects and issues tackled in the various chapters by our disparate team of authors. The volume itself is divided into three major sections: Ethical Theory, HRIR Applications, and Ethics in Practice; each section is focused on the subject of its title.

Section I, Ethical Theory, begins with our general overview of the importance of philosophical and ethical approaches to the whole field of human resources and industrial relations. This first chapter establishes the benchmark laissez-faire ethos of competition, profit-maximization, and efficiency that is rooted in utilitarian and libertarian ethical theories and sketches four alternative Western ethical theories. Chapter 1 also ties these ethical theories into theological and human rights scholarship on the employment relationship and introduces the reader to the important concepts of cultural relativism and ethical subjectivism. Varying theoretical perspectives that take issue with the benchmark utilitarian and libertarian ethical theories are discussed in more detail in the three remaining chapters in section I.

Chapter 2 is an extensive review by Bruce Kaufman of the narrow "scientific" viewpoint of 19th-century American economic orthodoxy and the range of moral and ethical objections raised by the institutional economists (exemplified by Ely, Commons, and the Wisconsin School) who were either forebears or founders of the then-new discipline of industrial relations. Its unifying ethical precepts were centered around the implications to be drawn from the conclusion that "labor is not a commodity." Kaufman notes that the field included a broad range of scholars and practitioners from personnel management across the spectrum to proponents of unionism and collective bargaining. By the end of the 20th century, Kaufman claims, this breadth had been replaced by a redefinition of industrial relations to focus solely on the "preferred option" of unions and collective bargaining. With this redefinition, industrial relations has lost sight of the broad ethical approach of the founders and may account for the crisis the field is confronting.

The next chapter in the Ethical Theory section brings Norman Bowie's neo-Kantian view to bear on aspects of the employment relationship in North America. Even though Kant's categorical imperative (developed here in three formulations) would certainly support the contention that labor should not be treated like a commodity—the initial position of the founders of industrial relations—Bowie's analysis of a wide range of contemporary employment practices shows that many of them are problematic in a Kantian view. Whether one agrees or disagrees with the finding that layoffs, the lack of meaningful work, and other prevalent practices are unethical, Bowie's chapter indisputably demonstrates the applicability of rigorous ethical analysis to central HRIR issues.

In chapter 4, the final chapter in the Ethical Theory section, James Scoville, John Lawler, and Xiang Yi outline three non-Western ethical frameworks—Confucian, Hindu, and Muslim approaches—and apply them to the employment relationship. The Confucian approach emphasizes relationships and connections, the Islamic approach focuses on justice, and the Hindu approach introduces the concepts of *dharma*, stewardship, and the business *ashram*. These non-Western frameworks provide rich contrasts to utilitarianism and libertarianism (and some other Western approaches) and are also increasingly important to understand because of globalization, especially outsourcing and migration. In a world where United States companies utilize call centers in India and Indian telephone companies outsource technical support to Sweden (Ericcson) and the United States (IBM), understanding major non-Western frameworks is imperative.

With a strong theoretical foundation established in section I, section II devotes four chapters to applying ethical theories to two specific topics (globalization and technology) and broader domains (human resource management and labor relations) within the broad field of HRIR. Hoyt Wheeler's chapter 5 on globalization identifies some of the major impacts of the growth of multinational business organizations that defy control by any nation-state. Fierce international competition in goods and services markets has been associated with worldwide pressures on labor standards and unionization. Wheeler discusses the ethical connections between these pressures and the push for corporate social responsibility and codes of conduct. While there are concerns with enforcement, these initiatives clearly underscore the importance of ethics in debates over globalization.

The tenor of chapter 6 by Richard Rosenberg, which examines the effects of technology on the workplace, is best summarized by the use of the word "assault" in his title. The technologies we work with have direct implications for the deskilling of jobs and loss of privacy rights in the workplace. Other technologies, especially those related to genetic testing, and pressures on employers to contain medical costs threaten the employability of whole segments of the labor force. To date, the law has not made much adjustment to these technological developments, which makes ethical discourse imperative. Like other key HRIR topics, technology should not be divorced from ethical analysis.

Ethical issues and practices in human resource management are the subject of Elizabeth Scott's chapter 7. She comprehensively addresses the questions of ethical approaches to the wide range of functional areas covered by human resource management: recruitment, training and development, motivation, retention, and termination. Special attention is paid to the HR manager's need to be cognizant of the organization's interests while treating employees as more than simply productive resources.

In chapter 8, John Delaney develops a similarly comprehensive analysis of ethical issues across the vast spectrum of important labor relations topics. Readers will be reassured to know that Delaney does not address the oft-beaten horse: is it ethical to bluff in bargaining? Instead, he addresses a number of more ethically serious issues related to employee voice, freedom of association, employer opposition to unions, the rights of strikers and nonstrikers, exclusive representation, and minority dissenters in majority-rule environments. Delaney's chapter explicitly reinforces an important theme that underlies the entire volume— different ethical theories frequently lead to different evaluations of HRIR practices, but it is better to confront these ethical debates directly than to suppress them. In other words, ethical analysis is not a magic bullet that solves longstanding conflicts, but such analyses can help us better understand the complex world of HRIR.

Section III of the volume focuses on ethics in practice. Chapter 9 by Jonathan Booth, Ronald Heinz, and Michael Howe presents a firsthand examination of key ethical issues in Allina Health System, a $2-billion health care system with more than 22,000 employees. In parallel fashion, chapter 10 by Linda Ewing presents a firsthand examination of key ethical issues in the United Auto Workers. While the authors recognize some challenges and limitations, these corporate and union case studies ultimately conclude that explicit ethical expectations—such as Allina's published values and the UAW's published Ethical Practices Codes—can positively shape individual action within organizations.

The final chapter by Gordon Lafer provocatively argues from a much more critical perspective that "business ethics" (and its subcomponent, "HRIR ethics") is necessarily an oxymoron in a capitalist world. If ethical behavior is costless, then it is meaningless; when a conflict arises between ethics and profits, then profits win. Ewing's chapter on the United Auto Workers is not a clear refutation of Lafer's stance, since unions do not subscribe to the profit orientation of a corporation. Booth, Heinz, and Howe's study of Allina Health System possibly comes closer to being the answer. Allina is a nonprofit organization, but the need to compete in the market for health care means that controlling costs is a constant consideration. In Allina's case, we see some cases where improved ethical approaches and standards—for example, moving from a punitive system to a more positive approach to dealing with medical mistakes—may yield returns to all. But the broad concern advanced by Lafer with squaring ethical considerations with the profit motive still lurks in the shadows. Lafer's closing chapter therefore serves as a sharp reminder that ethical issues in the employment relationship are complex and rich with competing perspectives.

In our view, issues of ethics in HRIR have been overlooked for far too long. These 11 chapters demonstrate that wide-ranging HRIR research, practice, and teaching can benefit significantly from increased positive and normative ethical analyses. Ethical scholarship warrants a place of prominence in the Labor and Employment Relations Association (LERA), and ethically informed debates over both private and public policies are needed. Through this volume, we hope to stimulate scholarly and practical consideration of ethical issues in all aspects of the employment relationship.

Acknowledgments

For their help and sacrifices in this endeavor, we are greatly indebted to the authors—without whom this volume would obviously not exist, and all of whom produced excellent chapters while meeting our deadlines in the face of their many other commitments—and to our families. We want to extend a particular note of thanks to Linda Ewing, Ron Heinz, and Mike Howe (the labor and management professionals who authored chapters 9 and 10), who took time from the demands of their professional lives to candidly share their real-world experiences. If dialogue on the ethics of human resources and industrial relations results, we trust all of the contributors will agree that it has been well worth it.

John W. Budd and James G. Scoville
Minneapolis, Minnesota
February 2005

CHAPTER 1

Moral Philosophy, Business Ethics, and the Employment Relationship

JOHN W. BUDD
University of Minnesota

JAMES G. SCOVILLE
University of Minnesota

Suppose a company is considering implementing a mandatory-overtime policy, in which workers are fired if they refuse a supervisor's order to work overtime. How is this action to be evaluated? Is it acceptable because it will improve economic efficiency, or because business owners have a right to establish working conditions as they choose? Alternatively, is such a policy troubling because it treats workers simply as factors of production or ignores relationships and communities that have been established? Or is it unfair because some (shareholders) benefit at the expense of others (workers)? Perhaps it just doesn't seem like the right thing to do. Each of these possibilities represents a different moral standard, or ethical theory.

Using ethical theories to evaluate behavior is an important normative application, but ethics can also be used for positive analyses. Consider the hypothetical managers as they wrestle with whether to implement a mandatory-overtime policy. Do they implement it for efficiency reasons? Or do they try to avoid it out of a concern for workers as humans, or a concern for the community, or for other reasons? Used in this way, ethics can help us *understand* actions in a positive, or analytical, sense, rather than *judge* them in a normative, or prescriptive, sense.

There is a wealth of normative and positive ethical problems in the field of human resources and industrial relations (HRIR)—the full range of issues and intellectual perspectives on the employment relationship, from human resource management policies to industrial relations institutions, from theories of the labor movement to theories of government regulation, from property rights to human rights, and from unitarist to pluralist to critical schools of thought.[1] Many examples jump out of the chapters in this volume: the standards of the employment relationship (chapter 2), employee participation (chapter 3), gender issues (chapter 4), international labor standards (chapter 5), employee monitoring (chapter 6), compensation (chapter 7), strikes (chapter 8), values-based HR decision making (chapter 9), union representation on corporate boards of directors (chapter 10), and the profit motive (chapter 11), to name just one example from each.

Such issues are sometimes explicitly analyzed in ethical terms. Budd (2004) and Muirhead (2004) root their standards of the employment relationship in Aristotelian, Kantian, and Rawlsian ethical theories. Legge (1998, forthcoming) and Schumann (2001) also analyze a selection of human resource management problems using these and other ethical theories, while Bowie (1999) focuses on the Kantian implications for contemporary employment practices. Provis (2000) explores the ethical implications of deceptive labor negotiations, and a number of human resource management issues are analyzed in Winstanley and Woodall (2000). But echoing the findings of some of these authors (e.g., Winstanley and Woodall 2000; Schumann 2001; Budd 2004), we note that scholarship on ethics in HRIR is rare. This is unfortunate.

The lack of attention paid to ethics in HRIR scholarship stems partially from the liberal market ethos of free choice; recall the quote from Ryan (1912:5) at the start of the preface that an employment outcome is typically perceived as fair if "it is free and made under rule of competition." This deeply ingrained belief that "impersonal market forces . . . produce efficient and equitable results" undermines the importance of ethical analysis and has created a "moral vacuum" with respect to employment issues (Osterman et al. 2001:12). The problem is that this emphasis on free choice is not ethics-free; rather, it reflects a specific ethical theory.

One might also be tempted to argue that work is required for survival— "a necessary response to nature's stinginess" (Muirhead 2004:4). If work is natural or in some sense preordained, then there is little basis for discussing the ethical aspects of work. But this is overly simplistic. "Work of some sort is necessary for survival, but modern employment—working for someone else in a limited-liability corporation—was created by society to serve human and social ends" (Budd 2004:33). "Work may be necessary, but our organization of it is not; as such it invites evaluation and justification" (Muirhead 2004:6). The modern employment relationship should clearly be open to ethical analysis and debate.

In academia, the moral vacuum surrounding employment issues is reinforced by the allure of value-free scientific analysis. But employment research is implicitly shaped by our underlying values. Research that focuses exclusively on whether outcomes are efficient, or whether practices and institutions improve productivity, embodies a normative judgment that efficiency concerns are paramount. Scholarship that is rooted in narrowly defined utility functions assumes that self-interest is more important than other motivators. An emphasis on economic transactions and markets reflects a belief that other types of relationships are not as important. But even setting aside the criticism that research is not value free, the lack of ethics in HRIR research misses the potential for ethical theory to help us understand behavior from an analytical and explanatory perspective. For example, variations in the ethical work climate can be hypothesized to relate to employee decision making and therefore help explain organizational outcomes (e.g., Barnett and Vaicys 2000). So the omission of ethics from HRIR scholarship is problematic even in a positivist vein.

In the practice and scholarship of HRIR, it is important to make the implicit ethical theories explicit. To say that the "one and only one social responsibility of business [is] to use its resources and engage in activities designed to increase its profits so long as it stays within the rules of the game" (Friedman 1962:133) is not amoral—it is very much a moral conjecture, rooted in specific ethical theories. To design public policies or research studies from this same perspective is to embrace specific ethical theories. Ethical perspectives should be made explicit by the incorporation of business ethics scholarship into the practice and research of HRIR. Business ethics focuses on the application of moral philosophy to business institutions, practices, and decision making. While business ethics partly involves normative evaluations of specific actions as either right or wrong, moral or immoral, it also analyzes the underlying bases for decision making (Solomon 1992). In providing an overview of how moral philosophy and business ethics can be applied to the employment relationship, the remainder of this chapter constructs the intellectual foundations for this volume on *The Ethics of Human Resources and Industrial Relations*.

The Practical Importance of HRIR Ethics

If the field of HRIR does not add serious ethical analyses to its domain, it risks falling out of step with a significant area of practical concern. In short, HRIR must keep up with contemporary trends in business practices and management education. In the wake of recent corporate scandals—the collapse of Enron, bankruptcy of WorldCom, arrest of the CEO of Adelphia, charges against the CEO of Tyco International, the collapse of the Italian giant Parmalat—business ethics has mushroomed into high profile in corporations and business schools. According to the mainstream magazine *BusinessWeek*, "corrupted by the chase for an ever-greater piece of the action, accountants, lawyers, analysts, and managers have shirked their duty on a scale not seen since the 1920s" (Nussbaum 2002:32). In response to the multiple scandals, Congress enacted the Sarbanes-Oxley Act of 2002, which promotes greater transparency in an effort to promote ethical corporate behavior. Had any HRIR scholars been engaged in this debate, they could have pointed out that this was the philosophy that the Landrum-Griffin Act applied to unethical union practices in 1959.

Many companies also appear to have bolstered their efforts to portray themselves as ethical contributors to society. Raytheon has a vice president for business ethics and compliance, and its website indicates that "we must do more than be compliant with laws, regulations and policies; we must work according to our ethical principles and endeavor to conduct ourselves in a manner beyond reproach" (Raytheon Corporation n.d.). At ChevronTexaco, a 2002 glossy pamphlet on "The "ChevronTexaco Way" emphasizes that "[o]ur company's foundation is built on our Values, which distinguish us and guide our actions. We conduct our business in a socially responsible and ethical manner. We respect the law, support universal human rights, protect the environment, and benefit the communities where we work."

The values listed could almost have been created by Aristotle: integrity, trust, diversity, partnership, high performance, responsibility, growth. Citigroup issues an annual full-color, 50-page citizenship report emphasizing its "corporate citizenship accomplishments" with respect to the community, environment, workplace, and corporate governance. Its corporate code of conduct is available on its website in 14 languages; the first item listed is the responsibility of all employees to maintain ethical standards. The implications for HRIR are underscored by the fact that one of the suggested contacts when employees have ethical concerns is "Your Human Resources Representative." Various labor unions also have codes of conduct; the best-known U.S. example—the United Auto Workers Ethical Practices Code—is discussed in chapter 10 of this volume.

Various professional associations relevant to HRIR also have codes of conduct (Scoville 1993). The American Arbitration Association, the National Academy of Arbitrators, and the Federal Mediation and Conciliation Service jointly publish a "Code of Professional Responsibility for Arbitrators of Labor-Management Disputes." The Society for Human Resource Management (SHRM) has a "SHRM Code of Ethical and Professional Standards in Human Resource Management." As

TABLE 1
The Society for Human Resource Management (SHRM) Code of Ethics

The Six Core Principles of the SHRM Code of Ethical and Professional Standards in
Human Resource Management

- *Professional responsibility:* As HR professionals, we are responsible for adding value to the organizations we serve and contributing to the ethical success of those organizations. We accept professional responsibility for our individual decisions and actions. We are also advocates for the profession by engaging in activities that enhance its credibility and value.

- *Professional development·* As professionals we must strive to meet the highest standards of competence and commit to strengthen our competencies on a continuous basis.

- *Ethical leadership:* HR professionals are expected to exhibit individual leadership as a role model for maintaining the highest standards of ethical conduct.

- *Fairness and justice:* As human resource professionals, we are ethically responsible for promoting and fostering fairness and justice for all employees and their organizations.

- *Conflicts of interest:* As HR professionals, we must maintain a high level of trust with our stakeholders. We must protect the interests of our stakeholders as well as our professional integrity and should not engage in activities that create actual, apparent, or potential conflicts of interest.

- *Use of information:* HR professionals consider and protect the rights of individuals, especially in the acquisition and dissemination of information, while ensuring truthful communications and facilitating informed decision making.

Source: http://www.shrm.org/ethics/code-of-ethics.asp (accessed on February 25, 2005).
The full code also includes a description of each principle's intent and guidelines for implementation.

shown in Table 1, this code emphasizes professional responsibility, professional development, ethical leadership, fairness and justice, conflicts of interest, and the use of information. From the SHRM website, HR professionals can even download the code to their Palm Pilots.

Important questions about the extent to which such initiatives are intended to shape public opinion rather than actual behavior are certainly legitimate. But we don't think that there is much debate that the initiatives demonstrate that ethics are a high-profile issue, one that HRIR scholars and professionals ignore at their own peril. To stay relevant in business and other arenas, it is imperative that HRIR expand the use of ethical analysis into teaching as well as into research, policymaking, and professional practice. In fact, AACSB—the association responsible for accrediting U.S. business schools—is pushing very hard for business ethics to be included in management education (e.g., AACSB 2004).

One example of a textbook that incorporates ethics into HRIR teaching is Budd's new *Labor Relations: Striking a Balance* (2005a). Six rigorous ethical theories are presented in an early chapter, and an ethical template is presented to help students work through ethical problems. In subsequent chapters students are asked to apply the ethical theories to varied labor relations issues, including bargaining, strike replacements, union shop clauses, globalization, and ethical leadership. Other HRIR textbooks also include ethical discussion, but they often lack a foundation rooted in ethical theories. Business ethics, and the direct connections with many areas of HRIR, are too important for us to ignore or to trivialize in research, teaching, and practice.

The Ethics of the Laissez-Faire Employment Relationship

Corporate scandals and codes of ethics notwithstanding, the dominant liberal market ethos of the 21st century emphasizes the laissez-faire employment relationship based on employment-at-will, well-defined property rights, maximizing individual utility, and maximizing corporate profits. Government regulation is seen as harmful interference that prevents the optimal allocation of resources. Physical and intellectual property rights trump labor rights. Rational, self-interested behavior and economic incentives are emphasized and celebrated. Inequality is seen as a motivator and reward for extra effort and ability.

Because of the fundamental emphasis on freedom and consent, there is a tendency to view this laissez-faire model as amoral. Individual freedom is seen as a natural right—that is, rooted in a universal law of nature:

> Man being born, as has been proved, with a title to perfect freedom, and an uncontrolled enjoyment of all the rights and privileges of the law of nature, equally with any other man, or number of men in the world, hath by nature a power . . . to preserve his property, that is, his life, liberty and estate, against the injuries and attempts of other men (Locke 1690:341–2).

As a natural right, freedom is divorced from ethical debate. And mainstream economists style themselves as value-free scientists studying the allocation of scarce resources in a non-ethical or non-ideological fashion (Gallaway and Vedder 2003; compare Budd 2005b). But the laissez-faire employment relationship is not amoral, natural, or value free. Rather, it is rooted very strongly in two specific ethical theories: utilitarianism and libertarianism.

Utilitarianism focuses on maximizing aggregate welfare or utility by producing the greatest benefits at the least costs (Beauchamp and Bowie 1997). Jeremy Bentham and John Stuart Mill started with hedonistic utilitarianism—maximizing aggregate pleasure or happiness. Modern utilitarianism focuses on preference satisfaction. However utility is measured, utilitarianism is a teleological ethical theory (from the Greek word for "ends") and a consequentialist ethical theory (actions are judged solely by their consequences). Actions that maximize aggregate utility are ethical; others are not. The calculation of Freeman and Medoff (1984) of the social costs and benefits of labor unions is a utilitarian calculation; if, on net, labor unions are socially harmful, they should not be allowed, says utilitarianism. In human resource management, designing policies to provide workplace equity and voice solely because of their instrumental value in increasing efficiency and competitiveness is similarly rooted in utilitarianism.

Libertarianism emphasizes individual freedom—the negative right to noninterference. Only actions that harm others are unethical. A strong emphasis on freedom means that the definition of harm to others is quite narrow while property rights are quite broad. Providing unsafe working conditions is not considered harmful as long as the dangers are not hidden from employees and they freely accept employment; taxation to redistribute resources from the wealthy to the poor is a violation of private property. Whatever a free exchange between consenting adults produces is viewed as fair.

The combination of utilitarianism and libertarianism is a powerful philosophical foundation for the laissez-faire employment relationship. Utilitarianism supports competitive labor markets because of the belief that this is the best way to achieve efficiency and to maximize aggregate welfare. The first fundamental theorem of welfare economics demonstrates that every perfectly competitive equilibrium is "Pareto optimal," meaning that no one can be made better off without someone else being left worse off. In other words, the utilitarian ideal of "the greatest good for the greatest number" is achieved in competitive markets through free exchange. Libertarianism supports competitive labor markets because of the primacy of liberty. Workers should be free to work for whomever they choose; companies should have the freedom to hire and fire whomever they choose. Both utilitarianism and libertarianism therefore advocate strong property rights, the freedom to contract, and free exchange without interference. In fact, in writings on the employment relationship, it is sometimes difficult to separate the two philosophies (e.g., Friedman 1962; Epstein 1983; Baird 2000).

The ethical element of the laissez-faire employment relationship is underscored by the fact that justice has become marginal-productivity justice (McClelland 1990). Standard economic theory predicts that in competitive markets with rational agents, each factor of production will be compensated at the value of its marginal product. The wage rate for labor, for example, equals the value to the firm generated by hiring the last unit of labor. Utilitarianism and libertarianism turn theoretical assumptions and predictions into normative statements: "one *ought* to be rational" (Hausman and McPherson 1996:41, emphasis in original) and "factors of production *ought to be paid* the value of their marginal product" (McClelland 1990:19, emphasis in original). In other words, "the enterprise of business harbors a fundamentally utilitarian conception of the good society" (Beauchamp and Bowie 1997:22). It is worth emphasizing that the laissez-faire employment relationship is not devoid of ethical content; it is, in fact, premised on very specific ethical theories.

The Ethics of the Fully Human Employment Relationship

The logic of the utilitarian–libertarian–neoclassical economics nexus is powerful: free individuals pursuing their self-interests in unregulated competitive markets create efficient outcomes in which profits and welfare are maximized, each factor is rewarded with its value, and individual autonomy and freedom are preserved. This view can be criticized, however, for its narrow conception of freedom. Why does the freedom from harm to private property always override the freedom to work or the freedom from hunger (Donnelly 2003)? And in the context of work, freedom of choice for its own sake is excessively narrow; rather, "work worthy of free choice requires the kinds of work roles that are fitting for free, equal, and proud democratic citizens" (Muirhead 2004:94).

Also, industrial relations scholars have long questioned whether labor markets are sufficiently (yet not overly) competitive to make workers equal to corporations and therefore free (Commons 1919). This undermines not only libertarianism but also utilitarianism, because aggregate welfare is not necessarily maximized if markets are not perfectly competitive. In fact, with market imperfections and other inequalities within society, the libertarian–utilitarian nexus reduces to ethical egoism in which ethical behavior is the unabashed pursuit of individual self-interest irrespective of the greater good. Ethical egoism, however, is not accepted as a legitimate ethical theory by moral philosophers, for it rests on the unsupportable assumption that each of us possesses interests that are more special than everyone else's (Rachels 2003).

But even if markets are competitive (or aggregate welfare is maximized in other ways) and even if one can measure welfare, especially troublesome to critics of utilitarianism is that the ends justify the means (Solomon 1992; Hausman and McPherson 1996; Beauchamp and Bowie 1997; Bowie 1999). Rights and virtues are irrelevant, distributive justice and minimum living standards are not a concern, and procedural justice, communities, and relationships are important only so far as they increase aggregate welfare. Only the consequences matter.

Other major ethical theories address these criticisms in one way or another. Chapter 4 in this volume analyzes three non-Western ethical frameworks that contrast sharply with the ethics of the laissez-faire employment relationship. To provide a foundation for the remainder of this volume, four Western theories—the ethics of duty, fairness, virtue, and care—are discussed here and are summarized in Table 2.[2] These theories can be broadly labeled the ethics of the fully human employment relationship, because relative to the narrow property rights freedom of libertarianism and the "ends justifies the means" consequentialism of utilitarianism, these theories embrace work as a fully human activity and emphasize the importance of human dignity. Note further that the importance of human dignity implies that ethical analyses apply to both substantive work rules and outcomes on the one hand, and the governance or formative processes by which they are developed on the other.

Kantian Duty

The most important contrast to utilitarianism is the ethics of duty, in which normative judgments are based on the character of the action, not on its consequences. Most literally, people have a duty to act in certain ways, for example, not to lie, even if it does not produce the best outcome. The ethics of duty is rooted in Immanuel Kant's categorical imperative "Act only on that maxim by which you can at the same time will that it should become a universal law," which in turn is rooted in the belief that humans are rational beings capable of self-determination and self-governance (Bowie 1999). Every responsible person is therefore entitled to dignity and respect.

A common example in business ethics is employment discrimination—discriminatory treatment for arbitrary reasons violates the equal sanctity of all human life. Treating someone only as a means—for example, to increase your own or even aggregate wealth or utility—violates the intrinsic value and sanctity of human life. To fire a union supporter because you are afraid a union will increase wages and lower profits treats a worker as a means and is unethical. We therefore have a duty not to act in such ways. Kantian moral philosophy has other far-ranging and rich applications to HRIR ethics and is the focus of chapter 3 in this volume.

Kantian moral philosophy is not without its critics. Common, if oversimplified and inaccurate (Korsgaard 1996), criticisms of Kantian ethics attack the emphasis on universal, unwavering, rational rules for ignoring virtues and the meaning of a good person in everyday life (Solomon 1992). Scenarios like protecting an innocent person by lying are also used

TABLE 2
Six Western Ethical Frameworks for Human Resources and Industrial Relations

Ethical framework (founders)	Central element	Unethical actions	HRIR applications
Utility (Jeremy Bentham, John Stuart Mill)	Welfare or utility maximization through cost-benefit analysis	Inefficient or welfare-reducing behavior	Using HR policies solely to enhance efficiency; "union-free" strategies based on a cost-benefit analysis
Liberty (John Locke)	Negative right of freedom and liberty from noninterference through strong property rights	Forcing individuals to use themselves or their property against their will (including taxation for redistribution)	Employer participation in the union organizing process because of an employer's rights of private property and free speech
Duty (Immanuel Kant)	Respect for human dignity through the Kantian categorical imperative	Treating others in ways you would not want to be treated; treating people only as means, not also as ends	HR policies and labor standards based on employees as human beings and not solely as means to an end
Fairness (John Rawls)	Justice as liberty, equal opportunity, and concern for the least well-off through the veil of ignorance and the difference principle	Placing efficiency above liberty, equal opportunity, and concern for the least well-off	Concerns with inequalities between workers with respect to income, health insurance, and other compensation elements
Virtue (Aristotle)	Moral character to achieve flourishing through virtues and community	Actions contrary to virtues (vices), which prevent flourishing	HR policies based on excellence, integrity, and personal growth
Care (Carol Gilligan)	Nurturing personal relationships through caring for people	Failing to develop special relationships; relationships based on exploitation, disrespect, or injustice	Union initiatives to organize workers by developing special relationships with the workers, especially in female-dominated occupations

Source: Adapted from Table 4.1 in Budd (2004:68) and Box 3.4 in Budd (2005a:77).

to question the validity of ethical duties. Proponents of property rights and liberty object to the Kantian concern for others in lieu of a focus on individual liberties. Others note that Kantian moral philosophy ignores the development of relationships or concerns of distributive justice.

Rawlsian Fairness

John Rawls (1971) famously augmented the Kantian standard of inherent human equality with concern for the distribution of outcomes and thereby developed an ethical theory of distributive justice or fairness. Rawlsian justice is based on a veil of ignorance: individuals must determine the principles of justice behind a veil of ignorance in which they do not know their own characteristics (such as race, gender, social status, and abilities). Rawls (1971:83, 250) asserts that under such conditions, rational, self-interested, and equal individuals will agree to the following (ignoring intergenerational concerns):

1. Each person is to have an equal right to the most extensive total system of equal basic liberties compatible with a similar system of liberty for all.

2. Social and economic inequalities are to be arranged so that they are both:

   a. to the greatest benefit of the least advantaged, and

   b. attached to offices and positions open to all under conditions of fair equality of opportunity.

Principle 1 is the highest priority. This liberty principle includes private property rights, the right to vote, freedom of speech, and freedom from oppression and arbitrary seizure. Principle 2a is the difference principle, which allows inequalities in outcomes if these inequalities benefit the least-well-off members of society. Principle 2b requires equal opportunity—differential outcomes are acceptable only if they reflect legitimate differences in ability and effort, not arbitrary or discriminatory factors.

The ethical theory of Rawlsian fairness is very significant for HRIR ethics because it raises the importance of social justice and the nature of work (Budd 2004; Muirhead 2004). The veil of ignorance means that "what counts for the justice of work is not the actual consent we give when we take a job, but the consent we *would* give under ideal circumstances" (Muirhead 2004:31, emphasis in original). Individuals are unlikely to agree from behind the veil of ignorance to hierarchical, authoritarian workplaces, sweatshop working conditions, work that is not meaningful, and other elements of the modern employment relationship (unless the alternatives are even worse); hence such practices are difficult to justify against the Rawlsian liberty and difference principles. Efficiency is important, but it does not trump political liberties, equal opportunity, and concern for the least well-off.

Aristotelian Virtue

Utilitarianism, libertarianism, Kantian ethics, and Rawlsian ethics rely on outcomes, rights, and duties; missing is a concern with virtue and character (Solomon 1992). Tracing all the way back to Aristotle, the ethics of virtue emphasizes the type of person each individual ought to be—virtues are the characteristics that make a person a good human being and are necessary to live a good life as part of, and in service to, a social community (in Aristotle's lexicon, to flourish). Important virtues highlighted by Aristotle include courage, temperance, generosity, friendliness, truthfulness, and proportionality. This is not an ethical framework of atomistic individuals, and contemporary definitions of virtues echo this importance of community and interaction.

In the context of business ethics, virtue ethics sees corporations as human communities with a vital sense of purpose that both contribute to and have responsibilities in the larger social community. A corporation should be a collection of mutually dependent individuals in which individual excellence and virtues play a role in community success. Contributing to the community via the provision of quality goods and services will result in profits if done well, but a blind focus on profits should not be the sole driving force: profit is "a means of encouraging and rewarding hard work and investment, building a better business, and serving society better," not "an end in itself" (Solomon 1992:47).

Industrial relations scholars might recall that John R. Commons emphasized forbearance and the interdependence of individuals' utility functions (Kaufman 2003). Forbearance is essentially an amalgamation of Aristotelian virtues, so it should not be surprising that the Aristotelian emphasis on social purpose and interdependence is consistent with Commons's critique of neoclassical economics and its emphasis on profits and individual self-interest. Aristotelian justice also includes a central industrial relations belief: might does not make right (Solomon 1992). More generally, virtue ethics implies that employment should be characterized by cooperation, integrity, honesty, fairness, and tolerance. Work should fit with individuals so as to promote flourishing and self-development (Muirhead 2004).

Feminist Caring

Carol Gilligan (1982:79) asserts that the feminine voice consists of "defining the self and proclaiming its worth on the ability to care for and protect others." This yields an ethical theory rooted in caring—not caring about something, but caring *for* someone and nurturing that person's well-being. Ethical judgments are based not on rules or principles but on each particular situation's implications for relationships (Gilligan 1982; Noddings 1984). In some respects, the ethics of care is a special case of the Aristotelian tradition that emphasizes virtues and community, especially the virtues that are central to personal relationships (Beauchamp and Bowie 1997). In HRIR ethics, then, the application of the ethics of care is similar to the application of virtue ethics. The importance of the community has clear implications for managerial attitudes toward employee; for example, deceiving employees for personal gain is unethical because of the lack of care demonstrated (Schumann 2001).

But relative to virtue ethics, the ethics of care places special emphasis on particular relationships, such as parents, neighbors, co-workers, and friends. It is acceptable, even encouraged, to treat those people differently. A concrete HRIR application of legitimizing such special treatment would be to give priority to existing relationships with current workers and the local community when deciding whether to invest in an existing plant or open a new plant in another location. The strategy to create support for a union among Harvard University's largely female population of clerical and technical workers by developing one-on-one relationships was inspired by Gilligan's (1982) feminine voice and the ethics of care.

Ethics, Theology, and Human Rights

The four Western ethical theories that underline the ethics of the fully human employment relationship—the ethics of Kantian duty, Rawlsian fairness, Aristotelian virtues, and feminist caring—are all ultimately rooted in varying conceptions of human dignity. They are thus closely related to other areas of HRIR scholarship that are connected to theology and human rights.

Judeo-Christian views on the sanctity of human life and respect for human dignity often closely resemble secular ethical conceptions of human dignity. (Recall that non-Western traditions are discussed in chapter 4.) In the form of papal encyclicals, the Catholic Church has explicitly linked theology to the ethics of the employment relationship. Pope Leo XIII's *Rerum Novarum* ("On the Condition of Workers," 1891) asserts that "justice demands that the dignity of human personality be respected in [workers]. . . . It is shameful and inhuman, however, to use men as things for gain and to put no more value on them that what they are worth in muscle and energy" (§31). Why? Because "no one may with impunity outrage the dignity of man, which God Himself treats with great reverence, nor impede his course to that level of perfection which accords with eternal life in heaven" (§57).

Rerum Novarum therefore explicitly calls for a living wage, a limit on work hours, health standards, and restrictions on child labor. In *Laborem Exercens* ("On Human Work," 1981), Pope John Paul II also explicitly affirms the right of workers to a living wage, social insurance, safe work, and formation of labor unions. In Judaism, "a social justice imperative appears repeatedly in Talmudic decisions concerning worker rights" (Perry 1993:1). This yields important standards regarding the payment of wages, hours of work, and sick and disability pay (Weisfeld 1974; Perry 1993). Jewish doctrine is also very supportive of labor unions (Schnall 2001).

Human rights scholarship in employment research (e.g., Gross 1999, 2003; Santoro 2000; Adams 2001; Budd 2004) has also raised the profile of human rights in the HRIR context. The Judeo-Christian teachings on work parallel those found in the United Nations' Universal Declaration of Human Rights (1948) and the International Labour Organization's (ILO) Declaration on Fundamental Principles and Rights at Work (1998).[3] In particular, in the Universal Declaration, human rights include just and favorable conditions of work, including pay sufficient for an existence worthy of human dignity, equal pay for equal work, reasonable working hours, periodic paid holidays, unemployment and disability insurance, and the right to form labor unions. The eight fundamental ILO conventions specify that freedom of association and collective bargaining, the abolition of forced labor, equal opportunity and pay, and the elimination of child labor are "fundamental to the rights of human beings at work."

Judeo-Christian traditions, the human rights movement, and ethical theories beyond utilitarianism and libertarianism all "share a universal interest in addressing the integrity, worth, and dignity of all persons, and, consequently, the duty toward other people" (Lauren 1998:5). The common concerns are clearly articulated by principle 4 of the ILO's 1944 Declaration of Philadelphia: "[A]ll human beings, irrespective of race, creed or sex, have the right to pursue both their material well-being and their spiritual development in conditions of freedom and dignity, of economic security and equal opportunity" (International Labour Organization 1944).

Underlying this inherent dignity are the common beliefs of the major religions that humans are created in the image of God and the common beliefs of the intrinsic value and equality of human beings in diverse writings on natural law, moral philosophy, and political theory.

These commonalities have two important implications for ethical analysis in HRIR. One, through the use of theology and human rights, ethical analysis implicitly exists in HRIR scholarship. As such, ethical theory has already been accepted as relevant to HRIR, so it is not misguided to advocate for greater ethical scholarship in the field. Two, HRIR scholarship on human rights can be strengthened by the explicit rather than implicit use of ethical theory. Important concepts in moral philosophy and business ethics can enrich the human rights scholarship in HRIR, and perhaps give this scholarship broader impact.[4] For example, human rights scholarship in HRIR often recites the list of international human rights instruments (such as the Universal Declaration of Human Rights) that protect workers' rights (e.g., Gross 2003), but what's missing are careful explorations of the conceptions of human dignity that underlie these instruments. In the meantime, the reader of this volume is reminded that the ethical issues discussed throughout often have strong connections with religious thought and the human rights movement.

Ethical Subjectivism and Cultural Relativism

The ethical theories outlined in this chapter can be used both to analyze and understand behavior across the diverse span of HRIR and to make normative evaluations. In making evaluations, if we declare that someone did something ethically wrong or that a law should prevent certain actions, we are asserting that there are *universal* ethical standards that everyone should follow. Whenever a labor leader argues that business leaders should adhere to a Kantian moral philosophy or whenever a business leader maintains that labor leaders should embrace utilitarianism, an assertion is being made that one ethical standard is superior than the others.

Ethical subjectivism, however, asserts that moral judgments are really feelings, not facts, that there are no right and wrong answers and each person is entitled to his or her own views. Cultural relativism tends to reach the same conclusion: no single ethical theory is universal, either because of specific historical or cultural factors or because people's reasons for differing ethical beliefs are equally valid. The normative use of ethics through universalism, therefore, must overcome the challenges posed by ethical subjectivism and cultural relativism.

The apparent diversity in ethical codes over time and across cultures combined with a desire to be tolerant and respect cultural diversity lends support to the subjectivist and relativist critiques to universalism. But these critiques do not stand up under closer scrutiny (Donnelly 2003; Rachels 2003; Brannigan 2005). The existence of a diversity of views does not imply equal validity. Taken to their logical conclusions, subjectivism and relativism prevent condemnation of Nazi Germany's unconscionable atrocities in the Holocaust, or allow slavery. Moreover, tolerance is itself an ethical standard—to assert that everyone should be tolerant of all views, as in the extreme versions of subjectivism and relativism, is a universalistic view and therefore contradicts the basis of subjectivism and relativism.

Lastly, some alleged cultural differences in ethical standards are actually differences in implementation (Beauchamp and Bowie 1997). Consider, as an example, autocratic and high-performance human resource management systems. At first glance, these two systems appear to reflect different ethical standards—the autocratic system pays little attention to how workers are treated while the high-performance one pays close attention to distributive and procedural justice, employee voice mechanisms, and other issues. And yet, if both systems are simply seeking to maximize organizational performance (in particular, if the high-performance system treats workers with respect only to increase their performance), then the two in fact share a common ethical framework.[5] The differences are not in ethical standards, but in implementation.

Thus, it is widely accepted that at least some universal ethical standards exist. There is, of course, significant debate over the content of these universal standards, but we cannot dismiss these debates out of hand by falling back on arguments of ethical subjectivism or cultural relativism. Labor and management may have different ethical systems, but this does not mean that each is right or that it is futile to try to establish a societal standard. At the same time, there is value in respecting cultural diversity because implementation of ethical standards can vary, because not all issues involve ethical standards, and because there is value in considering new standards. As in other areas of HRIR, one must strike a balance, in this case between strict universalism and extreme relativism.

Conclusions and Future Directions

This chapter seeks to motivate ethical analyses in the field and practice of HRIR by sketching the important theories in moral philosophy that have been profitably applied to business ethics and by connecting these ethical theories to the employment relationship. Normative evaluations of HRIR issues are nothing new, but the ethical standards underlying such evaluations are not always clear. The six ethical frameworks outlined in this chapter provide a set of rigorous standards.

Consider again the vignette from the opening of the chapter in which a company implements a mandatory-overtime policy. The six evaluative responses presented there reflect the six theories in this chapter. Under utilitarianism, a mandatory-overtime policy is ethically acceptable if it improves economic efficiency and aggregate welfare. Under libertarianism, it is acceptable because business owners have a right to establish working conditions as they choose. In a Kantian ethical framework, such a policy is troubling because it treats workers simply as factors of production (as means, not ends). In a Rawlsian framework, the policy is troubling because some (shareholders) benefit at the expense of others (workers). In Aristotelian ethics, a mandatory-overtime policy might be unethical because it doesn't seem virtuous or consistent with human flourishing. And in the ethics of care, the policy is troubling because it doesn't respect the community and the relationships that have been established.

Ethical theories describe what should be of fundamental importance in society and provide a rigorous avenue for evaluating specific HRIR practices and outcomes. It almost goes without saying that there are differing views of which ethical standards are best, but the underlying theories provide the basis for debating these standards. Applying moral philosophy and business ethics to the employment relationship will not provide easy answers to the difficult debates in HRIR, but it will help us more fully identify and evaluate the consequences of alternative policies and practices.

In addition to being applied for such normative, or prescriptive, evaluations, ethical analysis in HRIR should also be used for positive, or analytical, applications. Natural, social, and behavioral research indicates that humans "will be inclined, conditionally, toward cooperation with others, toward concern with how we are viewed by others, toward hostility to those who fail to reciprocate our cooperation, and toward receptivity to moral reasoning that is consistent with these and other propensities." (Ben-Ner and Putterman 1998:5; also see Frank 2004).

Research has shown that ethics are an important determinant of behavior (Rest and Narváez 1994). The ethical dimensions of an organization's work climate moderate the relationship between ethical judgment and intended behavior (Barnett and Vaicys 2000). Ethical climate is related to forms of organizational governance and control (Wimbush, Shepard, and Markham 1997).

Since the human resource management wing of the HRIR field is rooted to a certain extent in industrial and organizational psychology, it often emphasizes behavioral determinants of decision making. Since the industrial relations wing is rooted to a certain extent in economics, it often emphasizes environmental determinants. An integrated model of decision making should then pair behavioral with environmental determinants (Kaufman

1989, 1999). Such an integrated model provides a rich opportunity for HRIR scholars to incorporate ethical analysis (Budd 2004, 2005a). Ethical climate and social norms are part of the environment; an individual's ethical framework is part of the behavioral determinants of decision making.

Finally, consider the words of a prominent contemporary moral philosopher: "To later generations, much of the moral philosophy of the twentieth century will look like a struggle to escape from utilitarianism" (Korsgaard 1996:275). The same might be said of HRIR in that it seeks to move beyond utilitarianism by imbuing the employment relationship with a respect for human dignity and justice and by imbuing research with realism beyond narrow utility-maximizing models. Explicit incorporation of ethical scholarship into employment research and practice—that is, recognizing the ethics of the human resources and industrial relations— therefore provides a rigorous framework for this central feature of the field and profession of human resources and industrial relations.

Notes

[1] In the context of the employment relationship, the terms *unitarist* and *pluralist* are typically attributed to Fox (1974). The unitarist theory of the employment relationship emphasizes shared interests between employers and employees (as in the human resources management tradition), the pluralist theory rests on combination of shared interests and conflicts of interests limited to the employment relationship (as in mainstream U.S. industrial relations), and critical theories are rooted in broader assumptions of societal conflicts between labor and capital (or other competing groups) (as in mainstream British industrial relations) (Budd 2004).

[2] This section draws heavily on Budd (2004, 2005a). Similar, though not identical, taxonomies of ethical theories for human resource management are developed in Legge (1998) and Schumann (2001).

[3] For more on the ILO Declaration on Fundamental Principles and Rights at Work, see http://www.ilo.org/dyn/declaris/. For more on the Universal Declaration of Human Rights, see http://www.un.org/rights/.

[4] We also recognize that human rights are often ultimately rooted in political theory and struggles; therefore, while human rights and ethical theories are closely linked, they are not one and the same. Human rights pertain to what humans are entitled to; ethics pertain to how humans should act. Moreover, there is a broader international consensus on the accepted list of human rights than on accepted theological and ethical theories (Donnelly 2003).

[5] The common ethical framework in this example is utilitarianism if one assumes that maximizing organizational performance also maximizes aggregate welfare; otherwise, the common ethical framework is ethical egoism.

References

Adams, Roy J. 2001. "Choice or Voice? Rethinking American Labor Policy in Light of the International Human Rights Consensus." *Employee Rights and Employment Policy Journal*, Vol. 5, no. 2, pp. 521–48.

Association to Advance Collegiate Schools of Business. 2004. *Ethics Education in Business Schools: Report of the Ethics Education Task Force to AACSB International's Board of Directors*. St. Louis: Association to Advance Collegiate Schools of Business.

Baird, Charles W. 2000. "Unions and Antitrust." *Journal of Labor Research*, Vol. 21, no. 4 (Fall), pp. 584–600.

Barnett, Tim, and Cheryl Vaicys. 2000. "The Moderating Effect of Individuals' Perceptions of Ethical Work Climate on Ethical Judgments and Behavior Intentions." *Journal of Business Ethics*, Vol. 27, no. 4 (October), pp. 351–62.

Beauchamp, Tom L., and Norman E. Bowie, eds. 1997. *Ethical Theory and Business*, 5th ed. Upper Saddle River, NJ: Prentice Hall.

Ben-Ner, Avner, and Louis Putterman. 1998. "Values and Institutions in Economic Analysis." In Avner Ben-Ner and Louis Putterman, eds., *Economics, Values, and Organization*. Cambridge, UK: Cambridge University Press, pp. 3-69.

Bowie, Norman E. 1999. *Business Ethics: A Kantian Perspective*. Malden, MA: Blackwell.

Brannigan, Michael C. 2005. *Ethics Across Cultures*. Boston: McGraw-Hill.

Budd, John W. 2004. *Employment with a Human Face: Balancing Efficiency, Equity, and Voice*. Ithaca, NY: ILR Press.

_____. 2005a. *Labor Relations: Striking a Balance*. Boston: McGraw-Hill/Irwin.

_____. 2005b. "Ideas versus Ideology: The Origins of Modern Labor Economics-Comment on Gallaway and Vedder." *Journal of Labor Research*, Vol. 26, no. 1 (Winter), pp. 177-80.

Commons, John R. 1919. *Industrial Goodwill*. New York: McGraw-Hill.

Donnelly, Jack. 2003. *Universal Human Rights in Theory and Practice*, 2nd ed. Ithaca: Cornell University Press.

Epstein, Richard A. 1983. "A Common Law for Labor Relations: A Critique of the New Deal Labor Legislation." *Yale Law Journal*, Vol. 92, no. 8 (July), pp. 1357–408.

Fox, Alan. 1974. *Beyond Contract: Work, Power and Trust Relations*. London: Farber and Farber.

Frank, Robert H. 2004. *What Price the Moral High Ground? Ethical Dilemmas in Competitive Environments*. Princeton, NJ: Princeton University Press.

Freeman, Richard B., and James L. Medoff. 1984. *What Do Unions Do?* New York: Basic Books.

Friedman, Milton. 1962. *Capitalism and Freedom*. Chicago: University of Chicago Press.

Gallaway, Lowell, and Richard Vedder. 2003. "Ideas versus Ideology: The Origins of Modern Labor Economics." *Journal of Labor Research*, Vol. 24, no. 4 (Fall), pp. 643–68.

Gilligan, Carol. 1982. *In a Different Voice: Psychological Theory and Women's Development*. Cambridge, MA: Harvard University Press.

Gross, James A. 1999. "A Human Rights Perspective on U.S. Labor Relations Law: A Violation of the Freedom of Association." *Employee Rights and Employment Policy Journal*, Vol. 3, no. 1, pp. 65–103.

_____, ed. 2003. *Workers Rights as Human Rights*. Ithaca, NY: Cornell University Press.

Hausman, Daniel M., and Michael S. McPherson. 1996. *Economic Analysis and Moral Philosophy*. Cambridge, UK: Cambridge University Press.

International Labour Organization. 1944. *Declaration of Philadelphia*.

International Labour Organization. 1998. *Declaration on Fundamental Principles and Rights at Work.*

Kaufman, Bruce E. 1989. "Models of Man in Industrial Relations Research." *Industrial and Labor Relations Review,* Vol. 43, no. 1 (October), pp. 72–88.

_____. 1999. "Expanding the Behavioral Foundations of Labor Economics." *Industrial and Labor Relations Review,* Vol. 52, no. 3 (April), pp. 361–92.

_____. 2003. "The Organization of Economic Activity: Insights from the Institutional Theory of John R. Commons." *Journal of Economic Behavior and Organization,* Vol. 52, no. 1 (September), pp. 71–96.

Korsgaard, Christine M. 1996. *Creating the Kingdom of Ends.* New York: Cambridge University Press.

Lauren, Paul Gordon. 1998. *The Evolution of International Human Rights: Visions Seen.* Philadelphia: University of Pennsylvania Press.

Legge, Karen. 1998. "Is HRM Ethical? Can HRM Be Ethical?" In Martin Parker, ed., *Ethics and Organizations.* London: Sage, pp. 150–72.

_____. Forthcoming. "Ethics and Work." In Marek Kocsynski, Randy Hodson, and Paul Edwards, eds., *Social Theory at Work.* Oxford: Oxford University Press.

Locke, John. 1690. *Two Treatises of Government.* Edited by Peter Laslett, 1960. Cambridge, UK: Cambridge University Press.

McClelland, Peter D. 1990. *The American Search for Justice.* Cambridge, MA: Basil Blackwell.

Muirhead, Russell. 2004. *Just Work.* Cambridge, MA: Harvard University Press.

Noddings, Nel. 1984. *Caring: A Feminine Approach to Ethics and Moral Education.* Berkeley: University of California Press.

Nussbaum, Bruce. 2002. "Can You Trust Anybody Anymore?" *BusinessWeek* (January 28), pp. 31–32.

Osterman, Paul, Thomas Kochan, Richard Locke, and Michael J. Piore. 2001. *Working in America: A Blueprint for the New Labor Market.* Cambridge: MIT Press.

Perry, Michael S. 1993. *Labor Rights in the Jewish Tradition.* New York: Jewish Labor Committee.

Provis, Chris. 2000. "Ethics, Deception, and Labor Negotiation." *Journal of Business Ethics,* Vol. 28, no. 2 (November), pp. 145–58.

Rachels, James. 2003. *The Elements of Moral Philosophy,* 4th ed. Boston: McGraw-Hill.

Rawls, John. 1971. *A Theory of Justice.* Cambridge, MA: Harvard University Press.

Raytheon Corporation. n.d. "Our Reputation: A Foundation Built on Personal Integrity and Ethical Principles." <http://www.raytheon.com/about/static/node3564.html>. [February 25, 2005].

Rest, James R., and Darcia Narváez, eds. 1994. *Moral Development in the Professions: Psychology and Applied Ethics.* Hillsdale, NJ: Lawrence Erlbaum Associates.

Ryan, John A. 1912. *A Living Wage: Its Ethical and Economic Aspects.* New York: Macmillan.

Santoro, Michael A. 2000. *Profits and Principles: Global Capitalism and Human Rights in China.* Ithaca, NY: Cornell University Press.

Schnall, David J. 2001. *By the Sweat of Your Brow: Reflections on Work and the Workplace in Classic Jewish Thought.* New York: Yeshiva University Press.

Schumann, Paul. 2001. "A Moral Principles Framework for Human Resource Management Ethics." *Human Resource Management Review,* Vol. 11, nos. 1–2

(Spring/Summer), pp. 93–111.
Scoville, James. 1993. "The Past and Present of Ethics in Industrial Relations." *Proceedings of the Forty-Fifth Annual Meeting* (Anaheim, CA, January 5–7). Madison, WI: Industrial Relations Research Association, pp. 198–206.
Solomon, Robert C. 1992. *Ethics and Excellence: Cooperation and Integrity in Business.* New York: Oxford University Press.
United Nations. 1948. *Universal Declaration of Human Rights.* General Assembly Resolution 217 A (III).
Weisfeld, Israel. 1974. *Labor Legislation in the Bible and Talmud.* New York: Yeshiva University Press.
Wimbush, James C., Jon M. Shepard, and Steven E. Markham. 1997. "An Empirical Examination of the Multi Dimensionality of Ethical Climate in Organizations." *Journal of Business Ethics*, Vol. 16, no. 1, pp. 67–77.
Winstanley, Diana, and Jean Woodall, eds. 2000. *Ethical Issues in Contemporary Human Resource Management.* New York: St. Martin's Press.

CHAPTER 2

The Social Welfare Objectives and Ethical Principles of Industrial Relations

BRUCE E. KAUFMAN
Georgia State University

The field of industrial relations (or employment relations) is a three-dimensional project. It represents an intellectual field of inquiry in the social sciences, an area of applied practice and policy dealing with work and employment, and a normative value statement about the social objectives and ethical principles that should guide the structure and practice of work. Elsewhere (Kaufman 2004a) I have called these three dimensions the "three faces of industrial relations."

Of these three faces, the ethical dimension is the least explored and articulated in the literature of the field. Among modern works, the most significant and insightful discussion is presented in Budd's recent book *Employment with a Human Face* (2004), while several articles provide shorter overviews (e.g., Barbash 1991, Scoville 1993). Several other authors (e.g., Kochan, Katz, and McKersie 1986; Godard and Delaney 2000) have also described in summary form the ideological/normative premises of modern industrial relations, although generally without explicitly linking these premises to a foundational set of ethical principles. Finally, in recent years a small but burgeoning literature has emerged on the linkage between labor rights and human rights (Compa 1996; Adams 1999; Friedman and Wood 2001; Gross 2003). Beyond these studies, however, the subject of ethics and industrial relations largely languishes in neglect. Surprisingly, for example, to the best of my knowledge no person has surveyed the early literature of industrial relations to identify the ethical principles that guided the founders of the field, nor has anyone compared the ethical position taken in these early writings with the position taken by contemporary authors.

With this lacuna in mind, I use this chapter as an opportunity to canvass this early literature and reconstruct and delineate the social objectives and ethical principles upon which the field was founded. My primary resource material is the writings of the early institutional econo-mists, including Ely, Commons, and Slichter, dating from the 1880s to the 1930s. I conclude that the fundamental normative principle of the field is that labor is embodied in human beings, and thus should not be treated as are other inanimate commodities in production and exchange. Building on this premise, I examine the social welfare objectives of industrial relations and conclude they encapsulate a trilogy of variables: efficiency, equity (social justice), and human self-actualization and self-development. I then move to modern times and survey contemporary literature with regard to the ethical and ideological principles of the field, finding both overlap and divergence with respect to the principles enunciated by the field's founders. The chapter ends with a brief discus-sion of implications.

The Ethical Face of Industrial Relations

As a formal institutionalized entity, the field of industrial relations first emerged in the United States around the year 1920. At this time the term "industrial relations" was defined broadly and subsumed both labor–management relations and personnel (human resource) manage-ment, or what today go by the acronyms IR and HR.

By the early 1930s industrial relations had developed three distinct "faces," or dimensions. The first was as an area of scientific inquiry and scholarly research about the employment relationship. The second was as an applied area of practice and policy aimed at solving labor problems in industry.

Early industrial relations also had a third dimension, defined in terms of ethical values and ideological positions with respect to the performance of work, the structure of the employment relationship, and the solution of labor problems. This dimension may be called its ethical/ideological face, or simply "ethical face" in recognition of the main subject of this chapter. I note for the sake of clarity, however, that ethics and ideology are distinct concepts: ethics is a set of moral principles about right and wrong in human conduct; ideology is a structure of firmly held beliefs and premises about how the world works and should work. Both are normative constructs and are generally linked, although perhaps only loosely and implicitly.

One does not have to look far in the early literature of industrial rela-tions to find evidence of the ethical and ideological dimensions of the field. That industrial relations had an ethical dimension, for example, is well illustrated in this statement by Sumner Slichter:

> There are two ways of looking at labor problems. One is the scientific point of view. . . . It is aspired to by the scientist who

studies trade unions, child labor, unemployment, in order to find out what *is* or what *might be*, without speculating about what *should be*. . . . To the vast majority of people, however, even to the economists and sociologists, the labor problem is more than this. It is also a matter of ethics, a matter not simply of what is or what might be, but of what should be. . . . From the ethical point of view, therefore, the labor problem is concerned with two principal things: with the effect of the prevailing institutions . . . upon the conflict between life and work, and with the institutional change needed to harmonize men's activities as laborers with their interests as men (1928:287, emphasis in original).

One can also find numerous normative statements of a more ideological nature about how industrial relations should be practiced and what social and political goals it should promote. Commons (1934b), for example, states that his goal in industrial relations was "to save capitalism by making it good" (p. 143) and "What I was trying to do, in my academic way, was to save Wisconsin and the nation from politics, socialism, or anarchism, in dealing with the momentous conflict of capital and labor" (p. 170). Commons was clearly staking out a normative position for industrial relations that was opposed to radical, anticapitalist solutions to labor problems. In a similar vein, industrialist John D. Rockefeller Jr., another early participant in the field, writes that the goal of industrial relations should be "the discovery of some mutual relationship between Labor and Capital which would afford to Labor the protection it needs against oppression and exploitation, while at the same time promoting its efficiency as an instrument of economic production" (1923:47–48). The ideological position articulated here is one of long standing in industrial relations—that both greater efficiency and equity are desirable and the best outcome is a balance of the two.

Given that early industrial relations had an ethical face, the next question is exactly what principles and premises comprised it. The quotations from Slichter, Commons, and Rockefeller provide hints, but a more detailed examination is required.

In the academic world the field of industrial relations largely grew out of the writings of the economists and intellectual allies associated with the early institutional school of economics. Indeed, I have suggested elsewhere (Kaufman 2004a) that in many respects industrial relations is the intellectual child of institutional economics and could equally well be called "institutional labor economics." To reconstruct the ethical principles and social welfare objectives of industrial relations, I look in depth at the writings of early institutional economists, including Commons,

Slichter, and Richard Ely, and compare their position with that of their main adversaries—the economists and allies of the classical and neoclassical schools. In places, writers from the personnel management wing of industrial relations, such as Rockefeller and his industrial relations advisor, William Lyon Mackenzie King, are also introduced to promote an inclusive and balanced viewpoint.

Institutional economics emerged and grew in America in the first three decades of the 20th century, although its roots go back to the "new economics" introduced in America by Ely and others in the mid-1880s. Many of these men did graduate work in Germany, where opposition to orthodox economics was intense and dedication to constructing a new "ethical" type of political economy strong (Koslowski 1995). In addition to the German historical–social school of economics, the early institutional economists drew inspiration from the British historical/heterodox school (particularly the work of Sidney and Beatrice Webb), the newly formed social science disciplines of psychology and sociology, the field of law and the "legal realist" movement, and the Social Gospel movement among American Protestants (Fine 1956; Koot 1987; Gonce 1996; Fried 1998). The writings of the early institutionalists spanned a wide variety of subjects, but none was more important than labor.

The quest for a "new economics" was driven in part by dissatisfaction with the dominant orthodox school of classical and neoclassical economics. Consideration of the position of the classical/neoclassical economists on ethics and the social welfare objectives of economics thus helps to place the position of the institutionalists in better context. Further adding value to this discussion is the fact that many of these points of debate continue to separate modern industrial relations and neoclassical labor economics.

The Ethical Principles of Early Classical/Neoclassical Economics

The roots of classical and neoclassical economics are found in Adam Smith's *Wealth of Nations* (1776), as to some degree are those of the institutional school. The main body of classical and neoclassical economics, however, was developed and formalized by later generations of English economists in the 19th century, including Ricardo, Mill, Jevons, and Marshall, as well as by continental European economists including Walras (France and Switzerland) and Menger (Germany). Although American economists of the 19th century did relatively little to develop and extend the theoretical base of classical/neoclassical economics, most were adherents of the orthodox school, and a number wholeheartedly embraced its conservative policy implications.

General Orientation. Classical economics used deductive logic and a few canonical laws and assumptions, such as the centrality of self-interest, the law of diminishing returns, the wage fund theory, and the Malthusian population theory, to derive what were intended to be universalistic theories concerning the determinants of exchange value (the prices of goods and the factors of production), long-run economic growth, and the distribution of income. Neoclassical economics, started in the early 1870s by Jevons, Walras, and others but not fully formed until the publication of Alfred Marshall's *Principles of Economics* in 1890, maintained the same broad theoretical and methodological orientation but fundamentally recast economic theory around the marginal principle and shifted attention from long-run growth to the microeconomic analysis of markets, supply/demand, and price determination.

Although many of the classical and neoclassical economists were concerned about social reform and the conditions of labor, their outlook on these matters was heavily constrained by the conclusions and implications of their theory and dedication to philosophical and political principles such as freedom of contract, individualism, political liberalism, Social Darwinism, and laissez-faire (Coats 1971). Also important was their desire to make economics a true science, which led them to exclude as much as possible ethical considerations and model the subject along the line of the physical sciences, especially physics (Mirowski 1989). All of these considerations led to a reaction in the other direction by the early institutional economists.

The first point to make about classical/neoclassical economics is that it defined its subject matter narrowly around the subjects of wealth and value. Naturally, the focus then becomes generating the maximum amount of both from society's scarce resources. Walras's *Elements of Pure Economics* (1874) provides a good illustration. He states that the object of an economy is the "increase of social wealth" (p. 73) and that the production and distribution of social wealth "must be equitable" (p. 75) lest the economy and society fall into disorder. Yet Walras then quickly removes consideration of justice and other ethical standards from the corpus of economics on the grounds that they introduce a nonscientific element into the subject. In particular, he argues that scientific cause-and-effect relationships can be deduced only for the portion of economic activity that involves exchange, while the acts of production and distribution (what he calls "industry" and "institutions") are perforce nonscientific because production is essentially a human-learned art and distribution rests on politics and ethical precepts of right and wrong. The part of economics that is a genuine science, therefore, is the theory of exchange and, in particular, the theory of price determination. With this argument in mind, Walras maintains that "this pure theory of economics is a science which resembles the physico-mathematical sciences in every respect" (p. 71) and "our task then is to discover the laws to which these purchases and sales tend to conform automatically. To this end, we shall suppose that the market is perfectly competitive, just as in pure mechanics we suppose, to start with, that machines are perfectly frictionless" (p. 84).

Other classical/neoclassical economists followed along the same lines, in the process removing ethics from economics and narrowing the core subject matter to a theoretical analysis of price and value determination in (largely) competitive markets. For example, an American economics textbook popular in the late 19th century was Perry's *Elements of Political Economy* (1878). Perry tells readers that "value . . . is the sole subject of our science" (p. 82) and that there is "one universal law of value— . . . the Law of Demand and Supply" (p. 119). He goes on to give the study of supply and demand a moral justification, noting "the gratifying conclusion that the laws of exchange are based on nothing less solid than the will of God" (p. 129). Yet, having erected this ethical defense, Perry proceeds to deny a place for ethics in economics:

> [Economics] has no concern with questions of moral rights. If it favors morality, it does so because morality favors production. It favors honesty because honesty favors exchange. It puts the seal of the market upon all the virtues. It condemns slavery, not because slavery is morally wrong, but because it is economically ruinous. . . . Political economy appeals only to an enlightened self-interest, and exchanges are made because they are mutually advantageous, and for no other reason. . . . The grounds of Economy and morals are independent and incommensurable (pp. 61–2).

The Perry quotation points up another distinctive feature of the writings of the classical and early neoclassical economists: their strong defense of freedom of contract, private property rights, and laissez-faire in government policy. Illustrative of these commitments is the statement of American economist Simon Newcomb: "We now see very clearly that the policy to which individuals were led merely by following their own interests, and acting as circumstances dictated, was wiser, and tended more to the public good, than any system which had received the sanction of government" (1886:190). In a similar vein, Perry states, "the struggle [for freedom] will certainly never cease until liberty of contract and delivery, subject only to conditions of morals, health, and revenue shall be international and universal" (1878:143).

Perspective on Labor

The discussion now brings us to the subject of labor. In their effort to establish economics as a science and to develop a general theory of value and exchange, the classical and early neoclassical writers tended to treat labor in their writings as no different from other goods and services. Thus, late-19th-century economist Aaron Chapin states, "If labor and capital are free, the flow of each under the law of competition towards an equilibrium is as natural as that of the waters of the ocean under the action of gravitation" (quoted in Fine 1956:58). Marshall provides a similar statement: "The normal value of everything, whether it be a particular kind of labour or capital or anything else, rests, like the keystone of an arch, balanced in equilibrium between the contending pressures of its two opposing sides: the forces of demand press on one side, and those of supply on the other" (1961:526).

Viewing labor as similar to other commodities, and holding that social welfare is maximized by allowing the laws of supply and demand free and unfettered play, it was but a short step for the classical and early neoclassical economists to conclude that the labor market and relations between capital and labor were also best governed by the doctrine of laissez-faire. In this vein Perry states,

There is a way in which government may act most beneficially upon the matter of wages. By faithfulness to its peculiar trust, that is to say, by making the rights of person and property as secure as possible, it gives an impulse to enterprise, a spur to industry, makes the desire of accumulation effective, and thus indirectly but most powerfully contributes to the increase of capital, to the fund out of which wages are paid. . . . It is not denied that capital takes advantage of the ignorance and immobility of laborers, and sometimes secures their services at a less rate than the just relations of capital to labor then and there would indicate, but the remedy for this is not in arbitrary interference of government in the bargain, but in the intelligence and self-respect of the laborers which shall fit them to insist on a just bargain. In this whole sphere of exchange, the just and comprehensive rule always will be, that when men exchange services with each other, each party is bound to look out for his own interest, to know the market-value of his own service, and to make the best terms for himself which he can make. Capital does this for itself, and laborers ought to do this for themselves, and if they are persistently cheated in the exchange, they have nobody to blame but themselves (1878:199–200).

The dictum laid out by Perry was widely accepted by American classical/neoclassical economists in the late 19th century, albeit with certain caveats. The most important exception was with regard to the protection of children and (with moderately less unanimity) women as laborers, for it was widely held that these groups were incapable of protecting their interests in market exchange. Thus, Arthur Hadley, a future president of the American Economic Association, states, "We have to take care of our women and children by special legislation; but any attempt to apply the same policy to men's labor is a different matter" (quoted in Fine 1956:60). Edward Atkinson goes further and limits the proper role of protective labor legislation to only children, stating, "I am opposed to any and all statutes which take from adult men and adult women the liberty to make their own contracts" (quoted in Fine 1956:61).

Not unexpectedly, since the classical and early neoclassical economists opposed government regulation of wages and labor conditions, they also saw no good coming from the activities of labor unions. Their critique of trade unions rested on several grounds.

One criticism was that unions foment conflict and disrupt the otherwise amicable relations between workers and employers. Newcomb, for example, refers to them as "a kind of war waged against society" (quoted in Fine 1956:62), while Perry argues they "embitter relations between employers and employed which ought to be cordial and free" and the employment contract "ceases to be a bargain at all, and becomes a sort of robbery" (1878:204).

A second prong of their critique was that the activities of unions are at best ineffective in helping workers and are frequently counterproductive to their best interests. In this regard, Perry (1878:204) claims strikes "rarely or never are permanently advantageous to the workmen themselves," in part because even if unions win higher wages this only reduces the gross returns to capital and thus diminishes the ability of employers to maintain and increase employment and future wages.

A third criticism of unions is that that their activities promoted the sectional (or class) interests of workers but harmed the larger public welfare. Newcomb states in this regard, "Every kind of action which gives the public at large a better supply of the necessaries and comforts of life promotes our prosperity. We have, therefore, only to inquire whether more or less service is rendered to the public" (1886:41–2). He then concludes that "I have seldom, if ever, heard of their [unionized workmen] combining to render better service to the public. Such of their rules as I have seen are rather in the direction of rendering as little service to the community as they conveniently can" (p. 47). Based on this reasoning (what might be called "Newcomb's Rule"), trade unions are antisocial because they restrict rather than promote the production of goods and services (wealth). Of course, government labor legislation, such as a child labor law or workplace safety law, is also in most cases likely to run afoul of Newcomb's Rule.

The major thrust of these arguments against trade unions and government legislation was that in various ways these institutional interventions interfere with the efficient operation of the market and conflict with well-established legal principles such as freedom of contract and the sanctity of private property. To a significant degree, however, these arguments sidestepped the most damning indictment made against the regime of private property and a competitive market system by socialist and heterodox critics. As most forcefully argued by Karl Marx (Feuer 1959) but also espoused by a variety of social radicals, heterodox economists, and trade unionists, the fundamental defect of capitalism is not inefficiency but systemic *injustice* toward labor. Justice, they argued, requires that the producers of wealth be paid for the full value of their creation. But, Marx contended, in capitalism workers are paid only a fraction of the value created, and employers skim off the remainder as profits or "surplus value," creating a systemic condition of exploitation and injustice. Other critics of capitalism, although not necessarily subscribing to Marx's labor theory of value or other specific parts of his theory, agreed that under the market wage system workers are underpaid relative to their contribution to the production of social wealth (Dickman 1987).

The initial tack taken by the defenders of capitalism, as earlier pointed out, was to either rebut the critics with a counter ethical argument—that private property is sanctioned by God and the workings of the market system reflect divinely given natural law or, alternatively, to argue that the entire issue of ethics has no place in science. Neither shield was entirely effective, however, and up to the end of the 19th-century capitalism continued to be dogged by the critics' charge that it could reproduce itself only by exploiting workers. Into the breach stepped American neoclassical economist John Bates Clark.

In 1900 Clark published *The Distribution of Wealth*. In the first chapter he tells readers,

> The welfare of the laboring classes depends on whether they get much or little; but their attitude toward other classes—and, therefore, the stability of the social state—depends chiefly on the question, whether the amount that they get, be it large or small, is what they produce. If they create a small amount of wealth and get the whole of it, they may not seek to revolutionize society; but if it were to appear that they produce an ample amount and get only a part of it, many of them would become

revolutionists, and all would have the right to do so. . . . If this charge were proved, every right-minded man should become a socialist; and his zeal in transforming the industrial system would then measure and express his sense of justice (p. 4).

Revolution and socialism, of course, were outcomes that Clark and fellow neoclassical economists sought to avoid, so much rested on finding a refutation to the socialist charge that capitalism exploited labor. This is exactly what Clark claimed in his book to have done. He declares that

[i]t is the purpose of this work to show that the distribution of the income of society is controlled by a natural law, and that this law, if it worked without friction, would give to every agent of production the amount of wealth which the agent creates. However wages may be adjusted by bargains freely made between individual men, the rates of pay that result from such transactions tend, it is here claimed, to equal the part of the product of industry which is traceable to the labor itself (p. v).

The natural law Clark refers to is now called the marginal productivity theory. To establish this law, Clark adopts what he calls the "mercantile theory of labor" (all units of labor are like homogeneous commodities) and a condition of perfect (frictionless) competition in markets. He concludes, "Wages tend to equal the product of marginal labor. . . . All of these men create a certain amount of wealth. Competition tends to give them the whole of it; and it also tends to make other laborers accept what these men create and get" (pp. 106–7).

Clark thus helped close the circle for defenders of a free-market, private-property form of economy and society. The principal focus of the classical/neoclassical economics was to raise the level of material prosperity (or "wealth") in society. Ostensibly a higher standard of living benefits all people in the nation, although a more nuanced view would note that consumers, higher income groups (being the largest consumers), owners of property, and the business class are the most favored. As Adam Smith first propounded, the route to increased wealth, in the classical/neoclassical view, is to promote free markets and private protection of property so that the invisible hand of self-interest and competition can achieve optimal prices, outputs, and resource allocations. In the classical/neoclassical social welfare function, therefore, pride of place is given to promoting economic *efficiency*, for efficiency is a necessary condition for achieving maximum consumer satisfaction and wealth creation. Labor, in turn, is viewed as a factor input and, largely, an instrumental means to an end (greater wealth production). In the pursuit of maximum efficiency, the dominant view held that labor markets should be free and largely unregulated, workers' wages and working conditions would automatically rise with economic growth, and devices such as trade unions and government protective legislation were disruptive to efficiency and counterproductive to workers' own economic interests. While justice and other ethical precepts were formally ruled out of economics as unscientific, Clark nonetheless claimed to show that as a happy by-product of competition and free markets, social justice is indeed served under capitalism because workers as a group receive the full value of their contribution to production of wealth. Efficiency could thus be the principal argument in the classical/neoclassical social welfare function, but with the assuredness that social justice—or at least one measure of justice, called by McClelland (1990) "marginal productivity justice"—was simultaneously served.

The Ethical Principles of Early Institutional Economics

The economic viewpoint just described dominated American economics and policy toward labor in the last part of the 19th century. As can be appreciated, it was largely conservative with respect to existing institutional arrangements and government involvement in economic and social life. Arrayed against the orthodox position were various movements and schools of thought that sought to change the status quo, through either reform or revolution. Their chief complaint and object of attention of the reformers and revolutionaries was the condition of labor under capitalism, which they regarded as oppressive and unjust and the source of much conflict and bitterness in society. They typically referred to this condition as the *Labor Problem* (Kaufman 2004a). The Labor Problem emerged in the 1880s and peaked in intensity in the years during and immediately after World War I—the peak being marked in the popular consciousness by the Bolshevik revolution in Russia in late 1917 and the subsequent Red Scare in the United States in 1918 through 1920. Emblematic of the threatening nature of the Labor Problem is the statement of Commons that "[i]f there is one issue that will destroy our civilization, it is this issue of labor and capital" (1919b:1).

General Orientation

The early field of industrial relations was essentially the labor branch of institutional economics, and both could trace their American roots to Richard Ely and his book *The Labor Movement in America* (1886). The object of Ely and other early institutionalists was to vent the pent-up steam created by the Labor Problem through progressive reform—a problem-solving program and ideology that crystallized as the new field of industrial relations around 1920. The ideology of institutional economics and industrial relations was thus opposed to orthodox economics and its laissez-faire labor policy, since the latter largely justified and protected the status quo while the former sought to fundamentally change the system and the position of workers in it.

To promote the cause of reform, the institutionalists sought to create an alternative body of economic theory that would challenge the doctrine of laissez-faire and provide a public interest rationale for pro-labor resource redistribution and greater government protection of labor. One of their points of reconstruction of economics was to broaden and enlarge its ethical and social welfare criteria. This aspect I now turn to.

Institutional economics did not coalesce into a formally recognized entity of this name until the late 1910s. But, as earlier noted, its roots go back to the 1880s when Ely, Henry Carter Adams, and a number of other young scholars returned from graduate study in Germany and launched the "new economics." Under the direction of a later generation of economists, such as Thorstein Veblen, Wesley Mitchell, John R. Commons, John M. Clark, and Walton Hamilton, the new economics metamorphosized into institutional economics—the term I henceforth use as a shorthand to describe both groups.

Ethical concerns ranked high with the institutionalists and provided a major impetus and guide to their reconstruction work in economics. Ely and Commons, for example, were very active in the Social Gospel movement and in their early years considered themselves Christian socialists (Gonce 1996), while Henry Carter Adams had trained for the ministry. Rather than disavow a place for ethics in economics, the new economists and their institutional successors claimed that economics as a science can never be disassociated from ethical concerns and, indeed, economics must openly avow and incorporate an ethical program if it is to provide useful policy guidance. Ely, for example, referred to the new economics as "sound Christian political economy" (quoted in Rader 1966:36), and Commons (1934a) later stated that the task of institutional economics is to "correlate economics, law and ethics." Their criticism of orthodox economics, in turn, was that it made a virtue of egoism, selfishness, and personal conquest and aggrandizement—practices that if fully adopted and without the restraint and modification of other ethical virtues would quickly lead to the unraveling of a market economy and civilization itself.

For the institutionalists, the starting point in economic analysis is this normative question: what is the end purpose of an economy? As they saw it, the answer of orthodox economics was to maximize human welfare by producing as efficiently as possible the goods and services desired by people in their role as consumers. The institutionalists saw this answer as too narrow and biased toward the interests of certain social groups (consumers, the wealthy) at the expense of others (workers, the poor and marginalized). They also concluded that even on these narrow grounds the American economy of the late 19th and early 20th centuries noticeably failed to perform. Out of this narrowness of objectives and failure of performance grew considerable social unrest and hardship, manifested most ominously by the Labor Problem.

Writing retrospectively in his autobiography, Ely (1938) provides this statement of the institutional diagnosis of the social problems confronting America and other industrial countries in this period:

> All important social movements have their crises; in the last quarter of the nineteenth century the American people witnessed a crisis in the labor movement. It was marked by a deep stirring of the masses—not a local stirring, not merely a national stirring, but an international, world-wide stirring of the masses. The manner of producing material goods was examined critically and pronounced faulty. The distribution of these goods among the various members of the social organism was also critically examined and pronounced iniquitous. Proposals were made for new modes of production and distribution of economic goods. The masses desired changes, not merely in surface phenomena, but in the very foundations of the social order (p. 66).

Ely then goes on to make an important observation about the social welfare objective of institutional economics. The objective of an economy, he states, is not merely more goods and services—although these are important—but the full development of each person's character and personality. Thus, he says,

> What was the labor movement of the nineteenth century? . . . The labor movement, in its broadest terms, is the effort of men to live the life of men. It is the systematic, organized struggle of the masses to attain, primarily more leisure and larger economic resources. The end and purpose of all is the true growth of mankind; namely, the full and harmonious development in each individual of all human faculties—the faculties of working, perceiving, knowing, loving—the development, in short, of whatever capabilities of good there may be within us (1938:66).

Ely then ends with this further observation. In it he ties the quest for human self-development to the attainment of a just and equitable society ("a righteous social order"), an ethical code that balances self-interest with a genuine regard for the welfare of others, and abolition of economic relations where a subordinate group or class is used as an instrumental means to promote the material ends of a superior group or class. In this regard he states,

> And this development of human powers in the individual is not to be entirely for self, but it is to be for the sake of their beneficent use in the service of one's fellows in a Christian civilization. It is for self and for others; it is the realization of the ethical aim expressed in that command which contains the secret of all true progress, 'Thou shalt love they neighbor as thyself.' It is directed against oppression in every form, because oppression carries with it the idea that persons or classes live not to fulfill a destiny of their own, but primarily and chiefly, for the sake of the welfare of other persons or classes. Men's interests are inextricably intertwined, and we shall never become truly prosperous so long as any class of the population is materially and morally wretched (1938:67).

Similar thoughts were voiced by other people from both the institutional economics and business management sides of what became the field of industrial relations. Representing business management, for example, William Lyon Mackenzie King (1918) observed that "the path of Industry is beset with human tragedy, for it is there that too often the workers are mistaken as means to an end, instead of being regarded as ends in themselves" (p. 62). Commons (quoted in Gonce 1996) claimed that the end goal of economic activity should be "[to] gradually develop all that is highest in every son of man." Elsewhere Commons stated that in the neoclassical view, workers are treated "as commodities to be bought and sold according to demand and supply," while in the institutional perspective "they are treated as citizens with rights against others on account of their value to the nation as a whole" (1919a:33). In a similar vein, Slichter remarked that "it is vitally important that the methods of production shall be planned not only to turn out goods at low costs but to provide the kind of jobs which develop the desirable capacities of the workers" (1931:651–2).

Labor: More Than a Commodity

These quotations call attention to the two most fundamental principles that distinguish the ethical face of industrial relations. The first and bedrock idea is the ethical precept that the labor of human beings should not be treated in law or practice as a *commodity*. The second is that the social welfare goal of higher *efficiency* must be balanced by concerns for *equity/social justice* and opportunities for individual *human self-actualization and self-development.* I start with the former.

The central fact about labor, as seen by the institutionalists, is that unlike other factor inputs (capital, land), it is embodied in human beings and thus brings to the workplace and labor market a much higher moral significance. The social interest may well be promoted by having inanimate objects such as steel, coal, and computers traded in competitive markets and their price and conditions of use determined by the impersonal forces of demand, supply, and maximum profit. But from an institutional point of view, social welfare is likely to be seriously harmed if labor is utilized and traded in such a manner.

Because coal and computers are inanimate objects, no compelling social interest exists concerning whether the price they command is high or low, the working conditions are good or bad, or the treatment by the owners is sensitive or harsh. Rather, they are used in production as an instrumental means to an end and have value only to the degree that they efficiently satisfy the wants of consumers. Labor is different, however, because a low wage may put workers and their families in dire poverty—a condition society cannot be indifferent to if it puts value on human life. Likewise, even if 16-hour workdays and child labor in mills and factories are efficient outcomes of demand and supply, from an ethical perspective the hardships these conditions impose on flesh-and-blood people are an affront to a civilized, progressive society. And, finally, while it may be efficient to have business owners make unilateral and unchecked decisions about the treatment of their coal and computers and how long and under what conditions they are used, to allow the same with respect to their employees violates widely shared ethical principles of justice and democracy. Thus, labor is not only a means to an end (production of goods and services) but also an end in itself, since the process and outcomes of work so directly and intimately affect the life and well-being of the people providing the labor. By similar reasoning, since people's well-being in life comes not only from the satisfaction of consuming more goods and services but also from the experience and outcomes of work, a public interest rationale exists for a certain degree of protection and regulation of labor conditions in order to achieve a balance between the interests of people as consumers and their interests as workers.

A major impetus for the founding of the "new economics" by Ely and other early institutionalists was to challenge what they saw as the amoral and harmful doctrine of "labor as a commodity." At an intellectual level, this led them to try to construct a new body of theory to supplant the classical/neoclassical school, given that it implicitly and to some degree explicitly sanctions this practice through its narrow focus on efficiency and advocacy of unregulated labor markets (Kaufman 2004b). At a level of policy, this led the institutionalists to favor a wide range of reforms and institutional interventions in labor markets that would collectively "humanize" (or "socialize") the workplace and work experience.

One reform method was to establish a floor of minimum socially acceptable conditions in labor markets, called by Sidney and Beatrice Webb (1897) the "Method of the Common Rule" and the "Standard Rate." Then, with the passage of time, this floor was to be gradually raised in line with economic and cultural advance, an idea Adams (1886) referred to as elevating "the plane of competition." An example that they favored is a minimum wage law (to provide a "living wage"); another is an unemployment insurance program (to prevent destitution and a bidding-down of wages to sweatshop levels). A second reform method was to increase the bargaining power of workers so they could negotiate with employers more reasonable and fair wages and work conditions. For this reason, the early institutionalists favored legal protection and encouragement of trade unions and adoption of government countercyclical full employment fiscal and monetary policies. A third reform method was to democratize the workplace, replacing industrial autocracy with industrial democracy, or what Commons (1905) called "constitutional government in industry." Thus, while the classical/neoclassical economists condemned trade unions as labor monopolies, the institutionalists favored them as a means to provide collective voice and due process of law in the workplace—objectives that also led them to later favor well-run employer-created plans of representation (Leiserson 1929; Kaufman 2000). A fourth industrial reform the institutionalists advocated was the adoption of progressive labor management methods—tools that according to Commons (1921b) represented the "opportunity of management" to "self-cure" the labor problem by using employment practices that replaced adversarialism and bitterness with cooperation and unity of interest. And, finally, ranked above all the other reform proposals were methods to stabilize the macroeconomy at full employment, given the institutionalists' view that the hardship, insecurity, and waste from large-scale unemployment and the "boom and bust" of the business cycle were the single greatest cause of labor problems (Commons 1921a, Kaufman 2003a).

In the years surrounding World War I the campaign to reform labor conditions reached a peak, witnessed by the birth of the field of industrial relations and the creation under the League of Nations of the International Labour Organization (ILO). A battle cry of the reformers was "labor shall not be treated as a commodity." This principle first appeared in American law when Congress enacted the Clayton Act of 1914. Its purpose was to promote fair trade in product and labor markets, and to further that objective, the act sought to exempt labor unions from the legal ban on monopoly contained in the Sherman Anti-Trust Act. To do so, a provision was inserted in the act that stated, "The labor of a human being is not a commodity or article of commerce" (Schwochau 2000).

The second and more far-reaching example is provided in the Versailles Peace Treaty of 1919 that created the ILO. The ILO was headquartered in Europe while the field of industrial relations was American in origin, but the two were tightly linked in purpose and philosophy (Kaufman 2004a). The treaty outlines nine principles that form the core of the ILO's mission (Solano 1920:273–4). They also represent a concise statement of the policy goals and normative principles of the new field of industrial relations:

- labor should not be regarded as a commodity or article of commerce
- the right of association
- payment of a reasonable wage to maintain a reasonable standard of living
- an eight-hour day or 48-hour week
- a weekly rest of at least 24 hours
- abolition of child labor
- equal pay for equal work
- equitable treatment of all workers in a country
- enforcement of laws for worker protection

The Trilogy of Social Welfare Objectives

The premise "labor shall not be treated as a commodity" was the foundational ethical principle of early industrial relations. On this foundation was then erected a second fundamental ethical precept. In neoclassical economics the purpose of work and the employment relationship is to promote maximum efficiency. The early institutionalists rejected this proposition and substituted a trilogy of social welfare objectives: efficiency, equity (social justice), and opportunities for individual self-actualization and development.

Classical and neoclassical economics seeks to maximize the utility consumers derive from the economy's output of goods and services. Neoclassical theory shows, in turn, that consumer satisfaction is maximized when an economy achieves *efficiency* in production and exchange—that is, when it is impossible to reallocate resources so as to increase the utility of one person without at the same time reducing the utility of another. In this schema, work and the people who perform it inevitably become an instrumental means to an end—a "factor input" to be bought as cheaply as possible, utilized to its maximum, and then discarded when no longer needed.

As suggested by the quotations from Ely and others cited earlier, the early institutionalists took a broader and more humanistic perspective on the social purpose of work and employment. Satisfaction of material needs is important and antecedent to all others, since otherwise the human organism will perish. It is thus important that work and employment be performed efficiently. But by itself this social welfare objective makes people servants of the economy rather than the economy the servant of people. Thus, efficiency and the satisfaction of consumers' material needs is a *necessary* condition for social welfare, according to the institutionalists, but not a *sufficient* condition. In this regard the institutionalists adhere to the biblical dictum that "man does not live by bread alone." Also important to social welfare, they believed, are two other objectives. The first is that work and employment satisfy the ethical criteria of fairness, equity, and justice; the second is that they provide individuals the opportunity to realize their full human potential. Translated into modern terms, the classical/neoclassical social welfare objective is equivalent to the bottom level of Maslow's five-step hierarchy of human needs, while the social welfare objectives of institutional economics and industrial relations include all levels of Maslow's hierarchy (Lutz and Lux 1988).

Modest elaboration will flesh out and make clearer the institutional perspective on the important ethical role played by equity and self-actualization and development in the operation of a modern economy. I start with equity and its relationship to efficiency.

Commons observes in his theoretical magnum opus *Institutional Economics* (1934a) that the foundational fact upon which all of economic science is built is the existence of material scarcity. He then states, "It is for this reason of scarcity that I make efficiency also a universal principal, because it overcomes scarcity by cooperation. But cooperation does not arise from a *presupposed* harmony of interests, as the older [classical/neoclassical] economists believed. It arises from the necessity of creating a new harmony of interests—or at least order, if harmony is impossible—out of the conflict of interests among the hoped-for cooperators" (p. 6, emphasis in original). The meaning of this passage, as I interpret it, is that efficiency is a desired objective for improving social welfare since it helps overcome scarcity. Efficiency, then, can be taken as the first and antecedent argument in the institutional social welfare function.

But Commons also stresses that efficiency does not arise automatically from a God-given, Invisible Hand type of competitive market system but must be socially constructed by getting people to cooperate in a world where conflicts of interest are endemic and people, markets, laws, and property rights are all highly imperfect. In other words, cooperation is encouraged by "goal alignment" (creating a "harmony of interests"), and both must be socially engineered. Fundamental to engendering and maintaining cooperation and social order, in turn, is that the economy's "rules of the game" (e.g., laws, distribution of endowments, access to markets) and "outcomes of the game" (e.g., wages, incomes, job opportunities) be judged by participants as falling within the bounds of "reasonableness," or what Commons (1934a) calls *reasonable value*. Reasonable value thus imposes an ethical constraint on the market system—that it generate not only efficient outcomes but also reasonable outcomes if participants are to be induced to continue their cooperation and not rebel against the existing system. Other closely allied terms for "reasonable" are "just" and "fair." In modern language (Shepphard, Lewicki, and Minton 1992), for example, the concept of reasonable rules of the game goes under the term *procedural justice,* reasonable outcomes are called *distributive justice,* and "reasonable value" may be translated into the concept of *social justice.* The second variable in the institutional social welfare function may thus be specified as *equity* (justice, reasonableness), introduced in a quasi-lexicographic ordering such that it serves as both a constraint on the range of socially acceptable efficient outcomes (efficiency being the antecedent social welfare objective) and as a higher-order social goal valued for its own sake.

Thus, institutional economics holds as normative propositions that both the procedural rules and the realized outcomes of the economy must pass the dual test of *efficiency* and *equity* and that efficiency outcomes that fail the equity test are against the social interest (Budd, Gomez, and Meltz 2004). In part this is judged to be true because injustice is an affront to basic human rights and universally accepted moral principles. But inequitable outcomes are also against the social interest because they produce dysfunctional forms of behavior that undermine not only efficiency but also the very legitimacy of the economic and social order. Although neoclassical economic theory, by the nature of its assumptions, holds that economic efficiency can be separated from economic justice (Stiglitz 2001), institutional economics and industrial relations claim the two are indissolubly connected. The Versailles Peace Treaty clearly illustrates this principle in its first section: "Whereas the

League of Nations has for its objective the establishment of universal peace, and such peace can be established only if it is based upon social justice. . . " Although the language of the treaty speaks of "social justice," one can just as well substitute Commons's term "reasonable value" and get the same implication.

It is important to point out that the personnel management wing of the early industrial relations field also subscribed to the institutional position on efficiency and equity. An important precursor movement to industrial relations, for example, was scientific management. Taylor (1911), in his *Principles of Scientific Management*, claims that his system increases productivity because it "has for its very foundation the firm conviction that the true interests of the two [employers and employees] are one and the same" (p. 10) and achieves this unity of interest because it promotes "justice for all parties through impartial scientific investigation of all the elements of a problem" (p. 139). Likewise, the "dean of industrial relations men" in industry was Clarence Hicks, an executive in charge of industrial relations at Standard Oil of New Jersey. He writes in his autobiography, "A barren ground for developing real co-operation, autocracy breeds resentment in those who come under its domination. This resentment may not be apparent, and at times may not be fully recognized by the worker himself, but it is inevitably reflected in lowered morale and efficiency" (Hicks 1941:67). Without exception the early writers on personnel management maintained that a necessary condition for high productivity is that workers feel they are getting a "square deal." Balderston (1935), for example, examined the personnel programs of 25 advanced companies in the early 1930s and concluded that "fair wages and fair dealing" are the "prerequisite" (p. 252).

Efficiency and equity are two of the fundamental arguments in the institutional social welfare function, but there is yet a third and higher argument: the objective of promoting maximum self-actualization and self-development for each human being. Efficiency and equity are in this regard necessary conditions for attainment of the ultimate objective which, according to Ely is "the true growth of mankind; namely, the full and harmonious development in each individual of all human faculties" (1938:66)

Self-actualization and self-development are themselves rather broad and open-ended goals, and for some purposes it is useful to further delineate them. One point of departure is suggested by Commons, who states that "the three most fundamental wishes of all mankind [are]: security, liberty, and equality" (1934a:706). The terms "liberty" and "equality," in turn, may for expository purposes be collapsed into one composite term, "democracy," partly on the interpretation that Commons uses "equality" to connote due process or "equal protection of the law." An alternative approach used by Budd (2004) in his theory of the employment relationship, largely equivalent in its analytical implications, is to telescope the various items in self-actualization and democracy into the concept of employee "voice."

Without security, posits Commons, human beings revert to a more primitive state of behavior where fear is the dominant motive and cooperation and social order are undercut by brutishness, fraud, coercion, and aggression. With security, on the other hand, people have sufficient material and emotional resources to cope with life and can thus expand and develop the higher side of human existence, such as love, peace, honesty, and artistic and cultural creativity. Commons states, for example, "Not until the capitalistic system, not until the great financial interests that control this country have learned that it is just as important to furnish security for the job as it is to furnish security for the investment will we have a permanent provision for industrial peace" (1921a:8–9). For this reason, the institutionalists promoted a variety of programs and laws to provide greater security to workers, such as unemployment and old age insurance laws, public works programs in times of depression, and protections against arbitrary and unfair dismissal.

Similar considerations apply to democracy. Autocracy places people in a servile and dependent state, exposes them to the insecurity of arbitrary and capricious harm to body and livelihood, blunts personal self-expression, and breeds feelings of resentment and injustice. Democracy, on the other hand, promotes self-actualization and self-development by giving people independence and autonomy, an opportunity for voice and participation in the polity, the protection of due process of law, and the development of positive emotions such as pride, commitment, and love. Commons, for example, says that an elemental part of democracy is giving workers "power enough to command respect" (1921b:69). Similarly, Rockefeller (quoted in *Survey* magazine, October 25, 1919, p. 36) said at the 1919 Industrial Conference, "Representation is a principle which is fundamentally just and vital to the conduct of industry. This is the principle upon which the democratic government of our country is founded. Surely it is not consistent for us as Americans to demand democracy in government and to practice autocracy in industry." To promote greater democracy in industry, the institutionalists and progressive business allies both advocated more widespread forms of *worker voice* in industry (Kaufman 2003b). Although the need and desirability for more worker voice was a central normative proposition in early industrial relations, opinions differed as to the best form of voice. Some of the institutionalists favored independent worker voice through trade unions, the progressive businessmen tended to oppose trade unions and instead favored employer-created shop committees and other forms of nonunion representation, while most in the field took the normative position that it should be left to the workers to decide what form of representation (if any) they wanted.

Let me summarize the discussion to this point. The normative social welfare position of institutional economists is that the end goal of an economy should be to provide the opportunities and conditions that allow each person to grow and develop their full range of human capabilities and emotions. Essential ingredients are efficiency, equity, and self-actualization and self-development, with the final two variables decomposable into objectives such as security and industrial democracy. To some significant degree these arguments in the social welfare function are complements—more of one promotes accomplishment of the others, such as when more security, justice, and voice promote greater efficiency in production (Meltz 1989). Inevitably, however, in a world of scarcity these social "goods" are also at times substitutes, and thus a trade-off is unavoidable. Whereas classical/neoclassical economics tends to give all the weight in the social welfare function to efficiency and thereby is led to oppose any sacrifice of efficiency for other social goals, institutional economics gives explicit weight to a broader range of human values and is thus willing to countenance trading off, if required, a certain decrement of efficiency for additional social justice, economic security, and industrial democracy.

As seen by the institutional economists in the late 19th and early 20th centuries, the American economy and labor market were prone to considerable inefficiency in production, inequity in the distribution of social and economic benefits and costs, and abridgement or nonfulfillment of fundamental human values. The classical/neoclassical strategy of laissez-faire was thus seen by institutional economists as socially harmful and dangerous because it propped up and defended a system that not only failed the tests of efficiency, equity, and human self-development but did so in a way so egregiously flawed that American capitalism and representative democracy were under growing threat from socialist and anarcho-syndicalist revolutionaries.

The Early Institutionalists on Ethics and the Legal Framework of Industrial Relations

The institutional strategy to solve the Labor Problem was to abandon laissez-faire and instead promote a wide-ranging but largely conservative program of political and economic reform through new institutional innovations, additional government regulation of labor markets, and a rebalancing of power and rights in the workplace. It was in this spirit that Wisconsin institutional labor economists Thomas Adams and Helen Sumner remarked, "The true ideal of society is not laissez-faire, but economic freedom, and freedom is the child, not the enemy, of law and regulation" (1911.15).

As the Adams and Sumner quotation suggests, the institutional attack on laissez-faire was inevitably a movement not only for economic reform but also legal reform and, indeed, the legal had to precede the economic. For this reason, the early institutionalists sought to justify their humanized social welfare objectives not only on principles of economics but also on principles of law (Fried 1998). This led them to found the "first great law and economics movement" in the early part of the 20th century (Hovenkamp 1990). But the study of law inevitably leads back to the subject of ethics, for law is itself a reflection and codification of a society's moral values and ethical principles.

The emphasis given by the institutionalists to the law arose from their conviction that the Labor Problem and, indeed, the behavior of the entire economy rested on the fulcrum of property rights—specifically the form, distribution, enforcement, and exchange of property rights. Similarly, a reason they believed that the science of economics always contains an ethical dimension is because law is inherently based on ethical precepts of right and wrong and the law, in turn, determines the entire structure and operation of markets and supply and demand. Thus, as expounded by Adams (1897) in his presidential address to the American Economic Association, and later amplified and extended by Commons (1924) in *The Legal Foundations of Capitalism,* property rights and laws of contract define each person's endowment of resources, liberties, and duties with respect to economic resources (including the physical self) and political participation, and conditions for the exchange of resources. Commons noted that the classical/neoclassical economists tend to take property rights, contract law, and the resulting distribution of resources as a "given" and then analyze via the workings of a competitive market the level of production and distribution of income. But this procedure, he and the other institutionalists argued, hides the underlying causes of the Labor Problem and malperformance of the economy. The problem, in a nutshell, is that property rights and the "rules of the game" are created by the rich and powerful in society and inevitably are structured to promote their interests, thus marginalizing and putting at a disadvantage "outsider" groups.

Several examples will make this argument more tangible and transparent. Neoclassical theory, for example, maintains that in a competitive labor market both the firm and individual workers are "wage takers" and thus have no bargaining power and, hence, ability to exploit the other. The institutionalists argued, however, that in reality workers in this time period often faced a marked *inequality* of bargaining power and, for this reason, suffered from exploitative and unjust wages. The law, for example, allows investors to combine together and form a corporation and then treats this amalgamation of capital as a fictitious "legal person" who then as the "employer" bargains the labor contract with the worker. While in legal and neoclassical eyes it is a case of an individual employer competitively bargaining with an individual worker, from an institutional perspective the bargaining is often quite unequal since in actuality the employer is a huge corporation that because of its size and resources needs the worker much less than the individual worker needs the job. Also, employers used their political power to obtain legislation that permitted unrestricted immigration into the United States. Such a law greatly expands the supply of labor in the market, shifting the labor–supply curve to the right and leading to a low wage for workers. Neoclassical theory, by taking the law as a "given" and focusing only on workers as individuals, sees an equality of bargaining power and a socially desirable competitive wage; institutional theory on the other hand looks at the effect of the law on labor as a group (or class) and sees that unrestricted immigration greatly undercuts labor's bargaining power and thus forces down the wage to a socially undesirable "cutthroat" or "distress sale" level. With these results in mind, Commons and Andrews ([1916] 1936:532) declare, "Thus it may be affirmed that the equality of bargaining power toward which the law of employer and employee is directed is a principle so important for the public benefit that it becomes in itself a public purpose." To achieve a greater equality of bargaining power, in turn, Commons and the other institutionalists recommended reforms such as greater trade unionism, child labor and minimum wage laws, and expanded social insurance programs.

A second example concerns work hours and conditions. Neoclassical theory assumes that the length of the workday and the speed and pace of work are bargained in a competitive labor market and thus are voluntarily chosen, efficient outcomes that therefore merit no government or union regulation. From an institutional perspective, however, a feature of the property rights regime in labor markets is likely to cause both the length of the workday and the speed and pace of work to be excessive and injurious. This feature is that the firm cannot own labor (because slavery is illegal) but can only rent it (by the hour, day, week, year, etc.), and as is well known, a buyer who rents an asset (relative to owning) has a much greater incentive to "overwork" it (or neglect its maintenance and repair). The result in early-20th-century labor markets was that many workers were "used up" and "put on the scrap heap" by the age of 40. Working conditions, such as workplace safety conditions and accidents, provide another example. Neoclassical theory presumes competitive markets will provide, via Adam Smith's theory of compensating wage differentials, the socially efficient amount of safety and injuries. The problem, from an institutional perspective, is that many such workplace "bads" have a public goods aspect and thus will be overproduced relative to the social optimum (because workplace "bads" have ill-defined property rights, individual workers will free-ride and not fully reveal their preferences to the employer). For this reason, the institutionalists advocated abandoning laissez-faire in the realm of industrial work conditions and instead promoted a variety of protective labor laws (e.g., a maximum hour law), an accident insurance program, and institutionalized forms of collective voice.

A final example concerns democracy and voice in the workplace. A firm will only provide democracy and voice in the workplace to the extent it adds to profit, say in the form of an employee involvement program or dispute resolution program. If workers want still more democracy and voice, then the free market gives them a way to get it— by "buying" it from the employer in the form of a lower wage offer. From an institutional perspective, however, this mechanism is inherently defective. Democracy and voice in the workplace, at least at some minimum level, are basic human rights that all firms should provide and respect. Viewed this way, it is illegitimate to ask workers to "buy" them in the market or allow firms to offer only the amount that "pays," suggesting that a non-market method is needed to guarantee a sufficient supply of these social goods. One method is collective bargaining. Thus, Commons (1919a:108) states of the union contract, "Like the Constitution of the United States, the agreement has become a 'government of law and not men.' A man is not deprived of his job without 'due process of law.' This is the difference between democracy and autocracy."

America in the late 19th and early 20th centuries was thus presented with three alternative legal policy regimes to solve the Labor Problem. At the right end of the spectrum was the legal regime of free market capitalism espoused by the classical/neoclassical economists and their conservative colleagues; on the left end was the legal regime of socialism, state ownership, and/or worker cooperatives espoused by the socialists and anarcho-syndicalists; and in the middle was the legal regime of humanized and regulated capitalism espoused by the institutional economists. The latter program sought to balance the social "good" of efficiency and wealth creation with the equally valuable social "good" of justice, security, democracy, and opportunities for human self-development and self-actualization.

To advocates of free markets, the program of the institutionalists appeared to be overly interventionist and destructive of personal liberties and economic opportunities; to advocates of socialism it looked like a doomed effort to fix the systemic contradictions and flaws of capitalism with a set of band-aid solutions. But to the institutionalists it promised to save capitalism and representative democracy by humanizing, stabilizing, professionalizing, democratizing, and balancing an otherwise skewed, unjust, and inhumane system through a limited but far-reaching program of reform. The field of industrial relations was born in the early 1920s to develop and implement this reform program. As previously described, the concrete elements of this reform program included greater trade unionism, expanded protective labor law and social insurance programs, the spread of progressive labor management methods, and government full-employment fiscal and monetary policies. These normative policy positions were, in turn, based on a well-articulated set of moral values and ethical principles. In particular, the institutionalists believed that labor is embodied in human beings and thus cannot be regarded in either theory or practice as merely a commodity factor input and intangible means to an end; rather, labor is a human essence, and thus the quality of the work experience is a vital determinant of human welfare that theory and practice must give due consideration. This insight, I believe, is the ethical touchstone of industrial relations as espoused by the founders of the field.

The Ethical Principles of Modern Industrial Relations

After reviewing the writings of the founders of the field of industrial relations on ethical values, I searched the modern literature for works on the same subject, finding only a smattering of contributions in addition to Budd's recent book. The person who has written perhaps the most since 1970 on the ethical values and ideology of American industrial relations is Jack Barbash. Thomas Kochan has also written on the normative principles of the field in a number of places. Also relevant are the three papers published in the 1993 Industrial Relations Research Association (IRRA) proceedings on "Teaching Ethics and Values in the IR Curriculum." In general, however, the modern industrial relations literature is relatively slim when it comes to explicit attention to the ethical foundation of the field. In certain respects it also paints a different picture of the field's normative values relative to the position staked out by the founders eight decades ago.

Modern writers clearly recognize that the field of industrial relations has a normative value statement. States Barbash, for example, "If we are not bound by one theory it is just possible that common values inform our work" (1989:3). Likewise, Kochan states, "I believe the primary feature that distinguishes the field from its counterparts lies in the normative assumptions and perspectives that underlie our conceptualization of the employment relationship" (1998:37).

The question then becomes this: what is this normative value statement, and to what degree is it based on an underlying set of ethical principles? Here one finds both an interesting normative bifurcation and an ideological shift relative to the early founding period of the field.

The key development in modern industrial relations, as I have described in detail elsewhere (Kaufman 1993, 2004a), is that the coalition of progressive labor reformers from the institutional labor economics and personnel management wings of the field gradually splintered and broke apart. From the founding of the field in the early 1920s to the early 1960s, the field was generally defined broadly to cover the entire employment relationship, the union and nonunion sectors, and the subjects of personnel/human resource management (HRM) and labor–management relations. The normative value statement of the field was sufficiently broad that it could include such diverse people as John Commons and Elton Mayo, give balanced weight to all methods to solve labor problems, and accept both independent and employer-created forms of collective worker voice. As time passed, however, the perceived domain of the field tended to narrow, until in the 1980s most participants considered the term "industrial relations" to be largely (but not completely) synonymous with labor–management relations and collective bargaining, while the management side dropped out and became the separate and competing field of HRM (Strauss and Whitfield 1998; Budd 2004). Illustrative of this trend is the title of Kochan's popular textbook, *Industrial Relations and Collective Bargaining* (1980), and his observation that "in practice researchers in this field have focused most of their attention on the role of unions, collective bargaining, and related institutions and policies" (1998:31). As the perceived subject matter of the field shifted toward labor–management relations, so too did the field's normative value statement, resulting in a more critical stance toward management and more favorable stance toward unions and independent forms of employee voice.

A search of the modern literature reveals normative value statements that are quite similar to those from the early 1920s, which is to say broad enough to include both the institutional economics and progressive personnel management wings of the field. The emphasis is on labor's human essence, the importance of balancing efficiency with equity, and providing employees with voice and due process. In this respect normative statements about ideology and policy continue to be linked to ethical principles. One such example is provided by Barbash: "Industrial relations' underlying value . . . is the human essence of labor as a commodity or factor of production and, in consequence, labor's right to equity in the employment relationship" (1991:91). He goes on to say that

> [t]he duality between labor as a factor of production and labor's human condition . . . becomes the moral premise which justifies (a) why the labor factor is entitled to equity, (b) why the market, left to its own devices, falls short of equity, (c) how trade unions and collective bargaining, public policy and management "human relations" can variously compensate for the market's equity deficiencies, (d) why equity is indispensable to the stability of an industrial order and (e) why industrial relations came into being as a field of study and practice primarily concerned with equity in the employment relationship (p. 108).

An example of a broad, relatively inclusive, and ethically based value statement in the modern literature of industrial relations is made by Osterman et al. (2001):

> The institutional perspective recognizes a set of moral values, which individuals seek to realize through work. These values are distinct from economic efficiency and are not necessarily promoted by the market. They include equity and due process in the management of the workplace, equal employment opportunity, work as a creative and dignifying activity, and the right of workers to a voice in the organization and governance of the workplace. An institutional perspective understands the economy as embedded in the social structure and as depending on that structure for its capacity to operate effectively (p. 3).

A third example in this spirit is provided by Budd (2004):

> My conclusion can then be restated by saying that property interests must be balanced with labor interests. In either case, the critical task is seeking a balance. In broader terms, this balancing paradigm for the employment relationship is additionally reminiscent of the old institutional labor economics, or Wisconsin, school's belief in reforming and refining market-oriented capitalism, not discarding it (p. 45).

But a number of American IR scholars, including Barbash and Kochan, soon pass on to a more narrow ideological perspective. This perspective is narrower in giving normative preference to one particular form of workplace governance and worker representation—trade unionism, collective bargaining, and independent worker voice—rather than to all methods that solve labor problems in an efficient and equitable manner. It is also narrower in the sense that this normative position is generally stated without reference to any deeper underlying ethical values—perhaps on the assumption these are already widely shared and understood, or perhaps because modern social science is not comfortable with explicit value statements.

According to Kochan, Katz, and McKersie, the normative tilt in modern industrial relations toward unions and independent employee voice originated with the Wagner Act (1935), which, in their words, made collective bargaining the "preferred institutional mechanism" (1986:24). This preference given to collective bargaining, I note, is not actually stated in the language of the Wagner Act—the purpose is said to be to "encourage and protect" collective bargaining, but it was taken on as a widely held ideological position by supporters of the act and the scholars most active in the field of industrial relations after World War II.

Illustrative of this new and narrower normative position in industrial relations are a number of quotations from well-known scholars. Gerald Somers, for example, describes the normative value statement of American industrial relations as "the uniqueness and value of the free collective bargaining system, voluntarism, liberal pluralism [and] consent" (1975:1). Barbash expresses a similar opinion, declaring, "As I see it, two leading principles govern the American ideology of American industrial relations: the adversarial principle and the principle of voluntarism" (1979:453). Barbash's emphasis on the presumed adversarial nature of the employment relationship is echoed by Kochan: "Industrial relations theory starts from an assumption that an enduring conflict of interests exists between workers and employers in employment relationships" (1998:37–8). Yet another indicator is a statement by Walter Franke: "It is probably fair to say that the distinctive character of many [IR] programs has been the study of trade unionism and collective bargaining and the value system that supported these institutions" (1987:479). And, finally, in a recent article Godard and Delaney offer this statement of the subject content and normative perspective of industrial relations:

> The field of IR has historically been distinguished by its concern to balance the competing interests of labor and management, and its recognition that the labor–management relationship is at least partly distributive. Accompanying this concern has been a belief that conflict will arise in organizations

and that labor institutions such as unions and collective bargaining provide an effective system of conflict resolution. In such systems, the two parties confront each other on relatively equal terms, and an effective system of workplace jurisprudence exists—one in which workers enjoy basic democratic rights and protections (2000:497).

That the majority of industrial relations academics actually subscribe to the positions just quoted is suggested by Godard's findings from a large-scale opinion survey. He states, "In general, the findings for the U.S. sample indicate that, despite U.S. economic and political realities over the past decade, the majority of [industrial relations] scholars evince considerable support and sympathy both for the plight of workers and their unions and for selected institutional reforms" (1995:143).

These statements seem to focus on three "-isms" as the central normative premises of modern American industrial relations: *pluralism* (divergence of interests between workers and employers and their compromise through representative voice and organized negotiation), *voluntarism* (government establishment of fair and balanced rules of the game and leaving employers and workers maximum space to negotiate acceptable terms and conditions), and *collectivism* in employment relationships (independent representation of workers' interests, typically through trade unions). At the center of this normative trilogy stands *free collective bargaining*, arguably the concept that over the last half century has defined both the positive and normative center of gravity for the field.

If modern industrial relations has a normative predisposition in favor of unions and collective worker representation, what does this imply about the field's normative stance toward nonunion firms and the practice of "unitarist" HRM? The evidence on this matter—admittedly slim and not entirely consistent—suggests as a broad generalization that both tend to be less favorably viewed, but perhaps with some diminished degree of skepticism and antipathy in recent years. Providing evidence of a positive attitude, for example, is the survey by Godard that finds a majority of industrial relations academics favor "cooperative" forms of employee relations and believe HRM practices promote improved economic performance (1995). Also on the positive side, many industrial relations academics (e.g., Kochan and Osterman 1994; Appelbaum, Berg, Kalleberg, and Bailey 2000) have studied and promoted the high performance work system (HPWS) model—a model based on intensive use of HRM practices and a unitarist strategy of cooperation and goal alignment.

But there is also evidence of a negative attitude toward HRM and nonunion employers, evidenced in part by a general belief that these subjects are not part of the industrial relations field and should not be. Regarding the unitarist model, for example, Godard and Delaney argue that industrial relations scholars (p. 493) "must adopt a critical and analytical posture toward the new [HRM/high performance] paradigm" (2000:493) and "at minimum adhere to a perspective and research agenda that distinguishes their work from the management-centered perspective associated with the human relations tradition" (2000:497). The existence of this type of critical attitude is also spoken of by Strauss et al. (1974) when they noted in the preface to the IRRA research volume *Organizational Behavior: Research and Issues* that "the question of whether to publish a book devoted to Organizational Behavior (OB) caused strenuous debate within the Executive Board. There was one group which felt that OB did not really belong within Industrial Relations. Another group was willing to provide an opportunity to test OB's relevance." Although Kochan (1998) does not explicitly state it, one also infers that he does not believe HRM/OB is a part of industrial relations, given his statement that normative assumptions about conflict in the employment relationship divide the field into two different schools of thought: the pluralists and the radical/neo-Marxists, with HRM omitted by implication. That HRM is outside (modern) industrial relations is also maintained by Budd (2004), who divides the employment field into HR and IR (unitarist versus pluralist/radical).

Regarding the field's less favorable attitude toward nonunion employers, Cappelli observes that

> [a]lthough it is hard to quantify, there is a clear sense among some faculty in IR that the WWII generation of scholars, who dominated both the field and the IRRA as an organization almost until the 1990s, saw the traditional union–management model of employment relations as the preferred form and resisted efforts to study alternative models. They saw nonunion systems, for example, not as emerging approaches but as the old-fashion models (e.g., "Welfare Capitalism" of the 1930s) that were tried and rejected once industrial unionism came along (1991:7).

In a similar vein, Jacoby describes the normative bias against nonunion employers in the industrial relations field following World War II in these words: "Liberal academics inevitably treated nonunion companies as socially retrograde and thus undeserving of scrutiny" (1997:8). Strauss says of unions and collective bargaining, "Except for the extreme right and left, these hallowed institutions were not questioned for almost forty years" (1994:3).

Different observers may well come to different conclusions on the details, but I suspect that most would agree with this broad conclusion: the modern field of industrial relations has had in the post–World War II period a normative preference for a pluralist, collective-bargaining-centered form of workforce governance. Most often this normative position has been asserted in the academic literature without explicit grounding on underlying ethical precepts.

In recent years, however, a discernible reemergence of an ethics-based discourse on labor policy has been evident. This movement was initiated by the ILO in the 1990s and has since been taken up by a number of participants in American industrial relations. The impetus for the ILO's involvement was its desire to gain broader government and public backing for observance of certain fundamental labor standards, particularly in the context of international trade agreements. To promote this goal, the ILO selected four areas of work as "core labor principles" and declared them to be fundamental human rights. As outlined in its 1998 *Declaration on Fundamental Principles and Rights at Work*, the four core labor areas are freedom of association and the effective right to collective bargaining, the elimination of all forms of forced or compulsory labor, effective abolition of child labor, and elimination of discrimination in employment and occupation (Kellerson 1998).

The ILO's strategy of equating core labor rights with fundamental human rights has found strong advocates in the United States and Canada, particularly among proponents of trade unionism and independent worker representation. Two recent reports, one by the ILO (2000) and another by the New York–based Human Rights Watch (2000), have been very influential in this regard. Friedman and Wood (2001) observe, for example, that "The Report [*Unfair Advantage*] points to the human rights perspective as the solution to the problems of the US system. Its foundation is the reformulation of collective bargaining as a basic right of all human beings" (p. 588). Also of note is this observation of Roy Adams: "Perhaps the most significant aspect of the appearance of these two reports is the intermingling of industrial relations and human rights dialogue. Until recently the two communities had pursued their agendas separately and in isolation from one another" (2001:203).

The emergence of this rights-based advocacy for collective bargaining is, in part, a response to the long-term decline of the union sector in the United States, the accompanying loss of public support for the New Deal labor policy that encourages collective bargaining, and the search for a more effective and compelling normative argument for unionism vis à vis the increasingly dominant neoliberal agenda of deregulated labor markets. The decline of unionism and the New Deal model has also negatively impacted the field of industrial relations, given its close intellectual and normative ties to labor–management relations in recent decades. Thus, a field that gives normative pride of place to pluralist employment relations and collective bargaining finds itself in an increasingly tenuous and somewhat marginalized position, evident in the substantial decline in LERA (IRRA) membership, the closing of numerous university industrial relations programs, and shrinking student and academic interest in traditional labor–management relations. No doubt with these events in mind, former IRRA president Thomas Kochan described the field as being in "a state of profound crisis" (1998:31).

Inevitably, when caught in crisis, institutions and the people who comprise them are forced to reexamine and perhaps readjust long-held, often deeply felt values and normative commitments—a process now under way in industrial relations but rarely explicitly discussed because of the uncomfortable and potentially divisive nature of the subject. Should the position of the field continue to decline, however, the subject of "values" may require more explicit attention and, perhaps, further adjustment.

A range of responses is possible. One option is to hold tight to the field's normative value statement. This option, however, could spell the further decline of industrial relations and possibly even its demise as a going concern, at least absent a rebound in the labor movement. My impression is that a portion of the field—often coming from the ranks of political leftists, trade unionists, and their intellectual allies—favors this option. A second option is an intermediate position—to maintain fidelity to the basic principles of the pluralist model but broaden the field's normative value statement so it includes not only traditional collective bargaining but also new forms of work organization and labor market intermediaries and a broader array of methods for providing workers with protection, due process, and participation. This seems to me to be the position broadly espoused by Kochan (2000) in his recent IRRA presidential address and expounded on in more detail in the book *Working in America* (Osterman et al. 2001). A third and more far-reaching option is to further open up the field's normative domain so it makes a balanced increase in efficiency, equity, and human self-actualization and self-development the principal objective of practice and policy and gives preference in a fairly pragmatic way to any and all methods and institutions that singly or in combination promote this goal. Thus, in some situations and time periods this objective may be best accomplished by trade unions and collective bargaining, in others by a unitarist HRM strategy, and yet in others by government legislation, macroeconomic policy, or greater reliance on market forces.

Hopefully the historical analysis provided in this chapter will help inform the debate and provide fruitful food for thought. Greater attention to core ethical principles, as Budd (2004) suggests, is an essential part of this process; indeed, it is crucial if ideology and ethics are to be closely aligned and mutually supportive.

References

Adams, Henry Carter. 1886. "The State in Relation to Industrial Action." *Publications of the American Economic Association,* Vol. 1, no. 6, pp. 7–85.
_____. 1897. "Economics and Jurisprudence." *American Economic Association Studies,* Vol. II, no. 1, pp. 1–48.
Adams, Roy. 1999. "Collective Bargaining: The Rodney Dangerfield of Human Rights." *Labor Law Journal,* Vol. 50, no. 3, pp. 204–9.
_____. 2001. "On the Convergence of Labour Rights and Human Rights." *Relations Industrielles/Industrial Relations,* Vol. 56, no. 1, pp. 199–203.
Adams, Thomas, and Helen Sumner. 1911. *Labor Problems.* New York: Macmillan.
Appelbaum, Eileen, Peter Berg, Arne Kalleberg, and Thomas Bailey. 2000. *Manufacturing Advantage: Why High-Performance Work Systems Pay Off.* Ithaca, NY: ILR Press.
Balderston, Canby. 1935. *Executive Guidance of Industrial Relations.* Philadelphia: University of Pennsylvania Press.
Barbash, Jack. 1979. "The American Ideology of American Industrial Relations." In *Proceedings of the 1979 Spring Meetings, Industrial Relations Research Association.* Madison, WI: Industrial Relations Research Association, pp. 453–7.
_____. 1989. "Introduction." In J. Barbash and K. Barbash, eds., *Theories and Concepts in Comparative Industrial Relations.* Columbia: University of South Carolina Press, pp. 3–6.
_____. 1991. "Industrial Relations Concepts in the USA," *Relations Industrielles/ Industrial Relations,* Vol. 46, no. 1, pp. 91–118.
Budd, John W. 2004. *Employment with a Human Face: Balancing Efficiency, Equity, and Voice.* Ithaca, NY: ILR Press.
Budd, John W., Rafael Gomez, and Noah Meltz. 2004. "Why a Balance Is Best: The Pluralist Industrial Relations Paradigm of Balancing Competing Interests." In B. Kaufman, ed., *Theoretical Perspectives on Work and the Employment Relationship,* Champaign, IL: Industrial Relations Research Association, pp. 195–228.
Cappelli, Peter. 1991. "Is There a Future for the Field of Industrial Relations in the United States?" In R. Lansbury, ed., *Industrial Relations Teaching and Research: International Trends.* Sydney: ACIRRT, University of Sydney, pp. 90–112.
Clark, John. 1900. *The Distribution of Wealth.* New York: Macmillan.
Coats, A. W. 1971. *The Classical Economists and Economic Policy.* London: Methuen.
Commons, John. 1905. *Trade Unionism and Labor Problems.* New York: Ginn.
_____. 1919a. *Industrial Goodwill.* New York: McGraw-Hill.
_____. 1919b. "Labor Demands Secure Jobs." Newspaper article, Reel 19 of the John R. Commons Papers, microfilm version. Madison: State Historical Society of Wisconsin.
_____. 1921a. "Industrial Relations." In J. Commons, ed., *Trade Unionism and Labor Problems,* 2nd series. New York: Augustus Kelly.
_____. 1921b. *Industrial Government.* New York: Macmillan.

_____. 1924. *The Legal Foundations of Capitalism.* New York: Macmillan.

_____. 1934a. *Institutional Economics: Its Place in Political Economy.* New York: Macmillan.

_____. 1934b. *Myself.* Madison, WI: University of Wisconsin Press.

Commons, John, and John Andrews. [1916] 1936. *Principles of Labor Legislation,* 4th od. New York: Harper.

Compa, Lance. 1996. *Human Rights, Labor Rights, and International Trade.* Philadelphia: University of Philadelphia Press.

Dickman, Howard. 1987. *Industrial Democracy in America.* LaSalle, IL: Open Court Press.

Ely, Richard. 1886. *The Labor Movement in America.* New York: Thomas Crowell.

_____. 1938. *Ground Under Our Feet.* New York: Macmillan.

Feuer, Lewis. 1959. *Basic Writings on Politics and Philosophy by Karl Marx and Friedrich Engels.* Garden City, NY: Doubleday.

Fine, Sidney. 1956. *Laissez-Faire and the General Welfare State.* Ann Arbor: University of Michigan Press.

Franke, Walter. 1987. "Accommodating to Change: Can IR Learn from Itself?" *Proceedings of the Fortieth Annual Meeting, Industrial Relations Research Association.* Madison, WI: Industrial Relations Research Association, pp. 474–81.

Fried, Barbara. 1998. *The Progressive Assault on Laissez Faire: Robert Hale and the First Law and Economics Movement.* Cambridge, MA: Harvard University Press.

Friedman, Sheldon, and Stephen Wood. 2001. "Employers' Unfair Advantage in the United States of America: Symposium on the Human Rights Watch Report on the State of Workers' Freedom of Association in the United States. Editors' Introduction." *British Journal of Industrial Relations,* Vol. 39, no. 4, pp. 586–90.

Godard, John. 1995. "The Ideologies of U.S. and Canadian IR Scholars: A Comparative Analysis and Construct Validation." *Journal of Labor Research,* Vol. 16, no. 2, pp. 127–48.

Godard, John, and John Delaney. 2000. "Reflections on the 'High Performance' Paradigm's Implications for Industrial Relations as a Field." *Industrial and Labor Relations Review,* Vol. 53, no. 3, pp. 482–502.

Gonce, Richard. 1996. "The Social Gospel, Ely, and Commons' Initial State of Thought," *Journal of Economic Issues,* Vol. 30, no. 3, pp. 641–65.

Gross, James. 2003. *Workers' Rights as Human Rights.* Ithaca, NY: Cornell University Press.

Hicks, Clarence. 1941. *My Life in Industrial Relations.* New York: Harper.

Hovenkamp, Herbert. 1990. "The First Great Law and Economics Movement." *Stanford Law Review,* Vol. 42, April, pp. 993–1058.

Human Rights Watch. 2000. *Unfair Advantage: Workers' Freedom of Association in the United States Under International Human Rights Standards.* New York: Human Rights.

International Labour Organization. 2000. *Your Voice at Work: Global Report Under the Follow-Up to the ILO Declaration on Fundamental Principles and Rights at Work.* Geneva: International Labour Office.

Jacoby, Sanford. 1997. *Modern Manors: Welfare Capitalism Since the New Deal.* Princeton NJ: Princeton University Press.

Kaufman, Bruce. 1993. *The Origins and Evolution of the Field of Industrial Relations in the United States.* Ithaca, NY: ILR Press.

_____. 2000. "The Case for the Company Union." *Labor History,* Vol. 41, no. 3, pp. 321–50.

_____. 2003a. "John R. Commons and the Wisconsin School on Industrial Relations Strategy and Policy." *Industrial and Labor Relations Review*, Vol. 57, no. 1, pp. 3–30.

_____. 2003b. "Industrial Relations Counselors, Inc.: Its History and Significance." In B. Kaufman, R. Beaumont, and R. Helfgott, eds., *Industrial Relations to Human Resources and Beyond: The Evolving Process of Employee Relations Management*, Armonk, NY: M.E. Sharpe, pp. 31–114.

_____. 2004a. *The Global Evolution of Industrial Relations: Events, Ideas and the IIRA*. Geneva: International Labour Office.

_____. 2004b. "The Institutional and Neoclassical Schools in Labor Economics." In D. Champlin and J. Knoedler, eds., *The Institutionalist Tradition in Labor Economics*. Armonk, NY: M.E. Sharpe, pp. 13–38.

Kellerson, H. 1998. "The ILO Declaration of 1998 on Fundamental Principles and Rights: A Challenge for the Future." *International Labor Review*, Vol. 137, no. 2, pp. 221–7.

King, William Lyon Mackenzie. 1918. *Industry and Humanity*. Toronto: University of Toronto Press.

Kochan, Thomas. 1980. *Industrial Relations and Collective Bargaining*. Homewood, IL: Irwin.

_____. 1998. "What Is Distinctive about Industrial Relations Research?" In George Strauss and Keith Whitfield, eds., *Researching the World of Work: Strategies and Methods in Studying Industrial Relations*. Ithaca, NY: ILR Press, pp. 31–50.

_____. 2000. "Building a New Social Contract at Work: A Call for Action." In *Proceedings of the Fifty-Second Annual Winter Meeting, Industrial Relations Research Association*, Madison, WI: Industrial Relations Research Association, pp. 1–25.

Kochan, Thomas, Harry Katz, and Robert McKersie. 1986. *The Transformation of American Industrial Relations*. New York: Basic Books.

Kochan, Thomas, and Paul Osterman. 1994. *The Mutual Gains Enterprise*. Cambridge, MA: Harvard Business School Press.

Koot, Gerald. 1987. *English Historical Economics, 1870–1926*. Cambridge, UK: Cambridge University Press.

Koslowski, Peter. 1995. *The Theory of Ethical Economy in the Historical School*. Berlin: Springer-Verlag.

Leiserson, William. 1929. "Contributions of Personnel Management to Improved Labor Relations." In *Wertheim Lectures on Industrial Relations*. Cambridge, MA: Harvard University Press.

Lutz, Mark, and Kenneth Lux. 1988. *Humanistic Economics: The New Challenge*. New York: Bootstrap Press.

Marshall, Alfred. [1890] 1961. *Principles of Economics*, 9th ed. London: Macmillan.

McClelland, Peter. 1990. *The American Search for Economic Justice*. London: Basil Blackwell.

Meltz, Noah. 1989. "Industrial Relations, Balancing Efficiency with Equity." In J. Barbash and K. Barbash, eds., *Theories and Concepts in Comparative Industrial Relations*. Columbia: University of South Carolina Press, pp. 109–14.

Mirowski, Philip. 1989. *More Heat than Light: Economics as Social Physics, Physics as Nature's Economics*. Cambridge, UK: Cambridge University Press.

Newcomb, Simon. 1886. *A Plain Man's Talk on the Labor Question*. New York: Harper.

Osterman, Paul, Thomas Kochan, Richard Locke, and Michael Piore. 2001. *Working in America: A Blueprint for a New America*. Cambridge, MA: MIT Press.

Perry, Arthur. 1878. *Elements of Political Economy.* New York, NY: Scribners.

Rader, Benjamin. 1966. *The Academic Mind and Reform: The Influence of Richard T. Ely in American Life.* Frankfort: University of Kentucky Press.

Rockefeller, John D. Jr. 1923. *The Personal Relation in Industry.* New York: Boni and Liverwright.

Schwochau, Susan. 2000. "The Labor Exemption in the Antitrust Law: An Overview," *Journal of Labor Research,* Vol. 21, no. 4, pp. 535–55.

Scoville, James. 1993. "The Past and Present of Ethics in Industrial Relations." In Industrial Relations Research Association, *Proceedings of the Forty-Fifth Annual Meeting,* pp. 198–206. Madison, WI: Industrial Relations Research Association.

Sheppard, Blair, Roy Lewicki, and John Minton. 1992. *Organizational Justice: The Search for Fairness in the Workplace.* Lexington, MA: Lexington Books.

Slichter, Sumner. 1928. "What is the Labor Problem?" in J. Hardman, ed., *American Labor Dynamics in Light of Post-War Developments,* New York: Harcourt Brace, pp. 287–91.

_____. 1931. *Modern Economic Society,* 2nd ed., New York: Henry Holt.

Smith, Adam. 1776. *An Inquiry into the Nature and Causes of the Wealth of Nations.* New York: Modern Library.

Solano, E. 1920. *Labor as an International Problem.* London: Macmillan.

Somers, Gerald. 1975. "Collective Bargaining and the Social-Economic Contract." *Proceedings of the Twenty-Eight Annual Meeting, Industrial Relations Research Association.* Madison, WI: Industrial Relations Research Association, pp. 1–7.

Stiglitz, Joseph. 2001. "Democratic Development as the Fruits of Labor," *Perspectives on Work,* Vol. 4, no. 1, pp. 31–38.

Strauss, George. 1994. "Reclaiming Industrial Relations' Academic Jurisdiction." In *Proceedings of the Forty-Sixth Annual Meeting, Industrial Relations Research Association.* Madison, WI: Industrial Relations Research Association, pp. 1–11.

Strauss, George, Raymond Miles, Charles Snow, and Arnold Tannenbaum. 1974. "Preface." In G. Strauss et al., *Organizational Behavior: Research and Issues.* Madison, WI: Industrial Relations Research Association, p. iv.

Strauss, George, and Keith Whitfield. 1998. "Research Methods in Industrial Relations." In K. Whitfield and G. Strauss, eds., *Researching the World of Work: Strategies and Methods in Studying Industrial Relations.* Ithaca, NY: ILR Press.

Taylor, Frederick. 1911. *Principles of Scientific Management.* New York: Harper.

Walras, Leon. 1874. *Elements of Pure Economics* (English translation). Homewood, IL: Irwin.

Webb, Sidney, and Beatrice Webb. 1897. *Industrial Democracy.* London: Longmans Green.

CHAPTER 3

Kantian Ethical Thought

NORMAN E. BOWIE

University of Minnesota

Kantian ethics is often viewed as extremely intimidating and as too abstract and austere to apply to everyday life. Moreover, some might question why ethical theory is even needed in discussions of human resources and industrial relations. However, I believe that ethical theory has a valuable role to play. Moreover, as I shall demonstrate throughout this paper, Kantian moral theory coheres extremely well with a pluralist theory of industrial relations (Budd, Gomez, and Meltz 2004).

One of the main functions of ethical theory is to provide justification for ethical positions. It is one thing to say that we should treat employees fairly. It is quite another to show what fairness would require in any given context. One of the strengths of Kantian ethics is its justificatory power. Kant tries to show that making an exception of oneself and failing to treat people with respect is self-contradictory or irrational. Showing that reason itself requires doing or not doing something is powerful justification. After all, the only remaining question is "Why be rational?" But that question is a strange one; it asks for a reason for the very thing that is being questioned. As we shall see, Kant's rational approach to ethics provides a justification for two of the most basic principles of ethics: the golden rule and a respect-for-persons principle.

Ethical theory also provides a test for proposed practice and can help industrial relations practitioners shape policies that will be ethical. Consider drug testing. If respect for employees is a fundamental moral principle, then a drug testing policy will take a certain shape. Issues of consent, voice in formulating the policy, guaranteeing the integrity of the results, and protecting privacy as much as possible all become central concerns. There will be many opportunities in this chapter to show how Kantian ethical theory would shape industrial relations policy.

In this chapter I provide a concise workable statement of the three formulations of Kant's categorical imperative, then show how that categorical imperative can be applied to human resources and industrial relations so that the treatment of employees can be considered ethical as well as efficient. The strategy will be very familiar to the pluralists. A Kantian business enterprise organized as a moral community would require a balance among the competing interests of different stakeholders—the central tenet of pluralist theory. Although a Kantian theory of ethical industrial relations is compatible with efficiency, or so I argue, it justifies the pluralist contention that employees should not be treated as mere commodities and that the workplace should be more democratic. (Budd, Gomez, and Meltz 2004).

Kant's Categorical Imperative

The First Formulation

Some years ago the book *All I Really Need to Know I Learned in Kindergarten* was very popular (Fulghum 1988). Many of Fulghum's examples focused on ethical behavior. Kantian ethics is not quite that simple, but close. Kant started with the assumption that we normally know right from wrong and that we want to do what is right. The purpose of philosophical ethics was to help people who wanted to be ethical but were perplexed in difficult situations, where the right choice was not obvious. For example, Kant believed that everyone knows that lying is generally wrong. However, would it be wrong to make a lying promise when you were in desperate financial straits? To answer questions like that, Kant argued, we need to appeal to the *categorical imperative*.

The tradition in Kantian scholarship is to point out that there are three formulations of the categorical imperative. The first formulation is a philosophical version of the golden rule: you should do to others what you want others to do to you. The problem with that statement of the golden rule is that sometimes people have weird desires and beliefs. A sadomasochist willing to have pain inflicted on him would be able to inflict pain on others. A business executive who looked at the business world as a jungle and was willing to have people try to cheat her would, under the traditional formulation of the golden rule, be able to cheat others.

Kant would identify the problem in the traditional formulation with stating the rule in terms of wants. Kant built his ethics on reason, not on wants and desires. Kant's first formulation of the categorical imperative said, "Always act on the maxim which one can will to be a universal law." A maxim for Kant was a principle of action. If the principle of your action cannot be willed universally, then it is not moral. Consider the question of whether a person in dire financial straits is morally permitted to make a lying promise—say, to promise to repay a loan while having no intention of doing so. The maxim for that action would be "It is ok for a person in desperate financial straits to promise to repay a loan with no intention of doing so." Could such a maxim be universally willed? No, because if it were universally willed no one would lend money. It is not simply the fact that there would be bad consequences because no one would lend money. Kant is not a utilitarian. Rather, the lying promise cannot be consistently willed. The person making a lying promise and permitting the universalization of lying promises undercuts himself. The only reason a lying promise could succeed is because there is no universal maxim permitting lying promises. Unethical behavior often involves making an exception of yourself, permitting yourself to do something that you could not permit everyone else to do. If you did, you could not succeed in your aim. A universal maxim permitting lying promises would undercut your attempt to make a lying promise. Kant put it this way:

> Would I be content that my maxim of extricating myself from difficulty by a false promise should hold as a universal law for myself as well as for others? And could I say to myself that everyone may make a false promise when he is in difficulty from which he otherwise cannot escape? Immediately I see that I could will the lie but not a universal law to lie. For with such a law there would be no promises at all, inasmuch as it would be futile to make a pretense of my intention in regard to future actions to those who would not believe the pretense or—if they overhastily did so—would pay me back in my own coin. Thus my maxim would necessarily destroy itself as soon as it was made a universal law ([1785] 1990:19).

Using this formulation of the categorical imperative, it is easy to show that stealing and cheating are wrong. A maxim that would universalize stealing is inconsistent with the notion of private property; it would necessarily destroy itself. A maxim that permitted universalized cheating would make testing impossible—logically impossible. What Kant has done is to show why certain activities are considered wrong. When the maxim permitting those activities is universalized, the maxim becomes self-defeating.

Kant's point can be generalized so that it covers a wide range of human activity. A person can use this first formulation of the categorical imperative to show that whenever someone, including someone in business, agrees to follow the rules of cooperative behavior and then violates the rules for personal gain, she is acting immorally. A maxim that permitted universal violation of the rules is self-defeating. A universally violated rule is not a rule.

This kind of analysis shows that free-loading is morally wrong. A freeloader is one who accepts the rules for cooperative behavior but then either violates the rules or fails to contribute his share in supporting them. This analysis shows how ethical theory can establish that something normally considered to be wrong, such as free-loading, really is wrong.

In more contemporary language, the first formulation shows how much unethical behavior involves making an exception of oneself. The unethical person does what she could not agree to having done universally. Once one works with the categorical imperative, one can see why transparency is an essential moral value. Lack of transparency undermines those very institutions that depend on it. A Kantian is not surprised to see the stock price of a company plunge when accounting irregularities are revealed. The virtue most often associated with the first formulation is integrity—transparency in thought and action.

The Second Formulation

The second formulation of the categorical imperative states that "one should always treat the humanity in a person as an end and never as a means merely." Just as the first formulation can be seen as a version of the golden rule, the second formulation is a version of the principle that we should respect people. This principle is woven into the very fabric of American moral thought and is a foundation of American civil society. Any moral disagreement about the principle is disagreement about how it should be applied and not with the principle itself. (I recognize, of course, that despite the acceptance of this moral principle, respect for people is not always fully practiced in the economic and business arenas.)

Since the principle is so well accepted in moral discourse, there is seldom much demand that it be justified. But Kantian moral theory has a justification, and that justification assists us in applying the principle even in economic and business arenas, where it is frequently ignored. Kant asks what it is that distinguishes humans from other things on the planet. Humans are free. For Kant they are free in two senses. They have what is called "negative freedom," when they are free from causal necessity. People are not like billiard balls, whose movement is determined and whose actions can be explained solely by the velocity and angle of impact. People make decisions; billiard balls do not. But in Kant's view, negative freedom is not freedom in its fullest sense. Some events cannot be given a causal explanation because they are random, but these events are not truly free. William James thought he could explain human freedom by showing how a person who always went home a certain way suddenly made a decision to take an alternative route home. ([1884] 1962). For James that random change in the pattern of behavior showed that the event was free. Not for Kant. There was no reason for the change in pattern, for positive freedom actions must be done for a reason. For Kant, humans are positively free because they can conform to laws they give themselves. A free act, then, is one that is done not out of causal necessity but on the basis of a law (or reason) that the agent gives himself.

The fact that we are free in this sense is what gives us dignity—a dignity that is beyond price. We are aware of our freedom, and we all have a sense of dignity. Of course, what I ascribe to myself as a human being, I must logically ascribe to others who are human beings. A reason in one case is a reason in all similar cases. Hence, when I act from a law of my own making, it must be a law that other human beings could accept. It is a law that can be universalized. But that law is the categorical imperative in its first formulation. Thus humans are free because we are not bound by causal necessity and we can act from the moral law. That is what makes us special and why the humanity in a person should be respected.

Violating the humanity in a person is a great moral wrong in Kantian ethics. One violates a person's humanity when one violates her negative or positive freedom. The two basic means of violating negative freedom are coercion and deception. As the contemporary Kantian Christine Korsgaard has put it:

> According to the Formula of Humanity, coercion and deception are the most fundamental forms of wrongdoing to others—the roots of all evil. Coercion and deception violate the conditions of possible assent, and all actions which depend for their nature and efficacy on their coercive or deceptive character are ones that others cannot assent to. . . . Physical coercion treats someone's person as a tool; lying treats someone's *reason* as a tool. That is why Kant finds it so horrifying; it is a direct violation of autonomy (1996:140, 141).

Kant's point is accepted by persons of nearly all political persuasions. Coercion and deception are a violation of negative freedom because they block a person from choosing ends he would have chosen had the coercion or deception not occurred.

Lack of coercion and deception is not sufficient to treat persons with respect. We have positive obligations to further the humanity of people; we have obligations to take positive action to help people. Thomas Hill, Jr. has argued that in particular there is a positive obligation to help humans develop the following capacities:

1. the capacity and disposition to act on the basis of reasons

2. the capacity to act on principles of prudence and efficiency so long as these principles do not violate the categorical imperative

3. the power to set any end whatsoever which includes the ability to see future consequences, adopt long range goals, resist immediate temptation, and even to commit oneself to ends for which one has no sensuous desire

4. the capacity to accept categorical imperatives

5. some ability to understand the world and to reason abstractly (1992: 40–41)

For Hill, respecting and supporting the development of these capacities are what Kant means by respecting the humanity in a person.

Although I accept Hill's account, I think respecting the humanity in a person requires some additional things. In both the *Foundations* and *The Metaphysics of Morals*, Kant is clear that we have duties to develop our talents and to give aid to the needy. We also cannot be indifferent to people. To be indifferent is not to treat the humanity in a person with respect. Thus, in addition to supporting the development of the capacities identified by Hill, respecting the humanity in people requires that we support the development of their talents and provide aid when they are in need. By doing these things we show that we are not indifferent to them.

It is important to note here that some duties in respecting the humanity in a person are more stringent than others. Kant distinguishes perfect duties from imperfect duties. Perfect duties are duties that are always required, such as the duty not to coerce and the duty not to deceive. Imperfect duties are duties that one must honor on some occasions but can ignore on others, such as the duties to develop one's talents and to aid. You do not need to aid people whenever aid is required, but there is some requirement to aid. In terms of the discussion here, the duties not to violate negative freedom are perfect duties, and the duties to aid positive freedom are imperfect duties.

The Third Formulation

The third formulation of the categorical imperative is sometimes called the "kingdom of ends" formulation. Loosely put, this formulation says that you should act as if you were a member of an ideal kingdom of ends in which you were both subject and sovereign at the same time. What did Kant mean here? Kant recognized that human beings interact with other human beings (ends). This arena of interaction is the kingdom of ends. A business, like any other organization, is composed of individual persons; since persons are moral creatures, the interactions of persons in an organization are constrained by the categorical imperative. Any organization, whatever its purpose, must be governed by morality. In that sense an organization should be a moral community.

How are the relations in a moral community to be governed? They must be governed by laws that all can accept. Only those laws are consistent with human freedom. Since all members of the community in some sense create the laws that govern them, all members are sovereign. However, all members of the community are subject to the law. That is how you can be subject and sovereign at the same time. Strictly speaking, in any organizational context any rule proposed for governing the organization must be acceptable to all. Since this may not be possible as a practical matter, Kant's requirement might best be changed to the requirement that an organization be governed by a process that can be acceptable to all.

What Kant suggests is that we ask moral beings to act from rules that are publicly acceptable in the sense that they seem reasonable to any rational person. Let us apply this to business. Since all persons in economic affairs are moral agents, they are equal with respect to possessing dignity and intrinsic value. Thus, morally, the interests of any one member in a business community are equal to the interests of any other member. What is needed are specific suggestions for principles and processes that can gain the assent of all, even when individual interests may be in conflict.

A note on duty: Students of Kant realize that I have not said anything about Kant's insistence that an action must be done from a moral motive if it is to be a truly moral act. In other words, an action must be done because it is right and not for some other reason. The *Foundations* open with this central notion: "Nothing in the world—indeed nothing even beyond the world—can possibly be conceived which could be called good without qualification except a Good Will" (Kant 1990:9). In the minds of many, this would mean that even the benevolent actions of corporations would not be truly moral, because they are usually done on the grounds that they are right and because they are right they will be profitable in the long run. But doesn't the appeal to profit in the long run contaminate the motive? Not if seeking profit is one of the moral duties that managers have. The tendency in the public is to see profit-seeking as purely a prudential or even a selfish motive. But given U.S. law regarding the duties of the officers of a firm— the notion that the management is in a contractual relationship with the stockholders and that managers are fiduciary agents for the stockholders—it is clear that one of the duties of management is to seek profits for stockholders. And that duty is a moral duty (Bowie 1999).

On this point I am in partial agreement with Milton Friedman, who has maintained that the only proper function of business is to maximize profit consistent with law and ordinary morality. At one point Friedman put it this way:

> In such an economy [free], there is one and only one social responsibility of business—to use its resources and engage in activities designed to increase its profits so long as it stays within the rules of the game, which is to say, engages in open and free competition, without deception or fraud (1962:133).

What distinguishes the Kantian approach is an expanded notion of "rules of the game" based on a coherent moral theory. For example, a human resource manager ought not to gain profit by treating the humanity of a person merely as a means. However, the duty to seek a profit for shareholders is surely one of the duties that a human resource manager has.

And equally important, because there is a managerial duty to seek a profit, none of the attempts in this essay to show that Kantian ethics in human resource management is good business run afoul of Kant's central belief that an act can only be truly moral if it is done from the right motive—because it is right. Of course to be right, any action that leads to profitability must also be consistent with the three formulations of the categorical imperative.

Ethical Human Resource Management in the Kantian Tradition

Respecting the Humanity of a Person

Many of the moral objections to human resource management amount to the fact that employees are treated as merely a means to increase profits for stockholders. If enlightened human resource management techniques lead to greater profit, then they should be adopted. If they do not lead to greater profit then they should not be adopted. This was the view allegedly held by Jack Welch. In his early days at GE, he was known as "neutron Jack" because he left the buildings but fired so many employees. Later he discovered enlightened human resource management and became convinced that GE could be more profitable with that approach. Welch was asked, If later evidence nullified the greater profitability of the enlightened approach, would he give it up? "Of course" was his answer. Welch's view regarding human resource management is purely instrumental.

The Kantian argues that employees must not be treated in certain ways even if profitability could be increased by doing so. For example, the use of coercion or deception is wrong. The charge that employees are routinely lied to in the business context is a serious indictment of the morality of management. Retirees have been promised health benefits only to have them denied. Employees have been promised a certain level of pension contribution only to have management renege. Enron management urged employees not to sell Enron stock even though they knew that Enron was in serious financial trouble and even though they sold their own stock. The list of companies that have engaged in such conduct is seemingly endless. From a Kantian perspective that conduct is wrong. These actions violate not only the second formulation of the categorical imperative but the first formulation as well. Since all the actions involve lying or deception, they cannot be consistently universalized. Thus one of the ways to treat the humanity in a person with respect is to be transparent in word and deed.

One goal of Kantian human resource management should be an increase in transparency, for it is transparency that provides the proper antidote to deception. One of the most transparent management practices is open book management. Developed by Jack Stack at the Springfield Manufacturing Company (Stack 1992), open book management won a prestigious business ethics award. The goal of open book management is to make everyone a mini-CFO; employees are given all the financial information about the company. Needless to say, open book management is not soft. Imagine a business in which everyone in the organization focused on the profitability of the firm. Thus, open book management is supposed to be good business. With complete information and the proper incentives, employees behave responsibly without the usual layers of supervision. The success of open book management can be dramatically increased when it is combined with a profit-sharing program. As one foreman put it, where there is a profit-sharing plan and complete sharing of information, no one is likely to order extra inventory or make other choices that will undercut the profitability of the firm.

However, the case for open book management is not just profit related. In a video exploring the practice, employees speak of their increased freedom and responsibility. One woman sums it up: "I'm not just a name on a time card. I am somebody. I am a person." That is just the kind of statement a Kantian wants to hear. Obviously the employees under open book management do not feel that they are treated as a means merely. They feel treated as autonomous responsible adults—as persons (Case 1995).

Though much has been written about profit sharing, few have recognized that profit sharing *throughout the business* could be a means for reducing coercion and deception. Profit-sharing plans that extend to the entire workforce could allow everyone to share in the gains that result from increasing productivity. Since everyone would have an interest in the success of the firm, there would be demands for access to information to make sure that the profit-sharing plan is handled fairly (Ben-Ner and Jones 1995).

In theory, companywide profit-sharing plans also allow everyone to share the risks of an economic downturn—specifically, by avoiding layoffs. Many critics of capitalism argue that layoffs are coercive. Defenders of layoffs argue that they are often an economic necessity, one that every employee understands when agreeing to employment, and that an employee who freely accepts an employment contract cannot complain of coercion when a layoff occurs. That response raises an interesting philosophical issue about the nature of coercion.

The overwhelming number of people need to work to survive, at least for a large portion of their lives. There is a sense in which people are forced to work. When an assailant says, "Your wallet or your life," you technically have a choice. However, for many this situation is the paradigm of coercion. How close is the analogy between the assailant and the requirements of the employer? Admittedly, in good times the balance of power shifts somewhat, but in hard times the balance of power is with the employer. Most people have to take the terms of employment as they get them (Manning 2003). Someone wanting employment does not negotiate about whether or not to be tested for drugs, for example. If drug testing is the company policy, you either submit to the test or forfeit the job. If you want a job, you agree to employment at will and to layoffs if management believes they are necessary. Survival for yourself and any dependents requires it. As with the assailant, you technically have a choice, but most employees argue they have little choice about multiple important terms of employment. A Kantian, in common with the pluralist school of industrial relations, maintains that the imbalance between employer and employee ought to be addressed. Otherwise, industrial relations rests on an unethical foundation.

Layoffs are psychologically devastating to most employees. You can lose many of the goods you purchase with your salary without feeling a loss of respect. However, in Kantian terms, a layoff damages self-respect. The person who loses a job feels herself diminished and someone who is not fully worthy. I suspect that some of this results because the person who loses a job also loses some of her freedom or autonomy, and autonomy is a central human value. Thus a Kantian would argue on moral grounds that there is a prima facie case against layoffs. Layoffs are somewhat coercive and are damaging to employee self-respect, so unless they are absolutely necessary, they are wrong.

Profit sharing is a way of avoiding layoffs. If profits fall, everyone suffers a diminished paycheck. However, unless the fall-off in profits is incredibly severe, no one need lose a job. Indeed, if there were no profits to be shared, there still are alternatives to layoffs. Rather than anyone being laid off, everyone can take a cut in pay. In other words, in troubled economic times, the pain can be spread rather than fall completely on those who are laid off.

Sometimes layoffs are an economic necessity, and the moral presumption against them is overridden. However, a Kantian does not like to fire people and seeks alternatives to layoffs wherever possible. Moreover, the Kantian approach makes sound business sense. Research, including that by Jeffrey Pfeffer and Frederick F. Reichheld, has documented the payoffs that result when management seeks alternatives to layoffs (Pfeffer 1994, 1998; Reichheld 1996). Another study shows that the stock prices of companies that downsize do more poorly than those that don't (Dorfman 1991). Companies that do not downsize have also been found to have a productivity advantage (Pfeffer 1998). Managers also often overlook the cost of training. Reichheld (1996) has demonstrated the cost savings that result from a stable and loyal workforce.

Sometimes a negative case tells as much as a positive one. Apple Computer serves as a poignant example. Under Steve Jobs, Apple had a unique culture that was characterized by high employee morale. Apple was known for employee accessibility to management, recognition of employee milestones, and bagels and cream cheese on Fridays. Employment was stable. The employee handbook celebrated the importance of people to the firm's success.

But Apple was under extreme competitive pressure from Microsoft. How should management handle this pressure? The company behaved in a traditional and destructive manner. John Scully replaced Steve Jobs and introduced a new management philosophy that traditionally pleases Wall Street. Scully saw employees as costs, not as responsible moral beings deserving of respect. Layoffs were made in 1985, with a second round in 1991. By then Apple had eliminated 10% of its workforce. But Apple's competitive position did not improve, and Scully was fired. The approach to employees remained the same, however; they were viewed as costs and the layoffs continued. By 1997 Apple had less than half of its original workforce.

Treating people as costs had the unpleasant effect of treating them without respect. Pfeffer describes the dismissal process as follows:

> The dismissal process occurred on a single day. Each employee was told to be at their desk at 9:00 a.m. in the morning. Those who received early calls into their managers' offices were laid off. They were given pink slips, final checks and severance information. They were then escorted to the door. The remaining employees were gathered into a room at 11:00 a.m. to discuss their new jobs, since restructuring began immediately (1998:25).

Naturally the bagels and cream cheese had long disappeared as well. They were a cost that could be eliminated. Presumably the cost-obsessed management could not justify what they could not quantify—namely, the benefits of people getting together periodically over free food to discuss and resolve issues. Needless to say, employee morale at Apple was terrible. It continued to lose ground to Microsoft, and many predicted Apple's demise.

In desperation, Apple convinced Steve Jobs to return as CEO. He reversed course, focusing on improved quality and new products and competing on quality rather than reduced costs. Recently the company's iPod and iTunes have been great commercial successes. So have the Apple stores opened in major urban centers, including Manhattan and the Mall of America near Minneapolis–St. Paul. In February 2004 Steve Jobs was once again on the cover of *BusinessWeek*. The story of the decline and resurrection of Apple has much to tell us about corporate strategy, the importance of job stability, and the ethics of respecting people. Indeed, it casts light on a philosophical debate that is raging about the very purpose of the firm.

A Note on Stakeholder Theory Versus Stockholder Theory

MBA students are told again and again that the purpose of the firm is to contribute to (i.e., maximize) stockholder wealth. The managers are agents of the stockholders, and what the stockholder–owners want is more return for their investment. MBA students also learn that there are other constituencies—stakeholders—whose support is needed if the firm is to be profitable. A manager cannot make money for stockholders if there are no customers. However, these other stakeholders are treated instrumentally, merely as a means to stockholder wealth, rather than as ends in themselves, as a Kantian ethic would demand.

Management from the perspective of Kantian ethics takes a very different noninstrumental approach to the other stakeholders. Kantians argue that everyone affected by the firm has a moral claim to be treated with respect, though they realize that not all those affected by firm behavior stand in the same relationship to the firm. As William Evan and R. Edward Freeman have pointed out, some stakeholder groups are essential to the very survival of the firm (Evan and Freeman 1988). In addition to stockholders, those stakeholder groups traditionally include customers, employees, managers, suppliers, and the local community. Given the centrality of these groups to the success of the corporation, management has special obligations to them. Kantian moral philosophy requires that all those affected by the firm be treated with respect. Kantian business ethicists have spelled out in more detail what treating the humanity in a person requires when managers interact with these six essential stakeholder groups. This paper, of course, is outlining what is required when managers treat the humanity in employees with respect. A full-blown Kantian theory of business ethics would outline those obligations for all the stakeholder groups.

Building a Business as a Moral Community

If managers were to treat the employment relationship in the context of a moral community (a "kingdom of ends," in Kant's language), human resource policy would look very different. Corporate America's standard mode of organization is hierarchical. To see who reports to whom, you look at the organization chart, and in most organizations the reporting lines are pretty clear. The employer–employee relationship also is often covered by the doctrine of employment at will. An at-will employee can be fired for any reason—good, bad, or immoral— and may resign for any good, bad, or immoral reason. Certain exceptions do or may apply, however: One, employees have been given statutory protection against being fired on the basis of religion, race, sex, old age, or disability. An explicit employer–employee contract also can constrain the at-will relationship, as does employee membership in a labor union. Finally, a public policy exception protects employees from being fired when they are ordered to do something in violation of the law (but courts have interpreted this exception very narrowly). What is clear is that hierarchical organization combined with even a constrained employment at-will labor contract is not conducive to the exercise of employee autonomy or to employee participation. Kant requires that members of the kingdom of ends agree to the rules that govern them. Hierarchical management typically gives orders; it does not seek agreement.

A Kantian is a moral critic of the standard employer–employee relationship. What would a Kantian manager put in its place? Recall that for Kant, human autonomy is the central feature of humanity. Freedom is required for both our rational and ethical decision making. As the Kantian scholar Onora O'Neill points out:

> [Kant] argues not from reason to autonomy but from autonomy to reason. Only autonomous self-disciplining beings can act on principles that we have grounds to call principles of reason. . . . [I]t [the categorical imperative] is a fundamental strategy not just of morality but of all activity that counts as reasoned. The supreme principle of reason is merely the principle of thinking and acting on principles that can (not do!) hold for all (1989:57, 59).

Since autonomy is the foundation for both rationality and morality, autonomy is the central value for Kant. The most direct way to show respect for the humanity in a person is to respect or support the development of autonomy. Contrast what Kant says about reason and authority with the hierarchical view:

> Reason depends on this freedom for its very existence. For reason has no dictatorial authority, its verdict is always the agreement of free citizens, of whom each one must be permitted to express, without let or hindrance, his objections or even his veto ([1781] 1963:593).

The most obvious way to support autonomy is to support employee participation in the workplace. Kantian ethics demands that the workplace be more democratic, consistent with a main contention of pluralist human relations.

The traditional way for employees to obtain voice is through unionizing. The right to unionize is considered a universal one. It is endorsed in the United Nations (1948) Declaration on Human Rights and in all subsequent UN treaties and declarations relating to the workplace. It is endorsed by the Caux Round Table (1994) Principles for Business and by the International Labour Organization's Declaration on Fundamental Principles and Rights at Work (1998).

Despite the normative endorsement of unions, union membership has declined steadily in the United States during the last 40 years, and in the U.S. business context, "union" has become a dirty word. Union membership in other industrial countries, such as Canada, Japan, Australia, the United Kingdom, Ireland, France, and Italy, was under 50% at the end of the 20th century (Katz and Darbishire 2000). But a Kantian can endorse a union, so long as it is not corrupt and is governed by democratic principles. Since unions provide for voice and participation in the workplace and can protect workers from unjust and arbitrary dismissal, I believe their decline, especially in America, is tragic. And in North America, there is no more effective antidote to arbitrary at-will decisions than a union contract.

Fortunately, however, unions are not the only way to provide voice and participation in business organizations. An alternative that might be considered is one advanced by William Evan and R. Edward Freeman: a stakeholder board of directors (1988). Under this proposal the board of directors of a publicly traded firm would comprise representatives from five stakeholder groups: employees, customers, suppliers, stockholders, and the local community. There would also be a person who represented the corporation as an entity. The function of this kind of board is to manage the corporation for the benefit of all the stakeholders and to make sure that no one stakeholder group is unduly harmed. Since the interests of stakeholder groups often conflict, the stakeholder board would have to convince the various groups that its policies were in the interest of the long-term health of the corporation, even if a particular stakeholder group might suffer in the short run.

The deliberations of such a stakeholder board would also serve transparency. For example, the employee representative would see financial information, hear about planned mergers, and see executive compensation packages. In Kantian terms, the stakeholder board of directors would meet a minimum condition for the democratization of the business firm: that each person in the firm be represented by the stakeholder group to which she belongs and that the various stakeholder groups consent to the rules and practices that govern the organization. These stakeholder groups would also need to consent to the procedures for changing the rules. Under a Kantian regime, a contractual, cooperative, representative model of management would replace the hierarchical model.

Ideally, however, democratization should go further. Teams should replace some hierarchical layers of management. Decisions made in teams should be consensual or at least a product of the majority. The persons in a firm organized in a Kantian model would share the goals of the firm. Since its rules and procedures would have the approval of the various stakeholder groups, the firm would have the look of a representative democracy. To that extent the employees would be both subject and sovereign with respect to the rules and procedures that govern them, as required by the kingdom-of-ends formulation of the categorical imperative. Democracy at the team level would approach direct democracy, and an ideal for team decisions would be unanimous consent.

Business executives normally are very critical of calls for a more democratic workplace. Williamson (1985) thinks that hierarchical firms are the most efficient and that, in a competitive economy, hierarchical structures would win out in the end. Getting consensus—even when that consensus is limited to stakeholder groups—is time consuming. In addition, corporate executives like to be seen as "in command." Power in an organization is not easily shared. Thus, it might seem as if more democratic business organizations are doomed from the start.

I think such conventional wisdom is mistaken, however. First, there are business advocates for more democratic workplaces, and there are many anecdotal success stories. German law, for example, requires that employees are entitled to be one third of the representatives on the supervisory board of companies with more than 500 employees and to nominally equal parity consisting of one half of the representatives in companies with more than 2,000 employees. That means that managers are required to meet regularly with employees for purposes of dialogue and decision making. Cadbury's in the United Kingdom has a long tradition of participative management. The airline with the greatest customer satisfaction is Singapore Airlines. Joseph Pillay, the chairman in 1988, described his management philosophy as follows:

> First, we are above all, a democratic organization. . . . We are not authoritarian, autocratic or paternalistic. There has to be delegation of authority down the line. . . . We endeavor to create an environment in which responsibility . . . can be exercised effectively at all levels (quoted in Stewart 1998:112).

Sometimes financial exigency can turn traditionalists into democrats. In Maine a Pratt and Whitney plant was threatened with closure because of inefficiency and quality control problems. The new plant manager, Roger Ponchak, adopted a profit-sharing plan and imposed a program of extensive worker retraining. Though both of those reforms are consistent with Kantian ethics, neither was adopted democratically, and workers resisted. Then Ponchak had difficulty introducing a new production scheme. At that point he opted for workplace democracy. He appointed 22 representatives from both factory and clerical employees to leave their jobs and come up with a new pay and job classification scheme that linked pay to learning the new techniques. (Kantians would argue that it would have been better had the representatives been elected. In addition, the National Labor Relations Board, in its 1992 *Electromation* and other decisions, has developed standards to prevent the manipulation of workplace democracy plans.) The group succeeded, with the result that the plant was saved from closure (White 1996).

Authoritative research likewise documents the success of a participative environment. Studies documenting the adverse effects of hierarchical authoritarian management stretch back over a 50-year period. Rensis Likert of the University of Michigan distinguished four types of organizations: the exploitative authoritative, the benevolent authoritative, the consultative, and the participative group (Likert 1967). The participative group form of organization is highly democratic, with employee involvement in setting the goals of the organization and meeting them. Compensation plans are decided by group participation. Communication is initiated at all points in the organization, and the flow of information is multidirectional. There is a high level of teamwork in a participative group organization.

Which of the four Likert types of organization was the most productive? The participative group had lower absenteeism; produced less scrap, loss, and waste; had more interaction among its members; and had more accurate information. These factors are of course tied to greater productivity and profitability (Likert 1967). The extensive research literature in human resources and industrial relations that has come since Likert's work often concludes that high performance work practices can increase organizational performance. (For example, see Huselid 1995; Ichniowski, Shaw, and Prennushi 1997; and Batt 1999.) At the same time, it must be admitted that these conclusions are not universal (Cappelli and Neumark 2001). Should the less optimistic research concerning the connection between high performance work practices and increased organizational performance prevail, then a Kantian organization has a moral obligation to try to figure out how to make high performance work practices effective and therefore good for both firms and workers.

The late W. Edwards Deming is widely regarded as authoritative on developing processes to deliver quality. Most people emphasize the quantitative side of Deming's "14 points." What is often overlooked is Deming's strong advocacy for a more democratic workplace. He thought that workers were often unfairly blamed for the mistakes of management (Gabor 1990). Calls for a more participative democratic workplace may not be utopian after all; indeed, corporations that embody these characteristics might be more competitive rather than less so.

Kantian Leadership

One might wonder about the implications of this emphasis on employee autonomy for leadership. Doesn't effective leadership require someone who makes decisions and then successfully gets everyone on board to achieve the organization's goals? And if that is leadership, then doesn't an emphasis on autonomy undermine the stature of the leader?

I think not. What would Kantian leadership look like? Since Kant is committed to a view where respecting the humanity in a person is tied to respecting his or her autonomy I have argued that Kantian leadership involves driving decision making down the organization so that followers learn to become leaders (Bowie 2000). In that way a Kantian leader supports the development of autonomy among followers.

As with the discussion on a democratic workplace, the third formulation of the categorical imperative—the kingdom of ends—seems most relevant here. First, it acts as a significant restraint on leadership as leadership is traditionally understood. Most people think of a leader as "the boss," but a Kantian does not accept this view. To be consistent with the kingdom-of-ends formulation, the leader is a decision proposer rather than a decision imposer. A leader can propose ends as well as means for reaching those ends; he or she can propose decision-making rules as well. But the leader should not order these things or impose them on the basis of power. A Kantian is committed to reason, not power, as the basis for decisions.

In management terms the Kantian leader creates the conditions for participative management. Practitioners would say that the Kantian leader gets buy-in. However, this buy-in is not based on power or position. Nor should it be based on charisma. Rather it should be based on the merits of the proposal, on reasons that can be defended.

Kantian leadership would transform the traditional adversarial union–management relationship. The Kantian leader would be committed to cooperative attempts to resolve issues in the firm and find win-win solutions to problems. The Kantian is committed to integrative bargaining such as that described in *Getting to Yes* (Fisher and Ury 1981).

Again the Kantian needs to engage the critic who finds such notions as turning leaders into followers to be muddle-headed and inconsistent with running a successful, profitable company. However, the Kantian can appeal to solid research and to successful examples of such leadership to buttress the moral case.

Students of organizational behavior are familiar with the phenomenon of group-think, in which members identify so strongly with the position of the group—a position often inspired by the leader—that there is little critical discussion. As a result, strategic and/or moral disasters can occur. An excellent training film analyzes the Challenger space-shuttle disaster as an instance of group-think. The film vividly shows how the concerns of the engineers at Morton Thiokol got marginalized and then eliminated. At one poignant moment, engineer/manager Bob Lund is told, "Bob, take off your engineer's hat and put on your management hat."

What is the cure for group-think? In organizational behavior language, it is the appointment of "critical evaluators"—people charged with challenging the dominant idea of the group. In the Kantian model, critical evaluators occur naturally because people in the organization are encouraged to speak up and provide reasons for decisions—reasons that in principle could appeal to all. Simply put, in a firm where the task of the leader is to encourage others to be leaders, it is hard to imagine group-think getting a hold.

It seems easier to find examples of successful Kantian leaders in Europe than in the United States. One example is Jan Carlzon, former head of SAS Airlines. When Carlzon took over as CEO, the company had lost its way and was floundering. He undertook a number of steps that brought popularity and profitability to the airline. A characteristic of his leadership style was to empower others in the organization to make decisions. For example, persons checking in passengers could make decisions about upgrades, canceling penalties, and the like.

One anecdote in particular reflects Carlzon's leadership style. Carlzon realized he had not provided successful leadership the first time he went on vacation and got constant phone calls asking him to make decisions. Carlzon realized that he would only succeed when he went on vacation and no one called to seek his advice. He believed that his job as a leader was to encourage subordinates to make decisions on their own, and in that way he increased their autonomy on the job. Carlzon knew he had succeeded when eventually he went on vacation and nobody called.

Carlzon's experience illustrates the central thesis of a Kantian theory of leadership. Contrary to the popular stereotype of leadership, a Kantian leader is not the one to whom you look for a decision. Rather, the Kantian leader empowers others in the organization to take responsibility for making decisions. A central task of the leader is to respect and enhance the autonomy of followers. I have argued that one respects employee freedom by not coercing or deceiving them. Neither does one simply use authority or power to get employees to do the leader's bidding. That is what is wrong with hierarchical management from the Kantian perspective. Leadership that respects negative freedom (freedom from causal necessity) is leadership that increases an employee's autonomy in the organization. Kantian leadership empowers employees to make decisions rather than wait for orders. Indeed, its purpose is to turn followers into leaders. In addition to being required by the second and third formulations of the categorical imperative, that style of leadership simply makes good business sense.

Meaningful Work

In addition to respecting negative freedom, employers have an obligation to respect positive freedom, or the autonomy to follow laws people have made themselves. Employees who are positively free are as free from compulsions as they are from coercion. To honor positive freedom is to enlarge the realm of obligations. Treating the humanity of a person as an end in itself may require doing more than merely refraining from coercion and deception. Sometimes it requires taking positive action to help.

One positive action that a business can take to honor positive freedom is to provide meaningful work. Using Kantian texts as a guide, I have proposed that employers are obliged to meet the following conditions with respect to employees and that honoring them all is what is involved in providing meaningful work:

1. Meaningful work is work that is freely chosen and provides opportunities for the worker to exercise autonomy on the job.

2. The work relationship must support the autonomy and rationality of human beings. Work that unnecessarily deadens autonomy or that undermines rationality is immoral.

3. Meaningful work is work that provides a salary sufficient for the worker to exercise her independence and provides for her physical well-being and the satisfaction of some of her desires.

4. Meaningful work is work that enables a person to develop her rational capacities.

5. Meaningful work is work that does not interfere with a person's moral development.

6. Meaningful work is work that is not paternalistic in the sense of interfering with the worker's conception of how she wishes to obtain happiness (Bowie 1999:70–71).

Let us evaluate current human resource practices against these requirements to provide meaningful work. Condition 1 is a straightforward requirement: that work be freely chosen and that employees be given some autonomy on the job. Respect for negative freedom is sufficient here.

Condition 2 has a lot more bite because it challenges the morality of Taylorism, or the extreme division of labor. The classic case of division of labor is Adam Smith's pin factory, where the act of making a pin comprises 18 separate operations. Smith noted that without the division of labor, the individual output of pins would be somewhere between one and 20 pins a day. With the division of labor, hundreds of pins would be produced.

Fukuyama describes Taylorism as follows:

> [Taylor] tried to codify the "laws" of mass production by recommending a very high degree of specialization that deliber-

ately avoided the need for individual assembly workers to demonstrate innovative judgment or even skill. Maintenance of the assembly line and its fine-tuning was given to a separate maintenance department and the controlling intelligence behind the design itself was the province of white collar engineering. . . . The goal of scientific management was to structure the workplace in such a way that the only quality required of a worker was obedience. . . . A factory organized according to Taylorite principles broadcasts to its workers the message that they are not going to be trusted with significant responsibilities and that their duties will be laid out for them in a highly detailed and legalistic form (1995:225–6).

This form of Taylorism violates in a number of ways the Kantian injunction to respect the humanity of a person. Condition 1 is obviously violated. So is condition 2, because work done according to Taylor's principles of scientific management deadens autonomy and undermines rationality. Even the founder of specialization, Adam Smith, recognized the damaging effects of the pin factory:

The man whose life is spent performing a few simple operations, of which the effects are, perhaps, always the same, has no occasion to exert his understanding, or to exercise his invention in finding out expedients for removing difficulties that never occur. He naturally loses, therefore, the habit of such exertion, and generally becomes as stupid and ignorant as it is possible for a human creature to become. The torpor of his mind renders him not only incapable of relishing or bearing any part of rational conversation, but of conceiving any generous, noble, or tender sentiment, and consequently of forming any just judgment concerning many even of the ordinary duties of public life ([1776] 1976:part ii 303).

Most readers of Smith never get to book V, *Of the Expense of the Institutions for the Education of Youth,* where Smith makes these very provocative remarks. Both the autonomy and the rationality of the workers in the pin factory and in factories like the pin factory are impaired and indeed even deadened, violating condition 2.

Obviously some specialization in business is required to achieve efficiency and increased productivity. But surely it need not go as far as Taylor's scientific management. On that score the auto industry in the United States had something to learn from the teamwork of the Japanese. In general, teamwork both enhances autonomy and overcomes some of the deadening effects of specialization.

Condition 3 speaks to the issue of a minimum or living wage. In both of his major ethical works, *Foundations of the Metaphysics of Morals* and the second part of *Metaphysics of Morals,* popularly called *Metaphysical Principles of Virtue,* Kant argues that we have an obligation of beneficence, or a duty to aid others. This duty is an imperfect one in the sense that one does not have to help everyone all the time. That of course would be too demanding. But the obligation to help others must be taken seriously.

When taken to the business context, the most obvious way to be beneficent is to pay a living wage. In line with Kant's commitment to autonomy, a living wage is defined by its ability to allow a person to live independently. One cannot live independently if basic needs for food, clothing, shelter, and health care are not met. In addition to sufficient pay to cover these needs, there should be a bit left over for discretionary items. A wage that provides for basic needs plus a bit of discretionary income could be classified as minimally adequate.

In many cases business firms are clearly not providing living wages. It was recently pointed out that the $8 per hour earned by the average nonsupervisory employee at Wal-Mart would not meet the U.S. standard for a living wage—and the U.S. standard is below that required by Kantian ethics (Bianco and Zellner, 2000). Given the competitive power of Wal-Mart, its wage policy tends to bring down wages in the entire retail sector. As premiums for health insurance rise, more and more companies are dropping health insurance for their employees or, like Wal-Mart, are asking employees to pay a large part of the premium. Prima facie, American companies are adopting wage policies that move us away from what Kantian ethics requires rather than toward it.

I say prima facie because U.S. companies argue that they cannot pay the kind of wages for low-skilled or entry-level jobs that Kantian morality requires. If they did, they argue, they would go out of business. They are constrained by low-wage competition, both domestically and internationally. After all, it is a fundamental principle of ethics that "ought" implies "can," meaning that you can only be held responsible for events that are in your power. If so, then a business has an obligation to pay a living wage only if it has the capability to do so.

Though the adherents to this argument have a point, their case is hardly airtight. Pleading poverty seems disingenuous given the recent trend in executive pay. The ratio of average executive pay to the pay of the average factory worker went from 40 to 1 in 1990 to 400 to 1 in 2002 before falling back to 200 to 1 in 2003. I know of no ethical theory that can justify the skyrocketing executive pay of the 1990s. I recognize that lowering executive pay will not solve the living wage problem for everyone. However, such overinflated ratios stand as an affront to the hard-working Americans who are one paycheck from the street or are without health insurance and hope that no one in their family becomes seriously ill.

Suppose, however, that executive compensation was reasonable. What then? As I explained, Kantian morality requires that there is an imperfect obligation to help people attain a living wage. That obligation falls upon business, government, or both. It seems reasonable to hope that the economic system would enable businesses to pay living wages and that where they cannot, the government could serve a supplementary function. Business increasingly argues that competitive pressures prevent paying employees a living wage. If that is true, then it seems that business is morally required to urge government to take up the slack. Unfortunately, business owners often do just the opposite: they neither pay a living wage nor do they argue for the taxes on business that would provide for an adequate welfare policy. Such action, or inaction, runs contrary to Kantian ethics.

Conditions 4 and 5 for meaningful work require that employers try to structure the workplace so that both the rational and the moral capacities of employees are respected and indeed enhanced. As much has been said regarding the protection of the rational capacities of employees, let us focus on the moral capacities.

It goes without saying that employers should not order or request that employees do anything illegal or immoral. Despite the obvious immorality of such orders or requests, they are largely the source of business scandals. For decades I have asked my undergraduate business ethics students if they have ever been asked by an employer to do something illegal or immoral. I usually get around half the class to admit that such requests have been made. When asked if they complied, nearly 100% of the students indicate that they did, out of fear of losing their jobs—that despite the fact that nearly half of these requests to commit illegal acts involved felonies. Of course students have usually been only in entry-level positions and often in fields where borderline behavior is common, so we cannot generalize to the workplace at large. However, employers should note what kinds of introductory work experiences such students have had. Is it any wonder that there is such skepticism about business ethics?

Even if employees are not asked to act unethically, their moral capacity is threatened if they observe unethical conduct on the part of a superior. It is well known that employees take their cues on ethical conduct from their superiors. An employee with a developed conscience can find personal ethical standards eroded in an organization where superiors engage in unethical conduct. Employers have an obligation not only to themselves but also to others to behave in a highly ethical way. The unrelenting series of scandals that have been coming to light for more than two years is a serious indictment of employers. What can we expect of employees when they have witnessed such large measures of misconduct—if not in their own companies then in the business community in general?

Employers can have a negative effect on the moral capacities of employees by demanding so much overtime that employees cannot adequately meet other responsibilities. Overwork has become a serious problem in the United States (Schor 1991, Bailyn 1993). Harvard Business School case studies and articles in the business press provide many examples of employees forced to work late into the evening and/or on weekends. Spouses and children are neglected. Parents miss crucial events in the lives of their children (birthdays, graduations, major sports events). Few deny that there are serious social costs when family responsibilities are neglected because of the demands of the job. The 40-hour week should be considered a moral norm, and work in excess of that amount should be considered morally problematic. An employee's obligations to the job do not trump all of his or her other obligations.

The final condition for meaningful work is that the employer cannot be paternalistic regarding the employee. Managers should allow employees the latitude to pursue their individual conceptions of happiness in accord with their own desires. Insisting that employees do something they do not want to do on the grounds that it is for their own good is paternalistic, and paternalism with respect to adults is usually wrong. For example, there is nothing wrong with a company having fitness facilities for employees' use during lunch time or after work, but it is going too far to require that employees work out there so they can be more healthy. Many would consider such a practice enlightened, but a Kantian would reject it on moral grounds. Likewise she would normally consider it wrong for employers to forbid employees to smoke off the job or to avoid skydiving, race car driving, or other dangerous sports.

When activities away from the job have a serious impact on the cost of doing business, the issue of paternalism becomes more complicated. For example, the more employees a company has who smoke, the more expensive health insurance premiums become. Although a Kantian would argue that it is usually wrong to forbid employees to smoke off the job, he might accept charging employees who smoke more for their health insurance. In that way the employer could respect both the employees who choose to smoke and those who think it unfair to pay higher health insurance costs because of the habits of fellow employees. In situations where the desires of employees conflict, respecting the humanity in a person in all of them requires an exercise in moral imagination. Nonetheless that is what an employer is obligated to do.

Conclusion

In applying Kantian moral philosophy, I have rather severely critiqued American human resource management. Hierarchical organizations, extreme divisions of labor, lack of meaningful work, lack of voice, low regard for unions, and excessive time on the job have all come in for criticism. But the analysis is not all negative. I also asked what human resource and industrial relations would look like if they were governed by the three formulations of Kant's categorical imperative. Alternative human resource management practices have been suggested—practices that are acceptable both morally from a Kantian perspective and as practical business practices. Examples include teamwork, open book management, participative management, and shared responsibility. A Kantian perspective also shares with a pluralist theory of industrial relations a view of the business firm as a cooperative moral enterprise as well as an economic one. From one point of view, there is nothing new in these suggestions: human resource scholars have long known of their efficacy. This essay shows that such practices are morally sound as well as economically sound.

Note: Portions of this chapter are based on material in *Business Ethics: A Kantian Perspective* (Blackwell, 1999) and chapter 7 in *Employment and Employee Rights* (Patricia H. Werhane and Tara J. Radin, Blackwell, 2004). Some paragraphs on Kantian leadership are from "A Kantian Theory of Leadership" in the journal *Leadership and Organization Development* (2000; Vol. 21, no. 4, pp. 185–93).

References

Bailyn, Lotte. 1993. *Breaking the Mold: Women, Men, and Time in the New Corporate World.* New York: Free Press.

Batt, Rosemary. 1999. "Work Organization, Technology, and Performance in Customer Service and Sales." *Industrial and Labor Relations Review*, Vol. 52, no. 4 (July) pp. 539–64.

Ben-Ner Avner, and Derek C. Jones. 1995. "Employee Participation, Ownership, and Productivity: A Theoretical Framework." *Industrial Relations*, Vol. 34, no. 4 (October) pp. 532–54.

Bianco, Anthony, and Wendy Zellner. 2000. "Is Wal-Mart Too Powerful?" *BusinessWeek*, October 6.

Bowie, Norman E. 1999. *Business Ethics: A Kantian Perspective.* Malden, MA, and Oxford, UK: Blackwell.

_____. 2000. "A Kantian Theory of Leadership." *Leadership and Organization Development*. Vol. 21, no. 4, pp. 185–93.

Budd, John W., Rafael Gomez, and Noah Meltz. 2004. "Why Balance Is Best: The Pluralist Industrial Relations Paradigm of Balancing Competing Interests." In Bruce E. Kaufman, ed., *Theoretical Perspectives on Work and the*

Employment Relationship. Champaign, IL: Industrial Relations Research Association, pp. 195–228.

Cappelli, Peter, and David Neumark. 2001. "Do High-Performance Work Practices Improve Establishment-Level Outcomes?" *Industrial and Labor Relations Review,* Vol. 54, no. 4 (July), pp. 737–75.

Case, John. 1995. *Open-Book Management.* New York: HarperBusiness.

Caux Round Table. (1994). *Principles for Business.* <http://www.cauxroundtable .org/principles.html>.

Dorfman, J.R. 1991. "Stocks of Companies Announcing Layoffs Fire Up Investors, But Prices Often Wilt." *The Wall Street Journal,* December 10, pp. C1–2.

Evan, William, and R. Edward Freeman. 1988. "A Stakeholder Theory of the Modern Corporation: Kantian Capitalism." In Tom L. Beauchamp and Norman E. Bowie, eds., *Ethical Theory and Business.* Englewood Cliffs, NJ: Prentice Hall.

Fisher, Roger, and William Ury. 1981. *Getting to Yes: Negotiating Agreement Without Giving In.* Boston: Houghton Mifflin.

Friedman, Milton. 1962. *Capitalism and Freedom.* Chicago: University of Chicago Press.

Fukuyama, Francis. 1995. *Trust.* New York: Free Press.

Fulghum, Robert. 1988. *All I Really Need to Know I Learned in Kindergarten.* New York: Villard Books.

Gabor, Andrea. 1990. *The Man Who Discovered Quality: How W. Edwards Deming Brought the Quality Revolution to America.* New York: Random House.

Hill, Thomas E., Jr. 1992. *Dignity and Practical Reason in Kant's Moral Theory.* Ithaca, NY: Cornell University Press.

Huselid, Mark A. 1995. "The Impact of Human Resource Management Practices on Turnover, Productivity, and Corporate Financial Performance." *Academy of Management Journal,* Vol. 38, no. 3 (June), pp. 635–72.

Ichniowski, Casey, Kathryn Shaw, and Giovanna Prennushi. 1997. "The Effects of Human Resource Management Practices on Productivity: A Study of Steel Finishing Lines." *American Economic Review,* Vol. 87, no. 3 (June), pp. 291–313.

International Labour Organization. 1998. *Declaration on Fundamental Principles and Rights at Work.*

James, William. [1884] 1962. "The Dilemma of Determinism." In William James, ed., *Essays on Faith and Morals.* Cleveland and New York: Meridian Books.

Kant, Immanuel. [1781] 1963. *Critique of Pure Reason.* London: Macmillan.

_____. [1785] 1990. *Foundations of the Metaphysics of Morals,* 2nd ed. Lewis White Beck, trans. New York: Macmillan, Library of Liberal Arts.

Katz, Harry C., and Owen Darbishire. 2000. *Converging Divergences: Worldwide Changes in Employment Systems.* Ithaca, NY: ILR Press.

Korsgaard, Christine. 1996. *Creating the Kingdom of Ends.* New York: Cambridge University Press.

Likert, Rensis. 1967. *The Human Organization: Its Management and Value.* New York: McGraw-Hill Book Company.

Manning, Alan. 2003. *Monopsony in Motion: Imperfect Competition in Labor Markets.* Princeton, NJ: Princeton University Press.

O'Neill, Onora. 1989. *Constructions of Reason.* New York: Cambridge University Press.

Pfeffer, Jeffrey. 1994. *Competitive Advantage Through People.* Boston: Harvard Business School Press.

_____. 1998. *The Human Equation.* Boston: Harvard Business School Press.

rior appearing to the group to be in the wrong, which would cause loss of face for the superior.

Organizational citizenship behaviors have long been advertised as a face-gaining honor, and the pursuit of this honor sometimes goes beyond the desire for monetary reward, which is also influenced by the Confucian emphasis on social contribution and low regard for financial aspiration. In addition, publicly losing face is an extremely severe punishment that would normally not be a good option for leaders in the organization if the purpose is to motivate employees to work hard. Thus it has been noted that harsh criticisms tend to be avoided in performance evaluations in Asian organizations and "central tendency" is often a convenient means for the evaluator to try to avoid upsetting relationships.

Benevolence and Loyalty in the Workplace. The expectations associated with *ren* often mean that employers are obligated to take care of a wide variety of things for employees, far beyond what would be expected in the United States or Western Europe. The state-owned enterprises (SOEs) in China, although largely a product of China's post-1949 socialist system, operated through much of this period in such a manner. A typical large-scale SOE was like a local community. Stores, hospitals, and schools were run by the SOEs, housing was provided to employees, and job security was permanent. Employees enjoyed lifelong benefits, and their children could assume their positions after they retired. In return, *zhong* and *yi* were expected from employees in that they worked for minimal wages, showed reverence to superiors, and engaged in what the Western organizational behavioral scientists might term "organization citizenship behaviors" (Su, Zhang, and Hulpke 1998). Confucian beliefs hold that ethical individuals will do more than simply follow job requirements (Su, Zhang, and Hulpke 1998). Thus, those selected to work overtime would feel honored, as this was recognition of their contributions and would bring "face" to them and their families. While certainly the system was inspired in many ways by socialist thought and was modeled after the Soviet system, and it would not at all have been linked to the officially suppressed Confucian framework, it is clear that many aspects of Confucian values, the foundation of Chinese culture for more than 2,500 years, persisted in what came to be known as the "iron rice bowl" system.

There are many other variations of what would be considered *ren* in the workplace. For example, consistent with the organization-as-family metaphor, employers would not normally discharge employees, even if economic conditions warranted (Wah 2001). "Lifetime employment" is a well-known aspect of Japanese management, but it was until quite recently commonplace throughout much of East Asia. A person's job is not only a source of income but also integrally related to face. A job might be seen as a means of bringing prestige to the family as a whole, and the money earned by an individual might be shared with extended family members as needed. Thus to lose one's job can be a great source of dishonor. Employers would traditionally seek to avoid causing employees such loss of face and, indeed, discharging employees would reflect badly on the employer as well. Moreover, traditional Asian companies do little in the way of performance evaluation and, if they did, they focused more on an employee's loyalty and commitment to the organization than on task performance (Hui and Graen 1997). Thus, employees were generally not in danger of losing their jobs, at least for economic reasons or poor task performance. And corresponding to this, employees would be committed to their employers (often in a highly personal matter), so voluntary turnover would be very low as well.

Age and Seniority. The need to be increasingly competitive in the global economy has created organizational stresses throughout East Asia, as resulting changes in management processes often contradict traditional values and certainly many Confucian notions of ethical or appropriate behavior. Reverence for age and seniority is a fundamental aspect of Confucianism, and even slight differences in seniority can be important in determining status in an organization. Thus it is not surprising that seniority is a very important determinant of both pay and authority in traditional organizations. Important leadership roles are reserved for those who have reached a certain age. A retired owner or high-level manager of a company may still exert considerable influence behind the scenes because of his (or, very rarely, her) age and presumed wisdom.

Contemporary efforts in East Asia to introduce merit-based employment systems and assess organizations in terms of measurable financial goals, such as stockholder equity (Bae et al. 2003), are at odds with advancement and pay based on seniority. Many Asian-owned companies, following the lead of Western multinationals, are endeavoring to become more merit driven, which has immense implications for both HR and IR (see, for example, Kim and Bae 2004, who describe these efforts in Korea). Employees, and in some countries unions (e.g., Korea), have often reacted negatively to the substitution of merit for age in pay and promotion decisions, though not surprisingly this has generally been more widely accepted by younger workers (who are often more Westernized and less wedded to traditional values, as well as beneficiaries of these changes). Older workers who are passed over by younger workers, or even more humiliatingly, who become subordinates of younger workers, might well leave the company as a result. In Korea, for example, language issues can make transformation to a merit-based system difficult.

The honorifics that are used for organizational leaders and superiors often implicitly convey the notion that such individuals are senior to all of their subordinates. A manager of an Internet portal in Thailand shared an example of how her company shed its "older" workers (i.e., over 40), who the owner felt were too old to understand the needs of an Internet-based company. However, the owner felt uncomfortable firing them, as this would be considered inappropriate. Most were simply assigned to work groups with managers in their late 20s and early 30s. Virtually all of the older workers experienced loss of face by this affront and quit. Thus it can be problematic (though not apparently impossible) to introduce employment systems that stress merit over age or seniority.

The Role of Guanxi. Confucian societies, with perhaps the exception of Japan, operate through social networks in which family is the focal point. It is not uncommon that hiring, promotion, and pay are influenced by *guanxi*—that is, on the closeness of the employee and the decision maker (such as the supervisor) or someone who can influence the decision maker (such as an important government official who has the authority to create hardships for the business). This is also a process of fulfilling responsibilities and/or exchanging favors (*renching*), which could easily result in nepotism or favoritism. Although family-based connections are the strongest basis of *guanxi*, we have noted that other connections (such as having graduated from the same school, coming from the same town or region, or just simple friendship) can also establish relationships and impact significant employment-related decisions. Given what Hwang (2001) observed as one of the defining characteristics of Confucianism—"favor the intimate"—it is clear how employment decisions are particularistic, as individuals have the ethical obligation to act benevolently toward others in proportion to the strength of the relationship. *Guanxi* functions in many ways in lieu of the legal system as a means of enforcing interpersonal obligations.

Gender Issues

The chapters of this volume focusing on the several Western approaches to HRIR ethics deal with critical interpersonal behaviors, in particular those relating to sexual harassment and discrimination. Historically, however, neither Islam nor Hinduism has addressed these concerns, since women are not really supposed to be in the workplace (at least in mixed company): a family-centered *purdah* system is the Islamic model, and a gender-based division of labor the Hindu one. (Neither of these systems serves to spare women from arduous agricultural labor.)

Philosophically, the Islamic view is based in a demotion of women beneath the qualities of men. Summarizing the views of the philosopher al-Tusi (who died in 1274 CE), Fakhry writes that the woman's beauty "should not be the chief incentive for marrying her, rather the contrary. Due to her weak intelligence, the beauty of a woman is often a snare and a cross" (1991:135). Wives' attention should be kept focused on the family. Islamic traditionalists can appeal to verse 34 of the *sura* (a chapter of the Qur'an) on women: "Men have authority over women because Allah has made the one superior to the other, and they spend their wealth to maintain them." As Shahidian (2002:2) notes, this verse has been given legal status in the constitution of the Islamic Republic of Iran.

A much more recent and perhaps less negative view (although certainly equally paternalistic) has been expressed by Maulana Khan:

> What Islamic law lays down with regard to women is protective of their true nature, and is in no way cruel or repressive, as has been suggested by the uninitiated. When, after experimenting with a life and a career in the outside world, a woman finally realizes that her place is in the home, she has reached the point which Islam encourages every woman of marriageable age to reach at the very outset by way of following her natural womanly inclinations. Islamic law is designed to steer women away from the ordeals of the crassly competitive and brazenly immoral world in which only men can successfully make their way (1995:86).

On the Hindu side, women are seen as very polluting, perhaps largely due to the connection with blood, and hence it is good to keep them at a distance.[8] It is significant that, in a rather startling Internet report on the appearance of women in the Hindu priesthood, all three women mentioned by name are well beyond the age of menopause (Radhika 2002).

Of course, women do work outside the home (and in mixed company often) to a greater or lesser degree throughout the Muslim and Hindu worlds. Even in Taliban-run Afghanistan, there were some occupations for women. Kabeer (1994:176ff.) has described four "cultural strategies" by which Muslim women are able to "de-sexualize the factory floor": co-workers are brothers and sisters, the boss is an old uncle, and so on. Thus, the conflicts between the principles of *purdah* and mixed-gender factory work are eased. But there appears to be little Islamic or Hindu management literature about the possible problems of sexual harassment. As shown in Table 1, Beekun's (1997) code of ethics for Muslim businesses explicitly states that employees should be protected from any type of harassment; that sexual harassment is included is made clear in the text.

Our research has found one practitioner-oriented article on sexual harassment by a female Indian plant manager. Here is how it begins: "Sexual harassment is a social problem, involving a very real issue in the work place and which is crying out for proactive HRM intervention. *It is, in sum, an offence against the dignity of a human being*" (Jayashree 1999:202, emphasis added). Could Immanuel Kant have put it better? We are smack in the middle of Western thought; indeed, dignity has been a recurring theme in this chapter. Make no mistake, however: this is important subject matter for managers. Kanekar and Dhir state flatly that "sexual harassment of women appears to be more blatant and endemic in India than in Western countries, probably because of the very low status of Indian women, the high dominance of Indian men, and the relative lack of free interaction (e.g., dating, dancing, and other Western forms of courtship) between the sexes" (1993:119). Their study of the reactions of 540 Bombay undergraduates regarding sexual harassment found that male students attributed more blame to the victim and recommended milder punishment for the harasser than did female students.

Gender also enters the Confucian picture, with women cast in a generally subordinate role in those societies. Of course, one of the five cardinal relationships states that wives should be subordinate to their husbands. However, the extent to which women confront discrimination and a lack of equality of opportunity varies across Asia: women in Korea and particularly Japan seemingly are in the least favored position, while opportunities for women in the workplace are far greater in those countries where Chinese culture dominates.

Despite laws prohibiting discrimination based on gender in both Korea and Japan, women in both countries are clearly at a disadvantage in the labor market. In Japan, for example, more educated women often seek employment in subsidiaries of Western multinationals, where mobility opportunities for women are normally much higher. Employment discrimination against women is seemingly far less extensive in the Chinese societies of East Asia, as well as countries where Confucianism is less significant than other moral and ethical traditions, such as Thailand and the Philippines. The reasons for this are complex. In mainland China, the impact of Maoism certainly was important, as reflected, for example, in the "unisex" clothing styles common during the Cultural Revolution and the general expectation that both men and women would work (coupled with a social support system to care for children and elderly parents). But it is also true that Chinese intellectuals have been questioning many aspects of Confucianism since the late 19th century, and Chinese society underwent considerable modernization and liberalization (unlike Korea and Japan) after the establishment of the

Chinese Republic in 1911. In comparison to Japan and Korea, women in almost all other parts of East and Southeast Asia have far higher labor force participation rates and also are more apt to have higher status jobs, including high-level management positions (for example, both the Philippines and Indonesia have had female presidents in recent years). Taiwan passed legislation in 2002 prohibiting gender-based discrimination. The national constitution of Thailand that was adopted in 1997 included an antidiscrimination clause (although to date, it has only been implemented for public sector jobs).

It is still commonplace in many parts of Asia for job postings in newspapers to specify gender restrictions. A study by Lawler and Bae (1998) on such advertisements in Thailand found quite significant variations across occupations with respect to gender-based restrictions, with "male only" restrictions most common in management and engineering jobs, while "female only" restrictions were common in selected professional jobs (e.g., bookkeeper) and clerical–secretarial jobs. In addition, they found substantial variation across companies as a function of a company's country of origin. Subsidiaries of Japanese multinationals had by far the highest likelihood of imposing such restrictions, while subsidiaries of American multinationals virtually never included such gender-restrictive language. Both subsidiaries of European multinationals and locally owned Thai companies had discrimination rates higher than American subsidiaries but far lower than Japanese. Wu, Yi, and Lawler (2000) extended this work to Taiwan and found similar results. In addition, the ILO has expressed concern that one negative consequence of China's economic reforms and the growth of a largely unregulated private sector has been an increase in employment discrimination toward women in these private sector companies (as well as increased discrimination against China's many minority groups).

Concluding Observations: Universalism Challenged?

This chapter has described the central tenets of the Muslim, Hindu, and Confucian traditions and their implications for HRIR ethics. Such descriptions are important because of the need to understand other cultures in a globalizing world and the growth of Hindu and Muslim populations in Western countries. Moving beyond descriptions into cross-cultural evaluations raises difficult and important questions surrounding the metrics for such analyses and the extent to which such metrics are universal.

We can certainly ask how the Muslim, Hindu, and Confucian traditions (and Tata's practice) address the basic dimensions on which workplaces and their quality are commonly judged. Budd (2004), for example, argues that the three basic dimensions are efficiency, equity, and voice. Efficiency is for the most part assumed, although we should recall Sialkoti's strictures against loafing or, worse, featherbedding. In the Confucian view, where wisdom and order are the ultimate goals, efficiency is less clearly a principal objective. Efficiency would appear to be at least partially offset by equity considerations in the interests of clean, safe workplaces and the natural environment in the Hindu and Muslim traditions and in the Tata Code. Islam's strong emphasis on justice (and its close relative, dignity) yields a commitment to equitable and adequate compensation. Equity is less strongly emphasized in Hindu traditions, although clearly present in the Gandhian stewardship concept as regards wealth. Equity has its own peculiar meaning in the Confucian framework, deriving from neither meritorious work nor equality but from age and other status variables. Voice is the topic least well developed. Only Beekun's sample code of ethics for Islamic business gives employees explicit rights to some form of voice. In the Tata code, voice in governance is at most implicit. In Chakraborty's Hindu vision, we are left unclear about how, precisely, the members of the business *ashram* participate in its governance. Voice is not an important element in the Confucian view, centered as it is in authoritarian hierarchicalism.

As a second set of standards, the four core human rights in the workplace according to the ILO Solemn Declaration of 1998 are the right to organize and bargain collectively, abolition of forced labor, elimination of all forms of discrimination, and abolition of the worst forms of child labor. The three traditions examined in this chapter only partially fulfill these four standards. Both the Tata code and the Islamic sample code (with a somewhat mixed voice, however) are clear on avoiding discrimination, while Hindu traditionalism is built on it, however much change is under way in present-day India. The Confucian view, at least classically, embraces important elements of age and gender discrimination. The use of forced labor and the worst forms of child labor are probably incompatible with all four patterns: the Tata and sample Islamic codes provide for equitable or adequate compensation; Chakraborty's business *ashram* is presumably composed of consenting adults. The duties of benevolence and paternalism in Confucian thought would likely preclude these practices. The right to organize and bargain collectively is explicitly recognized nowhere, although we do note that Tata has had a long and generally harmonious relationship with labor organizations representing its employees (Lala 1992).

By these two sets of standards, therefore, the Muslim, Hindu, and Confucian traditions have important shortcomings—for example, in the areas of employee voice and nondiscrimination.[9] We have noted earlier that the three traditions traditionally have had problems with full equality for women. We know that some Islamic regimes (Saudi Arabia, for example) have serious restrictions on women's rights to work, to drive, and to move about outside the home. We know that independent labor unions do not exist in China and various Muslim states like Syria, Iran, and Turkey.

But are the standards of the ILO declaration and of efficiency, equity, and voice applicable only to Western societies, or are they universal standards that can and should be applied to all? The ILO declaration asserts that some workplace rights are human rights and are therefore universal. Ignatieff, however, observes that "the cultural challenge to the universality of human rights arises from three distinct sources—from resurgent Islam, from within the West itself, and from East Asia. Each of these challenges is independent of the others, but taken together, they have raised substantial questions about the cross-cultural validity—and hence the legitimacy—of human rights norms" (2001:102). In 1947 and 1948, Saudi Arabia did not accept the Universal Declaration of Human Rights because of articles providing for freedom in marriage and of religion. "In Islamic eyes, universalizing rights discourse implies a sovereign and discrete individual, which is blasphemous from the perspective of the Koran" (Ignatieff 2001:103–4). It seems that we face—unsurprisingly—a world where not all human rights are universally recognized.

Thus, recalling the story of General Boykin, we are generally correct to stress the importance of culture and ethical values in shaping behaviors and attitudes in the workplace. This is particularly true with regard to appropriate gender roles. The especially troublesome area of voice in workplace governance reveals a gulf between universal best practice and non-Western traditions that is wide and challenging. In the other key areas of efficiency and equity (including "fairness" to the environment), all non-Western traditions seem to see the trade-offs involved, although in different ways and for differing reasons.

Acknowledgments

Scoville acknowledges the helpful assistance of David Faust (Ames Library of South Asia), Ying Liu (graduate assistant), and Zuleqa Husain (undergraduate assistant), all of the University of Minnesota. Lawler and Yi acknowledge the research assistance of Bing Bai (graduate assistant, University of Illinois) and the comments of Shyh-jer Chen (National Sun Yat-Sen University, Taiwan).

Notes

[1] The thumbnail sketches of Islam, Hinduism, and Confucianism that follow are undertaken with some trepidation. There must surely be as many strains of Islam

and Confucianism as there are of Christianity, and Hinduism is probably even more variegated. Some will quarrel with the very idea of making the attempt. But, since ethical teachings derive at least in part from the core religious or philosophical teachings, it seems essential that we seek to identify some of them, much as other authors in this volume have dealt with those stemming from other philosophical or religious traditions.

2 Women are seen as pursuing traditional family roles throughout their lives.

3 Going beyond the Indian context, Perrett (1998) has even contended that some of the concepts that may initially seem to render Hindu ethical thought useless for Western thinkers—*dharma, karma* (rebirth in a status at least partially dependent on how one's previous life was lived), *moksa* (freedom in one's life, contrasted with goodness)—may pose more apparent than real obstacles. Perrett concludes that principles of Hindu ethical thought may be useful to modern-day Westerners, presumably to deal with modern-day Western ethical issues.

4 There appear to be parallels between Chakraborty's position and Aristotelian virtue ethics. See Solomon (1992) for a virtue ethics exposition of the roles cooperation and community ought to play in business.

5 It was in this tradition that one of J. N. Tata's sons, Sir Dorab Tata, in 1917 invited Sidney and Beatrice Webb to "write a memorandum on Medical Services in the Welfare Work at Sakch'" (Lala 1992:140). In industrial relations mythology (at least in the United States), the Webbs' role has been expanded to developing the whole Tata code of ethics and social responsibility, but this seems inaccurate. The Webbs did know the Tatas and other Indian notables reasonably well and reported that they spent some time with them during their trip through India in 1911 (Webb and Webb 1987).

6 There is some parallel with the Western ethics of care. See Gilligan (1982) and Noddings (1984), in which moral principles rely on the deeper context of each particular situation—especially the implications for relationships.

7 In the market economy that modern China is trying to adopt, in which the use of contract is the common practice, violation of contract is also a common phenomenon. People are yet learning to honor contracts, and the making of professional contracts in most situations is still at a fledgling stage. Even in Asian countries with more developed institutions for handling commercial relationships (with perhaps the exception of Japan), contracts are often seen as little more than a general framework for a business relationship that should be open to change as conditions warrant. The ability to enforce contracts in court is quite limited for this reason in many Asian countries.

8 For a review of patriarchal control and its "interplay with culture and religion" as related to schooling, see Chanana (2001).

9 Of course, not all Western countries necessarily fulfill these standards—the United States, for example, has been criticized for an excessive emphasis on efficiency (Budd 2004) and a failure to conform to international standards on freedom of association and collective bargaining (Human Rights Watch 2000).

References

Bae, Johngseok, Shyh-jer Chen, David Wan, John J. Lawler, and Fred Ochieng Walumbwa. 2003. "Human Resource Management and Firm Performance in

Pacific Rim Countries." *International Journal of Human Resource Management*, Vol. 14, no. 8 (December), pp. 1308–1332.

Ball, Carolyn, and Akhlaque Haque. 2003. "Diversity in Religious Practice: Implications of Islamic Values in the Public Workplace." *Public Personnel Management*, Vol. 32, no. 3 (Fall), pp. 315–330.

Beekun, Rafik Issa. 1997. *Islamic Business Ethics*. Herndon, VA: International Institute of Islamic Thought.

Bouma, Gary, Ali Haidar, Chris Nyland, and Wendy Smith. 2003. "Work, Religious Diversity and Islam." *Asia Pacific Journal of Human Resources*, Vol. 41, no. 1 (April), pp. 51–61.

Budd, John W. 2004. *Employment with a Human Face: Balancing Efficiency, Equity, and Voice*. Ithaca, NY: ILR Press.

Carroll, Hunter C. 1997. "Damned If They Do, Damned If They Don't: The Collision Between Religion and the Workplace Has Employers Caught in the Middle." *American Journal of Trial Advocacy*, Vol. 20, no. 2 (February), pp. 353–380.

Cash, Karen C., and George R. Gray. 2000. "A Framework for Accommodating Religion and Spirituality in the Workplace." *Academy of Management Executive*, Vol. 14, no. 3 (August), pp. 124–134.

Chakraborty, S. K. 2000. "Corporate Governance for India—Some Pointers." *Productivity*, Vol. 40, no.4 (January–March), pp. 507–510.

———. 2003. *Against the Tide: The Philosophical Foundations of Modern Management*. Oxford and New York: Oxford University Press.

Chanana, Karuna. 2001. "Hinduism and Female Sexuality: Social Control and Education of Girls in India." *Sociological Bulletin*, Vol. 50, no. 1 (March), pp. 37–63.

Chen, Min. 1995. *Asian Management Systems: Chinese, Japanese and Korean Styles of Business*. London: Routledge.

Chen, Ming-Jer. 2001. *Inside Chinese Business: A Guide for Managers Worldwide*. Boston: Harvard Business School Press.

Chopra, Anil. 2003. "Management of Business Ethics: Sowing the Seeds." *11th Annual International Anti-Corruption Conference* (Seoul, May 26, 2003).

———. 2004. "Management of Business Ethics: The Progress." *Conference Board Asia Conference on Business Conduct* (Mumbai, February 17, 2004).

Council on American-Islamic Relations. 2003. "Top U.S. General Says Muslims Worship Idol." <www.cair-net.org/asp/article.asp?id=154&page=AA>. [January 3, 2004].

Earley, Christopher P. 1997. *Face, Harmony, and Social Structure: An Analysis of Organizational Behavior Across Cultures*. New York: Oxford University Press.

Erez, Miriam, and Christopher Earley. 1993. *Culture, Self-Identity, and Work*. Oxford: Oxford University Press.

Fakhry, Majid. 1991. *Ethical Theories in Islam*. Leiden, New York, Copenhagen, and Cologne: E. J. Brill.

Garcia-Zamor, Jean-Claude. 2003. "Workplace Spirituality and Organizational Performance." *Public Administration Review*, Vol. 63, no. 3 (May/June), pp. 355–363.

Gilligan, Carol. 1982. *In a Different Voice: Psychological Theory and Women's Development*. Cambridge, MA: Harvard University Press.

Guha, Ramachandra. 2002. "The Past and Future of the Environmental Movement: Its Social and Ethical Perspectives." *Management and Labour Studies*, Vol. 27, no. 1 (January), pp. 7–20.

Hui, C., and George B. Graen. 1997. "Guanxi and Professional Leadership in Contemporary Sino-American Joint Ventures in Mainland China." *Leadership Quarterly*, Vol. 8, no. 4 (Winter), pp. 451–465.

Human Rights Watch. 2000. *Unfair Advantage: Workers' Freedom of Association in the United States under International Human Rights Standards.* Washington, DC: Human Rights Watch.

Hwang, K.K. 2001. "The Deep Structure of Confucianism: A Social Psychological Approach." *Asian Philosophy,* Vol. 11, no. 3 (November), pp. 179–204.

Ignatieff, Michael. 2001. "The Attack on Human Rights." *Foreign Affairs,* Vol. 80, no. 6 (November–December), pp. 102–116.

International Labour Organization. 1998. *Declaration on Fundamental Principles and Rights at Work.*

Jayashree, S. 1999. "Sexual Harassment at Work: An HRM Perspective." *Indian Journal of Industrial Relations,* Vol. 35, no. 2 (October), pp. 202–216.

Kabeer, Naila. 1994. "Women's Labour in the Bangladesh Garment Industry: Choice and Constraints." In Camillia Fawzi El-Solh and Judy Mabro, eds., *Muslim Women's Choices: Religious Belief and Social Reality.* Providence and Oxford: Berg.

Kanekar, Suresh, and Vidyut Lata Dhir. 1993 "Sex-Related Differences in Perceptions of Sexual Harassment of Women in India." *Journal of Social Psychology,* Vol. 133, no. 1 (February), pp. 119–120.

Khan, Maulana Wahiduddin, 1995. *Woman between Islam and Western Society.* New Delhi: Islamic Centre.

Kim, Dong-One, and Johngseok Bae. 2004. *Employment Relations and HRM in South Korea.* London: Ashgate.

Krishna, R. Suresh. 1999. "Ethics: A Survival Need for Business." *Management and Labour Studies,* Vol. 24, no. 2 (April), pp. 127–134.

Lala, R. M. 1992. *The Creation of Wealth.* Bombay: IBH Publishers.

Lawler, John, and Johngseok Bae. 1998. "Overt Employment Discrimination by Multinational Firms: Cultural and Economic Influences in a Developing Country." *Industrial Relations,* Vol. 37 (April), pp. 126–152.

Mathias, T. A. 1997. "Business Ethics in a Developing Country." *Management and Labour Studies,* Vol. 22, no. 2 (April), pp. 75–81.

Minehan, Maureen. 1998. "Islam's Growth Affects Workplace Policies." *HR Magazine,* Vol. 43, no. 12 (November), p. 216.

Noddings, Nel. 1984. *Caring: A Feminine Approach to Ethics and Moral Education.* Berkeley: University of California Press.

Perrett, Roy W. 1998. *Hindu Ethics: A Philosophical Study.* Honolulu: University of Hawaii Press.

Radhika, V. 2002. "Her Holiness: Overcoming the Gender Barrier to Priesthood." <www.indiatogether.org/women/worklife/priest.htm>. [November 20, 2003].

Shahidian, Hameed. 2002. *Women in Iran: Gender Politics in the Islamic Republic.* Westport and London: Greenwood Press.

Sialkoti, M. Sadiq. 1984. *Morals and Manners in Islam.* Idaratul-Buhoosil Islamia: Varanasi.

Solomon, Robert C. 1992. *Ethics and Excellence: Cooperation and Integrity in Business.* New York: Oxford University Press.

Su, Dongsui, Yang Zhang, and John Hulpke. 1998. "A Management Culture Revolution for the New Century?" *Journal of Applied Management Studies,* Vol. 7, no. 1 (June), pp. 135–138.

Tsui, Anne S., and J. L. Farh. 1997. "Where *Guanxi* Matters: Relational Demography and *Guanxi* in the Chinese Context." *Work and Occupations,* Vol. 24, no. 1 (February), pp. 56–79.

Wah, Sheh Seow. 2001. "Chinese Cultural Values and Their Implication to Chinese Management." *Singapore Management Review*, Vol. 23, no. 2 (2nd half), pp. 75–83.

Webb, Sidney, and Beatrice Webb. 1987. *Indian Diary*. Delhi and New York: Oxford University Press.

Wu, Cindy, Xiang Yi, and John J. Lawler. 2000. "Age and Gender Discrimination in Hiring in Asia: Cultural Effects in Taiwan and Thailand." Paper presented at the Seventh Bargaining Group Conference, East Lansing, Michigan.

CHAPTER 5

Globalization and Business Ethics in Employment Relations

HOYT N. WHEELER
University of South Carolina

In the absence of mandates of law, a community must rely on ethical norms, supported by moral suasion, to induce those behaviors that are necessary for the welfare of the community In national systems, ethical norms on moral rights can become enforceable legal rights. Since in the global setting there is no body of enforceable law on employment relations to provide legal entitlement to moral rights, ethical norms are more important. It is not surprising, therefore, that there is a rather intensive ongoing effort to identify and codify norms for business ethics pertaining to employment relations in the world community. These norms create moral rights, which are those rights that persons *ought* to have. They carry with them moral obligations on the part of others to respect them (Santoro 2000).

To proceed with an analysis of business ethics in employment relations in an international setting, it is helpful to first think in general terms about the nature and effects of globalization in order to get a handle on the context of the problem. Next, I will consider some conceptualizations of business ethics. Finally, I will move on to identify and analyze the various sources of ethical standards for international employment relations and discuss their implementation.

Globalization

Stated most simply, globalization represents a "world without walls" (Friedman 2000:133) in which information, capital, and goods move easily across national boundaries. More formally, it has been defined as "the inexorable integration of markets, nation-states and technologies to a degree never witnessed before" (Friedman 2000:9). The Organization for Economic Cooperation and Development (OECD) has defined the phenomenon in economic terms as "an evolving pattern of cross-border activities of firms involving international investment, trade and collaboration for purposes of product development, production and sourcing, and marketing" (Leisink 1999:4). It can be seen as a qualitatively new system in which multinational corporations are the main actors, which neither national nor transnational governmental mechanisms can effectively regulate. Logistic chains, which run from raw materials to the distribution of finished products to the ultimate consumers, have come to have links in multiple countries. Although a brand name attaches to the goods, the ultimate seller to the retailer or consumer may do little more than market goods made and transported by others (Beukema and Coenen 1999). In the most extreme form, this means that the company whose name goods are identified with may be a mere virtual corporation.

The global or "new" economy is seen as involving "financially oriented capitalism" in place of the old "production-oriented capitalism" and is characterized by a "global economic division of production" (Vilrokx 1999:58). Under this regimen, financial considerations and shareholder interests become increasingly important. Capital flows seamlessly around the world, landing where it produces the maximum return.

Effects of Globalization

Many observers believe that globalization is a totally new and overwhelmingly powerful force. It is said to be "the dominant international system" and a "worldwide shaping force" (Friedman 2000:9, xxi). There is, however, a minority view that globalization is really nothing new and that the global nature of corporations has been wildly exaggerated (Hirst and Thompson 1999). The weight of the evidence appears to favor the view that globalization is a very powerful new phenomenon. It has created a situation in which we are all influenced in our day-to-day lives by events elsewhere in the world (Leisink 1999). The cost of labor in China may affect the price of the shirt that we buy at Wal-Mart or our very job security. A protest in Seattle may improve working conditions in India.

One feature of globalization is an extraordinary increase in the mobility of production facilities. When a company locates a plant in a place where labor costs are low and regulations are lax, a firm with higher costs for labor and regulatory compliance can be placed at a competitive disadvantage. With the liberalizing of the international trading system, there are fewer and fewer barriers to firms' moving their production facilities around the world on this basis. The danger of this movement is, of course, a race to the bottom—what the Europeans call "social dumping." A recent report by the World Bank recognizes that the need to "find solutions that cut poverty through both growth and better distribution of income is becoming increasingly urgent in an era of globalization" (2003:2).

One critic of globalization says that its "most unsavory companion is the fast-widening divide between rich and poor, not only within nations but also between rich nations and poor" (Gates 2001). This is shown by the fact that in 1999, 80 countries reported lower per capita incomes than a decade before. In 1960, the fifth of the world's population living in the world's richest nations had incomes 30 times greater than the fifth in the world's poorest nations; by 1998, the gap had widened to 74 to 1 (Gates 2001). It is rather clear that the "polarization in the distribution [of wealth] between states has increased" (Leisink 1999:20). Within both advanced and developing countries, "income inequality has increased and poverty has grown everywhere" (Leisink 1999:20). A report by the World Bank (2003) reaches the same conclusion. One Global Union Federation (GUF, formerly called International Trade Secretariats) claims that globalization is "skewed in its effects and in fact generates conflict, poverty and social injustice over the greater part of the globe" (International Federation of Chemical, Energy, Mine and General Workers Unions [ICEM] 1996:5).

A World Commission on the Social Dimension of Globalization was established by the International Labour Organization (ILO) in 2002. In its 2004 report, the commission stated that "the current path of globalization must change. Too few share in its benefits. Too many have no voice in its design and no influence on its course" (World Commission on the Social Dimension of Globalization 2004:2). It produced an extensive report that, while recognizing the many positive benefits of globalization, documented in some detail its negative effects.

There is some concern in the developed countries that less developed countries (LDCs) will attract all of the manufacturing capacity, leaving the developed countries with nothing to sell abroad. In this scenario, the developing countries are only sellers, since their workers cannot afford to buy what they, or others, produce. Hirst and Thompson (1999:43) call this "madhouse economics" that would lead inevitably to a massive shortage of demand for goods on a world basis as well as deflation. In their view, the more likely long-term result is a rise in living standards in LDCs, turning them into buyers as well as sellers. Yet this may not prevent a transfer of manufacturing to LDCs from causing short-term economic and social turmoil in the West.

As the service sectors of the Western economies have grown, a new threat to their jobs has arisen, namely, the competition mounted by firms in LDCs, particularly India. Everything from computer programming to telephone call center operations have moved from the United

States and Britain to India—where employees are English speaking and well educated and can perform these services at much lower cost.

The new competitive environment has had dramatic impact on employment relations in the developed countries (Cappelli et al. 1997). Firms in LDCs can produce goods that compete effectively in price-sensitive markets, given their much lower labor costs. Also, because of the degree of customization made possible by computer-based technology, the historic advantages of American mass production methods are no longer important (Appelbaum and Batt 1994). Even relatively sophisticated products such as automobiles can be manufactured in LDCs at a level of quality equal to those produced in the United States In this environment, firms in the United States and Europe have adopted all or part of the techniques of Japanese lean production, which is "a sophisticated cost-cutting philosophy" (Cooke 1993:81) that produces high quality goods at low cost. Although lean production's egalitarian style and increased degree of participation appeal to many workers, the management by stress involved in lean production puts considerable pressure on them.

In many countries, governments "favor a neo-liberal redesign of labour relations without corporatist participation of collective actors involving deregulation, decentralization and curbing labor costs" (Leisink 1999:16). What Thomas Friedman (2000:105) has called the "Golden Straitjacket" that countries have to don in the globalized environment includes deregulation and privatization, both of which place downward pressure on wages and working conditions.

The effects on trade unions are very powerful. Unions are forced to restrain wage demands to keep labor costs competitive with those in other countries. This decreases the incentive for workers to belong to or otherwise support unions. In Western Europe, unions have to some degree accepted employers' calls for more management flexibility by, among other things, agreeing to decentralization of collective bargaining from the national level to the firm level. The European movement to performance-related pay has been a part of this emphasis on management flexibility. Union density has declined virtually all over the world (Leisink 1999).

On the other hand, most economists continue to hold the view that globalization is a positive force in the world economy. They base their arguments on the fundamentals of neoclassical economic theory and on some rather penetrating analyses of the practical positive effects of free trade. The relatively high wages paid by multinational enterprises and the resulting effects on the prosperity of LDCs are cited as beneficial effects of globalization (Irwin 2002).

A more nuanced argument for the benefits of free trade, and in particular foreign direct investment in developing countries, holds that whether these lead to benefits, such as increasing democratization of a society, depends on the strategic orientation of the firm operating in the country. Economic prosperity, which the operations of a multinational enterprise often bring about, is strongly associated with democracy. Western multinational enterprises' notions of rewarding individual merit, giving importance to information sharing and teamwork, encouraging workers to take initiative and assume leadership roles, and recognizing the need for continuous change are all useful in bringing a developing country into the modern world. These practices have the effect of producing a "human rights spin-off" (Santoro 2000:43). However, this can occur only where the strategic orientation of the multinational enterprise is toward the building of markets in the developing country, and not simply minimizing costs.

So it is in a highly distuibed and complex environment, about which there is much disagreement, that ethical questions are arising. But what do we mean when we speak of the ethics with which this paper deals—business ethics?

Business Ethics?

One might argue that the term *business ethics* is an oxymoron, in that it makes no sense to talk about business and ethics as being related. Most business, particularly international business, is done by corporations. The traditional view of a corporation is that it is a legal fiction (Paine 2003), having only those characteristics that are given to it by the human beings who form it. It is argued that, since the character of the modern corporation is that it is put together, and chartered by government, for the purpose of earning money for its owners, the shareholders, this is all that can be expected of it. It has no "soul to damn" (Paine 2003:83). It is a golem—an artificial being that has no moral compass. Within this view, therefore, any attempt to assign moral responsibilities to it is fundamentally misguided.

This "realist" view of corporations (Donaldson 1989:11) is deeply embedded in the American law of corporations (Paine 2003). It is supported by the thinking of neoclassical economists, such as Milton Friedman. According to Friedman (1962), the only social responsibility of a corporation is to make a profit. The very idea that it has moral responsibilities to employees, customers, or the society at large is anathema. A corporation is simply not "a proper subject for moral assessment," since "moral responsibilities attach only to human beings" (Paine 2003:87). The role of the corporation in society is seen as being "to maximize profits and financial value for the primary benefit of its shareholders" (Clarkson 1998:1).

The realist view has been under attack for a number of years, and it is not shared by most modern scholars in business ethics. An especially popular alternative is "stakeholder theory" (Clarkson 1998), built upon the idea that the traditional view states an undesirable "economics of irresponsibility" (Clark 1916:216). Stakeholder theory in its place asserts a positive economics of responsibility where the corporation is seen as obligated to serve interests in addition to those of its stockholders. However, the theory does not tell us how to weight the interests of the various stakeholders (Donaldson 1989). More importantly, it does not speak to the idea that when economic *interests* are weighed against fundamental *human rights,* rights should always trump interests (Werhane 1985). So the shareholder interest in maximizing returns, for example, must necessarily yield to the fundamental human right to free expression or to freedom of association (as in a labor union).

Ethics has to do with "rules without laws" (Donaldson 1989:149). If we are willing to accept the proposition that corporations, as well as their managers, are "moral actors—responsible agents that carry out their business within a moral framework" (Paine 2003:x), then our inquiry turns to the question of what their moral obligations are. The obverse of this is the question of what the rights are of others to whom these duties are owed (Donaldson 1989).

It is argued that the problems of corporate ethics can be solved by hiring ethical individuals. After all, it is the individuals who do the acting. The problem with this is that in a private corporation there are duties owed to the corporation, which is itself lacking in any inherent moral compass. A moral individual can be placed in a situation where the pressures to do immoral things are irresistible.

What are the moral duties of a corporation? A useful description is provided by Paine (2003), who distinguishes between *basic* and *full* commitments to the values of *justice* and *humanity.* Under the heading of obligations relating to justice, those reflecting only a basic commitment include avoiding wrong, fulfilling contracts, avoiding theft, avoiding fraud, and obeying the letter of the law. A full commitment to justice includes doing right, keeping promises, being fair, being honest, and obeying the spirit of the law.

Paine (2003) places under the heading of obligations relating to humanity, at the basic level, maintaining oneself, not harming others, respecting human rights, avoiding damage to the community, and being considerate. A full commitment to humanity involves developing oneself, actively helping others, promoting human dignity, contributing to community improvement, and being courageous.

In its 2004 report, the International Labour Organization (ILO) World Commission on the Social Dimension of Globalization argues for a stronger ethical framework for globalization. It proclaims that "[g]lobalization has developed in an ethical vacuum" and that "[t]here is today a deep-seated desire by people to reaffirm basic ethical values in public life, as seen, for example, in calls for a more 'ethical globalization'" (World Commission on the Social Dimension of Globalization 2004:7).

Ethical Standards in a Globalized World

It would appear, then, that globalization creates a challenging environment for the application of business ethics. What are the standards for ethical behavior in employment relations in global business? Where do they come from? What efforts are being made to cause them to influence corporate behavior?

What has been labeled a "'fair share' theory of moral responsibility for human rights" (Santoro 2000:143) provides a useful framework for identifying the moral rights for which multinational enterprises should be held responsible. The theory holds that "human rights are special kinds of moral rights because they create duties throughout the international community" (Santoro 2000:147). The duty to respect human rights attaches to individuals, but it is "most effectively discharged through collective enterprises" (Santoro 2000:151). Corporations are among the most powerful of these enterprises. Multinational enterprises "are in a potent position to uphold human rights, particularly the labor rights of workers, because they can control and direct their own personnel actions and those of their business partners" (Santoro 2000:156). Because these rights are under the control of the multinational enterprise, their fair share of responsibility includes a duty to ensure them. Basic worker rights are human rights, and are recognized by numerous international bodies to be such. They deserve this status primarily because they are necessary to human dignity (Wheeler 1994).

One ethical question that one does not find in the scholarly literature is whether it is morally wrong for a corporation headquartered in a country to ignore the national interests of its homeland. For example, is it wrong for a U.S. corporation to move jobs out of the United States when this works to the detriment of the American economy? Is there a patriotic duty to serve the interests of the corporation's home country? What if moving jobs overseas involves propping up a Communist dictatorship (e.g., China)? In political discourse in the United States, it seems to be assumed that it is wrong to move jobs from the United States abroad. Is this simply a question of national *interest*, or are moral rights and duties involved?

Corporate Social Responsibility

The broadest heading for an inquiry into the ethical responsibilities of business is the notion of corporate social responsibility (CSR), which arises from stakeholder theory (Justice 2003a). CSR has been defined as having to do with the corporation's role in society being to "exceed all laws, set *a higher ethical standard,* and help build a better society for all" (Environics International, Ltd. 2003:1; emphasis added). This stands in sharp contrast with the "realist" view that companies are in business solely to generate a profit for the benefit of shareholders. CSR has become a much discussed topic in the media and in international organizations of various kinds. It is a popular idea.

The European Community Economic and Social Committee's 2001 Green Paper on CSR declared it a "key theme" for the committee (Commission of the European Communities 2002:9). The report makes clear that the committee sees CSR as requiring companies to "go beyond simple compliance with existing laws" (Commission of the European Communities 2002:4). Business consulting groups and research foundations have spoken out in favor of the business and moral cases for CSR (Arthur D. Little, Ltd. and Business in the Community 2003; Environics International, Ltd. 2003; Frank Hawkins Kenan Institute of Private Enterprise 2003).

Socially Responsible Investing and CSR. Socially responsible investing (SRI) is one strategy for ensuring socially responsible performance on the part of a firm. It does this by either denying a company access to capital unless it establishes that it is conducting itself ethically or by influencing it to do so by shareholder activism.

SRI shareholder activism is the strategy adopted by the new Watchdog Fund as well as other funds with similar goals (Lens Fund, Relational Investors fund, and the California Public Employees Retirement System [CalPERS]; Baue 2003). Most groups involved in SRI take a less direct approach by simply screening out investments in companies that they deem to be socially irresponsible. A radical approach suggested by one academic is to give tax incentives to shareholders to encourage them to transfer the ownership of their company to citizen stakeholders over a period of 20 years (Turnbull 2003). As will be discussed, trade unions have a strong interest in SRI.

Unions and CSR. Both the International Confederation of Free Trade Unions (ICFTU) and the Trade Union Advisory Committee (TUAC) of the Organization for Economic Cooperation and Development (OECD) appear to have CSR high on their agendas as they respond to the challenges to labor posed by multinational corporations. Dwight Justice of the ICFTU Multinational Companies Department has cogently described the confederation's approach to CSR in the context of globalization. According to Justice, it is necessary to keep clearly in mind the difference between, on the one hand, "CSR as a form of business ethics or fad and [on the other hand] how society defines, sets and enforces socially responsible behavior by business" (Justice 2003a:1). CSR, which is generally seen as being voluntary for corporations, cannot replace the corporate accountability enforced by government regulation. Businesses should not be allowed to use CSR to redefine standards downward by seeking to have voluntary standards take the place of regulation.

As Justice notes, a stakeholder approach is not an unmitigated blessing for unions. Not all stakeholders should have the same status. Trade unionists argue that the worker interest is more akin to that of a shareholder, given that workers, unlike non-governmental organizations (NGOs), suppliers, and customers, have invested their lives and labor in the corporation. In addition, workers have a claim that is rooted in society's general interest in the dignity of its citizens and the general level of welfare. According to Justice, NGOs are, at best, surrogates for interests and are not truly representative organizations, whereas unions are. In Europe, management has utilized stakeholder analysis to escape treating unions as social partners, instead viewing unions as only one among many stakeholders rather than as an equal partner (Justice 2003a).

According to John Evans of TUAC (2002), unions have seen that consumer pressure and brand-damage concerns can be important in influencing corporate behavior. Issues involving supply chains of multinationals have risen to a new level of importance. The moral accountability of global corporations for their own actions and those of their suppliers has become a major theme of union actions.

U.S. and British unions have supported most of the attempts to build international labor standards through codes of conduct written by NGOs. Also, the European Trade Union Institute (ETUI) has declared itself in favor of social benchmarking within the European Community. It has produced a document (Benchmarking Working Europe) that provides extensive analysis of information relevant to benchmarking (European Trade Union Institute 2003).

Socially responsible investing is an area of considerable trade union interest and activity (Fung et al. 2001). Dwight Justice (2003b:6) of the ICFTU describes socially responsible investing as "part of the CSR phenomenon." As Justice argues (2003b), workers can pressure companies to behave in a socially responsible manner even where there is not a business case for it. This can be in the interests of workers because they may have a stronger interest in the sustainability of the society than do managers and some other investors. Sustainability is of greater concern to rank-and-file workers because they generally have stronger ties to the communities in which they live. Managers tend to be more geographically mobile. Particularly in the global economy, capital seems to fixate solely on profits without regard for where they are made.

The Trade Union Committee on Workers' Capital was formed by various national and international union groups to encourage socially responsible investing (Evans 2002). This group is supported by the AFL-CIO, the British Trades Union Congress (TUC), TUAC, and ICFTU, among others. It is headquartered in the TUC offices in London. The AFL-CIO has taken the lead in this collaboration, perhaps because in the United States there is more employee share ownership, particularly through pension funds, than in other countries. However, as private pension funds have come into existence in some countries (Germany and Italy) or become more important in others (France), European trade union movements have become more interested in using the power of these funds to influence corporate policy. In France, four of the five major trade union groups (all but the Force Ouvrière) have formed a consortium to review financial products (e.g., mutual funds and the like) for social responsibility, with the hope that company pension funds will more likely be invested in products that meet with union approval.

American labor has been active in using the power of pension funds to influence corporate policies (Wheeler 2002). Through its corporate affairs office, directed by Ron Blackwell, the AFL-CIO has adopted a strategy of educating pension fund trustees in socially responsible investing. The International Brotherhood of Carpenters and Joiners and other craft unions have moved beyond involvement during corporate shareholder meetings to even picket companies in which they own shares. This is in addition to efforts by the AFL-CIO Office of Investments to make labor the leading voice in the United States for reforms in corporate governance (*BusinessWeek* 2003).

Particular International Standards for Corporate Ethical Conduct

Where do we look to define ethical conduct for an international business as it relates to its workers? There have been a number of efforts to articulate the social responsibilities of corporations and their agents in this globalized world, ranging from standards laid down by the UN to declarations of principles developed by NGOs to codes of conduct adopted by individual corporations.

UN Initiatives. Immediately after World War II, the UN began to specify principles to guide corporate behavior. Its 1948 Universal Declaration of Human Rights says that "recognition of the inherent dignity and of the equal and inalienable rights of all members of the human family is the foundation of freedom, justice and peace in the world" (United Nations 2003a:1). Article 20 of the declaration states that "[e]veryone has the right to freedom of peaceful assembly and association" (United Nations 2003a:2). Article 23 declares that everyone has "(1) the right to work, to free choice of employment, to just and favorable conditions of work and to protection against unemployment, (2) "without any discrimination . . . the right to equal pay for equal work, (3) . . . just and favourable remuneration ensuring for himself and his family an existence worthy of human dignity, and supplemented, if necessary, by other means of social protection, (4) . . . the right to form and join trade unions for the protection of his interests" (United Nations 2003a:5).

At the turn of the 21st century, the UN adopted its Millennium Declaration, which included an item on freeing "our fellow men, women and children from the abject and dehumanizing conditions of extreme poverty" (United Nations 2003b:4). Also in 2000, the UN created the Global Compact, with several of its nine principles dealing with labor rights. Principle 3 states that "businesses should uphold the freedom of association and the effective recognition of the right to collective bargaining" (United Nations 2003c:1). Principles 4, 5, and 6, respectively, declare that firms should support the elimination of forced labor, child labor, and employment discrimination.

"Sustainable development" is a term that the UN defines to include both labor and environmental standards. The UN World Summit for Sustainable Development (WSSD) was held in Johannesburg, South Africa, in 2002. Among the summit's many conclusions was an agreement that states should take into account the ILO Declaration on Fundamental Principles and Rights at Work when pursuing policies aimed at generating employment. It also agreed to the need for corporate accountability but said that it should be "enforced by private sector corporations" (United Nations 2002:10). (In response, I would note that it is difficult to understand how corporations could enforce accountability upon themselves.)

In connection with the 2003 meeting of the UN Commission on Sustainable Development, ICFTU, TUAC, and the GUFs published a document setting out their priorities for implementation of the WSSD principles. They strongly emphasized the joint labor–management process of workplace assessments as the preferred method of meeting the workplace-related goals of the WSSD. In addition to the UN conferences, the ILO reports that there were about 25 regional or other conferences during 2003 that addressed globalization and its social consequences (International Confederation of Free Trade Unions, Trade Union Advisory Committee to the OECD, and Global Union Federations 2003).

The most recent UN attempt to set standards of conduct for multinational enterprises was an August 2003 draft statement of "Norms on the Responsibilities of Transnational Corporations and Other Business Enterprises with Regard to Human Rights" (United Nations Sub-Commission on the Promotion and Protection of Human Rights 2003). The sub-commission starts out with the premise that states have the primary responsibility for protecting human rights but that business enterprises, both national and transnational, share this duty. Among the rights to be protected are the right to equality of opportunity and treatment as set out in national and international law. The rights of workers include having their employers do the following: (1) refrain from using forced labor; (2) protect the rights of children against "economic exploitation"; (3) provide a safe and healthy work environment; (4) provide "remuneration that ensures an adequate standard of living for them and their families" that takes "due account of their needs for adequate living conditions with a view towards progressive improvement"; and, (5) "ensure freedom of association and effective recognition of the right to collective bargaining," including the right to establish and join labor organizations for "protection of their employment interests and for other collective bargaining purposes," as provided by national laws and "relevant conventions of the International Labour Organization" (United Nations Sub-Commission on the Promotion and Protection of Human Rights 2003:5).

Although supported by NGOs, and generally viewed favorably by labor organizations (but see International Confederation of Free Trade Unions 2004), the norms have been vigorously attacked by employers and their associations (Chandler 2004). They criticize the norms for shifting the responsibility in international law from governments to employers, holding employers responsible for the actions of subcontractors, and requiring remuneration according to a standard that is overly vague (Gow 2004).

ILO Core Labor Standards. The ILO, a tripartite organization that includes representatives of governments, labor, and management, has long been the principal source of international labor standards. In general it has operated by adopting conventions, urging nations to adopt them, and reporting on the progress, or lack thereof, by nations in applying or adopting particular conventions.

In 1998 the ILO took the unprecedented step, in its Declaration on Fundamental Principles and Rights at Work, of stating that member countries subscribe to certain core labor standards by virtue of their membership in the ILO (International Labour Organization 2003). Before this declaration, countries were bound to meet a standard only if they adopted the particular convention that propounded it. The declaration was adopted without a dissenting vote, although a number of member countries or their labor and employer delegations abstained. The United States was one of the countries voting in favor of the declaration. The core labor standards are "(a) freedom of association and the effective recognition of the right to collective bargaining; (b) the elimination of all forms of forced or compulsory labour; (c) the effective abolition of child labour; and (d) the elimination of discrimination in respect of employment and occupation" (International Labour Organization 2003:2). There had earlier been an ILO Tripartite Declaration of Principles on Multinational Enterprises and Social Policy adopted in 1977 (Jordan 2003).

The ILO core labor standards form the foundation for numerous lists of principles for socially responsible corporate behavior. These have been distinguished from "cash standards" that "mandate particular outcomes—such as minimum wages, working hours, and health and safety conditions—that directly affect labor costs, and thus also potentially affect trade competitiveness" (Elliott and Freeman 2003:13). Yet without provisions for a living wage and a safe and healthful workplace (provisions in the 2003 UN norms), the standards seem to fall short of the conditions for human survival, let alone a basic level of human dignity.

The ILO has expanded its activities in the field of labor standards under the heading of an initiative for "decent work" that includes the core labor standards, job creation, and social safety nets. The initiative calls for social dialogue among the social partners—government, labor, and employers. The ILO has also expanded its efforts against child labor through its International Program on the Elimination of Child Labor (Elliott and Freeman 2003).

OECD Guidelines. In 1976 the OECD, which comprises the governments of industrialized nations, first adopted Guidelines for Multinational Corporations. Due to renewed interest in the conduct of global corporations in the 1990s, the OECD's 30 member countries approved revised guidelines in 2000. With respect to employment and industrial relations, the guidelines provide a broad set of rights for union and other employee representatives. Among other things, they prohibit a company from threatening to leave a country in order to impede union organization (Organization for Economic Cooperation and Development 2003a).

NGO Codes of Conduct. There has been a spate of standards being issued by NGOs, focused either solely on workers' concerns or on "triple bottom line accounting," which involves corporations' reporting on social and environmental as well as financial performance. Much of the rationale comes from a stakeholder approach to corporate responsibility, holding the corporation accountable to stakeholders other than shareholders.

Social Accountability International (SAI) is a U.S.-based nonprofit organization that develops, implements, and oversees voluntary, but verifiable, standards for social accountability. Its advisory board consists of representatives of business, unions, and NGOs. It certifies corporations that meet its standards, labeled SA8000. They are based on the ILO conventions, the UN's Universal Declaration of Human Rights, and the Convention on the Rights of the Child. SAI standards constrain child labor, prohibit forced labor, require a healthy and safe work environment, require respect for freedom of association in trade unions (where national law does not permit unions, a company is required to seek out "parallel means of association and bargaining"), prohibit abusive punishments, constrain working hours, require pay that is "sufficient to meet the basic needs of workers and their families," and go "beyond simple compliance to integrate the standard into their management systems and policies" (Social Accountability International 2004:4).

Worldwide Responsible Apparel Production (WRAP) is a nonprofit association formed by American apparel companies. Like SAI, it has a set of standards and certifies compliance with them (Worldwide Responsible Apparel Production 2004). Another U.S. group issuing standards is the Worker Rights Consortium (WRC), a nonprofit organization of university administrators, students, and labor rights experts that attempts to ensure that goods bearing the names of universities are made under conditions of respect for worker rights (Worker Rights Consortium 2004). In 1998, a subgroup of the White House Apparel Industry Partnership, created by Secretary of Labor Robert Reich and President Bill Clinton, formed the Fair Labor Association (FLA). The two unions that had been part of the original partnership—UNITE and the Retail, Wholesale and Department Store Union—as well as the Interfaith Center for Corporate Responsibility refused to join the FLA because of weaknesses in its code and compliance system (Sweatshop Watch 2003). Another U.S. group that has been active in the campaign for worker rights in the garment industry is Sweatshop Watch (Sweatshop Watch 2003).

Based in the United Kingdom, the Ethical Trading Initiative (ETI) is an alliance of corporations, NGOs, and union organizations that aims to promote best practices and implement labor practice codes. ETI does not issue certificates or audit performance. Rather, it focuses on helpin companies learn about best practices. It does have a "base code" that is agreed to by participating companies, unions, and NGOs (Ethical Trading Initiative 2003). The Clean Clothes Campaign (CCC), headquartered in the Netherlands, aims at improving labor conditions in the global apparel industry. Its code is very similar to that of ETI, although it goes beyond with respect to the right to collective bargaining (Clean Clothes Campaign 2004).

An important source of standards and pressure for compliance with them is the Global Reporting Initiative (GRI), whose "sustainability reporting guidelines" are standards similar to many of those described above. GRI, an official collaborating center with the UN, works in cooperation with the UN Global Compact and seeks to "harmonize and integrate" efforts to set standards and ensure compliance (Global Reporting Initiative 2004).

Benchmarking. A diverse coalition of religious and advocacy groups has come up with yet another method of influencing corporations to behave in an ethical, socially responsible manner. In 2003, "Principles for Corporate Responsibility: Bench Marks for Measuring Business Performance" were released by groups including the Interfaith Center on Corporate Responsibility in the United States and similar organizations in the United Kingdom, South Africa, Canada, and other countries. Delegates from 22 countries were involved in the process of benchmarking over a period of about 10 years. The Bench Marks document calls for, among other things, "corporate governance policies that balance the sometimes competing interests of managers, employees, shareholders and communities; and that are based on ethical values, including inclusivity, integrity, honesty, justice and transparency" (Bench-Marks 2003:1).

What is unique about Bench-Marks is its explicit basis in religious beliefs. It declares that, on the basis of religious faith, it views the global economy in terms of "its impact on the environment, how it touches human life, and whether it protects the dignity of the human person" (Bench-Marks 2003:2).

Corporate Codes of Conduct. Since at least the early 1990s, it has become increasingly common for large corporations, both domestic and multinational, to adopt their own codes of conduct. It has been estimated that some 60% to 70% of major American companies have these codes (Sethi 1999). Several hundred were identified by studies performed in the 1990s (Elliott and Freeman 2003). These are generally ~een as being voluntary, but it has been argued that all of the companies 'th these codes have been "dragged kicking and screaming" into having m (Maquila Solidarity Network 2004:1).

Implementation and Enforcement of Standards

Although there is no lack of statements of the ethical standards that should be met by multinational enterprises, implementation and enforcement remain problematic. For example, the 2003 UN norms obligate enterprises to compensate those harmed by their violations. However, it is not clear what the mechanism for enforcing this remedy would be. The UN Global Compact has been accused of lacking any real power to enforce its principles, yet several prestigious human rights groups, unions, and union federations have supported it. It is said to be a "learning community" in which dialogue can take place among NGOs, firms, and government officials (*Social Issues Reporter* 2002:8). The organizers of the compact claim to have made discussions of labor and human rights less divisive and to have made possible "a truly global, multi-stakeholder dialogue" on these issues (*Social Issues Reporter* 2002:8). Under the compact, companies make submissions with respect to practices that are consistent with the principles. In its first two years it received 30 submissions. Examples include Nike's identifying and constructing plans to eradicate violations of the Global Compact's principles in its operations in Indonesia and Royal Dutch Shell's being recognized by the Brazilian government for discouraging child labor (*Social Issues Reporter* 2002).

OECD standards represent a body of principles to which member governments subscribe. The 2000 guidelines contain an interesting new set of implementation procedures. Countries are required to establish organizations to serve as "national contact points (NCPs). NCPs are obligated to promote the guidelines and make them known and available to investors. If a violation of the guidelines by a company is alleged by a trade union or other party, the NCP must attempt to resolve the issue. If the matter is not resolved, the NCP must make a public statement on the case (Organization for Economic Cooperation and Development 2003b).

Corporate codes have been criticized on a number of grounds related to their enforcement. First, they are said to involve the "fox guarding the chicken coop" (Compa 2001). Second, they seldom state how they will be monitored to secure compliance (Elliott and Freeman 2003). Third, they often consist of little more than "public statements of lofty intent" (Sethi 1999:9). Fourth, they generally fail to provide for communicating to the public the results they have achieved or failed to achieve (Sethi 1999). Last, they often fail to guarantee freedom of association and collective bargaining (Elliott and Freeman 2003).

Yet for all their failings, it appears that the corporate codes ha~ been of some use. Publicly declaring a set of principles exposes a cor

ration to criticism for not living up to them. Those whom Elliott and
Freeman call "human rights vigilantes" (2003:59) have been able to pressure firms to hold common standards and accept independent monitoring. While some firms have utilized international accounting firms as
monitors, others have accepted monitoring by FLA, WRAP, SAI, WRC,
and other NGOs that exist for this purpose. A number of groups, including women's organizations in Asia and Central America, have been able
to use corporate codes in their efforts to improve labor standards
(Maquila Solidarity Network 2004). A number of the more recent codes
have included provisions for independent verification of compliance
(Maquila Solidarity Network 2004).

Labor Standards and Trade

It has long seemed obvious to proponents of labor standards that the
most effective way to enforce them internationally is to link them to the
privilege of trading with developed countries. Since no hard international law carries penalties against a firm or a country that fails to meet
labor standards, there is no clear remedy for workers whose rights have
been abused, and therefore little incentive for employers to comply with
labor standards. The prospect of losing access to desirable markets such
as the United States and Western Europe, on the other hand, could be a
powerful incentive for compliance. Not surprisingly, this idea has been
met with accusations of protectionism from the developing world. LDCs
argue that developed countries did not comply with such standards
when they were industrializing and that it is unfair to insist that LDCs
be denied the freedom to develop in the same manner. From the standpoint of developed countries, many economists argue that trade restrictions are always to the disadvantage of the country imposing them (Irwin
2002).

A good argument has been made by Elliott and Freeman (2003)
for distinguishing between labor standards that affect foreign trade
and those that do not. There would certainly seem to be a stronger
case for standards on goods and services that are traded internationally. As is stated in the ILO's founding documents, "the failure of any
nation to adopt humane conditions of labor is an obstacle in the way
of other nations which desire to improve conditions in their own
countries"(quoted in Elliott and Freeman 2003:4).

Since 1984 the United States has had labor standards as part of its
Generalized System of Preferences, which permits duty-free access to
the American market for selected goods from selected LDCs. The North
American Free Trade Agreement (NAFTA) has a side agreement, the
North American Agreement on Labor Cooperation, requiring each

country in the pact to enforce its own labor laws. The free trade agreements of the United States with Jordan, Chile, and Singapore all have labor standards in the main text of the agreement (Elliott and Freeman 2003). Most recently (May 28, 2004), the U.S. trade representative signed the United States–Central American Free Trade Agreement (CAFTA) and announced plans to sign a similar agreement with the Dominican Republic. This agreement contains an obligation for the countries to enforce their own laws but no other labor protections. U.S. Senator John Kerry, during his Democratic candidacy for president, opposed the pact because of its inadequate labor and environmental protections (Bureau of National Affairs 2004b). Whether obtaining the agreement of a country to enforce its own laws meets the moral obligation of the United States to enforce human rights depends on the content of that country's laws. In the case of NAFTA, it appears that, in principle, this would be sufficient. However, there is the further question of whether this obligation is enforceable as a practical matter. It is here that such agreements pose real difficulty.

A number of protests at World Trade Organization (WTO) and World Bank meetings have aimed at the various effects of globalization. A great deal of the impetus behind these protests comes from concerns over the effects of globalization on labor conditions and rights. The United States has unsuccessfully attempted to place labor and environmental standards on the agenda of the WTO (Irwin 2002).

Critics of the idea of enforcing labor standards through trade sanctions argue that (1) low labor standards do not give countries an unfair advantage in international trade (it is low productivity that determines wage levels, so their low productivity compensates for their wage advantage); (2) standards such as limitations on child labor will only harm workers in developing countries, and the problems of child labor are best solved by eradicating poverty and improving educational opportunities; and (3) forcing a raising of standards by WTO action would cost workers in developing countries their jobs or would, at best, create an elite of workers in the export sectors of their national economies (Irwin 2002). It is argued that linking trade and labor standards is impractical because of a lack of international consensus on the meaning of the standards and on how to decide whether the standards have been violated (Bureau of National Affairs 2004a). However, as suggested by labor unionists, the need for rules exists in the global society, just as in national societies (Bureau of National Affairs 2004b). Indeed, the logic of the international antilabor standards argument could be applied at the national level as well. Yet, except for some extreme neoclassical economists, few students of employment relations issues would seriously argue that no regulation of the employment relationship at the national level is needed. There are two separate sets of questions to consider with respect to labor standards and trade. First, do labor standards involve human rights, and, if so, which labor standards rise to this level of importance? I have noted my belief that, as stated by numerous international organizations, the standards do involve human rights (see also Wheeler 1994). The UN norms adopted in 2003 are probably the most complete list. Perhaps the most controversial standard is the right to freedom of association as it relates to unions and collective bargaining. As I have argued elsewhere (Wheeler 2001), this is a basic human right necessary to assure human dignity in a setting where it is likely to be under attack.

The second inquiry is whether trade sanctions, certainly a blunt instrument, are the best method of enforcing these rights. In principle, free trade has many advantages, and unnecessary impediments are generally to be avoided. However, given the absence of hard international law, there appears to be little alternative to trade sanctions for imposing a real cost on companies or nations that fail to respect human rights. So there is a dilemma posed by attempting to have the benefits of free trade and yet guarantee human rights. But if we truly believe that we are dealing with fundamental human rights, there seems to be no choice but to use the means available to enforce them, even at some cost to free trade. Human rights trump other considerations (Werhane 1985). Until the dream of a world government is fulfilled, we must make do with what we have—trade sanctions.

Conclusions

What has been the result of the great deal of recent activity regarding ethical norms in employment relations for corporations operating globally? There does appear to be consensus among the UN, other international agencies, NGOs, and the many corporations that have adopted codes that companies face moral obligations in their international operations. It is important to note that this consensus is not limited to governments. The ILO, for example, consists of representatives of employers and trade unions as well as governments. Some NGOs have corporate representatives on their governing bodies. Corporate codes have been set out by companies themselves.

The obligations included in this consensus exceed those imposed by the laws of any particular country. Indeed, one of the ideas underlying corporate social responsibility is that a common body of ethical principles exists transcending national cultures. It is this idea, however, that is called into question by the LDCs, who argue that the standards are not only Western ones but that they are being applied to LDCs only after no longer affecting the countries now insisting on them. This is a fundamental philosophical question, long familiar to scholars of jurisprudence debating the existence of universal natural law.

Assuming that it makes sense to have universal standards, it is reasonably clear what they should be, at least in the most general terms. The ILO core labor standards state minimum worker rights; there would appear to be little argument that the worst forms of child labor, forced labor, and discrimination on grounds of race, sex, and other characteristics should be prohibited. I believe it equally clear that freedom of association in unions and collective bargaining is also a fundamental and unalienable human right (Ogle and Wheeler 2001; Wheeler 2001).

Other statements go further than the ILO standards. As to collective bargaining rights, the OECD guidelines include the obligation of employers to engage in "constructive negotiations" with worker representatives, make company facilities available to them, provide them with information, "promote consultation and co-operation" with them, and "provide information to employees and their representatives." SAI requires employers to find "parallel means of association and bargaining" where national law interferes with the employees' right to have a union. The WRC model code requires a company not to cooperate with government prohibitions of collective bargaining, to give union organizers free access to employees, and to recognize a union selected by employees. The CCC requires employers to "adopt a positive approach" and have an "open attitude" toward trade unions. In my view the right to freedom of association is so fundamental to the guarantee of a free and democratic society, and to other rights in the workplace, that the expanded version of collective bargaining rights contained in these documents is the one that should be adopted. In Paine's (2003) terminology, it is deserving of employers' *full*, rather than merely *basic*, commitment.

There are at least two other areas in which the ILO standards appear to be lacking. The first is pay. The UN norms require pay at a level that ensures an "adequate standard of living" (United Nations Sub-Commission on the Promotion and Protection of Human Rights 2003:5). A number of other sets of standards address pay, with references to a living wage (Bench-Marks 2003; Ethical Trading Initiative 2003); "just and favorable remuneration ensuring for [the worker] and [his or her] family an existence worthy of human dignity" (United Nations 2003a:5); pay "sufficient to meet the basic needs of workers and their families" (Social Accountability International 2004:4); pay that "provides for essential needs and establish[es] a dignified living wage for workers and their families (Worker Rights Consortium 2004:2); and wages that "meet basic needs of workers and their families and . . . provide some discretionary income" (Clean Clothes Campaign 2004:5). Here again, the expanded version of the employer obligation is required.

Of equal or greater importance is the requirement for a safe and healthful workplace, which is not included in the ILO Standards but is in the UN norms and a number of NGO codes. Also crucial are hours of work and overtime pay, which are directly connected to pay and affect workers' quality of life.

To what degree should these rights be respected? I suggest that worker protections against child and forced labor and discrimination and the rights to freedom of association, a living wage, and a safe workplace are fundamental human rights. Accordingly, these rights are entitled to a full commitment on the part of employers and should not be balanced against an employer's economic interests (see Wheeler 1994; Wheeler 2001; Ogle and Wheeler 2001). That is to say, where an employer cannot provide these conditions to employees, society is better off for that employer to go out of business and for the capital invested in it to be invested elsewhere.

As argued by Dwight Justice of the ICFTU, a stakeholder approach is of only limited help to workers. In Europe, where unions have been social partners, it is a step backward to be only one of a number of stakeholders. Elsewhere, being a stakeholder is perhaps better than being irrelevant to the goals of the firm, but unless a nuanced approach to stakeholder theory is taken, the special claim of workers as investors of their lives in a firm can be lost by being placed in the same category with suppliers and customers.

How are the *ethical* obligations of corporations and their agents to be enforced? By definition these obligations are beyond the law. Therefore, they exist independently of legal sanctions such as criminal punishments or the requirement of compensating those who are damaged by a corporation's failure to meet them. In practice, the primary enforcement device has been public opinion, which works best in the realm of consumer goods, where there is a valuable identifiable brand such as Nike, a retail store such as Wal-Mart, or a public figure such as Kathy Lee Gifford. Nation-states appear to be only weakly responsive to concerns about their national image around the world. Connecting violations of norms of socially responsible behavior to trade sanctions is making some halting progress as public protests have an effect on governments. International trade union pressure on a multinational enterprise has some potential where unions are in a position to impose costs on a company.

Given the difficulty of making ethical norms operate so as to effect a real difference in corporations' activities in their global operations, is it worthwhile to direct attention to them? Is this just a diversion from the real issues? Is the idea of corporate social responsibility just a scam being used by firms as an alternative to regulation that would force them to do what they say they want to do voluntarily?

All things considered, it appears that the activity with respect to corporate social responsibility is valuable. First, as is often the case in human societies, norms eventually become laws. Second, corporations' recognizing that they have obligations subjects them to criticism for not behaving accordingly. Third, socially responsible investing backed by shareholder activism by unions controlling substantial blocks of shares has real potential for change. Fourth, the fear of regulation may cause corporations to behave in a socially responsible manner. An example of how this can work is the European Community (EC) Social Dialogue, where such things as parental leave, fair treatment of part-time workers, Europe-wide works councils, and regulation of fixed-term contracts have resulted from the prospect of regulation by the EC government (Wheeler 2002). Extending the social dialogue beyond the European Community would, of course, require a very different structure of international governance than we have at present.

On the other hand, it would be unwise to expect too much of efforts pushing for corporate social responsibility. I believe that the nature of the corporate beast remains unchanged in both law and reality. It is a golem that is called into existence for the purpose of making money for its owners. If it fails in its charge, it ceases to exist. Serving other stakeholders may feed the need to make a profit, but if serving them interferes unduly with this basic goal, their interests will inevitably be ignored. To the contrary, no matter how well the corporation serves other stakeholders, if it fails to serve the interests of capital it will fail.

As can be seen from the discussion of globalization, the tendency of corporations to avidly pursue profits is accentuated in the global environment, and there is no effective international legal framework to constrain them. This combination bodes ill for those who would like to tame this beast to make it serve public, and other, purposes. The answer for national societies has been to regulate corporate behavior by laws and to encourage the growth of countervailing power in the form of trade unions. The greatest difficulty with both governments and trade unions is that they have remained largely national while corporations have become international. Also, it remains true that regulation is more likely to make a difference in the daily lives of workers than voluntary social-responsibility initiatives of any kind. The corporate lust for profits may be too powerful to be overcome by voluntary codes (Justice 2003a).

There is some hope for both government and trade union action to deal with this problem. The norms that are becoming more widely accepted are beginning to resemble a body of international law. The more that this is true, the more corporations are susceptible to being influenced by world public opinion. The authority of the UN, the ILO, and the various NGOs can serve as a basis for public pressure. If their standards are flaunted too shamelessly, the demand for international regulation will likely grow. Also, it should not be forgotten that human beings control corporations. They, unlike the corporation itself, have "souls to damn." Perhaps they can be made more sensitive to avoiding actions that are condemned by the international community—to avoid doing wrong.

As for trade union action, it appears that international labor organizations have taken on new life. In recent years, five of the Global Union Federations have entered into some 26 framework agreements with multinational firms (International Confederation of Free Trade Unions 2004). So for the first time we have a significant amount of something very similar to international collective bargaining going on. There had already been a start on this on a regional basis in Europe (Wheeler 2002). The work of the ICFTU and TUAC on corporate social responsibility has given them new visibility in global policy making. The international union action on socially responsible investing taps a source of real power within corporations—shareholder voting rights. To the extent that workers can add the power of their capital to the power of their labor, they may be able to change the basic nature of the corporation.

Change in international institutions comes slowly. They do appear to be moving in the direction of dealing with the phenomenon of globalization. As they do so, ethical concepts have assumed increasing importance in the discourse on globalization. This surely is a positive development.

References

Appelbaum, Eileen, and Rosemary Batt. 1994. *The New American Workplace.* Ithaca, NY: ILR Press.

Arthur D. Little, Ltd., and Business in the Community. 2003. "New Report Says Corporate Responsibility Builds Competitiveness—But Companies Are Failing to Recognise the Benefits." <http://www.csrwire.com/print.cgi/sfArticleId=2324>. [March 2, 2005].

Baue, William. 2003. "Watchdog Fund Established to Take a Bite Out of Corporate Governance Malfeasance." *CSRWire.* <http://www.csrwire.com/sfprint.cgi/sfArticleId=1290>. [March 2, 2005].

Bench-Marks. 2003. *Principles for Global Corporate Responsibility: Bench Marks for Measuring Business Performance.* <http://www.bench-marks.org/execsumm.shtml>. [December 10, 2003].

Beukema, Leni, and Harry Coenen. 1999. "Global Logistic Chains: The Increasing Importance of Local Labour Relations." In Peter Leisink, ed., *Globalization and Labour Relations*. Cheltenham, UK: Edward Elgar, pp. 138–157.

Bureau of National Affairs. 2004a. "Enforcing Compliance With Labor Standards in Trade Agreements Problematic, Forum Told." *Labor Relations Week*, Vol. 18, no. 22 (May 27), p. 740.

————. 2004b. "United States, Central American Nations Sign U.S.-Central America Free Trade Pact." *Labor Relations Week*, Vol. 18, no. 23 (June 3), p. 762.

BusinessWeek. 2003. "Labor Sharpens Its Pension Sword." November 24, p. 62.

Cappelli, Peter, Lauri Bassi, Harry Katz, David Knoke, Paul Osterman, and Michael Unseem. 1997. *Change at Work.* New York: Oxford University Press.

Chandler, Geoffrey. 2004. "Commentary on the United States Council for International Business 'Talking Points' on the United Nations Norms on the Responsibilities of Transnational Corporations and Other Business Enterprises with Regard to Human Rights." <http://209.238.219.111/Chandler-commentary-on-USCIB-Talking-Points.htm>. [June 2, 2004].

Clark, J. Maurice. 1916. "The Changing Basis of Economic Responsibility." *The Journal of Political Economy*, Vol. 24, no. 3, pp. 209–29.

Clarkson, Max B. E. 1998. "The Corporation and Its Stakeholders: Classic and Contemporary Readings." In Max B. E. Clarkson, ed., *The Corporation and its Stakeholders.* Toronto: University of Toronto Press, pp. 1–9.

Clean Clothes Campaign. 2004. "Codes, Monitoring, and Verification: Why the CCC Is Involved." <http://www.cleanclothes.org/codes.htm>. [January 15, 2004].

Commission of the European Communities. 2002. *Opinion of the Economic and Social Committee on the "Green Paper: Promoting a European Framework for Corporate Social Responsibility."* Brussels: Official Journal C 125.

Compa, Lance. 2001. "Wary Allies: Trade Unions, NGOs and Corporate Codes of Conduct." *The American Prospect* (Summer), pp. 8–9.

Cooke, P. 1993. "The Experiences of German Engineering Firms in Applying Lean Production Methods." In *Lean Production and Beyond: Labour Aspects of a New Production Concept.* Geneva: International Institute for Labour Studies, pp. 77–93.

Donaldson, Thomas. 1989. *The Ethics of International Business.* New York: Oxford University Press.

Elliott, Kimberly Ann, and Richard B. Freeman. 2003. *Can Labor Standards Improve Under Globalization?* Washington, DC: Institute for International Economics.

Environics International, Ltd. 2003. "The Millenium Poll on Corporate Social Responsibility: Executive Briefing." Toronto.

Ethical Trading Initiative. 2003. "What Is ETI?" <http://www.ethicaltrade.org/z/abteti/index.shtml>. [March 2, 2005].

European Trade Union Institute (ETUI). 2003. "Benchmarking Working Europe 2003." <http://etui.etuc.org/Projects/PSheets2004/2004/141-03_MJ-KS.cfm>. [March 2, 2005].

Evans, John. 2002. Trade Union Advisory Committee, Organization for Economic Cooperation and Development. Personal interview. Paris, January 25, 2002.

Frank Hawkins Kenan Institute of Private Enterprise. 2003. *Promoting Global Corporate Social Responsibility.* Washington, DC.

Friedman, Milton. 1962. *Capitalism and Freedom.* Chicago: University of Chicago Press.

Friedman, Thomas L. 2000. *The Lexus and the Olive Tree.* New York: Anchor Books.

Fung, Archon, Tessa Hebb, and Joel Rogers. 2001. *Working Capital: The Power of Labor's Pensions.* Ithaca, NY: Cornell University Press.

Gates, Jeff. 2001. "Tapping the Logic of Globalization to Relieve Human Misery and Restore the Environment." *Deep Democracy* (September).

Global Reporting Initiative. 2004. "About GRI." <http://www.globalreporting.org/about/brief.asp>. [January 15, 2004].

Gow, David. 2004. "Business Cries Foul over UN Rights Code." *Guardian Weekly.* March 11–17, p. 12.

Hirst, Paul, and Grahame Thompson. 1999. "Globalization—Frequently Asked Questions and Some Surprising Answers." In Peter Leisink, ed., *Globalization and Labour Relations*. Cheltenham, UK: Edward Elgar, pp. 36–56.

International Confederation of Free Trade Unions. 2004. "Global Union Federation Framework Agreements with Multinational Corporations." <http://www.icftu.org/displaydocument.asp?Index=991216332&Language=EN>. [January 20, 2004].

International Confederation of Free Trade Unions, Trade Union Advisory Committee to the OECD, and Global Union Federations. 2003. *WSSD Implementation Priorities of Global Unions.* Brussels: International Confederation of Free Trade Unions.

International Federation of Chemical, Energy, Mine and General Workers' Unions (ICEM). 1996. *Power and Counterpower: The Union Response to Global Capital.* Chicago: Pluto Press.

International Labour Organization. 2003. "ILO—Declaration on Fundamental Principles and Rights at Work." <http://www.ilo.org/dyn/declaris/DECLARATIONWEB.ABOUTDECLARATIONHOME?VAR_language=EN>. [February 28, 2005].

Irwin, Douglas A. 2002. *Free Trade Under Fire.* Princeton, NJ: Princeton University Press.

Jordan, Bill. 2003. "Trade Unions and Multinationals: The ILO Points the Way Forward." <http://www.icftu.org/displaydocument.asp?Index=990917145&Language=EN&Printout=...>. [April 15, 2003].

Justice, Dwight. 2003a. International Confederation of Free Trade Unions. Telephone interview. Brussels, Belgium, December 22, 2003.

———. 2003b. "The Corporate Social Responsibility Concept and Phenomenon: Challenges and Opportunities for Trade Unionists." Unpublished paper, International Labour Organization.

Leisink, Peter. 1999. "Introduction." In Peter Leisink, ed., *Globalization and Labour Relations.* Cheltenham, UK: Edward Elgar, pp. 1–35.

Maquila Solidarity Network. 2004. "Codes Primer." <http://www.maquilasolidarity.org/resources/codes/primer1.htm>. [January 5, 2004].

Ogle, George E., and Hoyt N. Wheeler. 2001. "Collective Bargaining as a Fundamental Human Right." *Proceedings of the Fifty-Third Annual Meetings* (New Orleans, Jan. 5–7, 2001). Champaign, IL: Industrial Relations Research Association, pp. 246–53.

Organization for Economic Cooperation and Development. 2003a. *A Users' Guide for Trade Unionists to the OECD Guidelines to Multinational Enterprises.* Paris: Organization for Economic Cooperation and Development.

———. 2003b. "The OECD Guidelines for Multinational Enterprises." *OECD Observer,* June, pp. 1–8.

Paine, Lynn Sharp. 2003. *Value Shift.* New York: McGraw-Hill.

Santoro, Michael A. 2000. *Profits and Principles: Global Capitalism and Human Rights in China.* Ithaca, NY: Cornell University Press.

Sethi, S. Prakash. 1999. "Codes of Conduct for Global Business: Prospects and Challenges of Implementation." In *Principles of Stakeholder Management: The "Clarkson Principles."* Toronto: The Clarkson Centre for Business Ethics, pp. 9–20.

Social Accountability International. 2004. "About Social Accountability International." <http://www.sa-intl.org/AboutSAI/AboutSAI.htm>. [January 15, 2004].

Social Issues Reporter. 2002. "Global Compact Turns Two, Assesses Progress." September [LexisNexis, pp. 1–9].

Sweatshop Watch. 2003. "About Us." <http://www.sweatshopwatch.org/swatch/about>. [December 18, 2003].

Turnbull, Shaun. 2003. "A New Way to Govern: Organisations and Society After Enron." <http://papers.ssrn.com/sol3/papers.cfm?abstract_id=319867>. [May 22, 2003].

United Nations. 2002. "Report of the World Summit on Sustainable Development, Johannesburg, South Africa, 26 August-4 September 2002." <http://daccessdds.un.org/doc/UNDOC/GEN/N03/204/23/PDF/N0320423.pdf?OpenElement>. [March 1, 2004].

———. 2003a. "All Human Rights for All: Fiftieth Anniversary of the Universal Declaration of Human Rights, 1948–1998, Universal Declaration of Human Rights." <http://www.un.org/Overview/rights.html>. [December 10, 2003].

———. 2003b. "United Nations Millenium Declaration." <http://www.un.org/millenniumgoals>. [December 10, 2003].

———. 2003c. "The Global Compact, Principle Three." <http://www.unglobalcompact.org/content/AbouttheGC/TheNinePrinciples/prin3.htm>. [March 1, 2005].

United Nations Sub-Commission on the Promotion and Protection of Human Rights. 2003. "Norms on the responsibilities of transnational corporations and other business enterprises with regard to human rights." <http://daccessdds.un.org/doc/UNDOC/GEN/G03/160/08/PDF/G0316008.PDF?OpenElement>. [March 1, 2005].

Vilrokx, Jacques. 1999. "Towards the Denaturing of Class Relations? The Political Economy of the Firm in Global Capitalism." In Peter Leisink, ed., *Globalization and Labour Relations.* Cheltenham, UK: Edward Elgar, pp. 57–77.

Werhane, Patricia H. 1985. *Persons, Rights and Corporations.* Englewood Cliffs, NJ: Prentice-Hall.

Wheeler, Hoyt N. 1994. "Employee Rights as Human Rights." *Bulletin of Comparative Labour Relations,* Vol. 28, pp. 9–18.

———. 2001. "The Human Rights Watch Report from a Human Rights Perspective." *British Journal of Industrial Relations,* Vol. 39, no. 4 (December), pp. 591–595.

———. 2002. *The Future of the American Labor Movement.* New York: Cambridge University Press.

Worker Rights Consortium. 2004. "Model Code of Conduct." <http://www.workersrights.org/coc.asp>. [January 15, 2004].

World Bank. 2003. "Labor Standards and Their Role in Economic Development." <http://web.worldbank.org/WBSITE/EXTERNAL/NEWS/0,,contentMDK:20091472~menuPK:34457~pagePK:34370~piPK:34424~theSitePK:4607,00.html>. [March 2, 2005.]

World Commission on the Social Dimension of Globalization. 2004. *A Fair Globalization: Creating Opportunities for All.* Geneva: International Labour Office.

Worldwide Responsible Apparel Production. 2004. "Welcome to WRAP." <http://www.wrapapparel.org.>. [March 3, 2005].

CHAPTER 6

The Technological Assault on Ethics in the Modern Workplace

RICHARD S. ROSENBERG
University of British Columbia

According to the U.S. Department of Labor, about one-third of the nation's nearly 40,000 private investigators work for corporate employers. In addition to using Web search engines like Google to do background checks, some corporate PIs excel at "social engineering." By worming information out of customer service departments and other trusted contacts, PIs obtain confidential data—including credit card, phone, and medical records—on unsuspecting employees ("Examples of Employee Surveillance" 2003:no page).

With the aid of information and communication technology (ICT), the modern office has evolved into a structure with great promise but with much stress as well. In this chapter, some of the factors contributing to this stress will be explored and located within the contexts of workplace ethics and long-term conflicts between management and employees. As the factory has continued to decline as a source of employment, the office as well as the service industries have taken up the slack. In a relatively short period the office has been transformed from an environment in which the typewriter and telephone rule into one in which the computer and the Internet are pervasive. A number of important questions have arisen as a result, including the following:

- Has productivity increased?
- Has the office environment been improved?
- Are workers encouraged to employ the new technologies in creative and interesting ways?
- What ethical challenges, if any, have accompanied the introduction of new pervasive technologies into the workplace?

A full answer to these questions is beyond both my resources and the scope of this chapter; I will emphasize the final question, related to "ethical challenges." Of primary interest is the assault on privacy in the workplace, a study of employee expectations and employers' responses, mediated by the use of technology to enforce management policies. Among the ethical issues and controversies to be presented are typical current office practices, existing and predicted technologies of surveillance, state and federal laws with respect to surveillance in the workplace, pre-employment testing, major legal cases explicating workers' rights (or rather lack of rights), and examples of office policies.

It is important at the outset to recognize that management's drive to control the workplace is frequently justified by the need to ensure that it is not subject to legal action because of questionable behavior by employees. Such behavior could include downloading material protected by copyright (for example, music and movies using peer-to-peer software), using instant messaging and e-mail to threaten individuals from the workplace, surfing sexually oriented websites, and inadvertently downloading viruses and spyware, thus threatening company security.

Another area of interest to be briefly discussed is deskilling, or reducing the scope of worker skills by parallel expansion in the complexity of work organization and the employment of sufficiently complex technologies. As Braverman (1974) has written, it is the long-term goal of management to extract the skills of workers and embed them in the work process, where they can be controlled. Since such challenges are global, it is not surprising that the International Labour Organization has developed recommendations on respecting the ethical autonomy of workers. Such principles should play an important role as surveillance technologies spread.

I have compared (Rosenberg 1999) the state of the office at the end of the 20th century with predictions made some 10 years earlier by the now defunct Office of Technology Assessment (1987). Many of the practices and threats discussed in 1987 are expanded upon and new issues introduced. From the early practice of monitoring keystrokes to the current tracking of websites visited, the office has become as controlled and controlling as the factory floor from the days of the first assembly line. It may have been naïve to assume that the computer and its associated technologies would liberate workers to contribute more fully of their talents and expertise. In some areas of work such liberation is in fact taking place, but for many workers the workplace offers little in the way of exercising individual creativity but much in the way of creating ethical concerns and challenges. In her book *White Collar Sweatshop*, author Jill Andreskey Fraser (2001:76) writes that "technological developments, meanwhile, have permitted corporations to extend their control over employees to an oppressive degree: all in the interest of keeping men and women at maximum productive efficiency, whether they find themselves in their cars or commuter trains, hotel rooms, or even master bedrooms." Among the more recent challenges, the use of global positioning technology to monitor the locations of mobile workers and even teleworkers now extends the employer's reach beyond the traditional workplace.

Cases and Reports of Workplace Conditions

Hundreds of McDonald's workers in Winnipeg now begin each shift by placing their hand on a scanner that confirms their identity and records the exact moment when they arrived at work. They finish each day with another scan (Smith 2004:A8).

As a context for the discussion to follow, I will present a few examples and illustrative legal cases to help show what employers want from their office employees and what employees might expect. The simple thesis to be substantiated is that in the modern workplace workers have almost no rights, and clearly this situation is ethically unacceptable. Civil liberties are shed as the worker enters the workplace, largely devoid of basic protections. Telephone conversations are monitored, website visits are logged and stored, e-mail messages are tracked and catalogued, and instant messaging contributions are recorded. Closed circuit television monitors are pervasive, "active" badges as well as global positioning devices embedded in cell phones reveal workers' locations, drug tests are performed both randomly and on a schedule, psychological tests are given to determine stability, genetic tests are administered to predict the possibility of terrible diseases, background checks are carried out prior to employment, and skills are gradually identified and extracted. And the intrusions all began with keystroke monitoring, shortly after computers were introduced.

I will briefly describe a series of legal cases, beginning in 1993 and ending in 2003, and evaluate their implications for privacy rights in the workplace. My purpose is not to provide legal guidelines to worker rights, or better lack of rights, nor to imply that what is legal is necessarily ethical. Rather, I want to roughly characterize the current legal situation with respect to the imbalance of employer powers and employee rights.

Bonita P. Bourke et al. v. Nissan Motor Corporation

The facts of the case are taken from the decision rendered by the Court of Appeal of the State of California on July 26, 1993 (*Bonita P. Bourke et al. v. Nissan Motor Corporation* 1993). Note that this decision, as well as others, is labeled "Not to be published" in its Internet source and is referenced here for educational purposes only. The Court of

Appeal upheld the original decision of the trial court in favor of the defendant, Nissan Motor Corporation in USA, against the charge of the plaintiffs, "alleging wrongful termination, invasion of privacy and violation of their constitutional right to privacy in connection with Nissan's retrieval, printing and reading of E-mail messages authored by plaintiffs" (no page).

This case is important because it occurred early in the use of e-mail for office business practices. Apparently, in a training session, one of the plaintiffs' co-workers used as an example of e-mail an unfortunately highly personal message sent by Bourke. The message was reported to management, and many other messages containing personal content involving Bourke and her colleague Hall were discovered. After receiving rather low performance ratings on periodic evaluations, Bourke and Hall filed grievances against Nissan's human resources department. Subsequently, they sued Nissan for "common law invasion of privacy, violation of their constitutional right to privacy, and violation of the criminal wiretapping and eavesdropping statutes" (no page). The trial court found in favor of Nissan on two grounds, of which one is substantive: "Based on the undisputed facts, plaintiffs had no reasonable expectation of privacy in their e-mail messages" (no page). Nissan presented additional arguments that have by now become familiar in the workplace, namely that only company business should be carried out on company computers and that if warnings of lack of privacy are made generally available, workers have little to complain about.

Alana Shoars v. Epson America, Inc.

Again, a State of California Appeals Court upheld a decision in favor of the employer. The employer apparently assured the plaintiff, in her role as an instructor in the use of Epson's e-mail system, that "their [employees'] e-mail was private and confidential" (*Alana Shoars v. Epson America, Inc.* 1994:no page). However, Shoars claimed that "beginning in August 1989 her supervisor at Epson, Hillseth, acting on Epson's behalf tapped the e-mail, printed it, and read it" (no page). Finally, the plaintiff maintained that she had been fired because of "refusal to go along with Hillseth and Epson's intercepting the e-mail, which in turn violated the public policy [etc.]" (no page). Although the case is somewhat more complicated than the present description, the point continues to be clear that management reserves the right to set the rules in the workplace and to punish employees for violating them. However, it was with the next case, probably the most influential in this area, that workplace control was firmly set within management's grasp.

Bill McLaren Jr. v. Microsoft Corporation

The Court of Appeals of Dallas, Texas, upheld the trial court's decision against Bill McLaren Jr. in May 1999. In brief, the circumstances of the case follow:

> McLaren was an employee of Microsoft Corporation. In December 1996, Microsoft suspended McLaren's employment pending an investigation into accusations of sexual harassment and "inventory questions." McLaren requested access to his electronic mail to disprove the allegations against him. According to McLaren, he was told he could access his e-mail only by requesting it through company officials and telling them the location of a particular message. By memorandum, McLaren requested that no one tamper with his Microsoft office workstation or his e-mail. McLaren's employment was terminated on December 11, 1996 (*Bill McLaren Jr. v. Microsoft Corporation* 1999:no page).

McLaren's suit involved an invasion claim against Microsoft's "breaking" into his computer files. However, among Microsoft's argument in defense was that "[t]he common law of Texas does not recognize any right of privacy in the contents of electronic mail systems and storage that are provided to employees by the employer as part of the employment relationship" (*Bill McLaren Jr. v. Microsoft Corporation* 1999:no page). So once again, the control of the workplace by management precludes any claim for individual privacy, a legal result outweighing ethical considerations.

Recent Surveys Related to Workplace Issues

A recent privacy poll found that 81 percent of the public believe employers have no right to monitor phone calls at work. However, employers do have a right to monitor phone calls as long as it is within "the ordinary course of business." A 2001 survey by American Management Association estimated that 12 percent of major U.S. corporations periodically record and review telephone calls, 8 percent store and review voice mail messages and 43 percent monitor the amount of time employees spend on the phone and check the numbers that have been dialed ("Examples of Employee Surveillance" 2003:no page).

Based on a review of surveys published in the past few years, an argument can be made that surveillance in the workplace has become the normal state of affairs and that most employees should probably assume that this condition exists as part of their jobs. Probably the most publicized series of surveys is that carried out by the American Management Association (AMA). In its 2001 survey of workplace monitoring and surveillance among a wide range of companies, AMA found the overall percentage of companies engaged in all forms of electronic monitoring and/or surveillance to be 82.2, up from 67.3 two years earlier (2001 AMA Survey 2001). The following types of surveillance and monitoring were included: "recording and review of telephone conversations, storage and review of voice mail messages, storage and review of computer files, storage and review of e-mail messages, monitoring Internet connections, video recording of employee job performance, telephone use (time spent, numbers called), computer use (time logged on, keystroke counts, etc.), and video surveillance for security purposes" (no page).

Although new full surveys in this series have not been carried out by the AMA, other results have been reported, in particular with respect to e-mail practices. Consider the following sample of results of a 2003 survey in which the AMA participated; this survey included over 1,100 companies and organizations (2003 E-Mail Rules, Policies and Practices Survey 2003).

- 52% of the organizations carried out some form of e-mail monitoring, 35% did not, and 13% did not know.

- Of those that did carry out some form of e-mail monitoring, 51% monitored incoming mail, 39% monitored outgoing mail, and 19% monitored internal e-mail between employees.

- 75% had written policies concerning e-mail, 48% trained their employees on those policies, and 34% had written e-mail retention and deletion policies.

- 59% used some form of enforcement of their e-mail rules and policies. Of these, 50% used discipline, 25% performance reviews, 22% termination, 18% removal of e-mail privileges, and 4% legal action.

In 2004, the AMA again cooperated with the ePolicy Institute to explore the use of e-mail as well as instant messaging in the workplace. The resulting survey of 840 U.S. businesses (2004 Workplace E-Mail and Instant Messaging Survey 2004) revealed that the continuous diffusion of technological innovation generates an ongoing stream of associated problems because the technologies are frequently misused, from the employer's point of view at least. Results of the 2004 survey include some interesting findings. The use of software to monitor ingoing or outgoing e-mail has increased to 60%, but internal e-mail among employees is monitored by only 27% of companies surveyed. Of particular interest is the increasing use of instant messaging in the workplace, as shown the following results:

When it comes to fast and loose content, nothing tops instant messaging. The majority (58%) of workplace users engage in personal IM chat. Survey respondents report sending and receiving the following types of inappropriate and potentially damaging IM content: attachments (19%), jokes, gossip, rumors, or disparaging remarks (16%); confidential information about the company, a coworker, or client (9%); sexual, romantic, or pornographic content (6%). From the standpoint of content and retention, employers should view IM as a form of turbocharged e-mail, creating a written business record that must be monitored and managed. Employers are advised to take control of instant messaging risks today, or face potentially costly consequences tomorrow (2004 Workplace E-Mail and Instant Messaging Survey 2004:2).

Furthermore, "90% of respondents spend up to 90 minutes per workday on IM" (2004:2). The actions of employers in response to lack of compliance with existing polices are becoming increasingly severe, as this survey reveals, "with 25% of 2004 respondents terminating an employee for violating e-mail policy, versus 22% in 2003 and 17% in 2001" (2004:2).

In late 2003, *Wired* magazine surveyed a panel of privacy experts to determine which companies were the best (and the worst) in respecting their employees' privacy rights ("Ranking Privacy at Work," 2003). The top three companies were IBM, Hewlett-Packard, and Ford ("uses stringent European Union privacy laws as the basis for its global policies"; no page); the worst were Eli Lilly, Wal-Mart ("wiring managers to tape conversations with coworkers"; no page), and the New York Times Company. That a company would seek to protect its employees' privacy as a matter of course has become a rare and special event.

Finally, a recent survey of 1,240 British businesses reported the following striking results (Thomson 2004:no page):

- Employee misuse of technology top[ped] the reasons for security breaches, with 50 per cent of businesses having problems.
- The second highest cause, at 45 per cent, was poorly updated antivirus software.
- Only 18 per cent of organisations attributed problems to their own security policies.

The many consistent results of comprehensive surveys seem to provide ample reasons for management to institute monitoring and surveillance technologies. Nevertheless, there is no one best way to accomplish the aims of concerned employers. Establishing policies that carefully describe management expectations within a framework that also respects employees' basic rights is a necessary and ultimately rewarding action. Taking an ethical point of view in managing the workplace is not a formula for losing control. Treating employees with respect and creating an environment that encourages commitment, resourcefulness, and responsibility can be equated with capital investment to improve productivity. Establishing ethical ground rules and enforcing them fairly demonstrate a commitment of management to respect its workers and their efforts.

Privacy in the Workplace: Expectations and Practices

A software program called Investigator which has sold more than 200,000 copies allows employers to monitor every single keystroke an employee makes. It also maintains a record of dialogue boxes and takes periodic screen shots of what's being displayed on the computer. If the PC is equipped with a Web cam, the program can also be configured to take secret photos of the computer user ("Examples of Employee Surveillance" 2003:no page).

The cases discussed in the previous sections reveal an incorrect assumption prevalent among many, if not most, employees: that they enjoy certain basic privacy privileges in the workplace. In reality, workers enjoy almost no workplace privacy protection. The simple fact is that employees have virtually no rights and should behave as if every action is being observed. The psychological impact of constant observation is serious and represents a major assault on the ethical rights of workers. Furthermore, productivity may also be compromised as a by-product of the growth of surveillance in the workplace. So what should employers do? A brief survey of advice for employers, in part consisting of reminders of both their powers and their responsibilities over the past few years, may be informative.

Employer Concerns and Responsibilities

Prison sentences could await business bosses who do not do enough to stop the most serious abuse of computer networks by employees (Ward 2004:no page).

The control of the workplace has a long tradition in industrial, and, yes, postindustrial, societies. From a Marxist perspective, it is the long-term goal of owners to extract from workers even the smallest amount of their specialized knowledge of the work process. As work becomes routinized, workers become interchangeable and replaceable and unworthy of being treated ethically. Of course information technology, or information and communication technology, facilitates this process. It has become clear that there is a price to pay for this supposed control, namely responsibility for the actions of the employees. The substantial increase in the use of e-mail and instant messaging in the office means that there must be an associated increase in cases of harassment, uploading of company secrets, and trafficking in sexually explicit material, including child pornography. For managers, only an active surveillance environment can alleviate criminal responsibility. So there is a vicious cycle of employees' potentially using information and communication technology for possibly criminal purposes, obliging managers to implement and extend online surveillance procedures.

It is useful to explore in somewhat more detail the specific powers and responsibilities of owners and managers. The simple question posed in the lead of a piece in *Transform Magazine*—"Should You Read Employee Email?"—receives the following answer (Lunt 2003):

> The surprising answer is yes. The risks of e-mail abuse include litigation, business interruptions, viruses and lost productivity. Companies need to establish written e-mail policies and then educate employees on the use and misuse of e-mail. E-mail monitoring software adds an extra proactive measure in enforcing corporate policy.

In November 2003, *The Wall Street Journal* featured an article titled "Big Employer Is Watching" (Mahler 2003). The first two sentences set the tone: "It's 9 a.m. Do you know where your workers are?" (no page). Of course the answer is increasingly yes, especially as surveillance software and hardware continue to pervade the workplace. The general tenor seems to be that unless employees are regularly monitored with respect to their comings and goings using fingerprint or online technologies, they will not act responsibly. The model of punching a time card when entering and leaving the workplace is obviously alive and well and being extended to salaried workers.

In a subsequent section, I will discuss existing laws that do protect employees even to a limited degree; for the present, consider the following summary paragraph from an article written by a lawyer concerned with advising managers confronting a post–September 11, 2001 world.

> The use of advanced technologies to monitor employees and collect PII [personally identifiable information] can serve a variety of legitimate business objectives. In order to mitigate privacy law-related liability exposure, a company should determine the specific business objectives it seeks to accomplish by its use of such technologies in the workplace, adopt a comprehensive corporate privacy policy regarding the use, security and storage of PII, and appoint an individual accountable for

compliance. These steps should ensure that the use of such technologies in and of itself does not interfere with the larger business objectives of the enterprise (Martin 2003:2).

The purposes of collecting personally identifiable information through monitoring technologies include "employee training and evaluation, facilities management, and security-related objectives such as protection of tangible and intangible business assets and personnel" (Martin 2003:1).

Employee Expectations and Rights in the Workplace

What do employees want? Given that they are aware of existing surveillance technologies available to management, most presumably want to know the rules of the game. No one wants to be surprised by a new and unanticipated rule just announced by management to deal with a given situation. Thus, at the very least, management should design guidelines that accurately reflect its concerns and expectations as well as what is being monitored and measured. Employees certainly would like to be treated ethically. There should be few surprises. Ideally, the guidelines should be a product of an employer–employee team, responsible for the initial design and regular updates as well as for evaluating effectiveness and fairness. In the United States, this should be done in a way that is also consistent with section 8(a)(2) of the National Labor Relations Act.

The assault on assumed workers' rights has been described by Judge James M. Rosenbaum in the somewhat offbeat "Entertaining Journal of Law," *The Green Bag*. The opening sentence sets the tone: "A new 'legal principle' has emerged. It holds that if a corporation, business, or government entity owns a computer, and if an employee puts personal matter onto that computer, the author has neither a right nor an expectation of privacy in the computer stored material" (Rosenbaum 2001:169). Judge Rosenbaum is very concerned about challenges to individual privacy; in his commentary on a specific case of employees at the *New York Times* being punished for storing offending material on company computers, he clearly sympathizes with the punished: "The employees had no rights in the face of this electronic rummage though their lives. They had no rights, because an employee should not expect privacy on material residing in a company-owned computer" (2001:170).

The trend in the workplace is for more surveillance, more loss of privacy, more restrictions, more control by management, and necessarily less concern with ethical treatment, all of which seem simply wrong to Judge Rosenbaum. He concludes his rather short piece with the following, somewhat wistful, remarks:

The present regime, giving employers a near-Orwellian power to spy and snoop into the lives of their employees, is not tenable. The use of an employer's computer should not be equated with the loss of its operator's rights. A society which values individual freedom cannot function this way. It seems to me a simple notice, coupled with a short cooling off period, can go a long way to protecting a citizen's essential right to think without fear (Rosenbaum 2001:171).

A Selection of Relevant Privacy Laws

The basic question to be addressed relates to the existence of laws that protect individual privacy in the workplace. The simple answer is that, in general, there are no such laws. Nevertheless, it is necessary to describe, even briefly, what minimal protections do exist and what the prospects for the future are. If we turn to the National Workrights Institute and the question "Does the common law or the ECPA [Electronic Communications Privacy Act of 1986] protect employees who are subject to electronic monitoring in the workplace?" we find the simple response to be generally no. The somewhat more detailed answer is that the act gives the power to an employer who makes available "electronic communication service, whose facilities are used in the transmission of a wire or electronic communication, to intercept, disclose, or use that communication in the normal course of his employment while engaged in any activity which is a necessary incident to the rendition of his service or to the protection of the rights or property of the provider of that service" ("Electronic Monitoring in the Workplace: Common Law and Federal Statutory Protection" n.d.:no page).

It is important to note that the ECPA applies to the protection of messages only in transit, not in storage. Hence, the bottom line is that in the workplace, the ECPA plays almost no role. Managers and administrators have legal access to all messages residing on the systems used by employees in the workplace. In general, as has been discussed previously, the law basically protects the interests of the employer:

> In the vast majority of such invasion of privacy cases [electronic monitoring], courts have ruled in favor of employer-defendants, finding a reduced expectation of privacy in the workplace and that an employer's business interests outweigh an employee's privacy interest. Courts have upheld claims of invasion of privacy only where the employer's monitoring has been physically invasive and has had no legitimate business purpose, such as conducting video surveillance inside of a bathroom or locker room in the workplace. Otherwise, state common law tort claims concerning electronic monitoring in the workplace virtually

always fail. Similarly, when assessing a claim under ECPA, an employee's privacy interest in any electronic communications will fail when construed alongside any legitimate business purpose of her employer ("Electronic Monitoring in the Workplace: Common Law and Federal Statutory Protection" n.d.:no page).

Smyth v. Pillsbury

One case has become exemplary in illustrating the power of management, even when an employee appears to be following company policy with respect to monitoring. The following discussion is taken from Rosenberg (1999: 6–7). Michael A. Smyth sued the Pillsbury Company for being wrongfully discharged, based on information obtained from Smyth's supposedly protected e-mail in spite of the fact that the company "repeatedly assured its employees, including plaintiff, that all e-mail communications would remain confidential and privileged. . . . Defendant further assured its employees, including plaintiff, that e-mail communications could not be intercepted and used by defendant against its employees as grounds for termination or reprimand" (*Michael A. Smyth v. The Pillsbury Company* 1996:no page).

The judge found for the plaintiff, and his reasons are revealing, particularly in the context of the accepted wisdom that well-defined and publicized e-mail policies are an absolute necessity for management to create an equitable and predictable environment. Consider the final paragraph of his decision:

> In the second instance, even if we found that an employee had a reasonable expectation of privacy in the contents of his e-mail communications over the company e-mail system, we do not find that a reasonable person would consider the defendant's interception of these communications to be a substantial and highly offensive invasion of his privacy. Again, we note that by intercepting such communications, the company is not, as in the case of urinalysis or personal property searches, requiring the employee to disclose any personal information about himself or invading the employee's person or personal effects. Moreover, the company's interest in preventing inappropriate and unprofessional comments or even illegal activity over its e-mail system outweighs any privacy interest the employee may have in those comments (*Michael A. Smyth v. The Pillsbury Company* 1996:no page).

This decision has been disputed, however. "The determination in *Smyth* that employees should have no expectation of privacy in the contents of their e-mail communications in an employer's network is clearly erroneous" (Dixon 1997:no page). In the end, the safest use of e-mail is to treat it as the equivalent of a postcard; anyone who has any interest in the contents can read them with no difficulty and no moral equivocation. The worker must recognize, and for most this is only a confirmation of long-held beliefs, that in the workplace, many civil liberties must be temporarily abandoned.

One final point also worth considering is taken from an analysis of the decision by the National Workrights Institute ("Electronic Monitoring in the Workplace: Common Law and Federal Statutory Protection" n.d.:no page):

> The court in *Smyth* also engaged in a balancing test, noting that even if it were willing to recognize a privacy interest in e-mail communications (which it was not,) such an interest could not rise to the level where a "reasonable person would consider the defendant's interception of these communications to be a substantial and highly offensive invasion of his privacy." 914 F. Supp. at 101. The defendant in *Smyth* had alleged that the e-mails "concerned sales management and contained threats to 'kill the backstabbing bastards' and referred to the planned Holiday party as the 'Jim Jones Koolaid affair'" [The 1978 "Jonestown Massacre," in which over 900 members of a religious group led by the Reverend Jim Jones died in an apparent mass suicide].[1] Id. at 99 n.1. The court declared that:

>> once plaintiff communicated the alleged unprofessional comments to a second person (his supervisor) over an e-mail system which was apparently utilized by the entire company, any reasonable expectation of privacy was lost. [T]he company's interest in preventing inappropriate and unprofessional comments or even illegal activity over its e-mail system outweighs any privacy interest the employee might have in those comments.

Overall Review of Privacy Rights in the Workplace

At this point it is worthwhile reviewing the status of privacy rights in the workplace by considering the following comment:

> Employer monitoring of electronic mail constitutes an emerging area of the law that is clearly unsettled at this point in time. This iBrief [online legal brief] demonstrates that the privacy rights of non public-sector employees are relatively unprotected by the federal and state constitutions, broad judicial interpretations of enacted privacy legislation favor legitimate employer-monitoring practices, and many of the elements of

common law claims are difficult for employees to prove ("Monitoring Employee E-mail: Efficient Workplaces vs. Employee Privacy" 2001:no page).

For the immediate future, therefore, workers would be well advised to assume that *all* their communications in the workplace are readily available to their employers. Both employers and employees have responsibilities, but employers of course have by far more power under existing laws. The following excerpt briefly describes what employers and employees should be aware of to minimize liability and to maximize responsibility and flexibility:

> Employers desiring to avoid liability for monitoring employee e-mail usage should "take all necessary steps to eliminate any reasonable expectation of privacy that employees may have concerning their use of company e-mail . . . systems" (Lewis 2000). This can be done through a detailed and clearly written electronic communications policy that is distributed regularly to as many employees as practicable before any monitoring begins.
>
> Employees, on the other hand, need to understand that current laws governing workplace e-mail will not protect them from excessive personal use. Most employers seem willing to tolerate some personal e-mail use and will police violations by looking more at employee work product and ability to meet deadlines. In fact, employees will be safer using a personal e-mail account from work, as opposed to an employer-provided account, although employees must remember that excessive personal e-mail may still raise employer scrutiny as it will likely translate into a lower overall performance. However, employees should feel secure that excessive monitoring or other employer abuses of their monitoring privileges will almost certainly violate federal and state statutes and also create tort liability ("Monitoring Employee E-mail: Efficient Workplaces vs. Employee Privacy" 2001:no page).

Fraser v. Nationwide Mutual Insurance Co.

Finally, an important case, *Fraser v. Nationwide Mutual Insurance Co.*, appeared after my 1999 review that further consolidates the power of employers and the lack of privacy protection in the workplace for employees. For our purposes, it is the privacy issues in this case that are of interest. Judge Ambro of the U.S. Court of Appeals for the Third Circuit in his opinion delivered on December 10, 2004, states that

> Richard Fraser, an independent insurance agent for Nationwide Mutual Insurance Company, was terminated by Nationwide as

an agent. We decide whether: he has stated a viable claim for wrongful termination under Pennsylvania law; he is entitled to damages under the Electronic Communications Privacy Act and parallel Pennsylvania law for Nationwide's alleged unauthorized access to his e-mail account (*Richard Fraser v. Nationwide Mutual Insurance Co.* 2003:2).

Fraser lost on almost all the issues, however. In analyzing the findings related to privacy concerns, the lawyer Shannon P. Duffy reports the following results:

> An employer's decision to dig through an employee's e-mails in computer storage does not violate any provisions of the Electronic Communications Privacy Act since the law bans an "interception" only if it occurs at the time of transmission and exempts the owner of an e-mail system from any claim alleging an illegal "seizure" of stored e-mails, a federal appeals court has ruled.
>
> In *Fraser v. Nationwide Mutual Insurance Co.*, the 3rd U.S. Circuit Court of Appeals ruled that since Richard Fraser's e-mails were stored on Nationwide's system, any search by the company was authorized by an express exemption in the federal ECPA for e-mail service providers (Duffy 2003:no page).

The legal system currently does little to protect the privacy of workers, and this situation is unlikely to change. Adherence to basic ethical principles regarding the importance of individual privacy in human affairs has been abandoned at the entrance to the workplace. The implementation of privacy policy guidelines with respect to what employees can expect in regard to their personal communications and other information rests solely on the good will of their employers, hardly a recipe for an equitable working environment.

Model Corporate Privacy Standards

Is there any hope that current trends will be reversed, to think that just because it is possible to monitor most workplace activities, they will not necessarily be monitored? As long as employees are viewed as contributing to increased liability, the advice to management is to monitor and control. A lawyer at a New York firm writing on the responsibilities of both employees and employers characterizes the current situation in this way:

> The problem facing employers is how to balance the obvious benefits of online access for their employees with the risks inherent in providing those tools to employees. Many employers

have sought to achieve this balance by monitoring the use that their employees make of e-mail and Internet access. Monitoring however, brings into conflict the employer's legitimate interest in protecting against the risks associated with online access for employees and the privacy interests of the employees. The conflict between employers' need to monitor and employees' right to privacy is, of course, not limited to electronic communication; but certain characteristics of e-mail and the Internet such as the use of passwords to access communications and the apparent ability to delete files may create an illusion of a higher level of privacy than is actually the case with electronic communication. The most effective and simplest way for an employer to protect its ability to monitor employees' online activities and avoid legal challenges to that monitoring is to put in place a policy which clearly informs employees that their use of e-mail and the Internet will be monitored and ensure that all employees are aware of the policy (Bassett 2002:no page).

Policies and Frequently Asked Questions (FAQs)

The National Workrights Institute has produced a "Model Policy on Electronic Monitoring" that enunciates a concern for workers' rights. Such a policy must stand on a basic ethical foundation with a solid respect for worker autonomy. Unless workers are respected and their basic humanity valued, as reflected by the embedding of basic ethical principles in working policy, the workplace environment will be oppressive. Some highlights of the Model Policy are excerpted here ("Model Policy on Electronic Monitoring" n.d.:no page):

1. Personal Use of Equipment

   Workers can use company equipment for incidental purposes such as checking up on a sick child but not on a regular basis.

2. No Secret Monitoring

   Except for investigations into serious misconduct, there will be no secret monitoring.

3. No Personal Monitoring

   No personal communications will be monitored nor will non-work areas be monitored for other than safety issues.

4. Notice of Monitoring

   If monitoring takes place, notification must be made. If documents stored on an individual's computer are needed, the individual must be asked to retrieve it unless he or she is not available.

5. No Monitoring in Private Areas

No video monitoring in bathrooms, locker rooms, etc. will take place.

6. Personal Information

Personal information about employees is collected only for legal requirements or essential business operations.

A privacy organization in the United States, the Privacy Council, issued Top Ten Guidelines to Workplace Privacy in late 2001. Beyond the rights addressed by the National Workrights Institute, the Privacy Council guidelines include the following points (Sigvartsen 2001:no page):

- Identify an individual or group of individuals within your organization to proactively manage workplace issues.
- Distribute the policy to everyone, and have them acknowledge receipt in writing or through electronic verification.
- If misconduct is discovered, conduct an immediate factual investigation and take prompt remedial action if appropriate.

It is not surprising that these policies stress the humane treatment of employees—with respect to, and presumption of, innocence. Adherence to basic ethical principles would demand no less. It is therefore surprising that any meaningful workplace policy would not be rooted in such principles.

Even the U.S. Government Accountability Office (GAO, until recently known as the General Accounting Office) has explored some of these issues. After a review of existing research literature, the GAO conducted interviews with executives from 14 Fortune 1,000 private sector companies. Although no generalizations can be made from the results of this survey, "all 14 companies we reviewed store their employees' electronic transactions: e-mail messages, information of Internet sites visited, and computer file activity. These companies reported they collect this information to create duplicate or backup files in case of system disruptions; to manage computer resources such as system capacity to handle routine e-mail and Internet traffic; and to hold employees accountable for company policies" (*Employee Privacy: Computer-Use Monitoring Practices and Policies of Selected Companies* 2002:3).

Table 1, taken from this report, summarizes the "key elements" of a computer use policy that is probably quite representative of those currently in use in American businesses. The policy elements are blunt and make quite clear the power that management exercises over its employees. Computer use policies incorporating such elements should leave little doubt in workers' minds about what is permitted and what is not, but

TABLE 1
Key Elements of a Computer-Use Policy

Policy element	Type of statement
Monitoring use of proprietary assets	Statements that company computing systems are provided as tools for business and all information created, accessed, or stored using these systems is the property of the company and subject to monitoring, auditing, and review.
Establishing no expectation of privacy	Statements about the extent or limitations of privacy protections for employee use of e-mail, the Internet, and computer files.
Improper employee use	Statements that some uses of company computers are inappropriate—including specific notice banning offensive material (e.g., obscenity, sexual content, racial slurs, derogation of people's personal characteristics) and language relating e-mail and Internet use to general prohibitions of harassment.
Allowable employee uses	Statements explaining proper or acceptable uses of the company systems, including whether or not personal use is permitted.
Protecting sensitive company information	Statements providing instructions for handling proprietary information on company systems.
Disciplinary action	Statements that there are penalties and disciplinary actions for violations of company usage policy.
Employee acknowledgment of policy	A statement requiring that employees demonstrate they understand the company policy and acknowledge their responsibility to adhere to the policy.

Source: *Employee Privacy: Computer-Use Monitoring Practices and Policies of Selected Companies* 2002:10.

just in case, some companies include such statements as the following in their policies (*Employee Privacy: Computer-Use Monitoring Practices and Policies of Selected Companies* 2002:12, emphasis added):

- All users should understand that *there is no right or reasonable expectation of privacy* in any e-mail messages on the company's system.

- Our personal privacy is not protected on these systems, and we shouldn't expect it to be.

- [company] reserves the right to audit, access, and inspect electronic communications and data stored or transmitted on its Computer Resources.

The GAO report concludes with this sentence: "Such actions [monitoring unsolicited e-mail] reflect the widespread belief among the company officials we interviewed that the worst nuisance and most likely threat to company computer systems comes from outside trespassers with a capacity to paralyze a company's Internet infrastructure or disrupt business, rather than the company's own employees" (*Employee Privacy: Computer-Use Monitoring Practices and Policies of Selected Companies* 2002:14). As I will outline in the next section, surprises may still lurk with respect to the efficacy of computer use policies and the responsibilities of management to uphold and enforce those policies. Often, the necessity to adhere to relevant laws may result in a compromise or even an abandonment of a policy rooted in ethical principles, whether or not the laws require such an approach. Too many companies seem ready to use the excuse that existing laws require a narrow approach to the development of workplace policies with respect to worker privacy and autonomy.

The International Labour Organization (ILO) produced the report *Protection of Workers' Personal Data* (1997) as one of a series of ILO Codes of Practice in 1997. Such a code has no force in law but can be used in the enactment of legislation or the development of work rules. Workers' personal data consist of information supplied at the time of hiring as well as information gathered in the course of employment, including that obtained during surveillance of Internet activity. This code is firmly based on ethical principles, as can be seen in the following highlights (the numbers refer to specific sections of the report):

5.2.   Personal data should, in principle, be used only for the purposes for which they were originally collected. . . .

5.4.   Personal data collected in connection with technical or organizational measures to ensure the security and proper operation of automated information systems should not be used to control the behavior of workers. . . .

5.6.   Personal data collected by electronic monitoring should not be the only factor in evaluating worker performance. . . .

5.8.   Workers and their representatives should be kept informed of any data collection process, the rules that govern that process, and their rights. . . .

5.11.   Employers, workers and their representatives should cooperate in protecting personal data and in developing policies on workers' privacy consistent with the principles in this code. . . .

1.14.1   (1) If workers are monitored they should be informed in advance of the reasons for monitoring, the time schedule, the methods and techniques used and the data to be collected, and the employer must minimize the intrusion on the privacy of workers.

(2) Secret monitoring should be permitted only:

   (a) if it is in conformity with national legislation; or

   (b) if there is suspicion on reasonable grounds of criminal activity or other serious wrongdoing.

(3) Continuous monitoring should be permitted only if required for health and safety or the protection of property.

The adoption by companies of this ILO code would be a significant step in ensuring workers' rights in the technological workplace, based on a firm ethical foundation.

Workplace Testing: Polygraph, Genetic, and Drug

Although thus far I have focused on the role of electronic surveillance in the assault on individual privacy in the workplace, many other technologies are employed to evaluate potential employees for suitability as well as current employees for continuing employment. No one would argue against the employer's right to undertake measures to determine the accuracy of a job application, including references and experience. Presumably such a determination could include hiring private investigators as well as requiring that all prospective employees submit to polygraph and drug testing. Indeed, such tests have been incorporated as part of the ongoing conditions of employment at many companies. It is necessary, therefore, to explore procedures generally used by management for these purposes as well as any relevant laws.

Polygraph (lie detector machine) testing, drug testing, and genetic testing are intrusive workplace technologies that raise important ethical issues. The motivation for employing these technologies is a mixture of necessity—for most jobs, honesty, reliability, and consistency are mandatory and the legal requirements for quality work. Testing for the presence of genetically possible diseases would seem to raise obvious privacy concerns, and the motivations for carrying out such tests, with associated limitations, will be discussed later.

Polygraph Testing

Lie detecting machines, or polygraphs, have become commonplace in television dramas, where they are typically used to "prove" someone's innocence or guilt. However, as we are often told, the results are not admissible in court. How do they work? A polygraph machine records the body's involuntary responses to an examiner's questions in order to ascertain deceptive behavior. The test measures physiological data from three or more systems of the human body—generally the respiratory, cardiovascular, and sweat gland systems—but not the voice. There are other tests that test the voice for deception (*Polygraph Testing*: no date). Of course, polygraphs are subject to a variety of false positives and negatives as a result of artificially altering body responses through the use of sedatives, antiperspirants, and self-inflicted injuries.

To protect against the misuse of polygraphs, the Employee Polygraph Protection Act of 1988 (EPPA) was passed. The American Civil Liberties Union describes the benefits of EPPA as follows:

> The EPPA, with some exceptions, prohibits the use of "lie detectors" by private sector employers involved in or affecting interstate commerce. In the law, the term "lie detector" includes polygraphs, deceptographs, voice stress analyzers and "any other similar device that is used . . . for the purpose of rendering a diagnostic opinion regarding the honesty or dishonesty of an individual." The ban applies to all random, and most pre-employment, testing and will eliminate about 80 percent of the testing done in the private sector in the past. The EPPA does not prohibit drug tests or written honesty tests.
>
> Under the EPPA, employers may not require, request, suggest or cause any employee or applicant to submit to a "lie detector" test, nor may they discharge, discipline or discriminate against any employee or job applicant for refusing to take such a test, for "failing" such a test, or for filing a complaint or exercising any other rights conferred by the legislation. The EPPA also requires employers to post a notice informing employees of the Act's provisions in a conspicuous place at the work site ("Lie Detector Testing" 1996:no page).

However, there are many situations in which lie detector testing is permitted, primarily for government officials and for national security–related activities ("Lie Detector Testing" 1996):

- The Act permits "lie detector" testing of federal, state, and local government employees.
- The federal government may administer "lie detector" tests to certain government contractors engaged in national security–related activities.
- Private security firms and companies that manufacture and distribute pharmaceuticals are permitted to test certain job applicants.
- Any employer may administer "lie detector" tests in connection with an ongoing investigation of an economic loss or injury to his/her business on these conditions: The employee under suspicion must have had access to the property, and the employer must state in writing the basis for a reasonable suspicion that the employee was guilty.

It is important to note that the current state of polygraph technology is highly suspect with respect to accuracy and therefore is also clearly ethically suspect. A report from a panel of the National Academy of Sciences specifically charged "to conduct a scientific review of the research on polygraph examinations that pertains to their reliability" was released in 2002 (*The Polygraph and Lie Detection* 2003).

Among the conclusions is the following with respect to the use of countermeasures to defeat the accuracy of the test: "Basic science and polygraph research give reason for concern that polygraph test accuracy may be degraded by countermeasures, particularly when used by major security threats which have a strong incentive and sufficient resources to use them effectively. If these measures are effective, they could seriously undermine any value of polygraph security screening" (*The Polygraph and Lie Detection* 2003:no page).

Drug Testing

Given that drug use is a general societal problem, it is no surprise that the workplace is afflicted. The U.S. Department of Labor describes the situation regarding drug testing, very similar to the use of polygraphs, as follows:

> Drug testing is **NOT** required under the Drug-Free Workplace Act of 1988. The majority of employers across the United States are NOT required to test and many state and local governments have statutes that limit or prohibit workplace testing, unless required by state or Federal regulations for certain jobs. On the other hand, most private employers have the right to test for a wide variety of substances ("Drug Testing" n.d.:no page; emphasis in original).

The reasons for employing drug tests are not surprising but are worth listing:

- Deter employees from abusing drugs and alcohol
- Prevent hiring individuals who use illegal drugs
- Provide early identification and referral of employees who have drug and/or alcohol problems
- Provide a safe workplace for other employees
- Ensure general public safety and instill consumer confidence that employees are working safely

It is obvious that drug tests are intrusive, and the American Civil Liberties Union has pointed out three examples ("Privacy in America: Workplace Drug Testing" 1997:no page):

However routine drug tests have become, they're still intrusive. Often, another person is there to observe the employee to ensure there is no specimen tampering. Even indirect observation can be degrading; typically, workers must remove their outer garments and urinate in a bathroom in which the water supply has been turned off,

The lab procedure is a second invasion of privacy. Urinalysis reveals not only the presence of illegal drugs, but also the existence of many other physical and medical conditions, including genetic predisposition to disease—or pregnancy. In 1988, the Washington, D.C. Police Department admitted it used urine samples collected for drug tests to screen female employees for pregnancy—*without* their knowledge or consent.

Furthermore, human error in the lab, or the test's failure to distinguish between legal and illegal substances, can make even a small margin of error add up to a huge potential for false positive results. In 1992, an estimated 22 million tests were administered. If five percent yielded false positive results (a conservative estimate of false positive rates) that means 1.1 million people who could have been fired, or denied jobs—because of a mistake.

In January 2004, the *Washington Post* reported that "federal workers who submit to drug screening soon may have their saliva, sweat or hair tested as the Bush administration increases efforts to deter and detect illegal drug use among 1.6 million civilian employees" (Lee 2004:no page). For almost twenty years, drug testing consisted of urine testing; this extension was seen as yet another blow in the ongoing assault against workplace privacy. Although most of the discussion has focused on the United States, I will end this section with the conclusions of a report released by the ILO:

To sum up, workplace drug testing is an issue beset with technical, legal and ethical controversies. WDT policies may be unclear about the motivation for testing, which however determines what type of testing programme should be used. The most serious challenges to testing are based on privacy and data protection arguments. Employers however face a legal responsibility to provide a safe workplace and meet obligations to their shareholders which may not be possible if drug use is rife. How far should they go to meet these obligations? Do such obligations represent adequate grounds for employers to determine what employees do in their free time? What kind of sanctions should be in place and how should these relate to health care initiatives which may also be part of a drugs and alcohol policy? Should employers' policies distinguish clearly between the consequences for the use of different drugs? Should policies distinguish more clearly between users, abusers and people with chemical dependencies? (Shahandeh and Caborn 2003:9).

Genetic Testing

DNA has become a valuable tool to identify potential criminals and to free wrongfully accused or imprisoned individuals. What role might it play in the workplace?

Employers, either current or prospective, could have an interest in the results of such genetic screening in so far as these might be a predictor of the future health of an employee, particularly if they were to imply possible levels of future absenteeism or low work rate which might impact on profitability. An employee who develops heart disease, for example, would certainly be likely to require periods of absence from work and, in certain occupations, might not be able to sustain a normal work rate. There is also the possibility that sudden onset of a disease condition might result in a hazard for the employee, other employees or the public. An employer could use the results of such tests to exclude job applicants on the basis of predicted future health. This type of genetic testing, where there is no reason to suspect that the employee might possess any particular genetic constitution, is generally referred to as genetic screening ("Ethical Aspects of Genetic Testing in the Workplace" 2003:5).

The health insurance reason demonstrates the complex relationship between general societal situations and ethical workplace issues. In the United States, there are no universal heath care systems such as those in Europe and Canada. Thus, many companies must contract with private health providers to ensure that their employees have medical coverage. If it turns out that an employee has a genetic status with a reasonable probability of developing into a condition requiring expensive and long-term care, insurance premiums may become prohibitive, resulting in a possible loss of coverage for the company. Thus genetic testing in the workplace may become a necessary requirement to guarantee affordable medical coverage; those exhibiting possibly serious genetic defects may be dismissed or not even hired. Furthermore, genetic testing creates new sources of private information, whose disclosure could create serious problems for future employment.

Several attempts have been made in the U.S. Congress to deal with such possibilities. Late in 2003, the Senate unanimously passed S. 1053, the Genetic Information Nondiscrimination Act of 2003: "To prohibit discrimination on the basis of genetic information with respect to health insurance and employment." No action seems to have been taken in the House, so this act would have to be reintroduced if its proponents are still interested in the issues. It would be an important legislative step in recognizing the ethical implications of genetic information. In this act, genetic monitoring is defined as follows (Definition (5) under Title II, Sec. 201. Definitions):

> The term "genetic monitoring" means the periodic examination of employees to evaluate acquired modifications to their genetic material, such as chromosomal damage or evidence of increased occurrence of mutations, that may have developed in the course of employment due to exposure to toxic substances in the workplace, in order to identify, evaluate, and respond to the effects of or control adverse environmental exposures in the workplace.
>
> To indicate the concern that lawmakers have for the detrimental impact of improper uses of genetic information, consider the following section of the Act (Section 202. Employer Practices):(a) USE OF GENETIC INFORMATION.—It shall be an unlawful employment practice for an employer—(1) to fail or refuse to hire or to discharge any employee, or otherwise to discriminate against any employee with respect to the compensation, terms, conditions, or privileges of employment of the employee, because of genetic information with respect to the employee (or information about a request for or the receipt of genetic services by such employee or family member of such employee); or
>
> (2) to limit, segregate, or classify the employees of the employer in any way that would deprive or tend to deprive any employee of employment opportunities or otherwise adversely affect the status of the employee as an employee, because of genetic information with respect to the employee (or information about a request for or the receipt of genetic services by such employee or family member of such employee) (page 1).

Whether or not this act will become law remains to be seen, but it is clear that a consensus exists that constraints must be put in place to limit the power of management to require genetic testing as well as to limit how the results can be used. Several states have already responded with their own laws limiting the use of genetic testing. For example, consider the following brief descriptions of laws in Oregon and Texas:

> Oregon state law prohibits employers from using genetic information to distinguish between or discriminate against

applicants and employees and prohibits employers from subjecting applicants and employees to genetic testing. A recently enacted Texas law prohibits employers, labor organizations, licensing agencies, and employment agencies from discriminating against any individual on the basis of the results of a genetic test or because of the individual's refusal to submit to genetic testing (Genetic Information and the Workplace 1998:no page).

Conclusions

A McDonald's outlet is a machine that produces, with the help of unskilled machine attendants, a highly polished product (Cohon 1988:14).

Although not apparently related directly to the assault on privacy, the movement toward the "McDonald's-ization" of work does create an environment that facilitates close monitoring of the work process and hence raises all the issues related to surveillance. As computers were first introduced into the workplace, the immediate impact was to reduce the typical range of activities for employees, in a manner similar to the process involved in moving from craftsmanship to the assembly line in the early production of automobiles. One way to summarize some of the ethical issues related to deskilling follows:

Somewhat more abstract but obviously of concern is the growing uncomfortable relation between people and machines, especially when these machines may pose a challenge to human dignity. Thus it is all the more important that the introduction of sophisticated computers into the workplace be accompanied by proper training, which stresses the long term benefits of computer-aided work and assures employees of their on-going value. Part of the fear is that they will ultimately be replaced by the computer. Even though there is little likelihood of this occurring in the short run, sufficient evidence exists to warrant some apprehension. A more realistic concern is that an increasing number and variety of jobs will be deskilled—they will consist of nothing more than "tending" machines (Rosenberg 2004:571).

Thus monitoring can be seen not only as a threat to individual autonomy but as a sophisticated means to ascertain employee knowledge of the work process, a necessary step in increasing the level of automation to reduce the labor components of costs.

The workplace is rapidly changing as the impact of technology continues to grow in many unpredictable directions, but what is predictable is that for many workers the environment is increasingly hostile. Crossing the threshold to the workplace often means surrendering basic civil liberties, specifically the right to privacy. For a variety of reasons—some valid, it must be admitted—management has introduced an array of surveillance technologies. This phenomenon shows no signs of lessening, and for employees the stress levels associated with the abrogation of basic ethical principles continue to increase.

Ethical concerns require that management at the very least construct a well-defined and well-managed policy on workplace surveillance. Such a policy should ensure that all employees are informed about the rules of the workplace, sign off on their having been informed, and are involved in the evolution of these rules. However, the case of *Smyth v. Pillsbury* discussed earlier is sobering, as it shows that even with a surveillance policy in place, management's actions, contrary to its policies, prevail. Recall that a promise that no repercussions will follow from the interception of internal employee e-mails, although broken, was judged in management's favor.

In general, U.S. laws support the power of management to abrogate the privacy rights of employees for a variety of reasons, including the need to ensure that company computer systems are not used to harass, to threaten, to download illegal material, or to upload proprietary information. The range of surveillance includes storing and monitoring e-mails and instant messages, polygraph testing, drug testing, genetic testing, and more. It would not seem easy to be an employee in today's workplace, where the ethical rights of employees are regularly trampled.

One small hopeful note was raised in August 2004, when the California Assembly passed Senate Bill No. 1841, which declares that "employers will be required to inform employees if job site e-mail and Internet activities are being monitored" ("California Assembly Approves Employee E-mail Protection" 2004). The bill "requires employers to give employees a one-time written notice if they plan to read e-mail, track Internet use, or use other electronic devices to monitor employees on or off the job." The bill went back to the Senate and then to Governor Schwarzenegger.

Unfortunately for California workers, on September 29 Schwarzenegger vetoed the bill, saying that "for business purposes, employers should have the ability to monitor employee activity in order to ensure (internet and e-mail) access is not being abused" (Sullivan 2004:no page). Schwarzenegger was also reported to have said that "the legislation was too broad and did not define clearly enough the notification employers would have to give to their employees before electronically monitoring them" (Sullivan 2004:no page). Not surprisingly, the sponsor of the bill, Rep. Debra Bowen (D-Redondo Beach), disagreed: "The bill simply required companies that want to monitor their employees' e-mail or internet use to give them a one-time notice saying, 'Your computer use may be monitored at any time.'" (Sullivan 2004:no page). It is currently against California state law to monitor employees' telephone calls without giving them notice. It seems fair to ask why the newer technology, with its greater power to monitor, should not be governed by a similar law. Lawmakers, judges, companies, and employees all need to pay greater attention to the ethical ramifications of new technologies in the modern office. Passage of the California bill would have been a significant first step.

Note

[1] From the website "The Jonestown Massacre": No date. Jonestown: Examining the Peoples Temple. On November 18, 1978, over 900 members of a religious group led by the Reverend Jim Jones were killed in an apparent mass suicide. The megalomaniac Jones convinced most of his followers to drink a cyanide mixture. Some, including Jones, were shot, either in suicide or murder. <http://www.boogieonline.com/revolution/express/religion/jonestown.html>. [December 29, 2004].

References

2001 AMA Survey. 2001. *Workplace Monitoring and Surveillance: Summary of Key Findings.* American Management Association. <http://www.amanet.org/research/pdfs/ems_short2001.pdf>. [February 1, 2004].

2003 E-Mail Rules, Policies and Practices Survey. 2003. American Management Association, The ePolicy Institute, and Clearswift. May 14. <http://www.epolicyinstitute.com/survey/survey.pdf>. [February 1, 2004].

2004 Workplace E-Mail and Instant Messaging Survey Summary. 2004. AMA/ePolicy Institute Research. <http://www.epolicyinstitute.com/survey/survey04.pdf>. [February 2, 2004].

Alana Shoars v. Epson America, Inc. 1994. No. B073234. In the Court of Appeal of the State of California, Second Appellate District, Division Two, April 14. <http://www.law.seattleu.edu/fachome/chonm/CASES/shoars.html>. [January 10, 2004].

Bassett, Morgan J., 2002. *An Overview of E-Mail and Internet Monitoring in the Workplace.* New York: Ford Marrin Esposito Witmeyer & Gleser, LLP. <http://www.fmew.com/archive/monitoring/>. [January 3, 2004].

Bill McLaren Jr. v. Microsoft Corporation. 1999. No. 05-97-00824-CV. On Appeal from the 116th Judicial District Court, Dallas County, Texas, Trial Court Cause No. 97-00095-F, May 28. <http://cyber.law.harvard.edu/privacy/McLaren_v_Microsoft.html>. [January 10, 2004].

Bonita P. Bourke et al. v. Nissan Motor Corporation in USA. 1993. No. B068705. In the Court of Appeal of the State of California, Second Appellate District, Division Five. July 26. <http://www.loundy.com/CASES/Bourke_v_Nissan.html>. [January 10, 2004].

Braverman, Harry. 1974. *Labor and Monopoly Capital: The Degradation of Work in the Twentieth Century.* New York: Monthly Review Press.
California Assembly Approves Employee E-mail Protection. 2004. SiliconValley.com, August 17. <http://siliconvalley.com/mld/siliconvalley/news/editorial/9424741.htm>. [August 18, 2004].
Cohon, George. 1988. CEO of McDonald's Restaurants of Canada Ltd., quoted in "Report on Business" Magazine, *The Globe and Mail,* Toronto, Canada, April, p. 14.
Dixon, Rod. 1997. "Windows Nine-to-Five: *Smyth v. Pillsbury* and the Scope of an Employee's Right of Privacy in Employer Communications." *Virginia Journal of Law and Technology,* Vol. 2, no. 4 (Fall). <http://vjolt.student.virginia.edu/graphics/vol2/home_art4.html>. [June 15, 2004].
Drug Testing. No date. U.S. Department of Labor. <http://www.dol.gov/elaws/asp/drugfree/drugs/screen92>. [August 17, 2004].
Duffy, Shannon P. 2003. *Federal Law Allows Employer's Search of Worker's E-mails.* Law.com, December 12. <http://www.law.com/jsp/printerfriendly.jsp?c=LawArticle&t=PrinterFriendlyArticle&cid=1071091317140>. [April 8, 2004].
Electronic Monitoring in the Workplace: Common Law and Federal Statutory Protection. No date. The National Workrights Institute. <http://www.workrights.org/issue_electronic/em_common_law.html>. [February 2, 2004].
Employee Privacy: Computer-Use Monitoring Practices and Policies of Selected Companies. 2002. United States General Accounting Office, GAO-02-717, September. <http://www.gao.gov/new.items/d02717.pdf>. [January 2, 2004].
Ethical Aspects of Genetic Testing in the Workplace. 2003. Opinion of the European Group on Ethics in Science and New Technologies to the European Commission. July. <europa.eu.int/comm/european_group_ethics/docs/avis18EN.pdf> [March 21, 2005].
Examples of Employee Surveillance. 2003. American Management Association. <http://www.amanet.org/books/catalog/0814471498_examples.htm>. [February 12, 2004].
Fraser, Jill Andreskey. 2001. *White Collar Sweatshop: The Deterioration of Work and Its Rewards in Corporate America.* New York: W.W. Norton.
Genetic Information and the Workplace. 1998. Department of Labor, Department of Health and Human Services Equal Employment Opportunity Commission, and Department of Justice. January 20. <http://www.dol.gov/asp/programs/history/herman/reports/genetics.htm>. [January 16, 2005].
Lee, Christopher. 2004. "New Kinds of Drug Tests Weighed for Federal Workers." *Washington Post,* January 20, p. A17.
Lewis, Terrence. 2000. "Monitoring Employee E-Mail: Avoid Stalking and Illegal Internet Conduct." *Pittsburgh Business Times,* May 19. <http://www.pittsburgh.bcentral.com/pittsburgh/stories/2000/05/22/focus6.html>. [August 10, 2004].
Lie Detector Testing. 1996. American Civil Liberties Union Briefing Paper. <http://www.lectlaw.com/files/emp28.htm>. [January 24, 2004].
Lunt, Penny. 2003. "Should You Read Employee Email?" *Transform Magazine,* October. <http://www.transformmag.com/toc/?month=10&year=2003>. [December 3, 2003].
Mahler, Kris. 2003. "Big Employer Is Watching," *The Wall Street Journal,* November 4. <http://webreprints.djreprints/861950252181.html>. [December 2, 2003].
Martin, Marc S. 2003. "Workplace Privacy Issues Arising from Use of Advanced Surveillance and Biometric Technologies." *The Metropolitan Corporate Counsel,*

January. <http://kelly.com/resourcecenter/Internet-E-Commerce/Biometric Technologies.pdf>. [December 31, 2003].

Michael A. Smyth v. The Pillsbury Company. 1996. Civil Action No. 95-5712, United States District Court, E.D. Pennsylvania, January 23. <http://cyber.law.harvard .edu/privacy/smyth_v_pillsbury.htm/>. [January 25, 2004].

Model Policy on Electronic Monitoring. No date. The National Workrights Institute, <http://workrights.org/issue_electronic/em_model_policy.html>. [February 18, 2004].

"Monitoring Employee E-mail: Efficient Workplaces vs. Employee Privacy." 2001. Duke Law and Technology Review, Vol. 26, July. <http://law.duke.edu/ journals/dltr/articles/2001dltr0026.html>. [March 1, 2004].

Office of Technology Assessment. 1987. U.S. Congress. The Electronic Supervisor: New Technology, New Tensions, OTA-CIT-333. Washington, DC: GPO.

The Polygraph and Lie Detection. 2003. Washington DC: National Academies Press. <http://www.nap.edu/books/0309084369/html>. [August 10, 2004].

Polygraph Testing. No date. Electronic Privacy Information Center. <http://www.epic.org/ privacy/polygraph>. [March 21, 2005].

Privacy in America: Workplace Drug Testing. 1997. American Civil Liberties Union, December 31. <http://www.aclu.org/WorkplaceRights/WorkplaceRights. cfm?ID=9074&c=178>. [January 31, 2004].

Protection of Workers' Personal Data. 1997. International Labour Organization. <http://www.ilo.org/public/english/support/publ/pdf/protect.pdf>. [August 11, 2004].

"Ranking Privacy at Work." 2003. Wired Magazine. October. <http://www.wired.com/ wired/archive/11.10/start.html?pg=4>. [December 12, 2003].

Richard Fraser v. Nationwide Mutual Insurance Co. 2003. United States Court of Appeals for the Third Circuit, No. 01-2921. June 23. <http://caselaw.lp.findlaw. com/data2/circs/3rd/012921p.pdf>. [January 31, 2004].

Rosenbaum, James M. 2001. "In Defense of the Hard Drive." The Green Bag, Winter. pp. 169-171. <http://www.greenbag.org/rosenbaum_harddrive.pdf>. [February 9, 2004].

Rosenberg, Richard S. 1999. "The Workplace on the Verge of the 21st Century." Journal of Business Ethics, Vol. 22, no. 11, pp. 3–14.

———. 2004. The Social Impact of Computers, 3rd ed., San Diego: Elsevier Academic Press.

S. 1053. Genetic Information Nondiscrimination Act of 2003. <http://frwebgate.access. gpo.gov/cgi-bin/getdoc.cgi?dbname=108_cong_bill&docid=f:s1053es.txt.pdf>. [August 15, 2004].

Shahandeh, Behrouz, and Joannah Caborn. 2003. Ethical Issues in Workplace Drug Testing in Europe. International Labour Office, February. <http://www.ilo.org/ public/english/protection/safework/drug/wdt.pdf>. [July 17, 2004].

Sigvartsen, Ana Leticia. 2001. Guidelines to Workplace Privacy. Infosatellite.com, October 31. <http://www.infosatellite.com/news/2001/10/a311001workplace_ security.html>. [December 30, 2004].

Smith, Graeme. 2004. "Is Big McBrother Invading Workplace Privacy?" The Globe and Mail, Toronto, Canada. January 13. <http://www.Hartford-hwp.com/ archives/44/231.html>. [January 14, 2004].

Sullivan, Mark. 2004. "Arnold Vetoes Privacy Bill." Wired News, September 30. <http://www.wired.com/news/privacy/0,1848,65152,00.html>. [October 11, 2004].

Thomson, Iain. 2004. *You Are Still the Weakest Security Link*. VNU Business Publications, August. 05. <http://www.vnunet.com/1157129>. [June 8, 2004].

Ward, Mark. 2004. *Work Porn Risk for Businesses*. BBC News, May 17. <http://news.bbc.co.uk/go/pr/fr/-/2/hi/technology/3701907.stm>. [May 18, 2004].

CHAPTER 7

The Ethics of Human Resource Management

ELIZABETH D. SCOTT
Eastern Connecticut State University

In a time when most organizations claim that "our employees are our most important [most valuable, greatest] asset," the ethical challenge to human resource (HR) managers is clear: How do we avoid treating employees merely as *means*? The term "human resources" may be relatively new, but viewing employees as something to be used is as old as the Roman days, when the tools of production were classified as "dumb tools" (used of plows, shovels), "semi-speaking tools" (used of animals), and "speaking tools" (used of slaves). While many employees would prefer to be referred to as an asset rather than as an expense or liability, the phrase "human resources" still rankles among those who see it as evidence that employers have not changed over the millennia. Assuming, *arguendo,* that we are discussing HR managers who wish to be ethical, one of their main challenges is to belie their titles. That is, they must manage humans not as resources but as autonomous individuals with legitimate rights and interests.

Ethical Theories

Elsewhere in this volume, others describe ethical theories in depth. I will not repeat those theories, save to suggest that each has something to say about how HR managers do their jobs. HR managers face the Kantian ethical question of how to ensure that their treatment of employees, applicants, and former employees respects the autonomy of those constituents. Stakeholder ethics also requires that the HR manager consider the interests of employees, applicants, and former employees, at least if we are to accept Clarkson's definition that "stakeholders are persons or groups that have or claim ownership, rights, or interests in a corporation and its activities, past, present, or future" (1995:106). HR managers who judge ethics by fairness or justice must apply them to employees, applicants, and former employees, and they may even be required by Rawls's

(1971) conception of justice to ensure that the least well off are not disadvantaged by the policies they implement and also have a voice in decision-making processes.

Utilitarian HR managers must consider the outcomes of their decisions on everyone, including employees, applicants, and former employees. And virtue ethics would recommend developing habits that contribute to the flourishing of humans, as individuals and in community. While there might be special situations in which a particular ethical theory would prescribe behavior different from that prescribed by other theories, my interest is not in ferreting out those exceptions but in illustrating the claims these theories make on HR managers desiring to be ethical in performing their functions. Therefore, where I use such words as "fairness," "stakeholder," and "duty," I intend to invoke principles of ethics derived from the theories discussed elsewhere.

Types of Ethical Issues Addressed

Three different types of ethical problems face HR managers. The first type is the need for discernment—determining the right thing to do in very complex situations. The HR manager has both authority and the support of management to make and implement decisions, but he or she still must weigh options and make decisions with incomplete information. The second type of problem is a conflict between the HR manager's professional judgment of what is right and the responsibility as an agent of the employer to do what the employer asks. The third type of problem involves conflict of interest—or *appearance* of conflict of interest—when the HR manager's personal interest differs from the responsibility as an agent of the employer. The first type of problem has the potential to turn into the second or third type once the HR manager determines the appropriate course of action.

The common challenge with all three problems is recognizing them (Rest 1976). Often, in the day-to-day requirements of running a human resources operation, the manager does not have time to reflect on the ethical implications of an action (Moberg 2000). The more obviously "ethical" situations involve virtue or moral courage—the HR manager simply has to refuse to do that which is not right and choose to do what is. For example, an HR manager who looks the other way or even helps falsify the paperwork when a hiring manager uses slave labor is not facing an ethical issue but rather simply failing to do right. There are many cases, though, where HR managers do not know all of the facts, do not think about the implications of a decision, or do not see themselves as moral agents in the decision and thus do not recognize it as a moral issue.

One challenge, then, to HR managers who wish to behave ethically, is to find ways to increase their abilities to recognize moral issues. They can do this by setting time aside to reflect, by talking with other managers about issues, by reading journals and newspaper columns devoted to discussion of ethics, and by listening carefully to employees who voice concerns. The allocation of resources to this effort becomes an ethical issue in itself. How much time can an HR manager devote to better recognizing ethical issues before being guilty of neglecting other duties? Is once a year enough? Is every day too often? The more HR managers develop their moral sensitivities, though, the more difficult it may be to learn of ethical issues, because other employees in the organization may go out of their way to hide information. There may be a counterbalancing tendency of wronged individuals to seek out the HR manager known to be ethical (Trevino, Hartman, and Brown 2000), but since many of those wronged may be outside of the organization, they may never learn of the HR manager's reputation. HR managers wishing to behave ethically thus must also increase their abilities to discover hidden motives and activities.

Even after recognizing a moral issue, obtaining facts and determining right action is still difficult. Not all facts are available, and many that are cannot be obtained in a timely (or fiscally responsible) manner. Taking incomplete information, considering it, and making decisions are what managers do. Some decisions are just more difficult to make than others, especially when several different duties or interests are opposed and the information gap is large.

Problems related to fetal protection can fall in this category. While adults may be able to evaluate incomplete scientific data and determine whether the risks of working in a particular environment are worth the other benefits of engaging in that work, they may not be in a position to make those decisions for their future offspring. The HR manager must consider both interests as well as the interests of the firm and its stockholders and the firm's ability to mitigate potential harms, all in an environment where data are incomplete and the HR manager's power is limited. Knowing the history of industries where scientists withheld information about harm to consumers, such as the tobacco industry, the HR manager may be very skeptical of the scientific data that *are* available.

"Right action," once discerned by the HR manager, is sometimes translated into policy and procedure, to provide guidance to other managers and information to employees. Policies and procedures help HR managers ensure fairness by making the decision-making process more consistent and transparent. However, policies and procedures can also detract from HR managers' recognizing some ethical issues, because policy may be applied without regard for changes over time or for individual situations. One approach to that dilemma is to set up systems whereby employees review HR policies and practices regularly (Kochan 2002).

HR managers can also turn to their professional associations for guidance. Codes of ethics established by professional associations of human resource managers require certain levels of integrity, obedience to the letter and spirit of the law, contribution to the organization and the profession, loyalty, and confidentiality (Wiley 2000). A more skeptical view of these codes' usefulness has been expressed by Scoville (1993).

This chapter does not address the ethical issues faced by HR managers as managers dealing with their subordinates. Instead, it addresses their responsibilities with respect to the organization's policies and procedures and the special role of HR manager. This chapter also does not discuss the legal requirements affecting HR managers. It assumes that the HR manager has an obligation to obey the law unless the law itself is immoral. The chapter does address, however, ethical issues faced by HR managers when others violate laws, when laws are immoral, and when the letter and spirit of the law do not coincide.

Functions of an HR Manager

HR managers are taught that they have four basic functions with respect to employees: to recruit, to train, to motivate, and to retain. A fifth function, terminating, is also performed by HR managers, albeit usually after failing somehow at one of the other four functions. All of these functions are aimed at achieving the goals of the organization, and each has the potential for all three kinds of ethical issues. Some responsibilities (e.g., compensation, benefits, labor relations, record-keeping) cross several functions. For example, compensation is used to recruit applicants and to motivate and retain employees. Labor relations (addressed in another chapter) affect recruiting, training, motivating, retaining, and terminating employees. Practices in organizations vary widely, so not all of the descriptions of issues here will apply to every organization.

Recruitment

HR managers know all too well that, despite organizational rhetoric, they are not looking for *the* best qualified person for each job. They are looking for someone who can do the job well and, in some cases, for someone who shows promise for being promoted. To this end, HR managers are expected to outline minimum qualifications, set an entry salary range, advertise the position, refer applicants to hiring managers, and review selection decisions in a way that balances the organization's resources with the likelihood of finding a well-qualified person. The ethical challenge is to balance individuals' expectations of (and rights to) equal opportunities with the organization's obligation of resource stewardship.

Minimum Qualifications. To recruit employees, an HR manager needs a clear idea of qualifications needed to perform job duties. Before advertising a vacancy, the HR manager usually establishes the minimum knowledge, skills, and abilities a person must have to be considered for the position. Setting minimum qualifications is an ethical decision, but it is often approached as merely a strategic one. The strategic decision is certainly important. Setting the minimum qualifications too high will result in applicants unwilling to accept either the position or the salary offered. Setting the minimum qualifications too low will result, at best, in applications from so many people that extensive secondary screening procedures will be required and, at worst, in signaling to the most desirable applicants that they need not apply because they will be judged overqualified.

In addition, however, the HR manager is often faced with special requests—such as ensuring that the qualifications don't exclude the hiring manager's preselected favorite candidate—that further complicate the process of determining what qualifications to require. Ever since the days of (*Griggs v. Duke Power* 1971:424), it has been evident that managers can use minimum qualifications to exclude people who are perfectly capable of doing a job. While the *Griggs* decision outlawed these exclusions where they distinguish on the basis of race, sex, or other legally defined classification, there is no similar protection when the minimum qualifications exclude individuals who cannot claim "adverse impact" under *Griggs*. However, ethical principles would still require fairness.

It is sometimes difficult for the HR manager to discern why a hiring manager insists on a particular qualification that does not seem necessary for performance of the job duties. Sometimes the HR manager does not fully understand the job duties, but other times the hiring manager wants to avoid having to consider a particular employee. The hiring manager may have good reason not to want this employee, but manipulating the minimum qualifications is not the way to achieve that end. The HR manager has an ethical obligation to try to eliminate such managerial behavior—both because it can be disastrous for the employer and because it singles out individuals for unfair treatment. A typical example occurs when a hiring manager prefers a relatively new employee over more senior candidates. Observing that the more senior candidates have no college degrees, the hiring manager requests that a degree be one of the minimum qualifications—erroneously believing that in the end this will appear to be an "objective" reason why the junior person obtained the job and thus head off internal bickering. Unfortunately for the manager, the other internal applicants are not usually so easily fooled. Depending on the HR manager's authority within the situation, he or she may be able to refuse the hiring manager's request outright or may have to pursue another avenue (e.g., internal whistleblowing) to eliminate this kind of behavior.

Entry Salary Range. HR managers must balance several considerations in setting appropriate salary ranges. First, there is the question of what the current labor market demands. This is mainly a practical consideration. If the labor market demands more than the employer is willing to pay, it may be foolish to spend resources to recruit applicants. However, there are also ethical considerations associated with internal equity. If the current labor market demands more than it once did, employers may find themselves paying new employees more than long-term employees doing the same job. This fact may not always be apparent to the existing employees, who may not realize that they could command higher salaries elsewhere and may not have direct contact with other employees doing the same work. The ethical consideration for the HR manager then becomes whether to take steps to increase the salaries of the existing employees or change the job classifications of the new employees. If there are real differences between the skills and abilities of those in the external labor market and the existing employees, changing the job classification of the vacant position may be the appropriate action. The change may take the form of a higher classification for people with greater skills and abilities or of a lower classification to attract trainees who do not yet have the skills and abilities necessary. If there are no real differences, the ethical HR manager will address the question of internal equity before advertising the job, developing a plan to ensure that existing employees are not penalized with lower salaries for failing to seek jobs elsewhere.

The second question regarding entry salary levels relates to what has been called "comparable worth." If applicants would be hireable at lower salaries due to generalized discrimination against members of the labor market, does the employer have an ethical obligation to pay on the basis of the contribution made to the organization? An HR manager with limited resources is unlikely to conduct studies assessing the "worth" of jobs, but failing to do so because one wants to avoid legal liability would be, in Kantian terms, not produced by a "good will."

The third question is whether to advertise the salary range for the position and, if so what portion. Omitting a salary or salary range may simply be an effort to save on advertising costs. However, when it is done to enable employers to negotiate lower salaries for those most desperate for work, it violates the Rawlsian principle of setting up systems that protect the least advantaged. Similarly, advertising just the top of the salary range when most employees achieve only a small percentage of it is dishonest. When the vast majority of employees in a particular job make minimum wage, advertisements that claim employees can earn huge bonuses and commissions, even if true, mislead potential applicants to believe they *will* earn significantly more than is true.

Advertising. A position can be advertised very narrowly, such as by handing a vacancy announcement to one person, or very broadly, by putting a sign in the window, a link on a web page, an ad in the paper, or a commercial on television. The decision about how broadly to advertise has both strategic and ethical components. When the position would represent a promotion (or even a more desirable career path) for current employees, the strategic component involves considering the costs and benefits of going outside the organization. Possible costs include monetary expense for ads, lost productivity during the recruiting period, and turnover by disappointed employees. There also may be adverse effects caused by creating new vacancies and encouraging complacency by promoting from within. Organizations wishing to encourage employee loyalty often require posting positions internally first and going outside the organization only after all internal candidates have been rejected. Other organizations, hoping to encourage creativity and internal competition, routinely recruit outside. This assessment of costs and benefits remains in the strategic realm as long as the HR manager's concern is to maximize the welfare of the organization, but as the concern broadens to include maximizing the welfare of society, the analysis enters the realm of utilitarian ethics.

One of the ethical balancing acts an HR manager must perform regarding advertising is between fulfilling promises (or psychological contracts) regarding career advancement and providing legitimate opportunities for those outside the organization to obtain employment. Hiring managers sometimes request advertisements with no intention of considering anyone beyond a particular individual. Such pro forma advertisements waste applicants' time, energy, money, and hope, and they either encourage favored candidates to believe it is acceptable to mislead others or they cause favored candidates to feel insecure about jobs they have already been promised. Often the advertisement is placed at the behest of the HR manager, who insists that the position be advertised to provide equal employment opportunities. But since advertising does not ensure that the hiring manager will be any more open to considering all applicants, the HR manager's goal would be better served by establishing a procedure under which hiring managers can request exemption from any requirement to advertise vacancies by providing evidence that forgoing advertisement is appropriate in the particular case.

With a decision to advertise outside the organization made, the HR manager should consider the organization's stated values and choose methods that reflect them. Word-of-mouth advertising, for example, is most likely to generate applicants similar to current employees. If the organization claims to value diversity but is not already diverse, this form of recruitment would call into question the truth of the organization's claim. Similarly, website advertising may create a bias in favor of wealthier and younger applicants. If computer skills are not important to the job, such advertising diminishes the integrity of the process. The HR manager's job is to consider cost-effective outlets where qualified candidates are most likely to see or hear a vacancy announcement. In choosing among those outlets, the HR manager's ethical obligation is, foremost, not to bias the pool unfairly and, second, not to bias it in ways that conflict with the organization's stated values. (If the values themselves are unfair, the HR manager has no obligation to ensure that they are enacted in advertising positions.)

Adhering to the organization's stated values is, in ethical terms, promise keeping. If the organization promises in its stated values to promote from within, an initial advertisement beyond the bounds of the organization would violate that promise. The more difficult problem for the HR manager is determining when the inevitable bias caused by the choice of advertisements is significant enough to render the process unfair. One important consideration is the intentionality of the bias (Kant's notion of a "good will"). For example, it is impossible to ensure that no employee is on leave when a vacancy is announced, but if a hiring manager waits until a particular employee's vacation week to advertise a vacancy because the manager wants to avoid considering the person, that bias is unfair. A second important consideration is the potential effect of the choice of advertisement on society. Ethical theories put varying degrees of emphasis on the outcomes of an action, but they would suggest considering whether the bias caused by the advertising benefited those least well off in society, whether there was more good than harm done by the bias, and whether important stakeholders were considered in the decision. The advertisement of any particular vacancy is probably unlikely to affect society in an appreciable way, but a policy or practice of a large corporation to, for example, post all entry-level vacancies with the local employment service office or in shelters for battered women has the potential to affect local economies.

The HR manager sometimes faces the question of whether to recruit applicants from competitors, suppliers, customers, or regulators. HR managers should not encourage among potential or actual employees disloyalty, dishonesty, or violation of "noncompete" agreements that have been legitimately negotiated (i.e., by knowledgeable participants with relatively equal power). But they should also respect the autonomy of potential employees to choose to leave another employer. Whether an applicant has slighted, or even breached a duty to, a current employer is difficult for the HR manager to monitor, because such information is not always available. HR managers have a duty to scrutinize any decisions to hire people who have had prior dealings with the organization as employees of another organization, especially if the prior dealings resulted in unusually advantageous decisions for the hiring organization. And, since violations are so hard to find, those that are found should be punished sufficiently harshly to transmit the message that the behavior is contrary to any employer's values.

An issue currently in the forefront of business ethics is outsourcing. In order to determine the ethical stance in this discussion, an HR manager must clearly understand the anticipated outcomes regarding all of the stakeholders: employees, potential employees, local communities, external communities, and stockholders (Arnold and Bowie 2003). The manager also needs to clearly understand all of the contracts, both actual and psychological, surrounding the relationships with current employees.

Selection. The final step in the recruitment process is to select from among the applicants for a position. Selection is so important that it is sometimes listed as a separate function of HR managers. However, it is often performed by the hiring manager, after the HR department has collected applications and eliminated the people who clearly don't qualify. The HR manager establishes policies and procedures to be followed but may have little control over what occurs in the actual selection process.

Screening of applicants can be performed by HR staff. They may add a set of preferred qualifications that are more stringent than the minimum qualifications posted in the advertisement. They may use written or performance tests. In both of these cases, the HR manager has to worry not only about being fair but also about appearing fair. Tests or screening criteria that do not have face validity appear unfair to applicants, even when the employer knows that they are valid through extensive studies linking test scores with job success. One threat to test validity exists if applicants who take a test multiple times can do better on that specific test, but not necessarily on the job, just because they have practiced the test (Huasknecht, Trevor, and Farr 2002). If there are practice effects that are not related to on-the-job performance, to preserve fairness HR managers should consider whether to implement rules limiting the number of times an applicant can take the same test.

HR staff may conduct recruiting or screening interviews, and surely every HR manager has experienced having a CEO or other senior staff member send people to be interviewed "as a favor." In these cases, HR's role is to represent the organization well and to become familiar enough with the applicant's qualifications to help locate vacancies in the organization that might prove fruitful. The ethical HR representative must be careful not to overpromise to the applicant or to misread the degree of assistance promised by the senior staff member.

After the applicant pool is narrowed through evaluating preferred qualifications and testing, there is often a small set of applicants presented to the hiring manager for interviews and the selection decision. The HR manager bears some responsibility for training the hiring manager in interviewing technique and for reviewing the process to ensure that interviews are conducted and evaluated fairly. Many organizations are moving toward establishing work teams, with the team empowered to select its members. There is some evidence that teams are more likely to pick people like themselves, demographically, and thus engage in unlawful discrimination as agents of the employer (Goins and Mannix 1999). The HR manager has an obligation to create mechanisms that reduce this tendency.

An ethical issue associated with the interviewing process is the amount of privacy protection due applicants. Depending on the applicant's power in the situation, various ethicists have recommended eliminating all questions aimed at determining attitudes, motivations, and beliefs, arguing that applicants have a right to keep this information to themselves. Others see this position as paternalistic (Nye 2002). The HR manager's job is to discern the appropriate amount of privacy protection due applicants and convey this to hiring managers.

As genetic screening tests become available, employers face the possibility of having information that could be relevant to long-term employment decisions. Knowing that a particular employee has a greater likelihood of developing a serious disease can tempt an employer to pass over that person for promotions or for training requiring long-term investment. HR managers have a responsibility to ensure that these records are not available to anyone but the employee and that such data are not collected without the employee's knowledge and consent.

Many HR managers in industries with very low-wage jobs find themselves in the position of not knowing whether their employees are legally allowed to work—for example, because they are aliens, because they are below a minimum age, or because they have not obtained required licenses. In some cases, line managers obtain forged supporting documents (birth certificates, passports, etc.) proving eligibility to work. While lack of participating in the forgery may exempt the HR manager from legal liability, he or she still has an ethical obligation to take reasonable steps to ensure that neither line managers nor new employees violate laws that are themselves ethical. Random checks of original documents may eliminate widespread violations, but there may be no way to thwart the determined violator. Internal whistleblowing by the HR manager may be necessary to bring violations to the attention of someone with the power to enact sanctions. Clear and relatively harsh consequences for employees who are complicit in hiring illegally may be the only way to convey the organization's lack of support for such behavior.

Violating hiring laws would generally fall in the area of unethical behavior. However, HR managers sometimes must discern whether the law, various regulations, or court decisions are ethical. For example, organizations considering employing persons with disabilities whose conditions pose a threat to their own health and safety on the job but not the health and safety of others faced conflicting Equal Employment Opportunity Commission (EEOC) regulations and court decisions. The EEOC allowed employers to refuse employment on this basis, but the 9th Circuit Court of Appeals did not. While this controversy has been resolved by the U.S. Supreme Court, in favor of the EEOC regulations, it illustrates a case where the HR manager must balance concern for the health and welfare of the prospective employee against employees' rights to make decisions about their own health and welfare (Reed 2003). Similarly, HR managers of multinational corporations during apartheid in South Africa made decisions to violate local laws requiring separation of the races.

A common complaint from applicants is that they submitted applications and "never heard back" from the employer. This contributes to a perception of unfairness, and it may actually inhibit the freedom of an applicant who waits to hear about an employment application rather than go on vacation or accept other employment. At the conclusion of the selection process, the ethical HR manager will ensure that unsuccessful applicants are notified promptly and kindly of rejection decisions.

Successful Applicants. Having identified successful applicants, HR managers face several ethical challenges. The HR manager must carefully explain the employment contract. Some ethicists argue that "at will" contracts are not morally permissible (Werhane 1983; Radin and Werhane 2003; McCall 2003), while others argue simply that the employer should not sugarcoat the nature of the relationship (Roehling 2003). If a union represents the prospective employee's position, the collective bargaining contract must be provided to the applicant. While there is pressure on the HR manager to "woo" successful applicants, the ethical manager will provide an accurate picture of the job and the organization. There may also be pressure to negotiate the lowest possible salary, but ethics require that the manager not take advantage of applicants' vulnerabilities (Brenkert 1998), and fairness requires equal pay for equal work.

Determining the point at which to check references requires balancing the need to protect applicants' privacy against the need to obtain relevant information. In many industries, employees are fired if their employers learn they are even applying for other jobs. Reference checking is especially important in jobs where the incumbent will have unsupervised responsibility for children or elderly persons or access to large quantities of cash. If the applicant is internal, the HR manager must decide what information gained from within is appropriate to transmit to the hiring manager and what information is irrelevant to the hiring decision. If the applicant is external, an HR manager often draws upon personal or professional contacts to obtain reference information about an applicant. In this case, the HR manager has an obligation to balance the discretion due the informant and the fair hearing due the applicant.

Conflict of Interest. The recruitment function is not fraught with large conflicts of interest for HR managers. There may be a temptation to use the power of the position to provide jobs to friends or relatives or to ensure that recruiting trips include the HR manager's alma mater, but since there is usually a separation between functions of the HR and the hiring managers, the HR manager may find efforts to place family and friends thwarted.

Training and Development

Typically, training is divided into two types: general training, which will make an employee more flexible and adaptable within the organization and more marketable outside it, and specific training, which is unique to the organization or even the position. Employee development involves examining an employee's career prospects and offering support in his or her career path. The ethical challenge to HR managers is to devise systems of providing training and development opportunities that are fair to all employees.

General Training. Organizations are often reluctant to provide general training, because they see themselves as paying for training that an employee can then take to a competitor and use against them. There is no ethical obligation to promote general training programs, but doing so is one way to treat employees as more than a means to an end. One financial safeguard used by some employers is to require employees to sign agreements to repay the cost of their training if they leave within a certain period. The ethical issue facing the HR manager drafting such an agreement is to ensure that it is clearly explained and does not take unfair advantage of the employee.

Safety Training. While HR managers may have no ethical obligation to provide general training, they are obliged to ensure that all employees are aware of any safety hazards associated with their jobs or their work environments. Beyond simply providing safety warnings, HR managers have an ethical obligation to ensure that the warnings are clearly understood by employees, particularly those who may not be able to read the language of the warning or who otherwise may not understand the danger being identified in the warning. Literacy training may be a necessary precursor to safety training.

A special case of safety training involves protection against potentially contagious diseases, such as AIDS and hepatitis. When possible, safety training should be designed to prevent or reduce transmission of disease, whether or not the infection status of a person is known. Gloving, hand washing, and proper instrument disposal are all techniques that can be taught to employees. However, employees understandably want to be informed whenever their risk level increases. They expect employers to provide them with the identities of infected co-workers, clients, or customers. The HR manager must balance the likelihood that an employee will become infected against the infected person's right to privacy. In this balancing, the HR manager must consider that knowing the identities of some but not all people who are infected may actually put employees at a higher risk, because it will give them a false sense of security with any others who are infected but not known to be.

A second special case of safety training is balancing an employee's right to make decisions about undertaking risk and the employer's responsibility to protect others from harm. When an employee's job involves risk to bystanders if done incorrectly, an employer cannot stop after providing training and assume that the employee will bear the ethical burden of keeping others safe. The employer has an obligation to ensure that the job is performed as taught and that the employee is not provided with incentives to take unnecessary risks. Again, while the burden of legal liability may be on someone else, an ethical HR manager will implement systems to monitor the transfer of the training to the workplace and will build incentive systems that encourage safety.

Values Training. Some employees resent being required to attend values training because they see it as an attempt to indoctrinate them into a particular religion or to brainwash them. The HR manager, who presumably shares the organization's values, should ensure clear consistency both between values addressed in training and those supported by the organization and between these values and the organization's reward and discipline systems. The training should also recognize that new employees may intend to be ethical but may be less sophisticated than experienced employees in evaluating the implications of various behaviors (Stevens 2001).

There should also be some provision for employees to opt out of training they consider morally objectionable. However, enough such requests should give the HR manager pause. It could be simply the method of training and not the core value that is in question, but it could also be time to reexamine the underlying values or the employee selection methods. Ever since Weber (1930) described how religious beliefs can fuel corporate profits, employers have sought to select employees with some set of religious or quasireligious beliefs or to create it in them. The Kantian idea of a categorical imperative can guide HR managers trying to ensure that all employees accept certain values. Some values, such as participative management, tolerance, and diversity, create internal inconsistencies when organizations attempt to require them as "rules for all." Requiring all managers to use participative management, for example, does not allow managers to participate in the decision to use it. Requiring tolerance of all employees is intolerant of those who are themselves intolerant. Embracing diversity means embracing even those who do not embrace diversity. Rules that the HR manager either does not want applied universally or cannot imagine applying universally should not be implemented. The HR manager should periodically review values-training programs to ensure that they are consistent with all of the organization's values, not simply the one or ones being addressed in that particular session.

Employers have occasionally been required by law or court order to train employees in certain values, such as diversity. In these cases, the HR manager is faced with following the law, advocating for a change in the law, breaking the law, or resigning. Deciding among these options requires considering one's personal position and the organization's position. If they are not in concert, and neither party is convinced by the other to change, an ethical HR manager will resign. This is because ethical HR managers cannot abrogate their responsibilities to their employers by acting on behalf of an employer to violate a law the employer would have them follow or to follow a law the employer would have them violate. However, ethical HR managers also cannot abrogate responsibility to themselves by following a law they believe to be immoral or violating one they believe to be moral. If the HR manager and the organization are in concert, they can devise an approach together. Where the organization, the HR manager, and the law are all in concert, the decision-making process is relatively simple: the law is followed. Decision making becomes complex where the law differs from what the HR manager and organization believe. An organization should not take lightly the decision to violate a law or court order. Avenues of appeal and legislative influence should be exhausted first, but where the law is immoral (not simply inconvenient or costly for the employer to implement), the organization can ethically engage in civil disobedience. Laws or court orders that require employers to trample on employees' freedoms should give HR managers great pause. Some managers who have been too quick to follow such laws or too enthusiastic in sanctioning employees who object to the training have found that courts subsequently overturned the laws in question.

Conflict of Interest. Building a training staff large enough to provide any kind of training for the organization can contribute to the HR manager's personal influence and even compensation level. Being able to select from among consultants can give HR managers opportunities to assist friends or family in the consulting firm or to receive gifts or favors from the consultants. Both situations represent conflicts of interest that the ethical HR manager will avoid. Decisions should be made on the basis of the HR manager's professional judgment, not personal interests.

Career Development. Many organizations use mentoring programs to foster career development, pairing new (or at least junior) employees one-on-one with employees with significant experience. What was once an informal practice has become much more formal in many organizations. Mentors can take advantage of their positions of power with respect to the employees they are mentoring, so the HR manager's ethical responsibility is to ensure that abuses of power are minimized (Moberg and Velasquez 2004).

A typical career development program includes succession planning, in which the organization identifies employees who are prepared (or have the potential to be prepared) to step into vacancies as key staff retire, are promoted, or otherwise leave their positions. The organization provides training to prepare the designated employees for eventual vacancies and does not provide such training to those deemed not promotable. To ensure that such planning does not treat employees unfairly, HR managers should develop procedures that, at a very minimum, allow employees to indicate their interests in being promoted and notify those deemed not promotable of the decision. Employees remain with organizations with the belief that they will have a chance to compete for future vacancies on a level playing field. If a determination is made to give the inside track to certain employees, in terms of both training offered and preference for assignments, then the employees deemed not promotable should not be deceived into thinking that, if they are loyal employees, their tenure will be rewarded with promotions. They should be provided with clear feedback that enables them to consider whether they want to remain with the current organization without being promoted or to try their chances at another. If current trends continue, such that employees have reduced expectations that they will remain with the same employer for life, this may become less of an ethical issue (Cappelli 1999).

Motivation

In designing motivation systems, HR managers seek to align employees' goals with those of the organization. This can be done coercively or by convincing employees of the worthiness of the organization's goals and the value of employee contributions to them. Designing effective motivation systems is difficult; ensuring that they have no coercive element is almost impossible. The HR manager's ethical challenge is to consider the amount of coercion used and discern whether it is reasonably balanced against the employee's power in the situation and whether it serves the goals and values articulated by the employee. Taking the car keys away from a drunk would-be driver is coercive, but it properly considers other stakeholders as well as the values the driver has when sober. Similarly, docking the salary of an employee who fails to follow safety regulations is a coercive way to change behavior, but it can also be an ethical way to motivate a recalcitrant employee. On the other hand, offering huge sums of money to employees to work in dangerous environments may be an unethical form of coercion, especially if the technology exists to make the environment less dangerous. The problem of discernment for an HR manager wishing to behave ethically is determining the point at which "hazardous duty pay" stops being a reasonable recognition of risk freely undertaken by an employee and becomes an offer the employee truly *couldn't* refuse. Coercion removes the employee's freedom to choose, thus abridging the right to liberty (Greenwood 2002).

Systems to motivate employees are developed both by HR managers and by direct supervisors. While supervisory intervention may have the most significant effect on employee motivation, tools that the HR manager provides can make supervisors more effective. These tools can include compensation systems, performance appraisal systems, employee monitoring systems, organizational climate, charitable contribution campaigns, job design, work teams, progressive disciplinary systems, and others. Line supervisors can use the tools ethically or unethically; the HR manager's ethical responsibility is to design tools that are not easily used unethically and to develop procedures to monitor their use.

Compensation. Though compensation systems are designed to align the interests of employee and employer, they can also create conflicts of interest. Commission compensation systems can provide incentives to salespeople to disregard the interests of customers in order to obtain the highest commission (Robertson and Anderson 1993; Kurland 1999). Insurance agents, stock brokers, and real estate buyers' agents, for example, may urge clients to purchase a more expensive product to increase commissions. Supervisors who receive bonuses for number of days without a lost-time accident may pressure employees not to seek treatment for injuries. Managers whose performance is measured by staff productivity may require subordinate employees to work "off the clock" or to skip their breaks. In each of these cases, the organization motivates employees to perform well using some proxy (seniority, supervisor's assessment, hours worked, quantity of output) to estimate the value of the employee's contribution. There is nothing inherently unethical about any of these compensation systems, but other parts of the organization must be operated ethically in order for the compensation systems not to create conflicts of interest. Using seniority as a method of determining pay, for example, is often criticized as unfair. However, this criticism may arise because seniority no longer operates as a proxy for performance on the job. This could occur for one or a number of reasons: because employees who should have been fired were not, because technology has changed and long-term employees were not trained, because the selection system used in the past was faulty, because the cumulative effect of a number of years of working for the employer decreases employees' abilities. The HR manager has the responsibility to ensure that every compensation system contains effective mechanisms to reduce conflicts of interest.

HR managers face a personal conflict of interest in implementing and administering compensation systems. They might be tempted to implement systems that benefit them financially. For example, if the system establishes pay caps for jobs based on market analysis, the manager may be tempted to recommend eliminating caps as he or she approaches the limit, based on the desire to earn more money rather than professional judgment about the caps. The ethical obligation is to ignore such temptation and instead continue to develop a system that is best for the employer, administer it impartially, and build in checks and balances.

HR managers' problem of discernment requires determining a compensation system that is fair and just, and this may differ within and between organizations. Issues include the appropriate difference between pay for the CEO and for rank-and-file employees, systems for paying line versus staff employees, comparable worth, merit-based pay, team-based pay, power differences in salary negotiations, coercively high pay, unpaid work, paid breaks, travel pay, overtime pay, vacation pay, holiday pay, and sick pay, among many others. In some jurisdictions, local and national laws govern the treatment of some of these issues, and the problem becomes more complex in multistate and multinational organizations (Graham and Trevor 2000; Donaldson 2001).

Much of the current controversy regarding compensation addresses executive compensation, especially for CEOs in publicly held firms (Hannafey 2003). Decisions on executive compensation are almost always outside of the HR manager's job, though the manager may be able to use informal influence and earned authority to affect these decisions. In cases where the HR manager cannot create a fair compensation system because of decisions made by senior managers or the board of directors, the only ethical recourse may be to resign.

Performance Appraisal Systems. Performance appraisals are almost universally dreaded. Despite this, HR managers argue, at least publicly, that appraisals are valuable because they know that feedback is important to smooth organizational functioning and that informal feedback, while essential, is not remembered the same by both parties. At their best, performance appraisals motivate employees to continue the things they are doing well, to improve at things they are doing poorly, and to cease things they should not be doing at all. At their worst, they are used to attack or protect employees based on managers' likes and dislikes. Ethics dictate that the HR manager not create a system so complex, cumbersome, or unmonitored that supervisors ignore it or use it improperly.

Employee Monitoring. Many employers have systems of monitoring employees—to measure productivity, to prevent theft, or to protect others (Hoffman and Hartman 2003)—through videotaping, capturing keystrokes, reviewing e-mail, tapping telephones, collecting specimens for drug testing, or tracking locations (Mishra 1998). In all cases, the HR manager must weigh the employee's right to privacy against the reason for the monitoring. Some ethicists argue that monitoring systems offend against employees' freedoms and that the legitimate ends of monitoring can be achieved in less intrusive ways (Mishra 1998).

Climate and Culture. There is evidence that the organizational climate and subunit climate can motivate employees to engage in ethical or unethical behavior (VanSandt 2003; Weber, Kurke, and Pentico 2003). Insofar as the HR manager has control over climate, there is an ethical obligation to ensure that it is ethical. However, even when the HR manager cannot control climate, especially in subunits, he or she may set up systems to monitor climate and provide training or advice to managers on how to improve it.

Charitable Contribution Campaigns. Many employers seek to motivate employees by projecting an image as a caring, socially responsible organization. Some sponsor campaigns to encourage employees to contribute to charitable organizations, including, in the cases of qualified organizations, the employer itself. This practice, when carried out without coercion, can contribute to employees' sense that their employer does good, especially when the employer matches employee contributions. However, some employers pressure employees for contributions, eliminating the strategic purpose of motivation and reducing the overall good done by the organization. HR managers are usually removed from the solicitation activity, giving them freedom to lessen pressure on employees by reminding both solicitors and those solicited that contributions are truly voluntary. They should remind management, in particular, to discourage campaigns seeking 100% participation and to recognize employee charitable activities not connected with the organization's campaign.

Job Design. The HR literature argues that jobs need to be intrinsically rewarding to be motivating. Hackman and Oldham's classic set of factors is still used today (Hackman, Oldham, Janson, and Purdy 1975). Jobs must have skill variety, task identity, task significance, autonomy, and feedback to have the potential to be motivating. Some ethicists suggest that employers have an obligation to ensure that jobs are intrinsically rewarding. Others suggest that it is an obligation to design jobs in a way that makes them more accessible to people with disabilities. HR managers should consider such arguments in writing job descriptions. Similarly, there is considerable debate over the number of hours a week a person is expected to work. Flexibility in hours worked makes jobs more accessible to people with lower levels of stamina, with competing home responsibilities, or with restrictions on the income they can earn. Determining that a job is "part-time" has significant implications for most benefits contracts. Many organizations provide reduced or no benefits to people in part-time positions.

Teams and Quality Circles. Teams can make employees happier with their jobs and more likely to stay (Hunter, Macduffie, and Doucet 2002), and they have been used to motivate employees by giving them more control over their jobs. However, teams have also been shown to be related to increases in injuries (Brenner and Fairris 2004). HR managers have an ethical obligation to monitor the behavior of teams to ensure that the increased motivation is not misdirected toward activities that endanger team members.

Progressive Discipline. HR policies usually include a range of disciplinary actions that can be taken to motivate employees when more positive reinforcement fails, including such things as warnings, reprimands, docking pay, demotion, suspension, and firing. The HR manager's ethical challenge is to ensure internal equity in the selection of appropriate disciplinary action and to ensure that the person disciplined is treated with respect. For example, the Minnesota Department of Corrections failed to ensure internal equity when it reprimanded some employees for reading religious texts during training but did not reprimand others for reading magazines, doing paperwork, or sleeping (*Altman v Minnesota Department of Corrections* 2001).

Disciplinary action is often taken without consultation with the HR manager. An ethical manager will use mechanisms such as employee handbooks, training, and newsletters to provide notice of policies and performance requirements. It is especially important to provide such notice when it is not obvious that a behavior is proscribed. An HR manager need not provide notice to employees regarding the employer's objection to punching a supervisor, but organizations with rules against accepting tips or holding secondary employment have an obligation to put employees on notice. Consequently, much of the mechanism to ensure fairness must be incorporated in policy and supervisory training. If disciplinary actions are regularly overturned by arbitration panels or courts, HR managers should take steps to correct problems quickly. Otherwise, some actions warranting discipline may go unchecked because a supervisor does not want to go through the process of a disciplinary action only to be overturned. This would result in inequities in implementing discipline (and therefore even more decisions overturned) and might also result in employees suffering harassment or other abuse at the hands of co-workers because supervisors believe it is impossible to discipline anyone successfully. Some supervisors are very concerned about the effects of their actions on subordinates and their families, to the point where HR managers should be alert to instances where employees without families receive harsher discipline than those with families (Butterfield, Trevino, and Ball 1996).

Retention

The origin of many HR departments can be traced to Henry Ford's efforts to maintain a stable, trained workforce. He paid employees more money and offered them long-term benefits, such as retirement, that made it very difficult for them to quit. The first ethical challenge for HR managers is to examine the measures used to retain employees and to ensure that they do not make it so difficult to quit that employees will not leave or confront the organization even when put in untenable ethical positions. Do the on-site child care, company-subsidized mortgage, stock-option incentive pay, and family-friendly health plan tie employees so closely to the company that they are afraid to quit or to report irregularities? Even if the HR manager determines that the benefits offered have enough portability not to bind employees too closely, there are ethical issues surrounding the specific programs implemented and the amount of choice given employees.

Benefits. The negotiating power that a large employer has in providing benefits for employees helps drive the costs lower than they would be if they were purchased individually by the employees. However, HR managers must consider the ethical implications of reducing costs for their own full-time employees while increasing them for their part-time employees, the unemployed, and persons employed in the secondary labor market. This is probably irrelevant for some of the more trendy benefits, such as on-site dry cleaning and fitness centers, but for retirement and health insurance, the reflective HR manager whose ethical concern goes beyond the organization's boundaries must consider these implications. I do not mean to suggest that any individual HR manager has the power to reverse the dominant U.S. model for providing health benefits to employees. In fact, were any organization to cut its benefits significantly, it might be violating its duty to keep promises to employees unless it made arrangements for the same benefits to be provided through another source. HR managers in multinational firms, however, would do well to consider whether adding U.S.-style benefits might begin a trend to undermine functioning national systems.

The most common method of providing benefits to employees of large organizations is to offer them an array from which they can choose. In some cases, employees are given a fixed sum of benefit dollars to spend; in others, they are given the option to use part of their salary to purchase the benefit. Many benefits are available through salary reduction, which shields part of the employee's salary from income taxes.

Even where there is a choice in benefits, the HR manager must decide which benefits will be included and, usually, which carrier will provide them. An ethical issue facing HR managers in this arena is the potential for conflict of interest. It can take two forms. First, the HR manager, as an employee, can be tempted to select programs for the benefit smorgasbord that are personally appealing. Second, since large revenues hinge upon these decisions, insurance carriers can be tempted to offer kickbacks or other incentives for the HR manager to select them. In both cases, the HR manager has a clear ethical obligation not to allow personal considerations to affect professional choices.

HR managers also have to balance the welfare of employees against the cost of benefit plans, and they have to make decisions about the amount of choice employees can reasonably be given. Obviously, companies could go bankrupt offering employee benefits. The strategy of offering benefits thus must take into account the likelihood that offering a particular benefit will help the employer attract better employees, retain desirable employees at lower overall cost, and motivate employees to devote more hours to productive work. The strategic question is not easily answered by a formula. Some benefits have a very short half-life on the employee-motivation scale, after which they become minimum requirements. By offering "cafeteria" plans of benefit choice, employers reduce the need to up the benefit ante every year, but they also increase administrative costs and decrease their purchasing power. So even within their obligation to be good stewards of employer resources, HR managers have real choices to make that have ethical implications.

Over the past half century, the costs of benefits have skyrocketed, with health insurance costs accounting for a large portion of the increase. The introduction of health maintenance organizations (HMOs) and preferred provider organizations (PPOs) to the mix slowed the rise for some time, but some of the limitations imposed by these plans created very real problems for employees. HR managers were faced with angry employees, who felt that their psychological contract with the employer had been violated (Lucero and Allen 1994). As demand for lifting the restrictions increased, so did costs. In response, some companies are cutting benefits or increasing the portion of the costs paid by employees. The ethical implications of cutting benefits or increasing co-payments mean that even when employers offer benefits, many lower-paid employees (Rawls's "least advantaged") are unable to purchase them.

The amount of choice provided to employees can be overwhelming. HR managers can provide a real service by examining plans carefully and providing information to employees making choices. The problem of discernment the HR manager faces is determining when the restriction of choice infringes on employee freedoms.

Balance. There is considerable current research on the effects on workers of trying to balance work with "family" or "life" or "nonwork" activities. Organizations seeking to retain employees have instituted "work–family" benefits, including such things as on-site day care, work–family training, day-care referral programs, elder care assistance, and flexible schedules (Osterman 1995). These programs have generally been hailed by the business ethics literature as virtuous (Marchese, Bassham, and Ryan 2002), but the HR manager must address the issue of fairness, as employees with fewer dependents may begin to complain that they are shouldering more than their share of the work or receiving disproportionately fewer benefits.

Compensation Systems. Compensation systems are also important to retention (Gerhart and Trevor 1996). HR managers must ensure that employees perceive their jobs as being worth at least as much as any alternative employment available to them. Some ethicists suggest that employers who receive higher-than-average profits in an industry have a moral obligation to pay their employees higher-than-average wages for that industry (Koys 2001). Turnover is related not only to the amount of compensation but also to the growth of compensation over time (Trevor, Gerhart, and Boudreau 1997). Certain compensation systems are designed as "golden handcuffs" that force employees to stay even when they wish to leave. Stock options that don't mature for years, longevity salary increases, and other devices intended to link the long-term interests of the organization with the employee's interests can become coercive if they represent a sufficient percentage of the employee's compensation.

Employee Complaint Mechanisms. Hirschman (1970) suggests that people given the opportunity to voice complaints will be less likely to choose "exit" as their strategy. Many organizations have employee complaint procedures, administered through the HR department. Typically, they allow an employee to bring a formal complaint first to the supervisor or manager accused of wrongdoing, then to successively higher levels of management. One of the challenges facing HR managers is to ensure that the power differential between managers and employees does not quash complaints that should be heard. Unfortunately, one of the few ways to ensure this is to allow the expression of complaints that shouldn't be heard, taking up valuable staff time. An independent complaint investigator may lend credibility to the procedure. There is some evidence that having decision makers who are not part of management increases the number of grievances (Colvin 2003). However, even if the typical system is used, it is important for managers to receive training that enables them to see the employees' side of issues (Moberg 2003). An ethical HR manager will encourage legitimate grievances, will have them heard in a just platform, and will seek meaningful resolutions.

Termination

Not mentioned in the core responsibilities of HR managers but still a very real part of their jobs are employee dismissals, layoffs, resignations, and retirements. Employees who violate the organization's rules or fail to meet the standards established for their employment are dismissed. Those whose jobs are no longer needed, due to changes in organizational structure, goals, or finances, are laid off. The main difference between the two is that dismissal is person specific while layoff is job specific. In either case, the person affected is often devastated, and the HR manager has the ability to make the process less distressing. While the law in some places allows an employer to fire an employee for "a good reason, a bad reason, or no reason at all," Kant ([1785] 1981) would suggest that only actions done for good reasons can be good.

Dismissal. Dismissals for rule violations are different from dismissals for poor performance; the first is willful, while the second may not be. The distinction has implications for how an HR manager addresses dismissals. "Fault" and "blame" should not be ascribed to people who are unable to achieve the standards of the organization, especially if they have been able to achieve those standards for years or are new employees. In the first case, it is likely declining capabilities that cause the inability to meet standards, and blaming a person for a natural process is cruel. In the second case, the HR manager is perhaps more blameworthy, having assessed the person's qualifications and determined that he or she could perform the job duties. However, in cases where the employee has chosen not to meet standards or has intentionally violated a rule, the HR manager may take pains to explain that the dismissal was within the employee's control.

HR managers have an obligation to make sure that systems of dismissing employees for rule violations are fairly designed and administered and clearly articulated. While employees whose productivity is high may be given special dispensation to violate rules (for example, to come to work late), it is important for HR managers to ascertain that all similarly situated employees receive the same dispensation. It is easy to look at an individual's record and say, "Of course that person deserves to be fired," but fairness cannot be determined until the HR manager has compared that record to the records of those who are not being considered for firing. The manner in which the employee is informed of the dismissal, as well as treatment after the notice has been provided, must respect the dignity of the employee and the safety of co-workers. Cases where disgruntled people take up arms and attack former supervisors or co-workers are rare enough to make front-page news, but the HR manager's ethical responsibility is to take steps to make sure they stay rare.

Layoffs. When there are insufficient funds or orders to justify the size of the workforce, workers are laid off, either temporarily (until business picks up) or permanently. Layoffs are sometimes conducted under very strict rules, requiring people to be dismissed in reverse order from their hiring and providing "bumping rights" to people to return to previously held positions, forcing the incumbents to be laid off instead. The first job of the ethical HR manager is to provide alternatives to layoffs, outsourcing, or downsizing to the other managers considering the action. This requires clearly understanding the anticipated outcomes in terms of what might happen to all of the stakeholders: employees, potential employees, local communities, external communities, and stockholders (Arnold and Bowie 2003). The HR manager must also clearly understand all of the contracts, both actual and psychological, surrounding the relationships with current employees.

Assuming that a layoff does occur, the second job of the ethical HR manager is to provide notice, placement assistance, and recommendations for those being laid off. The specifics for each of these depend on the situation. The ethical HR manager should focus on looking out for those least advantaged by the decision. The third job is to provide for the emotional reactions of the "survivors," both rank-and-file co-workers and managers in the affected unit (Dewitt, Trevino, and Mollica 2003).

Resignation. Employees who quit their jobs sometimes leave because they haven't found an outlet where they can voice their complaints. One way an HR manager can help these employees is to provide exit interviews, which, though not completely satisfying, may at least help the employees to feel as if their departure could help those left behind. Assuming the HR manager investigates and acts on complaints voiced in these interviews, other employees can be helped by subsequent reforms. One practice prevalent in some industries is to process all resignations immediately, despite any employee attempts to give notice. Unless there is a compelling reason to do otherwise, HR managers should encourage practices that reward giving notice rather than punish it.

Death. Employees who die while employed leave family members in vulnerable positions with respect to the employer. The ethical HR manager can smooth the way for survivors by providing prompt and clear information on final paychecks, life insurance, continuation of health coverage, and other benefits that might be useful. Similarly, the HR manager can provide support for co-workers, including notices of the death and funeral arrangements and time off to attend the funeral, and can work with the direct supervisor to ensure smooth transitions.

Conclusion

Having been an HR practitioner for more than a decade, I have special sympathy for the pressures HR managers live under. It is rare that they can sit back and reflect on the many ethical issues involved in every decision they make. It is even rarer that they find other managers in the organization who are attuned to HR issues from an ethical perspective. While it may be easy for those removed from the situation to point to all of the ethical lapses of HR managers, I would hope that industrial relations and HR faculty would recognize their great potential to assist current practitioners and influence the behavior of future practitioners.

Teaching faculty can stress strategic or ethical considerations in their HR courses. Stressing ethical considerations would be one way to help develop an ethical sense among future practitioners. Faculty can make a course in ethics a prerequisite for their own HR courses and then address ethics regularly in relation to the topics they cover. They can invite ethicists to give guest lectures and local HR managers to talk about ethical issues they face. A few of the available HR textbooks address ethics in almost every chapter—choosing those over textbooks that ignore ethics or relegate it to a paragraph or two would be one way to underscore that students should consider ethics in all that they do. In "HR for the non–HR manager" courses, faculty can give other managers an appreciation for the multiplicity of ethical issues involved in their interactions with employees and with the HR department.

Research faculty have the opportunity to do considerably more work in the area of HR ethics. They have examined HR practices alone and in "bundles" to determine whether there are any that characterize more productive organizations. The consensus seems to be that there are "bundles" of best practices, but they are industry- or organization-specific (Macduffie 1995; Hunter 2000). That is, HR practices must work together toward the achievement of the organizational goal. How the ethics of human resources fits into this picture is not clearly understood. Researchers have yet to add what they know about ethics to what they know about bundles of practices. Similarly, researchers could examine the human costs of various HR practices.

In the end, though, the burden is on each individual HR manager to be reflective, always alert to the potential that what appears to be a routine decision may actually be a chance to do right.

References

Altman v Minnesota Department of Corrections, 251 F.3d 1199 (8th Cir., 2001).

Arnold, Denis G., and Norman E. Bowie. 2003. "Sweatshops and Respect for Persons." Business Ethics Quarterly, Vol. 13, no. 2 (April), pp. 221–43.

Brenkert, George G. 1998. "Marketing and the Vulnerable." Business Ethics Quarterly, The Ruffin Series [Special Issue], No. 1, pp. 7–20.

Brenner, Mark, and David Fairris. 2004. "Flexible Work Practices and Occupational Safety and Health: Exploring the Relationship Between Cumulative Trauma Disorders and Workplace Transformation." Industrial Relations, Vol. 43, no. 1 (January), pp. 242–67.

Butterfield, Kenneth D., Linda Klebe Trevino, and Gail A. Ball. 1996. "Punishment from the Manager's Perspective: A Grounded Investigation and Inductive Model." Academy of Management Journal, Vol. 39, no. 6 (December), pp. 1479–1512.

Cappelli, Peter. 1999. "Career Jobs Are Dead." California Management Review, Vol. 42, no. 1 (Fall), pp. 146–67.

Clarkson, Max E. 1995. "A Stakeholder Framework for Analyzing and Evaluating Corporate Social Performance." Academy of Management Review, Vol. 20, no. 1 (January), pp. 92–118.

Colvin, Alexander J. S. 2003. "The Dual Transformation of Workplace Dispute Resolution." Industrial Relations, Vol. 42, no. 4 (October), pp. 712–36.

Dewitt, Rocki-Lee, Linda Klebe Trevino, and Kelly A. Mollica. 2003. "Stuck in the Middle: A Control-Based Model of Managers' Reactions to Their Subordinates' Layoffs." Journal of Managerial Issues, Vol. 15, no. 1 (Spring), pp. 32–49.

Donaldson, John, 2001. "Multinational Enterprises, Employment Relations, and Ethics," Employee Relations, Vol. 23, no. 6 (November), pp. 627–42.

Gerhart, Barry, and Charlie O. Trevor. 1996. "Employment Variability Under Different Managerial Compensation Systems." Academy of Management Journal, Vol. 39, no. 6 (December), pp. 1692–712.

Goins, Sheila, and Elizabeth A. Mannix. 1999. "Self-Selection and Its Impact on Team Diversity and Performance." Performance Improvement Quarterly, Vol. 12, no. 1, pp. 127–47.

Graham, Mary E., and Charlie O. Trevor. 2000. "Managing New Pay Program Introductions to Enhance the Competitiveness of Multinational Corporations." Competitiveness Review, Vol. 10, no. 1, pp. 136–54.

Greenwood, Michelle R. 2002. "Ethics and HRM: A Review and Conceptual Analysis." Journal of Business Ethics, Vol. 3, no. 3 (March), pp. 261–78.

Griggs v. Duke Power 401 U.S. 424 (1971)

Hackman, J. Richard, Greg Oldham, Robert Janson, and Kenneth Purdy. 1975. "A New Strategy for Job Enrichment." California Management Review, Vol. 17, no. 4 (Summer), pp. 57–71.

Hannafey, Francis T. 2003. "Economic and Moral Criteria of Executive Compensation." Business and Society Review, Vol. 108, no. 3 (Fall), pp. 405–15.

Hirschman, Albert O. 1970. Exit, Voice, and Loyalty: Responses to Decline in Firms, Organizations, and States. Cambridge, MA: Harvard University Press.

Hoffman, W. Michael, and Laura P. Hartman. 2003. "You've Got Mail . . . and the Boss Knows: A Survey by the Center for Business Ethics of Companies' Email and Internet Monitoring." Business and Society Review, Vol. 108, no. 3 (Fall), pp. 285–307.

Huasknecht, John P., Charlie O. Trevor, and James L. Farr. 2002. "Retaking Ability Tests in a Selection Setting: Implications for Practice Effects, Training Performance, and Turnover." *Journal of Applied Psychology,* Vol. 87, no. 2 (April), pp. 243–54.

Hunter, Larry W. 2000. "The Adoption of Innovative Work Practices in Service Environments." *International Journal of Human Resource Management,* Vol. 11, no. 3 (June), pp. 477–97.

Hunter, Larry W., John Paul MacDuffie, and Lorna Doucet. 2002. "What Makes Teams Take? Employee Reactions to Work Reforms." *Industrial and Labor Relations Review,* Vol. 55, no. 3 (April), pp. 448–73.

Kant, Immanuel. [1785]. 1981. *Grounding for the Metaphysics of Morals.* Indianapolis: Hackett.

Kochan, Thomas A. 2002. "Addressing the Crisis in Confidence in Corporations: Root Causes, Victims, and Strategies for Reform." *Academy of Management Executive,* Vol. 16, no. 3 (August), pp. 139–42.

Koys, Daniel J. 2001. "Integrating Religious Principles and Human Resource Management Activities." *Teaching Business Ethics,* Vol. 5, no. 2 (May), pp. 121–39.

Kurland, Nancy. 1999. "Ethics and Commission." *Business and Society Review,* Vol. 104, no. 1 (Spring), pp. 29–33.

Lucero, Margaret A., and Robert E. Allen. 1994. "Employee Benefits: A Growing Source of Psychological Contract Violations." *Human Resource Management,* Vol. 33, no. 3 (Fall), pp. 425–46.

MacDuffie, John Paul. 1995. "Human Resource Bundles and Manufacturing Performance: Organizational Logic and Flexible Production Systems in the Automobile Industry." *Industrial and Labor Relations Review,* Vol. 48, no. 2 (January), pp. 197–222.

Marchese, Marc C., Gregory Bassham, and Jack Ryan. 2002. "Work–Family Conflict: A Virtue Ethics Analysis." *Journal of Business Ethics,* Vol. 40, no. 2 (October), pp. 145–54.

McCall, John J. 2003. "A Defense of Just Cause Dismissal Rules." *Business Ethics Quarterly,* Vol. 13, no. 2 (April), pp. 151–76.

Mishra, Jitendra M. 1998. "Employee Monitoring: Privacy in the Workplace?" *S.A.M. Advanced Management Journal,* Vol. 63, no. 3 (Summer), pp. 4–15.

Moberg, Dennis J. 2000. "Time Pressure and Ethical Decision-Making: The Case for Moral Readiness." *Business and Professional Ethics Journal,* Vol. 19, no. 2 (Summer), pp. 41–67.

———. 2003. "Managers as Judges in Employee Disputes: An Occasion for Moral Imagination." *Business Ethics Quarterly,* Vol. 13, no. 4 (October), pp. 453–78.

Moberg, Dennis, and Manuel Velasquez. 2004. "The Ethics of Mentoring." *Business Ethics Quarterly,* Vol. 14, no. 1 (January), pp. 95–133.

Nye, David. 2002. "The Privacy in Employment Critique: A Consideration of Some of the Arguments for Ethical HRM Professional Practice." *Business Ethics: A European Review,* Vol. 11, no. 3 (July), pp. 224–33.

Osterman, Paul. 1995. "Work/Family Programs and the Employment Relationship." *Administrative Science Quarterly,* Vol. 40, no. 4 (December), pp. 681–701.

Radin, Tara J., and Patricia H. Werhane. 2003. "Employment-at-Will, Employee Rights, and Future Directions for Employment." *Business Ethics Quarterly,* Vol. 13, no. 2 (April), pp. 113–30.

Rawls, John. 1971. *A Theory of Justice.* Cambridge, MA: Belknap Press.

Reed, Lisa J. 2003. "Paternalism May Excuse Disability Discrimination: When May an Employer Refuse to Employ a Disabled Individual Due to Concerns for the Individual's Safety?" *Business and Society Review,* Vol. 108, no. 3 (Fall), pp. 417–24.

Rest, James R. 1976. "New Approaches in the Assessment of Moral Judgment." In Thomas Lickona, ed., *Moral Development and Behavior Theory, Research, and Social Issues*. New York: Holt, Rinehart and Winston, pp. 198–218.

Robertson, Diana C., and Erin Anderson. 1993. "Control Systems and Task Environment Effects on Ethical Judgment: An Exploratory Study of Industrial Salespeople." *Organization Science*, Vol. 4, no. 4 (November), pp. 617–44.

Roehling, Mark V. 2003. "The Employment-at-Will Doctrine: Second Level Ethical Issues and Analysis." *Journal of Business Ethics*, Vol. 47, no. 2 (October), pp. 115–25.

Scoville, James G. 1993. "The Past and Present of Ethics in Industrial Relations." *Proceedings of the Forty-Fifth Annual Meeting* (Anaheim, CA, January 5–8, 1993). Madison, WI: Industrial Relations Research Association, pp. 198–206.

Stevens, Betsy. 2001. "Hospitality Ethics: Responses from Human Resource Directors and Students to Seven Ethical Scenarios." *Journal of Business Ethics*, Vol. 30, no. 3 (April), pp. 233–42.

Trevino, Linda Klebe, Laura Pincus Hartman, and Michael Brown. 2000. "Moral Person and Moral Manager: How Executives Develop a Reputation for Ethical Leadership." *California Management Review*, Vol. 42, no. 4 (Summer), pp. 128–42.

Trevor, Charlie O., Barry Gerhart, and John W. Boudreau. 1997. "Voluntary Turnover and Job Performance: Curvilinearity and the Moderating Influences of Salary Growth and Promotions." *Journal of Applied Psychology*, Vol. 82, no. 1 (February), pp. 44–61.

VanSandt, Craig V. 2003. "The Relationship Between Ethical Work Climate and Moral Awareness." *Business and Society*, Vol. 42, no. 1 (March), pp. 144–52.

Weber, James, Lance B. Kurke, and David W. Pentico. 2003. "Why Do Employees Steal?" *Business and Society*, Vol. 42, no. 3 (September), pp. 359–80.

Weber, Max. 1930. *The Protestant Ethic and the Spirit of Capitalism*. London: Allen & Unwin.

Werhane, Patricia. 1983. "Individual Rights in Business." In Tom Regan, ed., *Just Business*. Philadelphia, PA: Temple University Press, pp. 100–29.

Wiley, Carolyn. 2000. "Ethical Standards for Human Resource Management Professionals: A Comparative Analysis of Five Major Codes." *Journal of Business Ethics*, Vol. 25, no. 2 (May), pp. 93–114.

CHAPTER 8

Ethical Challenges in Labor Relations

JOHN T. DELANEY
Michigan State University

In the United States, life revolves around work. Over the past 25 years, average annual hours worked in the United States have increased about 2%, while declining 12% in other OECD (Organisation for Economic Co-operation and Development) countries (Mishel, Bernstein, and Boushey 2003:425). People work for many reasons—to secure money, to achieve self-actualization, even to escape problems of family life. As Alan Wolfe noted, however, "in a capitalist society, we value work to the degree that we establish a value for work" (1997:566). And in the establishment of work's value, society creates an intersection where ethics and workplace issues collide.

The field of labor relations, in particular, includes many issues with significant ethical dimensions. Today, for a variety of reasons, the resulting collision between ethics and labor relations is less audible, albeit more noteworthy. The nation's general devotion to capitalism has served both to discourage reflection on the equity of market-generated outcomes and to treat as heretical ethical questions raised about the economic system. At the same time, globalization has increased competition for jobs, especially for workers with limited education and skills. In combination with the decline in union density and employers' victories in labor–management battles, arguments for efficiency generally dominate concerns for equity.

There exists no widely accepted way to measure ethics in labor relations. The persistent struggle between unions and employers allows the ethical character of most labor relations outcomes to be challenged. At the heart of such challenges is disagreement over the extent to which a measure of efficiency or equity or voice or freedom or human rights or something else adequately captures all aspects of the interaction between employees and managers (see Budd 2004). Even if the parties agreed on common benchmarks for evaluating ethics, they would likely dispute their application.

In addition, in labor relations one side's gain is often perceived as the other's loss. Either side may complain that a situation or outcome is unfair when it does not achieve its preferred position. Any projection of ethical considerations into labor relations thus appears to be contextual, as each side strongly adheres to its objectives as moral and right while rejecting the other party's position as partisan and self-interested. The persistence of this "holy war" (see Delaney, Lewin, and Sockell 1985:46) virtually ensures that one side or the other will dispute any conclusion that some labor relations approach or outcome is ethical.

Identifying Benchmarks from Ethical and Economic Theories

Management has prevailed in its struggle with unions partly because the American people have generally accepted a narrow application of economic theory as the guarantor of prosperity. Prominent economists, such as Milton Friedman, have advanced a perspective that favors Adam Smith's ideal world of competition and equilibrium over competing views. In that world, the general good is advanced when every individual actively seeks his or her self-interest, which then serves the markets frequented by others. Friedman, in his classic book *Capitalism and Freedom,* noted that "there is one and only one social responsibility of business— to use its resources and engage in activities designed to increase its profits, so long as it . . . engages in open and free competition, without deception or fraud" (1982:133).

As Joseph Stiglitz has argued, however, the perspective of neoclassical economics is powerfully one-sided:

> One of the great "tricks" (some might say "insights") of neo-classical economics is to treat labour like any other factor of production. Output is written as a function of inputs—steel, machines, and labour. The mathematics treats labour like a commodity, lulling one into thinking of labour like an ordinary commodity, such as steel or plastic. But labour is unlike any other commodity. The work environment is of no concern for steel; we do not care about steel's well-being (2002:10).

By ignoring human nature, economic theory provides elegant theoretical models and mathematical tests. Stiglitz is correct, however, that it is a stretch to assume that people are like any other input.

Ethical theorists accepted centuries ago the unique nature of people and have attempted to build theories accordingly. As a result, although economists and ethicists study similar issues, they do not speak the same language. This is one reason why economists have not viewed positively the writings of Catholic theologians and papal encyclicals on work and workers' rights (see McGurn 2002). Indeed, economists have typically argued that the views advanced in such works harm more people than they help because their implementation would reduce the efficiency of the free market. It is deceptively seductive to take economists' lead and focus primarily on efficiency. Such an approach seems to apply a veneer of "truth" onto a world of shadows. As Wolfe concluded,

> Workers, particularly in unionized sectors, rightly have their suspicions about moral language—you don't strike against someone with whom you have close moral ties. But it is also true that capitalists share some of those suspicions, for you do not cut the benefits or fire without notice your moral partners either. Both those who speak for labor and those who speak for capital will not likely find themselves urging a return to the moral dimension of work (1997:569).

Wolfe's point reinforces the reality that just as union and management supporters take different perspectives, so do philosophers studying ethics. Readers might interpret the numerous and divergent perspectives as suggesting that morality is subjective. For example, philosophers have advocated both deontological perspectives (focusing on duties) and teleological ones (focusing on ends). Moreover, ethical discourse is often abstract and difficult to understand, making it easy to ignore in favor of arguments of a more primal nature.

Today, economic theory serves as a primal approach by providing an accepted way to categorize actions. Its unchecked dominance provides an imprimatur of ethics in a capitalist society. This view is best reflected in the words of character Gordon Gekko in the movie *Wall Street* (1987): "Greed is good." Economists are somewhat more pious, arguing the point with the word self-interest. In America and many other parts of the world today, it's widely accepted that free markets are good, that they create efficiency and promote the self-interested behavior of individuals that generates optimal economic outcomes. It is seen as wrong to advocate anything other than efficiency, such as equity or voice. In the best case, advocates of voice or equity are called liberals; in the typical case they are called much worse. As a result, there is little common ground across the disputing camps and little reason to develop a common measure of ethics in labor relations.

Advocates have staked their claims squarely in each of the theoretical camps (see Friedman 1982 and McGurn 2002, on the one hand, and Adams 1992, 2001, on the other). Each camp embraces and promotes its perspective and ignores or rejects the contrary view. Ultimately, this creates a battle of principles in which contradictory assertions are leveled as gospel by the disputing sides. Such battles cannot be won. Accordingly, no universally accepted metric is available to guide an analysis of ethics in labor relations.

Recognizing this, I examine selected labor relations issues using two general ethical benchmarks: the extent to which a society's freedom is aided or hindered and the extent to which fundamental human rights are protected by the actions of the parties. These benchmarks are not new or unique, though they differ from other approaches (see Budd 2004). Although the benchmarks do not overcome the inherent disagreements I have noted, they permit an examination of ethics in labor relations using consistent criteria. After providing some background on the criteria, I will apply them to selected labor relations issues.

The doctrine of utilitarianism provides strong support for the use of a freedom benchmark to examine ethics. Shaped by Jeremy Bentham and John Stuart Mill, utilitarianism holds that actions are judged right or wrong solely by their consequences, that consequences are measured according to the happiness or unhappiness they create, and that happiness is judged in the aggregate (i.e., no person's happiness is more important than another's; see Rachels 1999:107–8). Because of its examination of costs and benefits and its support for the notion of efficiency, utilitarianism has greatly influenced neoclassical economists. For example, Friedman advocates that freedom is the "ultimate goal" in society (1982:5). He believes it essential for government to promote freedom, as the "fundamental threat to freedom is the power to coerce" (1982:15). As Budd noted, "the logic of the utilitarian-neoclassical economics nexus is powerful: Individuals pursuing their self-interests in competitive markets create efficient outcomes in which profits and welfare are maximized" (2004:70).

Utilitarianism has often been questioned on the ground that it ignores that certain actions are right or wrong regardless of the outcomes they may produce. More importantly, utilitarianism does not capture or reflect humanity. People deserve certain respect and treatment simply because of the intrinsic worth or dignity that accrues because they are human. This has led some observers to suggest that certain labor rights are fundamental human rights. The work of philosophers and theologians supports that view.

Immanuel Kant's work supports the use of human rights as a benchmark for examining ethics in labor relations. Kant believed that humans should never be used as means to an end (Rachels 1999:132). Moreover, according to Kant, the moral worth of an action is derived not from its purpose but in the "maxim by which it is determined" ([1785]1959:16). This leads to his categorical imperative: "Act only according to that maxim by which you can at the same time will that it should become a universal law" ([1785]1959:39). Critical to derivation of the categorical imperative is recognition of the dignity of "human nature and every rational nature" ([1785]1959:54).

The Catholic Church and the International Labour Organization (ILO) have strongly promoted the human rights view. In *Rerum Novarum* ("On the Condition of the Working Classes"), Pope Leo XIII's encyclical letter (1891), obligations for employers and workers were clearly delineated. Workers were obligated to "perform entirely and conscientiously whatever work has been voluntarily and equitably agreed upon," cooperate with the employer, and protect the employer's property (Pope Leo XIII 1891:¶30). Employers were admonished not to treat workers as slaves or to corrupt them but to offer them the respect and dignity that they deserve as human beings (1891:¶31). Cooperation between workers and employers was encouraged to achieve better outcomes for all.

Forty years later, Pope Pius XI issued *Quadragesimo Anno* ("The Fortieth Year: On Reconstruction of the Social Order"), which proclaimed the need to treat workers justly. In addition to reinforcing *Rerum Novarum*, this encyclical asserted that workers should be paid a just wage and have the right to band together and enter into agreements with employers (Pope Pius XI 1931:¶92). Subsequently, Pope John Paul II issued two encyclicals on work and workers' rights (*Laborem Exercens* ["On Human Work"] 1981; *Centesimus Annus* ["The Hundredth Year"; 1991), and the U.S. Conference of Catholic Bishops published *Economic Justice for All* (1986), a pastoral letter on Catholic social teaching and the economy. These documents assert that workers are entitled to certain economic rights, fair treatment, state protection of efforts to organize, and just wages. The basis for these entitlements lies in Christian scripture and in the dignity of human life.

In June 1998 the International Labour Conference unanimously adopted the "Declaration on Fundamental Principles and Rights at Work." That document identified four basic rights, which all ILO members were bound to respect: "(a) freedom of association and the effective recognition of the right to collective bargaining; (b) the elimination of all forms of forced or compulsory labour; (c) the effective abolition of child labour; and (d) the elimination of discrimination in respect of employment and occupation." These rights were held as essential to the development of "universal and lasting peace," "social progress and the eradication of poverty," and "justice and democratic institutions" (ILO 1998). While not based in religion, this view inherently recognizes that people, by their birth, are entitled to basic rights and considerations in society, at home, and at work. Governments are expected to respect these rights, which cannot be granted or withheld by rulers or law. As asserted by the United Nations (UN) Universal Declaration of Human Rights (1948), "all human beings are born free and equal in dignity and rights" (Article 1), and "everyone who works has the right to just and favorable remuneration ensuring for himself and his family an existence worthy of human dignity ... [and] everyone has the right to form and to join trade unions for the protection of his interests" (Article 23). In essence, both the Catholic Church and the UN effectively argued that the inherent nature of humanity requires special status and consideration.

Although the benchmarks of freedom and human rights do not cover all aspects of ethics in labor relations, they permit a wide-ranging analysis. For example, to understand some of the links among these subjects, I empirically compared measures of economic freedom, political rights, civil liberties, human rights abuses, and union density. The measures were created and published by several organizations. (An appendix describing the analyses is available upon request.) In general, the results indicated strong positive correlations among measures of economic freedom, political rights, and civil liberties (each correlation was greater than .57 and statistically significant at the 1% level). Human rights abuses were negatively related to economic freedom ($r = -.56$; $p < .01$), political rights ($r = -.63$; $p < .01$), and civil liberties ($r = -.70$; $p < .01$). Union density was positively related to the economic and political freedom measures (two correlations were significant at the 10% level) and negatively associated with human rights abuses ($r = -.41$; $p < .05$). Because of measurement, causality, and other issues, these results should not be overinterpreted. However, they reinforce that the benchmarks are appropriate in an analysis of ethical challenges in labor relations. I will go on to identify some labor relations issues and their associated ethical challenges.

Free Association Rights, Self-Organization, and Labor Relations

In the United States, the notion that people have the right to associate with whomever they choose is almost universally accepted. Free association promotes freedom and honors an individual's human dignity. The principle of free association is seldom in dispute. Liberals and conservatives, workers and managers, union and employer organizations advocate the virtue of free association. Ethical challenges to the concept arise when people *exercise* their freedom to associate, especially when they choose to organize a union. In practice, association rights can impose costs on another's property or prosperity. This leads people and groups to oppose some free association activities and to seek to influence governmental regulations covering association rights. When individuals seek union representation, ethical questions may arise regarding the form of association or self-organization rights available, the mechanisms and metrics used to determine if the individuals have chosen to exercise their association rights, the activities available to those who organize, the rights of those who dissent, the governance principles followed by the organizations representing people, and the rights of individuals facing a group of people exercising free association. In this chapter I examine these issues.

Giving Workers a Voice at Work

A critical assumption of labor relations is that workers seek a voice at work. Data support the assumption, showing that a large percentage of nonunion U.S. workers desire a voice in the workplace (Freeman and Rogers 1999). Managers do not oppose giving employees voice—data suggest that employers believe benefits accrue when employee involvement programs are adopted (Kaufman 1999, Kaufman and Taras, 1999). Recent research also suggests that use of various employee-voice mechanisms (e.g., employee involvement programs, information sharing, due process procedures) is associated with better organizational performance (see Kleiner and Bouillon 1988, Cooke 1994, Huselid 1995, Appelbaum et al. 2000). Unfortunately, while few would disagree in principle with the idea that employees should have a voice at work, acrimonious conflicts arise as the precise nature of "voice" is defined.

In the United States, the traditional method for achieving worker voice is *collective bargaining*, as delineated and supported by law. Employers are required to bargain with the duly selected representative of employees, and workers cannot be legally fired for engaging in concerted activities. Historically, when workers banded together in groups at work, they sought to bargain collectively with their employer. One purpose of unionizing was to negotiate a contract that distributes resources in ways that employers may not prefer. In such instances, the contract dictates how workplace matters are handled, not the employer.

Few employers like such situations. Even when unions were at the peak of their strength in the United States, strong opposition to collective bargaining existed among private and public employers. As unions overcame the resistance of public employers in the 1960s and 1970s, organizing gains in the public sector masked the deunionization of the private sector. Over the past 30 years, private employers have aggressively sought to defeat unions, even if it was necessary to use illegal tactics (see Kleiner 2001). Public employers, by contrast, were less able to resist so strongly.

Instead, public employers relied on government bargaining laws that generally allowed negotiation over a narrower set of issues than was mandated in the private sector. The public sector is likely to remain the center of unionization in the United States, in part because the right of free association is enshrined in state constitutions.

Strong employer opposition to bargaining has created moral gray areas in labor relations. It has encouraged both sides to use any action—legal or otherwise—that might defeat the other side. It has also fueled general opposition to unions and has encouraged both labor and management to use political tactics to bolster their respective situations.

In efforts to fight unions and bargaining, employers have argued that bargaining is inefficient and bad for the economy. By allowing unions to extract monopoly rents, bargaining is allegedly associated with higher costs, lower profits, and decreased competitiveness (Freeman and Medoff 1984). Management arguments ignore the fact that bargaining produces higher wages for workers, which allow them to maintain a better standard of living, purchase more goods, and participate more vigorously in the economy (Mishel, Bernstein, and Boushey 2003). Employers rely on economic theory to oppose unions. Stiglitz (2002) asserted that economic theory effectively defends policies that favor the small number of wealthy people over policies aiding the large number of working people. Seemingly, economic theory has been accepted as religion, and employers have encouraged everyone to embrace the faith.

From the perspective of freedom, employers and employees legitimately have different feelings about the value of collective bargaining. Employers have used an appeal to economic theory, coupled with substantial political lobbying, to promote their view. It apparently does not matter to many employers or politicians that this view treats human workers as just another factor of production. The view that the owners of capital should have more rights or say than other people diverges substantially from perspectives holding to the sanctity of humans.

In turn, this is one reason why papal encyclicals and bishops' statements on work have advocated that "every economic decision and institution must be judged in light of whether it protects or undermines the dignity of the human person" (U.S. Conference of Catholic Bishops 1986:13). The ILO takes the religious element out of this argument simply by advocating that all people are entitled to certain fundamental human rights. For individuals accepting these views, wealthy people cannot be entitled to greater voice than other people. As I will articulate, the conflict arising from collective bargaining is magnified in questions involving workers' right to strike and engage in concerted activities and employers' right to oppose unions aggressively.

Although conventional wisdom suggests that relations between employers and unionized workers are usually adversarial, many examples exist of cooperative relationships that have benefited both sides (e.g., Southwest Airlines, Saturn Corporation, General Motors' Lansing Grand River Assembly Plant, Deere and Company). Indeed, once employers discovered that a little bit of voice goes a long way, they devised a variety of ways to give that voice to nonunion employees (see Jacoby 1997). Over time, scholars have shown that programs giving workers a voice provide tangible benefits to organizations (see Kaufman and Taras 1999).

Employers appear to prefer cooperative approaches that can be controlled. They do not desire to bargain with workers' representatives over wages, hours, and other terms and conditions of employment. In unorganized settings, employers can give employees input without having to bargain over anything. Managers can even use voice mechanisms to help shape the situation at work. This situation troubled New York Senator Robert F. Wagner when he drafted the National Labor Relations Act (NLRA) in the 1930s. To overcome the possibility that workers could be forced to accept a representative more supportive of the employer than the worker, Senator Wagner wrote precise safeguards into the law. Labor organizations were defined broadly—"any organization of any kind, or any agency or employee representation committee or plan" (NLRA §2[5])—and it was deemed an unfair labor practice for an employer "to dominate or interfere with the formation or administration of any labor organization or to contribute financial or other support to it" (NLRA §8[a][2]). This statutory language effectively made unions *the* participation program legally available to employees.

Recently, this situation has encouraged employers to lobby Congress to enact the "Team Act," a law that would amend the NLRA, giving employers wider latitude to engage in cooperation programs with their nonunion workers (for a history, see Kaufman 1999). The Act was passed by Congress but vetoed by President Clinton. That employers have aggressively pushed for the Team Act while relentlessly fighting union organizing and collective bargaining (e.g., by refusing to negotiate contracts; see Cooke 1985) raises another ethical issue. Specifically, collective bargaining, as promoted by U.S. law, is simply one means by which workers secure a voice at work. Admittedly, it is a means that guarantees employees an *independent* representative, not a company-sponsored one. Why do employers oppose independent voice so adamantly while advocating other forms? The answer likely involves consideration of the strength of voice employees secure through bargaining and other mechanisms.

In short, employers seem to enact a contradiction by fighting collective bargaining while advocating other ways to give employees voice at work. Interest in creating voice opportunities likely occurs because evidence indicates that worker involvement creates beneficial organizational outcomes (see Cooke 1994). Managers desire those outcomes, but they do not want to surrender control over work. This is self-interest, pure and simple. From the perspective of freedom, both employers and unions rightly seek an ability to shape activities in their workplaces. Such conflicting desires do not violate the freedom benchmark, though they generate an ethically indeterminate outcome. On the other hand, the human dignity metric is clear. Employer efforts to create participation mechanisms favoring management undermine the dignity of workers.

Employers' Right to Oppose Unions

Many people in the business community seem to hate unions. Managers generally prefer not to deal with unionized workers, and the subject of unionization provokes strong emotions. This opposition has been cited as a reason for the decline in the American labor movement (Fiorito and Maranto 1987) and has generated strong feelings on the part of union supporters (see Adams 2001). Interestingly, however, in some ways this perspective is one-sided. Unions don't hate employers in the way that employers hate unions because unions need employers and the jobs they provide for workers. This likely magnifies employers' disdain, as they see unions as outside third parties.

The manner in which an employer exercises opposition, however, is open to abuse. This has fueled intense debate about the extent to which employers oppose unions and whether it is moral to do so (see Adler and Bigoness 1992; Higgins 1996). Employers have many means available to them under U.S. law to oppose unions (Gould 2004). They can fight organizing campaigns aggressively and bargain hard for contracts serving management's interests. They may close unionized facilities and relocate operations as long as economic reasons serve as the basis for the decision (and they must bargain over the effects of the decision for affected employees). Managers may make comments to workers opposing unions and pointing out the faults of organized labor. Firms sometimes engage in sophisticated anti-union campaigns that subtly provoke workers to reject a union.

Using the benchmark of freedom, employers have considerable latitude to oppose unions and union activities. Where employers' methods of opposition impose difficulties on workers or others, the boundary of acceptable union-hating behaviors would seem to be delineated. Unfortunately, that boundary is not clear, and many employers have used the lack of clarity to infringe on workers' rights to select a representative for collective bargaining (Greer and Martin 1978; Kleiner 1984). From the perspective of human dignity, aggressive tactics followed by employers to oppose unions—such as illegally firing union supporters to teach other employees a lesson or using thugs to intimidate workers—must come under ethical scrutiny. To the extent that ILO conventions define the free association and collective bargaining as fundamental human rights, employer efforts to deny them would seem to be improper. From the perspective of the Catholic Church and inherent human dignity, it is likely that the actions taken by employers to oppose unions must be evaluated before it is possible to reach a conclusion about the morality of the opposition effort. But some employer tactics would surely be unethical.

Current employer resistance and government aversion to unions seem to be inconsistent with the ILO conventions on workers' rights. Although it might be speculated that this reality bodes poorly for the possibility of the United States ratifying ILO Conventions 87 or 98 any time soon, the free association and unionization rights enumerated in those conventions will be promoted as principles for the purpose of making judgments (see Gross 2001). In addition, "by virtue of US membership in the ILO, US worker rights policy on a formal and agreed basis will be measured by whether it meets the goals and objectives of the fundamental worker rights treaties" (Potter 2001:378–9). Debate will continue to swirl around this issue. Some observers have suggested that "debate over freedom of association and collective bargaining could galvanize the diverse forces opposing corporate led globalization" (McIntyre and Bodah 2002:25). In its extreme form, such galvanization could spawn visions of ILO sanctions against U.S. policies or labor law reforms consistent with ILO conventions. In reality, neither is likely any time soon. The current U.S. administration surely has no plans to enact laws or ratify treaties favoring what some will view as union rights. Absent that kind of jump-start, it will take many years of data gathering and analysis for substantive questions to be raised about U.S. performance on metrics of free association, organization, and collective bargaining. The ILO conventions will become a priority only if they are seen as fundamental to American economic interests. In this regard, the concerns of U.S. employers for achieving balanced competition in global markets could ironically propel the country in the direction of the conventions.

The Right to Strike or Engage in Concerted Activities

The principle of free association becomes meaningful when individuals take action to support their associational choices. In such instances, action often generates conflict because outcomes favor one group over another. In labor relations, a primary self-help mechanism used by employees and unions is concerted activity. Workers can strike or take other job actions designed to pressure employers to accede to their demands. But the strike is a double-edged weapon. Because a shutdown means the loss of production and profits, strikes are fearsome to employers. Because stoppages mean the loss of income (and potentially jobs), strikes are fearsome to employees. And because of divisive social conflict, as well as the loss of goods and services, strikes are fearsome to communities.

Strikes typically cause collateral damage, and for this reason work stoppages and lockouts generate a variety of subsidiary ethical concerns. Some of the concerns are related to the employers and workers involved in a stoppage. Will the business suffer seriously from the action? Could it result in employees losing jobs? Will nonstriking workers face sanctions from colleagues after the strike? A second and potentially more serious set of concerns arises because of other potential strike effects. Will the cessation of business harm the community? Will the stoppage generate violence? Will safety issues arise during the strike because replacement workers (supervisors or others) are unfamiliar with jobs? Will the community be divided between strikers and nonstrikers if the employer chooses to hire replacements? The controversy of strikes is greatly magnified because their reach extends beyond the parties directly involved in a dispute. This makes the ethical issues inherent in strike actions complex.

The strike has always been controversial. For example, *Rerum Novarum* argued that peace and order should prevail in relations between workers and employers (Pope Leo XIII 1891:¶¶53–6). *Quadragesimo Anno* was unequivocal: "strikes and lock-outs are forbidden" (Pope Pius XI 1931:¶94). Given the problems associated with a strike, the Catholic encyclicals have preferred that some form of dispute resolution be mandated. Ironically, in the U.S. public sector, many states have done just that to protect the public from the disruptions of public employee strikes. In disputes over interests in the private sector, however, few efforts to replace strikes with other dispute resolution mechanisms have been successful.

Strikes are effective when they impose costs. The freedom benchmark makes it morally acceptable for employees or employers to take a hard line in a dispute. Given the potential consequences of stoppages, it is unlikely that such actions are initiated unless the situation is serious and the issue important to the parties. In such instances, the parties may freely act until the pressure of the situation generates an outcome—which may or may not be in the favor of either side. Although a stoppage may infringe on the freedom of others to avoid the dispute (e.g., workers idled in other firms, consumers who temporarily lose access to a product or service, communities that lose tax revenues because of idle facilities), this concern is not typically dominant. Statutes limit or prohibit strikes deemed to be harmful to the public (e.g., strikes by police or firefighters or that threaten national health or safety). Strikes in violation of such statutes may or may not be ethical. A strike that truly endangered the population would be ethically unacceptable. In other situations, strikes are an unfortunate but necessary by-product of a free society.

The human dignity benchmark provides a similarly murky perspective on the morality of strikes. While free persons have the right to withhold their labor, they could choose to do so by quitting their jobs rather than by imposing costs on their employer and others. If a strike harms bystanders, observers are forced to analyze whether one group's inherent human rights are more important than another's—a no-win situation. It is clear, however, that incidents of violence cannot be justified in strike situations. Even when violence is precipitated by employers' actions, it is morally wrong. Deliberate employer efforts to incite violence are similarly wrong. A problem here is the need to hinge ethical conclusions on an assessment of the motivations of a party engaging in a stoppage. For example, if an employer precipitates a strike solely to hire replacement workers and eliminate the union, the action is immoral. If a union initiates a strike to force small nonunion employers in a local industry out of business, the action is unethical. In reality, it is impossible to know motivations with certainty, and there is an inevitable intertwining of legitimate and illegitimate objectives (e.g., an employer forces a strike to gain concessions but ends up replacing the workforce). Short of embracing a teleological approach to ethics (ends justify the means), which obviates the need to analyze motivations, strike actions will never lend themselves to an easy general assignment of ethical implications. It will be necessary to examine specific circumstances to make moral judgments.

That some workers inevitably choose not to strike almost always ensures that hard feelings develop among workers. Whether some workers disagree with the union in the first place, have a need to maintain their job and income, or have legitimate reasons for not striking, when they cross a picket line they subject themselves to potential retaliation and repudiation by their co-workers. The situation degenerates into one in which the right of one group to strike is valued more than the right of another group not to strike—or the reverse. And yet pragmatically, to enforce solidarity, unions have imposed penalties on workers who cross picket lines, and union members regularly impose social sanctions on their strikebreaking neighbors. From the perspectives of freedom and human dignity, there is not an easy way to overcome this problem. Moreover, this fact of life—that some workers will strike and others will not—ensures hard feelings across workers and between workers and managers during a walkout.

The Permanent Replacement of Striking Workers

Much attention has been directed at employers' decisions to hire permanent replacements for striking workers in the United States. This possibility exists because of the Supreme Court's *Mackay* decision (*NLRB v. Mackay Radio 1938*), which made it illegal for an employer to fire a worker for engaging in concerted activities, such as a strike, but legal to permanently replace the same worker (LeRoy 1995). As the court's theoretical and legal distinction between discharge and replacement is irrelevant to any of the workers losing their jobs for striking, the morality of this situation has been questioned.

For example, strike activity in the United States has declined dramatically in recent years (Delaney 2003), in part because of the belief that strikes are less effective now than they were in the past, primarily because of aggressive employer efforts to replace striking workers. Regardless of one's view on the morality of this issue, management's use of permanent replacements precipitated a bitter and ultimately unsuccessful effort from 1988 through 1996 to amend U.S. labor law to prohibit this tactic (for a review, see Logan 2004). Few other nations permit the permanent replacement of strikers (Budd 2005), as the policy is seen as undermining unions and employees' free association rights.

The permission to hire permanent replacements during strikes yields a mixed assessment on the freedom benchmark. The policy absolutely protects employers' freedom to operate without explicitly denying workers' right to strike. But it offers little freedom to workers wishing to exercise their rights. Indeed, the policy seems to negate the workers' ability to engage in protected concerted activities. From a human dignity perspective, the policy seems to fail. Although it provides dignity to replacements who otherwise would not have strikers' jobs, it ignores the dignity of the striking workers and exposes replacements to safety issues (e.g., because of inadequate training or prolonged working hours or both) and social sanctions by strikers during and potentially after a strike.

Majority-Rule Unionism

Most nations permit workers to form and join unions to advance members' interests. Wide national differences exist in the rights afforded unions and the protections offered to individuals. In the United States, unions organizing a majority of workers in a specific bargaining unit must represent all workers in the unit for purposes of collective bargaining. This notion of "exclusive representation" and its derivative duty of fair representation compel unions to gain the support of a majority of people in a bargaining unit defined by a governmental unit, typically in an election, and to represent all bargaining unit employees fairly and equally. Exclusive representation generally ensures that employers potentially need not deal with many small groups of workers seeking minority representation rights (for a contrasting view, see Morris 2005). Such groups could be fragmented across social, religious, class, or other lines.

The approach has fundamental consequences for the nature of labor relations in the United States. It restricts workers' free association rights by subjecting labor relations to majority rule. This helps ensure that employees do not use free association rights to form whatever groups they prefer (e.g., the Christian workers group, the machinists, the Irish workers group) and to seek special privileges for that group from employers. Even in small workplaces, employers would be disadvantaged if they needed to deal with each group formed by employees, both because of time costs and the reality that the groups would not have uniform preferences regarding outcomes. The result could be an administrative nightmare, especially if the employer were required to deal with the issues raised by each group. Whereas an approach advocating pure free association is akin to a parliamentary system of government, U.S. labor law mirrors our national political system, which elects officials based on their receiving a majority of the votes in their district. The system avoids the problems associated with multiple minority groups and multiple conflicting interests by subjugating those interests to the will of the majority. It assumes that responsiveness to a majority of the people is important, not responsiveness to each interest and issue of every small group (or person).

Significant ethical issues arise from the requirement of majority rule. The system restricts free association rights, and in so doing it ensures opposition within a group that achieves majority rule because it is unlikely that every member desires the same thing in a group defined by bargaining unit rather than by class, religion, or a narrow interest. Although it has been argued that the NLRA preserves the right of "members-only unions" (Morris 2005), such unions are rare. In reality, majority rule creates difficulties for unions, forcing them to organize a unit of workers rather than an interested group of employees. It creates a situation in which disputes are inevitable between the majority and minority groups. And labor organizations must represent all workers, whether or not they join the union.

Majority rule in union organizing in the United States is typically determined by a formal election. This differs from the procedures used in other nations, such as Canada (see Godard 2002), where card checks may be used to determine the preferences of employees (see also Eaton and Kriesky 2001; Johnson 2004; Riddell 2004). It is well known that the U.S. election procedure is subject to lengthy delays, electioneering, and intimidation campaigns designed to convince workers to reject union representation (Freeman and Kleiner 1990; Kleiner 2001). Observers have assumed that unionization rates in the United States are lower today than they would be if some other form of certification mechanism for bargaining units were in effect (see Freeman and Rogers 1999).

Given majority-rule requirements, it is interesting that employers fight unionization so aggressively. For example, in the hospital industry, employers for many years argued for large and inclusive units, essentially because they believed unions could not organize such groups. Once unions had success in those units, employers made contrary arguments (see Delaney and Sockell 1988). The real issue here is that employers have opposed unionization in virtually all instances, despite the fact that U.S. law advocates collective bargaining. Some employers have blatantly disregarded the law and fired workers who sought to unionize or closed plants that were organizing (Freeman and Kleiner 1990). Such actions promote neither freedom (they are intended to ensure that workers do not freely choose a representative) nor human dignity (workers are subjected to economic sanctions such as job loss for exercising their legal rights). They reveal a devotion to economic self-interest in its basest form, which undermines moral action.

Compulsory Unionism

The system of majority rule and exclusive representation often creates situations in which some key concerns of one group may not be addressed, giving certain employees economic incentives to refuse to join the union. Why pay dues for services that must be provided equally to all members of a bargaining unit? This free-rider problem is one reason unions have engaged, where legally permitted to do so, in negotiating contract provisions requiring all members of the bargaining unit to pay dues or representation fees to the union. While unions see this as an issue of fairness—people paying for the services they receive—many individuals see it as being forced to support outcomes, views, and political perspectives with which they disagree (Haggard 1990). This situation has extended the debate about majority representation into another about *compulsory unionism.*

Legitimate concerns arise when people are required to support—through their payments—an organization that they chose not to join. When the organization is a union, the concerns are magnified, in part because employees need their jobs, because employers openly discredit unions, and because of past union practices. There is evidence that unions have at times favored members over nonmembers. Unions have also been guilty of racial discrimination. The courts were so concerned about discrimination by unions that they imposed on labor organizations a "duty of fair representation" toward all individuals in a bargaining unit (see Steele v. Louisville & Nashville Railroad 1944, Brotherhood of Railroad Trainmen v. Howard 1952).

Union efforts to require represented workers to join the union—compulsory unionism—raise other moral questions. Once again, ethical perspectives differ depending on the individual's view. Union explanations of compulsory unionism are not convincing. The primary argument is that because the union must represent all workers in a bargaining unit, all workers should pay for that representation. Otherwise, some individuals will act like "economic man" and accept the benefits of representation without paying for it. This public-good argument is flawed, however, as it ignores the fact that nonmembers do not have the opportunity to vote for union officers, provide input into negotiations, or vote to ratify contracts with an employer.

Moreover, compulsory unionism puts unions in an awful public position of needing to argue that workers should be forced to pay for union representation. Anti-union individuals rightly ask why covered workers refuse to join if union representation is so good. After all, during representation campaigns, union organizers argue that everyone will be much better off if they join the union than if they reject it. If that is the case, the benefits do not disappear when an organizing campaign is over. Moreover, in settings with many pro-union workers, social norms make it difficult for people to refuse to join. The problems of compulsory unionism have even led unionists to argue that the labor movement lost its moral high ground when it advocated contract provisions requiring workers to pay union dues to retain their jobs (Brooks 1976). Ethically, unions are in a vulnerable position when arguing that everyone in a unit covered by bargaining should be forced to pay union dues (Delaney 1998).

Compulsory unionism makes unions more prosperous, but it produces a two-tier system. Individuals in the minority are forced to provide financial support to a union that responds to the views of the majority in the unit—even if those views will never reflect the will of the minority.

Compulsory unionism combined with majority rule is ethically ambiguous on the freedom criterion. It promotes freedom of the majority but imposes costs on the minority. Covered individuals are likely to assess this system differently depending on whether they are in the majority or the minority. The approach is ethically acceptable—and appealing—to individuals who value efficiency outcomes (and the primacy of business organizations) and ethically unacceptable to the people whose views are discounted (or who are required to pay union dues against their wishes). To the extent that the dignity of the person is viewed as paramount, decisions to adopt compulsory unionism are problematic. Not only do they create an environment in which some people's dearly held views are subjugated, they force some people to support financially perspectives they do not accept. This in turn generates considerable concern and anger.

Inconsistent Member Views and Political Action

Because labor law greatly influences the success of unions, both employers and unions have reason to be politically active. The involvement of unions and businesses in the political process, however, has long been controversial (see Sabato 1984). Although political action is often a form of free speech, Congress has restricted some union and business political activities. In general, the regulations focus on participation in electoral activities rather than on involvement in lobbying activities. Since the early 1970s, unions and other organizations have been allowed to establish political action committees (PACs) to raise money donated voluntarily and contribute PAC funds to federal candidates. In addition, unions are permitted to use treasury (dues) money for properly reported lobbying activities (for a description of the regulations, see Masters and Delaney 2005).

Unions regularly use political tactics to support bargaining activity. Involvement in the political process, however, raises a number of concerns. The issue is not that unions should be prevented from participating in the political system. Rather it is the problem arising when union members lack a uniform political view, a situation that occurs regularly. This means that some members will support and others oppose specific union political activities. Because unions are legally permitted to use dues money to fund lobbying efforts, the dues of some members may be spent supporting political positions they oppose.

Policymakers and the courts have imposed restrictions to protect the interests of members who object to union political spending. The restrictions are intended to protect the freedom of individual members—at the expense of their union. In its most recent incarnation, conservative legislators have proposed a "Paycheck Protection Act" to address this issue (Hogler 1998; Clark 1999). The proposed law would require unions to get permission from members before spending money on political purposes. This is an interesting concept given that it applies only to unions and union members and not to corporations or nonprofit groups, which could spend money lobbying for legislation opposed by some shareholders or members. A majority of legislators apparently see no double standard in laws that restrict union political efforts but provide corporations with political carte blanche. This blind spot is probably created by the fact that corporations donate significant sums to political candidates (see Masters and Delaney 2005). Restrictions on unions serve corporate donors by reducing the campaign accounts of office seekers who may be sympathetic to unions or workers.

It is difficult from the freedom benchmark to justify any restrictions on political expenditures that are voluntarily contributed. As U.S. law has long required that expenditures on electoral activities be voluntary, such union and employer contributions to political candidates would seem to be ethical. From the human dignity benchmark, the issue is less clear. Since many political efforts are aimed at securing outcomes viewed as beneficial to corporations or unions, it is possible that the interests of employees are not considered. To the extent that large sums are spent opposing positions that are relevant to workers (e.g., safety and health regulations, wage and overtime regulations), some restrictions seem ethical. Congress appears to have little interest in regulating these donations, except in instances involving unions. Treating corporations differently raises ethical questions.

Employers are the single most powerful political force in the United States today, contributing a disproportionate share of campaign contributions to candidates for public office. In 2002, according to the Center for Responsive Politics, businesses gave more than $800 million, or about 64% of total contributions, to candidates for federal office; during that same election cycle, unions contributed $97 million (about 8% of the total) to candidates (Masters and Delaney 2005). The amount of money spent to lubricate the electoral process in the United States is troublesome. Notwithstanding politicians' denials that contributions buy votes, the cost of running for office requires candidates to spend time with and listen to contributors—especially big contributors. Whether the contributions are from labor or management, serious ethical considerations arise from this donation free-for-all.

Role of Democratic Union Structures

It is necessary to consider the organizational structure of unions before reaching final conclusions about the ethical challenges in labor relations. Specifically, because unions are democracies by law, they must follow internal procedures designed to protect the rights of members. Although some of the majority-rule issues mentioned earlier may be relevant here, the most important aspect for purposes of this analysis is whether unions' democratic structure warrants special consideration relative to other organizations. Are unions inherently more ethical because they tend to be democratic organizations? There is no unequivocal answer to the question, as democratic organizations can act in ways that treat members or nonmembers unethically. Certain differences in treatment may promote the dignity of union members at the expense of nonmembers. Although unions are organized in a manner that differs from private-sector organizations, their organizational form does not immunize them from questions about ethical matters that can be legitimately raised with for-profit corporations. In addition, because unions grant rights to members but are required to represent all workers in a bargaining unit, there are instances in which represented nonmembers may have fewer privileges than members.

Labor history has provided many examples of democratic union rules being used to promote the interests of certain members or officials over the interests of others. In some cases, the "democratic" rules selected by unions serve to protect entrenched interests—for example, for many years the Teamsters union did not grant individual members the right to vote directly for their national leaders. The enacted rules were democratic, but they also served the entrenched union leadership. Thus, democratic structures do not protect organizations from confrontations with ethical issues. An examination of union constitutions and conventions provides evidence of democratic rules that serve multiple purposes (Jarley, Fiorito, and Delaney 2000). To my knowledge, although a similar examination of company bylaws and annual meetings has not been conducted, firms regularly impose rules that give corporate officers wide discretion in their decisions. Hence, various organizational structures can support unethical conduct.

The Problem of Labor Law

As noted above, U.S. labor law governs worker–management interactions. But the NLRA was enacted in a different era. Although §1 of the act indicates that collective bargaining and the protection of workers' exercise of their "full freedom of association" are "hereby declared to be the policy of the United States," observers have suggested that the law is interpreted in ways that protect neither (see Adams 1992). This shapes and reflects numerous ethical issues. Because the law seeks to balance the rights of unions, employees, and employers, it was inevitable that ethical questions would arise from legal interpretations. The lack of consensus on workers' rights has fueled a persistent battle among forces advocating employees' rights, union representation rights, and employers' rights at the workplace. American employers seem never to have accepted the legitimacy of employees' self-organization rights (see Wolters 1980; Kochan, Katz, and McKersie 1986; Freeman and Kleiner 1990). This has fueled countless battles in legislatures, courts, and labor tribunals to reinterpret labor law (see Adler and Bigoness 1992; Gould 2000, 2004) and has raised questions about the underlying fairness of U.S. labor law (Gould 2000), the seeming political partisanship inherent in decisions interpreting labor law (Cooke and Gautschi 1982; Cooke, Mishra, Spreitzer, and Tschirhart 1995), and the willingness of parties—especially employers—to violate the law and evade its requirements (Greer and Martin 1978; Kleiner 1984, 2001).

The existence of disagreement between unions and managers is not new or surprising. While the debate over labor law has always been highly charged and emotional, it has generated great bitterness and animosity in recent years. Throughout, however, little attention has been paid to the morality of rules imposed by Congress, tactics chosen by the parties, ethical dimensions of the objectives sought, or the implications of the opportunistic labor relations culture that such approaches have created. Thus, unlike the contemporaneous business ethics scandals, the situation has *not* precipitated substantial discussion of ethical and moral lapses that seem to pervade the labor relations system.

Conclusion

It follows from the examination of selected labor relations issues that no single ethical standard or approach will be acceptable to union and management proponents on all issues. Each observer's perspective colors significantly the evaluation of the ethics of various issues, strategies, and actions. Moreover, when freedom is used as an ethical benchmark, an overall unambiguous answer to ethical queries is often not possible. Since the perspective of freedom, as preached by economic theory, dominates the political landscape in the United States today, labor relations will continue to be controversial in the near future. The growth of global markets will probably worsen this situation, given that the quest for efficiency often requires more exertion (or attention) from workers with no guarantee of extra rewards—establishing a classic zero-sum game. When efficiency is favored, it is easy to adopt legal strategies (such as closing high-cost plants) and illegal ones (such as firing union sympathizers) that follow an ethically ambiguous path to a preferred organizational objective.

In recent years, across the globe, unions have been on the defensive. Businesses and institutions of capital have been celebrated. As a result, unions have lost protections in some nations, and employees' support for unions at the workplace level has not been sufficient to stem the decline in union density. The main reason for the changed perspective is a concern about improving the state of the economy and the reality of the brutal nature of global markets and competition. Unions have been viewed negatively in this light because of the assumptions that efficiency is the primary objective in an economy and that labor organizations reduce efficiency. More important, the perspective presents itself as objective and nonpartisan, while allowing the real interests and concerns of working people to be subjugated to the theorized interests of labor in an economy. Because these real and theoretical interests do not necessarily match, the interests of workers, especially those with low skill levels, are given less consideration than the interests of institutions (and wealthy individuals) holding capital (Stiglitz 2002). Devotion to economic orthodoxy provides a mechanism and theory to reduce the rights of some so that those of others can be protected. It allows those who benefit from the current situation to argue that the concept of human dignity is irrelevant, as promotion of a capitalist system will provide the greatest benefit to the greatest number of people.

All this means that ethical issues are inherent in labor relations across the legal systems used by governments to regulate worker–management relationships. No system is more or less ethical than another. Depending on the specifics of the systems, either unions or employers are advantaged. Only in instances of strong adherence to social democratic institutions, as is the case in Scandinavian countries, do managers and union officials seem to have similar views. And even in those nations, pressure from globalization is forcing consideration of the idea that efficiency is more important than equity in society.

The issue of ethics in labor relations boils down to the question of whether it is necessary to achieve morally correct actions and outcomes at work. This question is unanswered in practice. Ironically, because so much is at stake, competing groups (including unions and employers) engage in political and other activities to secure self-interested outcomes. This has reduced the amount of ethical reflection and increased the use of self-interested justifications for preferred positions, outcomes, and decisions. No labor relations legal system can remove the moral issues that arise when competing interests exist at work and in society. This means that nations increasingly seem to assume that economic efficiency promotes social equality and that government laissez faire is the precursor to efficiency in markets. Put differently, evidence of increasing inequality in society is seen as a good thing. In such an environment, the ethical challenges in labor relations are likely to grow.

Acknowledgment

I wish to thank John Budd, Jim Scoville, and Susan Schwochau for the helpful comments, insights, and advice they provided as this chapter was being written.

References

Adams, Roy J. 1992. "Efficiency Is Not Enough." *Labor Studies Journal*, Vol. 17, no. 1 (Spring), pp. 18–28.
_____. 2001. "On the Convergence of Labour Rights and Human Rights: A Review Essay," *Relations Industrielles*, Vol. 56, no. 1 (Winter), pp. 199–203.
Adler, Robert S., and William J. Bigoness. 1992. "Contemporary Ethical Issues in Labor-Management Relations." *Journal of Business Ethics*, Vol. 11, no. 5 (May), pp. 351–60.
Appelbaum, Eileen, Thomas Bailey, Peter Berg, and Arne L. Kalleberg. 2000. *Manufacturing Advantage: Why High-Performance Work Systems Pay Off.* Ithaca, NY: ILR Press.
Brooks, George W. 1976. "Stability Versus Employee Free Choice." *Cornell Law Review*, Vol. 61, no. 3 (March), pp. 344–67.
Brotherhood of Railway Trainmen v. Howard, 343 U.S. 768 (1952).
Budd, John W. 2004. *Employment with a Human Face: Balancing Efficiency, Equity, and Voice.* Ithaca, NY: ILR Press.
_____. 2005. *Labor Relations: Striking a Balance.* Boston: McGraw-Hill/Irwin.
Clark, Paul F. 1999. "Using Members' Dues for Political Purposes: The Paycheck Protection Movement." *Journal of Labor Research*, Vol. 20, no. 3 (Summer), pp. 329–42.
Cooke, William N. 1985. "The Failure to Negotiate First Contracts: Determinants and Policy Implications." *Industrial and Labor Relations Review*, Vol. 38, no. 2 (January), pp. 163–78.
_____. 1994. "Employee Participation Programs, Group-Based Incentives, and Company Performance: A Union–Nonunion Comparison." *Industrial and Labor Relations Review*, Vol. 47, no. 4 (July), pp. 594–609.
Cooke, William N., and Frederick H. Gautschi III. 1982. "Political Bias in NLRB Unfair Labor Practice Decisions." *Industrial and Labor Relations Review*, Vol. 35, no. 4 (July), pp. 539–49.
Cooke, William N., Aneil K. Mishra, Gretchen M. Spreitzer, and Mary Tschirhart. 1995. "The Determinants of NLRB Decision-Making Revisited." *Industrial and Labor Relations Review*, Vol. 48, no. 2 (January), pp. 237–57.
Delaney, John T. 1998. "Redefining the Right-to-Work Debate: Unions and the Dilemma of Free Choice." *Journal of Labor Research*, Vol. 19, no. 3 (Summer), pp. 425–43.
_____. 2003. "Contemporary Developments in and Challenges to Collective Bargaining in the United States." In John T. Addison and Claus Schnabel, eds., *International Handbook of Trade Unions*. London: Edward Elgar, pp. 502–30.
Delaney, John T., David Lewin, and Donna Sockell. 1985. "The NLRA at Fifty: A Research Appraisal and Agenda." *Industrial and Labor Relations Review*, Vol. 39, no. 1 (October), pp. 46–75.

Delaney, John T., and Donna Sockell. 1988. "Hospital Unit Determination and the Preservation of Employee Free Choice." *Labor Law Journal*, Vol. 39, no. 5 (May), pp. 259–272.

Eaton, Adrienne E., and Jill Kriesky. 2001. "Union Organizing under Neutrality and Card Check Agreements." *Industrial and Labor Relations Review*, Vol. 55, no. 1 (October), pp. 42–59.

Fiorito, Jack, and Cheryl L. Maranto. 1987. "The Contemporary Decline of Union Strength." *Contemporary Policy Issues*, Vol. 5, no. 4 (October), pp. 12–27.

Freeman, Richard B., and Morris M. Kleiner. 1990. "Employer Behavior in the Face of Union Organizing Drives." *Industrial and Labor Relations Review*, Vol. 43, no. 3 (April), pp. 351–65.

Freeman, Richard B., and James L. Medoff. 1984. *What Do Unions Do?* New York: Basic Books.

Freeman, Richard B., and Joel Rogers. 1999. *What Workers Want*. Ithaca, NY: ILR Press.

Friedman, Milton. 1982. *Capitalism and Freedom*. Chicago: University of Chicago Press.

Godard, John. 2002. "Institutional Environments, Employer Practices, and States in Liberal Market Economies." *Industrial Relations*, Vol. 41, no. 2 (April), pp. 249–86.

Gould, William B. IV. 2000. *Labored Relations: Law, Politics, and the NLRB*. Cambridge, MA: MIT Press.

———. 2004. *A Primer on American Labor Law*, 4th ed. Cambridge: MIT Press.

Greer, Charles T., and Stanley A. Martin. 1978. "Calculative Strategy Decisions During Union Organization Campaigns." *Sloan Management Review*, Vol. 19, no. 2 (Winter), pp. 61–74.

Gross, James A. 2001. "Discussion." *Proceedings of the Fifty-Third Annual Meeting, January 5–7, New Orleans*. Champaign, IL: Industrial Relations Research Association, pp. 373–4.

Haggard, Thomas R. 1990. "Union Security and the Right to Work: A Comprehensive Bibliography." *Journal of Labor Research*, Vol. 11, no. 1 (Winter), pp. 81–106.

Higgins, Susan H. 1996. "Towards Taming the Labor-Management Frontier: A Strategic Marketing Framework." *Journal of Business Ethics*, Vol. 15, no. 4 (April), pp. 475–85.

Hogler, Raymond L. 1998. "Unions, Politics, and Power: The Ideology of Paycheck Protection Proposals." *Labor Law Journal*, Vol. 49, no. 10 (October), pp. 1195–1204.

Huselid, Mark A. 1995. "The Impact of Human Resource Management Practices on Turnover, Productivity, and Corporate Financial Performance." *Academy of Management Journal*, Vol. 38, no. 3 (June), pp. 635–72.

International Labour Organization. 1998. *ILO Declaration on Fundamental Principles and Rights at Work and Its Follow-Up*.

Jacoby, Sanford M. 1997. *Modern Manors: Welfare Capitalism Since the New Deal*. Princeton, NJ: Princeton University Press.

Jarley, Paul, Jack Fiorito, and John T. Delaney. 2000. "National Union Governance: An Empirically-Grounded Systems Approach." *Journal of Labor Research*, Vol. 21, no. 2 (Spring), pp. 227–46.

Johnson, Susan. 2004. "The Impact of Mandatory Votes on the Canada–U.S. Union Density Gap: A Note." *Industrial Relations*, Vol. 43, no. 2 (April), pp. 356–63.

Kant, Immanuel. [1785] 1959. *Foundations of the Metaphysics of Morals*. Translated by Lewis White Beck. Indianapolis: Bobbs-Merrill.

Kaufman, Bruce E. 1999. "Does the NLRA Constrain Employee Involvement and Participation Programs in Nonunion Companies? A Reassessment." *Yale Law and Policy Review*, Vol. 17, no. 2, pp. 729–811.

Kaufman, Bruce E., and Daphne Gottlieb Taras, eds. 1999. *Nonunion Employee Representation: History, Contemporary Practice, and Policy.* Armonk, NY: M.E. Sharpe.

Kleiner, Morris M. 1984. "Unionism and Employer Discrimination: Analysis of 8(a)(3) Violations." *Industrial Relations,* Vol. 23, no. 2 (Spring), pp. 234–43

_____. 2001. "Intensity of Management Resistance: Understanding the Decline of Unionization in the Private Sector." *Journal of Labor Research,* Vol. 22, no. 3 (Summer), pp. 519–40.

Kleiner, Morris M., and Marvin L. Bouillon. 1988. "Providing Business Information to Production Workers: Correlates of Compensation and Profitability." *Industrial and Labor Relations Review,* Vol. 41, no. 4 (July), pp. 605–17.

Kochan, Thomas A., Harry C. Katz, and Robert B. McKersie. 1986. *The Transformation of American Industrial Relations.* New York: Basic Books.

LeRoy, Michael H. 1995. "Employer Treatment of Permanently Replaced Strikers, 1935–1991: Public Policy Implications." *Yale Law and Policy Review,* Vol. 13, no. 1, pp. 1–43.

Logan, John. 2004. "Labor's Last Stand in National Politics? The Campaign for Striker Replacement Legislation, 1988–1996." Unpublished manuscript.

Masters, Marick F., and John T. Delaney. Forthcoming. "Organized Labor's Political Scorecard." In James T. Bennett and Bruce Kaufman, eds., *What Do Unions Do? A Twenty-Year Retrospective.* Fairfax, VA: Olin Institute.

McGurn, William. 2002. "Pulpit Economics." *First Things* Vol. 122 (April), pp. 21–5. <http://www.firstthings.com/ftissues/ft204/articles/Mcgurn.html>.

McIntyre, Richard, and Matthew M. Bodah. 2002. "The U.S. and ILO Conventions No. 87 and No. 98: The Freedom of Association and Right to Bargain Collectively." Paper presented at AFL-CIO/Michigan State University Worker Rights Conference, East Lansing, Michigan, October 11.

Mishel, Lawrence, Jared Bernstein, and Heather Boushey. 2003. *The State of Working America, 2002/2003.* Washington, DC: Economic Policy Institute.

Morris, Charles J. 2005. *The Blue Eagle at Work: Reclaiming Democratic Rights in the American Workplace.* Ithaca, NY: Cornell University Press.

NLRB v. Mackay Radio and Telegraph Co. 304 U.S. 333 (1938).

Pope John Paul II. 1981. *Laborem Exercens* (On Human Work). <www.vatican.va/holy_father/john_paul_ii/encyclicals/>.

_____. 1991. *Centesimus Annus* (The Hundredth Year). <www.vatican.va/holy_father/john_paul_ii/encyclicals/>.

Pope Leo XIII. 1891. *Rerum Novarum* (On the Condition of the Working Classes). <www.vatican.va/holy_father/Leo_iii/encyclicals/>.

Pope Pius XI. 1931. *Quadragesimo Anno* (The Fortieth Year: On Reconstruction of the Social Order). <www.vatican.va/holy_father/pius_xi/encyclicals/>.

Potter, Edward E. 2001. "Discussion." *Proceedings of the Fifty-Third Annual Meeting, January 5–7, New Orleans.* Champaign, IL: Industrial Relations Research Association, pp. 377–79.

Rachels, James. 1999. *The Elements of Moral Philosophy,* 3rd ed. New York: McGraw-Hill.

Riddell, Chris. 2004. "Union Certification Success under Voting Versus Card-Check Procedures: Evidence from British Columbia, 1978–1998." *Industrial and Labor Relations Review,* Vol. 57, no. 4 (July), pp. 493–517.

Sabato, Larry J. 1984. *PAC Power.* New York: Norton.

Steele v. Louisville & Nashville Railroad, 323 U.S. 192 (1944).

Stiglitz, Joseph E. 2002. "Employment, Social Justice and Societal Well-Being." *International Labour Review,* Vol. 141, no. 1–2, pp. 9–29.
United Nations. 1948. Universal Declaration of Human Rights. <www.un.org/ Overview/rights.html>.
United States Conference of Catholic Bishops. 1986. *Economic Justice for All.* Pastoral letter. Washington, DC.
Wolfe, Alan. 1997. "The Moral Meaning of Work." *Journal of Socio-Economics,* Vol. 26, no. 6, pp. 559–70.
Wolters, Roger S. 1980. "Union-Management Ideological Frames of Reference in Bargaining." *Proceedings of the 33rd Annual Meeting, September 5–7, Denver.* Madison, WI: IRRA, 1981, pp. 211–18.

CHAPTER 9

Ethical Practice in a Corporation: The Allina Case

JONATHAN E. BOOTH
University of Minnesota

RONALD S. HEINZ
Allina Health System

MICHAEL W. HOWE
Allina Health System

Corporations and other organizations increasingly are having to address human resource issues within an ethical framework. As organizations deal with ethical decision making, they face a major dilemma in terms of the need to consider and reconcile the many different ethical perspectives used by interested parties in viewing and evaluating decisions made by the organization.

The organization certainly has its own framework, which originates from delivering on its corporate mission to shareholders, customers, employees, and other stakeholders; from prudent use of financial resources; from production of high-quality, reliable products or services; and so on. The employees in the organization have their own framework, often somewhat different from one employee to the next. The employees' framework is likely to be based on what they consider to be fair and considerate treatment of themselves and their families. The community has yet another framework, based on how the organization functions from a legal and regulatory standpoint, how the organization contributes to (or detracts from) society, and how the organization treats its various stakeholders.

One such organization is Allina Health System in Minneapolis, Minnesota. Allina is a nonprofit system of hospitals, clinics, and other health-care services, providing care throughout Minnesota and western Wisconsin. At the present time, Allina owns and operates 11 hospitals, more than 40 clinics, hospice services, pharmacies, medical equipment providers, and emergency medical transportation services. In 2004 the organization had net revenues of $2.0 billion and has more than 22,000 employees.

In 2000 Allina, which at that time also included a large million-member health plan/insurer called Medica, was notified that it was being investigated by the Minnesota attorney general. As a nonprofit organization, Allina fell under the attorney general's responsibility for overseeing charitable organizations. The original reason for the investigation arose out of a media inquiry and focused on allegations that Medica had provided excessive sales incentives to customers and holiday gifts to board members.

As the attorney general's audit continued, the investigation broadened under allegations that Allina had misused public money and charitable contributions. The allegations suggested that Allina/Medica had excessive travel and entertainment expenses, had provided lavish gifts to employees, had utilized high-paid consultants and contractors for long periods, and had established programs and practices that had resulted in excessive compensation to senior executives. The attorney general held numerous press conferences and television and radio interviews to detail the allegations of abuse.

The investigation culminated in the summer of 2001. Following an agreement with the attorney general, Allina undertook a complete change in control. The CEO and COO agreed to resign their positions, and the board of directors was disbanded and reconstituted with members who were personally approved by the attorney general. Allina also spun off its health plan subsidiary, Medica, an action that the company had already been contemplating. In addition, the new Allina board and the attorney general agreed to a formal "memorandum of understanding" (MOU), under which the organization agreed to certain policies and practices that would guide its business actions going forward.

Under the MOU, Allina could no longer pay for or reimburse club memberships for employees. No out-of-state travel or purchases of gifts at company expense were allowed without the approval of the chairman of the board. Allina was required to significantly restrict its use of outside consultants, and significant constraints were established regarding the development and approval of executive compensation programs.

With the new board being given oversight responsibility to put the MOU into practice, the company was required to periodically report to the attorney general on its progress and actions. After Allina had operated under the MOU for about a year, the attorney general lifted the sanctions with the assurance that the board would provide ongoing oversight. This action brought to a close a publicly embarrassing period in

Allina's history. It ended a tumultuous time during which the company was quite vulnerable and its leadership was distracted from focusing on its core purpose—providing excellent health care to patients and families. The experience reiterated to Allina the importance of promoting and ensuring the use of ethical policies and practices by all of its employees. Had ethical and transparent practices and decision-making processes been effectively instituted, Allina might have avoided some of the embarrassment and negative press associated with the investigation. Most importantly, Allina's leadership would have been more likely to have full knowledge about credibility issues and mishandling of resources and would have been more prepared to proactively remedy these situations had an ethical framework already been in place. By not having particular ethical standards, consistently monitored and executed, Allina's board and management were forced to shift their focus from providing consistent, quality health care and had to focus more on answering the attorney general's inquiries and making dramatic changes internally within a rather short time frame.

Allina's Ethical Strategy

In addition to assuring the economic sustainability of the organization, one of the first orders of business for the new board of directors was to rebuild Allina's credibility and reputation, both internally and externally. This rebuilding process began with the development of a new mission, vision, and values through a very thoughtful, deliberate, and comprehensive collaboration between the board and management. The process covered many months and included input from the full spectrum of stakeholders: the board, upper management, physicians, employees, unions, and the community.

A central theme that emerged while developing the mission, vision, and values was ethics and integrity. The organization recognized that rebuilding needed to start with the foundation of an ethical framework. Table 1 highlights the result of this work and articulates Allina's mission, vision, and values (Allina Health System 2004b).

The newly created values emphasize integrity, trust, respect, compassion, and stewardship. In the context of Allina's mission and vision, these values stimulate ethical discussions within the everyday work life of each employee. The mission and vision clearly guide employees toward Allina's desired end result with every stakeholder interaction. As a frame of reference, the values signal behavioral expectations enabling employees to support Allina's mission and vision. Allina expects all employees to act consistently with the company's values and encourages them to discuss any individual or organizational action that appears to conflict with

TABLE 1
Allina's Mission, Vision, and Values

Mission	We serve our communities by providing exceptional care, as we prevent illness, restore health and provide comfort to all who entrust us with their care.
Vision	We will:
	• Put the patient first;
	• Make a difference in people's lives by providing exceptional care and service;
	• Create a healing environment where passionate people thrive and excel; and
	• Lead collaborative efforts that solve our community's health care challenges.
Values	*Integrity*—we match our actions with our words.
	Respect—we treat everyone with honor, dignity and courtesy.
	Trust—we act in the best interests of our patients, physicians, communities and one another.
	Compassion—we create a caring environment for our patients and one another.
	Stewardship—we use our resources wisely.

the implications of the values. At Allina, actions should not deviate from what is promised (integrity); honor, dignity, and courtesy should occur in every stakeholder interaction (respect); care is at the forefront of every decision and action (compassion); and individuals should monitor, properly use, and distribute capital, human capital, and other intangible or tangible resources (stewardship). These values provide an ethical check to ensure that behaviors are appropriate and align with Allina's goals.

The mission/vision/values process had just been completed when the board of directors hired a new CEO. At that point, Allina turned its attention to a comprehensive effort to share the mission, vision, and values with every one of its 22,000 employees. All leaders conducted discussions with their work teams and solicited input about the values that were demonstrated when employees performed at their best. In addition, managers led meetings with their staffs to uncover situations and conditions in which Allina and its employees were not embracing and following the values. In many cases, these employee meetings served as a significant catharsis for the organization as a whole. Many discussions were intensely emotional, with employees expressing anger, sadness, guilt, or embarrassment over the experiences of the past. The meetings facilitated and developed a commitment by most to behave in an honest and ethical way moving forward. In addition to facilitating employees' reception of the new mission, vision, and values, Allina instituted new tools specifically to ensure ethical practices.

Implementing Ethics: Allina's Ethical Tools

Allina developed a very deliberate strategy to fulfill its new ethical framework, starting with creating a culture of transparency. To achieve transparency, Allina opened up many decision processes to employees, provided full disclosure of major decisions to the workforce, and introduced decision-making processes that always contemplate the workforce as an interested stakeholder.

Secondly, Allina leadership developed a process to systematically ensure that major organizational decisions are thoroughly evaluated against the Allina values. This values-based decision-making process aids the decision-maker in determining the most effective and ethical solution for each business decision or issue, where there may not be a clear right or wrong choice. The process provides a framework to explore the implications of a decision on each of the values. It also provides guidance to think thoroughly through situations in which values come into conflict with a particular decision. A cadre of leaders has been trained to guide decision-makers through the use of the process.

A third part of the strategy was to develop a "just culture" throughout the organization. Just culture introduced a new mindset and tools that encourage employees to report and deal openly with errors, especially medical errors. Moving away from blame and punishment when responding to errors, Allina has focused on reporting, systemic analysis, and process improvement. The organization believes and continues to stress that a "blaming" culture inhibits transparency.

Transparency and Leadership Style

Once Allina's new board had entered into the MOU commitments, met with stakeholders throughout the organization, and created a new mission, values, and vision, they determined that they should begin to rebuild the company's reputation and credibility by striving to be transparent both internally and externally. They had experienced the consequences of a culture in which the business strategy and leadership style prevented the organization from fulfilling its community mission. During the earlier period, Allina had lost the confidence of its core stakeholders: management, employees, unions, physicians, and community leaders. The new board was determined to create a new culture based on increased transparency. Their reasoning was that in closed cultures people look out for themselves, whereas in open cultures, they make decisions by considering other's perspectives as well as their own.

The seriousness with which the board undertook this effort was evident in the specifications used for the CEO search, in their openness in communicating their intentions during the search, and ultimately in the selection of the new CEO. Once on board, the CEO had a mandate from the board to transform and reinvent the corporation in service of the newly created mission, vision, and values. Under the new CEO's leadership, Allina implemented several steps to ensure the creation of this culture of transparency.

A group of approximately 75 senior leaders and board members participated in a three-day meeting in 2003 to develop a new strategic plan. This became a transparent exercise when the strategic plan was shared with all employees. The employee unions had varying interests in the plan and its implementation, so employee representatives were informed about the changes to ensure a smoother, open transition. Obviously, not all employees were directly involved in executing the strategy, but great care was taken to illustrate how it aligned with the mission and vision and connected, at least indirectly, with every employee. This transparency continues to be reinforced by sharing with all Allina employees quarterly updates of organizational progress against the strategic plan.

Another action that underscored the culture of transparency was the creation of the Physician Leadership Team (PLT). As in many healthcare organizations, nonphysician businesspeople constituted Allina's leadership. Allina's staff physicians and the independent physicians are critical to mission delivery, but they were not part of the senior decision-making process. The creation of the PLT rectified this missing influence, placing physicians at the leadership table. The PLT is part of the Allina Leadership Team (ALT), the company's top leadership group, led by the CEO and comprising key staff and line officers. The PLT offers a physician's perspective on each major issue and decision being considered by the ALT. The PLT is considered an equal and integral member of the ALT and is required to contribute to and maintain ownership of assigned business issues and decisions. An additional PLT responsibility is to be informational ambassadors, sharing the team's experiences and observations throughout the medical community. The establishment of the PLT has done much to open up Allina's decision making to a much broader set of stakeholders.

To eliminate redundancies and productivity problems that result in communication breakdowns and limited visibility into organizational issues, Allina has decided to move its corporate and shared services staff from various sites to one location. Enhancing communication, increasing productivity, and reducing costs will be achieved by integrating these groups at a single, central headquarters site. To further transparency, an employee advisory team was created to represent and educate all of Allina's staff about the facilities move and to provide perspective and suggestions to those charged with selecting and designing the new headquarters.

Additionally, the CEO created an internal website called "On My Mind" that is accessible to all employees, physicians, and directors. The site allows the CEO to share the direction of the organization and inter-act with all of Allina's stakeholders, to respond publicly to concerns and questions submitted by employees and other stakeholders, to educate everyone about key challenges, and to communicate what's keeping him up at night. The site has been used to solicit employee input into key issues and to inform everyone of prospective changes in a way that allows all to anticipate implications and react to issues if they so choose.

The CEO made an ultimate demonstration of transparency in post-ing on his "On My Mind" website a summary of the performance review he received from the board of directors. He essentially shared with all employees what, in the estimation of the board, he was doing well and not so well and what he needed to improve. This level of self-disclosure did much to assure the entire organization that no secrets were being withheld from stakeholders.

Allina recognized that it was necessary to ensure that the company's leadership broadly understood the new expectations and developed the competencies required to lead a more transparent organization. As a result, a set of leadership commitments and supporting competencies necessary to fulfill the commitments was established and communicated to all manage-ment. The Leadership Commitments and Competencies have been incor-porated into a patterned interview selection methodology used for each vice-president hire, have been incorporated into the CEO performance review format and used for 360-degree feedback in the process, have served as the core component in the leadership talent review and develop-ment process for all management (i.e., used for the business directors up to the CEO), and have been central in the recent Leadership Cornerstone Program that brought all 1,400 managers together to better understand expectations and learn essential skills to support the expectations.

Figure 1 illustrates Allina's Leadership Commitments and Competen-cies (Allina Health System 2003), which set high expectations for leaders to demonstrate a responsive, transparent, and engaging organizational culture. The wheel's core identifies Allina's expectation of all managers: performance excellence. Arising from the company's mission, the commitments, dis-played in the inner circle, lead to performance excellence and articulate the principal components that Allina's leaders must pledge to uphold.

Leaders are expected to act courageously to inspire high performance, build a collaborative culture, convey passion to the mission, foster joy and optimism in the workplace, and enable a caring community to inspire exceptional care. However, the decisive commitment that should guide a manager ethically is "live the values." The competencies, identified on the wheel's outer circle, align with a commitment and provide behavioral, defining dimensions and a skill set for each commitment. Table 2 defines

FIGURE 1
Allina's Leadership Commitments and Competencies Wheel

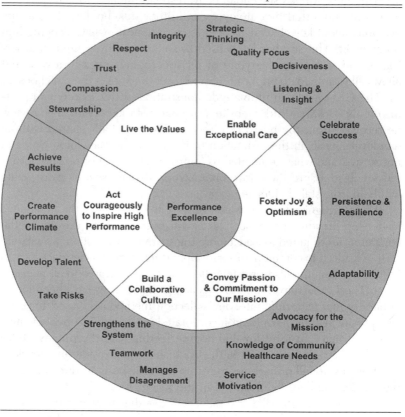

the competencies for "live the values" and specifies for leaders the behavioral expectations to which they should hold themselves and their team accountable (Allina Health System 2003). The value commitments and competencies are the cornerstone for ethical action within Allina; they are required for appropriate decision-making, use of Allina's ethical tools, and interaction with every stakeholder. Together, the commitments and competencies set the stage for demonstrating a leadership style that encourages an ethical culture and results in the discretionary employee effort necessary to provide exceptional patient care and service.

Values-Based Decision-Making

Allina has created a tool to help leaders and teams make better ethical and business decisions. The Values-Based Decision-Making (VBDM)

TABLE 2
Allina's "Live the Values" Competency Definitions

Commitment: Live the Values and Challenge Others to Live Them	
Integrity	Explicitly uses the values in decision-making; follows through and delivers on promises; takes accountability for decisions, works with others in an open and honest fashion; pursues and acts on feedback about his/her impact on others; knows own strengths and weaknesses and pursues personal growth.
Respect	Treats others with dignity and courtesy; respects and values the beliefs, traditions and cultures of others; recognizes and utilizes the skills and talents of others; values the opinions of others; supports opportunities for all.
Trust	Speaks openly about beliefs, values and intentions; matches actions with words; addresses problems in a consistent and fair manner; earns the confidence of co-workers; provides relevant information to others so they can make informed decisions.
Compassion	Offers help and conveys concern for others; has empathy for other's needs and feelings; supports the physical, emotional and spiritual well-being of colleagues.
Stewardship	Uses organizational resources wisely; practices sound financial management; nurtures the energy and talent of coworkers; shares credit with others; monitors demands on self and others and creates opportunities for renewal.

tool is intended to instill Allina's mission, values, and vision within each and every decision that is made throughout the organization. Allina believes that by incorporating the mission, values, and vision into everyday decision-making, they will create a more stable, secure, and honest environment. Figure 2 outlines the steps that Allina takes in its VBDM assessments (Allina Health System 2004a).

The first step of the VBDM tool is to determine if the decision has value-based implications. The leader or team must deliberately question the proposed decision to ensure that it does not affect patient care; does not compromise Allina's commitments to employees, physicians, and the communities that the company serves; does not affect the reputation of the organization; does not impede organizational goals and strategies; does not require exorbitant funding; or does not conflict with one's individual conscience or the group's collective conscience. If any one of these questions is answered yes, the manager or team must approach step two.

Step two utilizes one or more resource options that assure values-based reflection: using the values checklist, seeking a values-based consultation, or using the structured discussion format. With the values checklist, the leader or the team simply assesses the potential decision to see if it mirrors and achieves Allina's mission, values, and vision.

Values-based consultation asks that the leader or team locate a confidential in-house consultant who is trained and has experience with the appropriate application of Allina's values and healthcare ethical principles.

FIGURE 2
Allina's Values-Based Decision-Making Tool

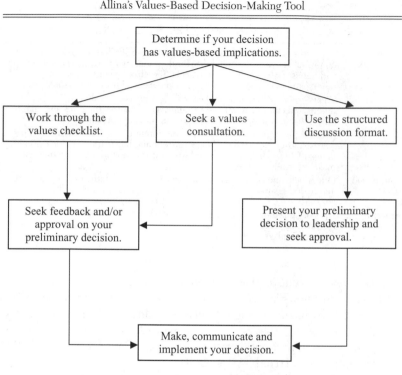

Allina has identified and trained consultative support staff ("value experts") to assist the manager with collecting needed information, creating a framework that accounts for crucial decision factors, and assisting with reflective discourse among all stakeholders.

According to Allina, decisions that significantly impact patient care, employees, and Allina's community commitments require a more comprehensive and disciplined decision analysis that should include all stakeholder perspectives; this element is called the structured discussion format. The format requires all stakeholders to be gathered for a dialogue and advises managers or teams to also involve Allina's in-house "value experts." Allina believes that multiple views and backgrounds are required at the table when values are being considered for a difficult and multifaceted decision. The structured discussion format is a deliberative approach that enables purposeful, unambiguous, and concise discourse. In addition, it is designed to facilitate prioritization of Allina's values for the particular decision in question. If values are in conflict or if consensus is not instantaneous, value prioritization tends to be useful. Identification of the more applicable values can assist further with developing a resolution or a consensus. The steps for the structured discussion format are outlined in Table 3 (Allina Health System 2004a).

After the completion of step two in the VBDM tool, Allina requires the decision-maker to seek feedback and/or approval on the preliminary decision. If the decision-maker used the values checklist or the values-based consultation, the leader or team must thoroughly examine the decision privately with trusted, knowledgeable peers who may provide thoughtful insight on how the decision may be perceived by or affect all key stakeholders. If the structured discussion format is used for decision assessment, the recommended decision must be presented and approved by leadership.

Finally, step four involves finalizing the decision and communicating and implementing it. Throughout the implementation, the decision-maker or team should always educate and conduct discussions with the stakeholders using values-based justifications.

Just Culture

Many healthcare providers function under a traditional punitive system: a staff member who makes a mistake pays for it. The individual may

TABLE 3
Allina's Values-Based Decision-Making Structured Discussion Format

1. Identify the preliminary decision and state the facts.
   Ensure that everyone understands the issue and the goal of the conversation. Clarify the issues, concerns, and challenges arising from the decision. Share the results of the Values Checklist process and name the values that may be in tension. State or represent the preferred outcomes and rationale for each stakeholder, attempting to preserve the "best interests" of stakeholders who are not present by thoughtfully weighing the benefits and burdens of each option.

2. Invite and identify options for consideration.
   Thoroughly discuss how the mission and vision statements and each value may inform the options. Invite reflective dialogue, honoring each person's perspective. Seek to build consensus among all participants, noting how the values can shape either consensus or compromise.

3. Prioritize the values.
   If necessary, ask the group which values seem most important to guide this decision. Have each participant openly vote for their top two preferred values, giving two points for the first choice and one point for the second choice. Use this point process to rank the top values.

4. Make the decision.
   Carefully reconsider the options in light of how you prioritized the values, building a consensus for the one option that most reflects the top value.

5. Create an action plan for communicating the decision.
   The plan should include the rationale that explicitly acknowledges how the mission, vision, and values played a role in your decision-making process, and strategies for informing all stakeholders of the decision.

be reprimanded, placed on probation, or fired immediately based on the severity of the error.

Healthcare professionals place a huge importance on conducting themselves professionally and providing patients with the best service and utmost respect. Often professionals self-inflict a lot of pressure to do their best jobs. They expect their peers to do the same and actually place added pressure on each other to perform.

The irony of this pressure is that healthcare professionals often believe that they are incapable of making medical errors and mistakes. Many believe that they are so dedicated that they are infallible. In fact, many think that an employee found to have committed an unintentional mistake should be fired immediately. At Allina, for example, a nursing manager stated that she would not bring her family to a hospital that did not enact punitive actions against personnel determined to have committed errors (even for first occurrences).

However, the pressures that healthcare providers place on themselves and each other in a punitive system can result in underreporting or covering up errors. A provider who self-reports an error fears losing his or her job and being ostracized by peers. Though healthcare professionals pressure each other, a sense of camaraderie does exist. A provider does not desire to be labeled a whistleblower within an organization or known as the one who "eliminated a friend's position" by reporting another for committing a violation. Thus, healthcare personnel may have a tendency to overlook errors that are not blatant.

Additionally, all employees understand the red tape, bureaucracy, and procedures involved when mistakes are identified. The individual potentially must go through an intensive investigation process with an extensive paper trail. Depending on the circumstances, a human resources department normally has an obligation to report the provider to his or her licensing board for further investigation. These processes take time and often remove affected individuals from their obvious passion—providing quality health care. Removing an employee who consistently provides exceptional care but may have made a minor error also can be costly to the organization. If management has to relieve an employee of duties, the likely result will be understaffing; the manager will have to either ask the other staff to fulfill the duties of the absent staff member or find a replacement. The staff member likely views these processes as obstacles and perhaps would rather ignore carelessness than undergo scrutiny.

These facets of the traditional system discourage expeditious and thorough reporting of errors, which is very problematic with respect to patient safety. Management cannot address errors quickly and appropriately train and educate staff to avoid further errors if errors are never reported. Late notice of errors does not just place patients in potential jeopardy; it also jeopardizes the facility and staff because the hospital is unable to mitigate issues in a timely fashion to stop or avoid further damage, such as lawsuits or investigations by governmental agencies.

These struggles and the nature of the healthcare culture prompted Allina to look for alternatives to the punitive system. Realizing that the system does not foster the reporting of errors and inherently hurts patients, Allina wanted to find a program that enables individuals to act ethically by reporting themselves or their colleagues while remaining confident that their jobs will be protected. However, the new program still needed to instill accountability and distinguish between the provider who gives consistent health care but due to human error makes a rare mistake and the repeat offender who has utter disregard for the oath to protect patients' interests (such as someone who consistently reports to work under the influence of drugs or alcohol). Ultimately, Allina needed a system that its employees and patients could trust and that would work seamlessly and effectively.

After thoroughly investigating the situation and inquiring how other hospital systems handle error reporting, Allina determined that a "just culture" would foster its core values of creating a safe environment for patients and employees. As well, just culture blends well with Allina's long-term organizational goal to implement a "blameless" culture. Just culture facilitates an environment in which it is safe to report and learn from mistakes; the organization as a whole is allowed further openness and mandates that errors be reported while ensuring that reported errors are dealt with in an environment of learning and continuous improvement. In addition, Allina received support for the implementation of "just culture" from the nurses' union. The union has concluded that the change is in the best interest of its membership and has encouraged immediate implementation of "just culture" throughout Allina's hospital network. Additionally, the union has been instrumental in notifying, educating, and supporting its membership throughout this cultural change.

Though the public's support of "just culture" is not fully known, some idea of the likely receptivity can be inferred from a recent event that occurred at a non-Allina hospital. Several weeks after surgery, a patient "discovered what looked like a tiny piece of metal poking out of her abdomen" (Lerner 2005). The patient visited her doctor to investigate her concern, and the physician found a "5 1/4-inch metal clamp inside [the patient's] abdomen" (Lerner 2005). The physician immediately informed the patient and her spouse and profusely apologized for such an oversight. Throughout the hospital's investigation of the error, the physician kept the patient informed of the investigative process and the steps the hospital was taking to ensure that this event would not occur again. The hospital also held a meeting with everyone involved in the surgery to conduct an analysis to determine exactly what went wrong. In addition, the hospital adopted a new policy to X-ray patients after all lengthy surgeries to verify that foreign objects are not left inside the body.

The patient chose not to sue the hospital and the physician because the hospital and staff were so forthright and apologetic about the medical error, included her in the investigative details and process, and provided her reassurance through a policy change that this mistake would not be repeated. Although this incident did not occur at an Allina hospital, the implications hold for Allina and all other hospitals. Patients value honesty and require immediate and detailed information about their situations. A simple apology and explanation with added assurance that faulty systems and processes have been remedied and improved can be adequate to please and comfort the patient. Though Minnesota hospitals are now required by state law to report all medical errors to the public via the Minnesota Department of Health, hospitals are realizing the benefits of an open and learning environment where errors can be reported. As noted in the newspaper account of this event, "For a long time, the idea of confessing medical mistakes was seen as professional suicide" (Lerner 2005). By breaking the silence, hospitals are enabled to treat their patients and staff more ethically and to decrease the risks of hurting other patients and of incurring financial damage to the institution.

In keeping with a new commitment to "just culture," Allina was one of several healthcare organizations in Minnesota to convince the state legislature to create the nation's first Patient Safety Registry that publicly reports medical errors. The first report issued by the Minnesota Department of Health was released on January 19, 2005. Through being instrumental in the creation of the registry, Allina has reiterated its goal of high reliability. By definition, to be a high-reliability organization a facility must be committed to reporting, learning, accountability, and justice. In essence, a high-reliability organization is one where learning and blame cannot coexist. Punitive cultures do not work in a high-reliability organization because the organization cannot reach the reliability level necessary to deliver consistent outcomes. If errors are not consistently and accurately reported, the healthcare facility will not be able to provide consistent safety of care. The key to achieving this new culture is understanding systems and understanding how they can fail and how they can maintain their reliability. Proper error reporting aids in this understanding; however, to ensure that reporting occurs, personnel must understand that they will not be held responsible for unsafe and unreliable systems. Thus, it has become Allina's goal to readjust its internal culture.

In August 2004, the Just Culture Implementation Team presented to the ALT key principles that are essential to carrying a just culture forward.

Allina must be committed to a learning environment that encourages reporting of all mistakes, errors, adverse events and system weaknesses. The organization must reveal its commitment to continuous improvement of work processes and systems to ensure the highest level of patient and staff safety. Allina must encourage and expect its staff to report all types of adverse events and good catches (an error being "caught" prior to harm or for any other reason). Reporting system weaknesses as a means to assess and improve processes that provide a safe environment for patients and employees must also be encouraged. A punitive culture inhibits reporting; thus, management must not intend to generate fear, impose punishment or retaliate when employees make or report errors. Finally, leadership must encourage the use of non-disciplinary actions (including coaching, non-disciplinary counseling, additional education or training, demonstration of competency or additional supervision) to address performance issues, correct skill or knowledge deficits, and prevent future errors (Balik, Peterson, and Watson 2004:1).

Critics of just culture may argue that a supposedly blameless or blame-free environment has no accountability element and is inherently more injurious to the patient base than a punitive system. But the report presented to the Allina management notes that accountability is key to successful implementation and survival of just culture. Thus, Allina holds its management accountable for the following activities:

- Set high performance standards, enable employees to achieve the standards, and coach employees to improve performance,
- Fully assess all errors and good catches,
- Correct work conditions and improve policies/procedures to reduce the chance that a patient might be harmed,
- Communicate to the employees frequently about safety concerns, issues and improvement plans,
- Implement appropriate staff recommendations for error prevention strategies,

- Train and educate individuals and provide equipment and resources so that each person's responsibilities can be completed safely and reliably,
- Promote a "just culture" of non-punitive error reporting and continuous safety (Balik, Peterson, and Watson 2004:1–2).

In addition, Allina has standards for which it holds all nonmanagerial employees accountable. Employees must notify their supervisors immediately of any adverse events, errors, and near-misses. They must comprehend and pursue all policies and procedures applicable to their jobs and perform duties properly to ensure that no harm to any patient occurs. Employee involvement is key in the just culture because employees are expected to share personal knowledge of what went wrong when an error occurs and to aid in improving systems to decrease the chances that an error will reoccur (Balik, Peterson, and Watson 2004).

To a critic, a just culture may sound like a free ride with no repercussions for intentional mistakes, repeated mistakes, or incompetence. It is important to remember that just culture hinges on nonpunitive reconciliation in the case of errors made when personnel are correctly following policy and processes or when policy and processes do not exist or are ambiguous. Gray areas and exceptions do exist, and they may merit punitive actions.

Borrowing from the Missouri Baptist Medical Center in St. Louis, Missouri, and from the work of James Reason, professor emeritus of psychology, University of Manchester, United Kingdom, Allina has modified a measuring instrument for assessing errors in a nonpunitive culture. The tool, "Assessing Unsafe Acts in a Non-Punitive Culture," is a linear spectrum; nonpunitive actions fall on the right of the spectrum, exceptions on the left, and gray areas at the midpoint. Allina defines a gray area as a lax compliance, an unintentional mistake with policy and processes, or straying from policy and processes. When approaching a gray-area mistake, leadership must ask if the act or omission was intentional, was a repeated occurrence, was knowingly a violation, and/or was due to personnel incompetence. An exception that receives immediate punitive action is one deemed reckless, intentional, a repeated violation of policy, related to drug or alcohol abuse, and/or a criminal act. In the new system, an individual found to have not reported an error is more likely to receive a reprimand than had he or she reported the mistake initially.

Ethics in Action at Allina

These three tools—transparency, the VBDM tool, and just culture—better enable Allina to act ethically. Transparency provides Allina the ability to exemplify that it is an open and truthful organization with all of its stakeholders. The VBDM tool is a standard for any Allina decision-maker to determine ethical choices that consider all perspectives. Finally, the change from a punitive system to a just culture allows Allina to better protect its patients, its employees, and itself. The tools are used in many ways, but to better reveal the tool applications, we will discuss three examples.

Error in Judgment: Using Just-Culture Practices

The application of just culture can result in gray areas, as we have discussed. However, by using the "Assessing Unsafe Acts in a Non-Punitive Culture" tool, Allina has reaped benefits in handling these gray-area scenarios. Consider an actual example that occurred in 2004.

A night nurse recommended that a family member leave an elderly relative in her room for the night. The nurse reminded the family member that it was the nurse's role to keep watch on the patient. Given the nurses on duty, the nurse insisted that the elderly patient would have no risk of climbing out of bed and potentially breaking a hip. The nurse sent the family member home to sleep.

Concerned that the patient needed quiet to sleep and not thinking of hospital policy, the nurse closed the door to the patient's room. During the night between patient checks, the patient climbed out of her bed and fell, breaking her hip. Because the door was shut, the nurses on the wing were unable to hear the alarm triggered by the patient's getting out of bed.

The nurse reported the situation immediately. In a punitive culture, the nurse would have been severely reprimanded and potentially placed on probation. However, by using the company's new error assessment tool, management was able to analyze the error and treat the nurse in a more ethical manner.

Management determined that the nurse did violate hospital policy by closing the door; however, the nurse's actions were not intended to harm the patient and had not occurred before. The nurse's actions were based on her thinking she was following correct procedure for the best interest of the patient. In this more ethical framework, management reviewed hospital policy with the nurse to reiterate the nurse's obligations and duties and verified that the nurse understood her error and the appropriate measures to follow if confronted with a similar decision in the future. The nurse was trained accordingly by management and allowed to continue working.

The treatment of the nurse was conducted in a transparent nature so that other employees could witness the truthfulness and dedication of management behind just culture. Due to the transparency, other nurses were able to learn from the mistake of this nurse. In addition, the values of Allina were upheld in treating the nurse ethically and reiterated to Allina personnel that the company does foster its mission, vision, and values.

Social Responsibility: Headquarters Relocation

Another example of ethical application within Allina is the process for deciding where to locate corporate headquarters. Allina's corporate, administrative, and operational services were housed in 13 buildings spread across eight different communities in the Minneapolis/St. Paul area. These facilities accommodated 1,450 employees in 432,000 square feet of space. Some locations were owned while others were leased.

Management presented a strategic plan to the Allina board of directors that recommended consolidating nine of the 13 sites into a centrally located facility. The other four sites were excluded because of minimal interdependencies with the consolidated functions and services and the financial implications associated with their co-location. Through consolidations and implementation of workplace standards, the space plan for the consolidated employees represented a reduction of approximately 90,000 square feet from currently used space.

Over a 10-month period, management conducted a comprehensive study of potential sites and evaluated them with an employee task force and a board subcommittee. From more than 80 possibilities, three sites were identified as being most viable.

Although it was a very difficult task, the board made a mission- and values-based decision highly influenced by the amount of stakeholder involvement and transparent communication practices established within the values-based decision-making process. The "Allina Commons Employee Advisory Team" was established to ensure that employee perspectives and input guided the design and implementation of the facility. Allina did not have consistent space standards or office practices prior to beginning this process. The drivers set by the team included cost, flexibility, and operational efficiency.

The advisory team focused on assuring that employee feedback mechanisms existed to ensure broad input into space design. The team implemented an internal communications plan that engaged affected employees and built understanding and support for relocation. Team-building activities were designed and put into practice that supported a positive, collaborative culture and reinforced the Allina mission and values.

Employees were surveyed about their interests and suggestions regarding overall objectives, location, space design, aesthetics, and office standards. Focus groups were conducted with employees to better understand brand issues, messages with stakeholders, motivations for working at Allina, expectations of the new space, and images they would like Allina to represent.

Management determined that five objectives were important to creating a new culture: embedding the mission, vision, and values into daily actions, behaviors, and decisions; implementing a philosophy of "systemness"; reflecting a common transparent style of leadership; supporting culture with symbols, rituals, and celebrations; and ensuring alignment of internal incentives. Allina consistently followed these objectives in making decisions related to the relocation.

The board valued the work of the employee advisory committee and weighted the VBDM process heavily as it received management's recommendations. In thoughtful but sometimes conflicting deliberations, the board ultimately chose a site based on Allina's mission and values. First, they selected one best site based on the desire to serve Allina's charitable objective of creating a positive impact on its neighborhood. In addition, the board wanted to meet corporate staff needs by locating the headquarters near a significant healthcare delivery site. Finally, the board was able to negotiate a long-term third-party lease that was financially advantageous to Allina.

Ultimately, the Allina Commons will be completely open space with no offices—even for the CEO. The headquarters will be located in the Minneapolis inner city, within an urban renewal area next to a major healthcare site. This extensive process included not only the Allina board but also major involvement with city, county, and state officials. While Allina's predominant financial responsibility to this project will be the construction of its corporate office building and parking facility, the company's commitment as a base tenant has facilitated further investment in the neighborhood by other corporations, and a much larger neighborhood revitalization program has been created. As a result, a freestanding 126-room hotel, 350 units of housing, 110,000 square feet of speculative office space, and 60,000 square feet of retail space will be located adjacent to the new Allina Commons area. The corporation has demonstrated leadership by aligning its interests with the communities it serves.

Redesign of Benefit Plans

In early 2004 Allina undertook an effort to redesign its benefit plans with a need to remove $100 million in projected cost increases over a five-year period. Cost management on this scale requires either significant benefit reductions or cost shifting to employees; both involve a number of ethical issues. Several of the aforementioned tools were utilized during the benefit redesign process to ensure an alignment of the decisions with the values framework.

At the beginning of the process, the CEO and business unit presidents created design principles that ultimately were approved by the Allina board. These principles, closely tied to the organizational values, included themes such as providing employees affordable choices and protecting them from financial catastrophe. An employee engagement survey and a specifically designed employee benefits survey were used to obtain feedback from both union and non-union employees and to assess employee readiness for the considerable change that was being introduced. Labor management committees that support bargaining units were consulted by Allina's leadership about the benefit changes. In all cases, union representatives were notified of the prospective designs. Though the unions were not keen about benefit changes, Allina's leadership did value their opinions and considered their reactions as input to the redesign decisions. In addition, Allina honored the union contracts that prohibited benefit changes during the contract period. Finally, the CEO used the "On My Mind" website to share his point of view and some very honest messages with employees about the coming changes and to solicit employee questions.

The final design recommendations were subjected to a values-based decision-making process with a group of senior managers, who considered the trade-offs of the recommendations with respect to values including stewardship, compassion, and integrity. The results of this process along with some associated advice were shared with all senior leadership as part of the final review and approval of the design recommendations.

At the end of the process, Allina believed that the benefit changes, although not popular with employees, were thoroughly rooted in the organizational values and had gone through an ethics "filter." Though the policies and practices guide Allina to act and make decisions in a more ethical manner, the ethical framework does not eliminate differences of opinion, nor does it dilute dispute resolution processes. A number of issues with ethical implications did surface and were considered during the benefit redesign process; they will continue to be studied and discussed during future benefit decision making. For example, the impact of changes for low-income versus high-income earners led to discussion of the percentage of take-home pay that medical benefits should cost Allina employees. Another question that was addressed is the differential impact between employees who are covered by a union contract and employees who are not covered (employees who are not covered by a union contract often pay more for the same benefits). Allina's leadership believes that the process allowed these issues to be identified and provided for sufficient consideration. In spite of the many efforts to include all parties in the process and discourse, Allina realizes that it may receive future grievances from the unions. However, given the transparency and values-based tools, senior leaders are comfortable standing behind the benefit changes. In addition, these ethical tools will continue to guide Allina in its future benefit considerations and in discussions with all stakeholders, both union and nonunion.

Conclusion

As a result of the initial investigation by the Minnesota attorney general's office, Allina determined that it had to reevaluate its ethical presence and the inclusion of all of its stakeholders. This reevaluation has provided a rebirth and restructuring of the company's mission, vision, values, and culture and the tools that it applies to ensure its ethical soundness. From the frontline employee to the CEO, Allina has created strategy and tools, including a new mission, vision, and values; transparency; leadership commitments and competencies; values-based decision-making; and just culture, with the goal of enabling each of its employees to act, behave, and decide in a more ethical manner. Allina's leadership continually is learning and demonstrating the business value of becoming a more ethical enterprise by following and building policies and practices that reinforce its ethical framework. By being more explicit and transparent about its internal ethical practices, Allina also has become a better citizen to the external community.

Given the nature of health care and care delivery, Allina's employees, management, and board undoubtedly will continue to face daily ethical dilemmas. Breakthrough technologies and the pressures for increased organizational efficiency and effectiveness of care delivery processes will continue to challenge all healthcare organizations. The strategies and tools this chapter has discussed, when hardwired into the organization, will better equip Allina to address future ethical issues in a transparent businesslike manner. Though growing pains are inevitable, Allina has learned from its former unfortunate experiences that it has the capacity to change and is positioned to adapt, take control, and proactively lead in the face of future adversarial conditions.

Allina's experiences could be encountered by any organization. Organizations must realize that they are not immune to ethical dilemmas and probably face ethical decisions daily. However, they should not become discouraged when confronted with ethical issues, because change is feasible.

As demonstrated by Allina, ethical transformations can be achieved through organizational perseverance, forethought, humility, creativity, accountability, and adequate funding commitments, as well as a "change" commitment and mindset that is fostered and embraced by all employees and stakeholders.

References

Allina Health System. 2003. *Allina Leadership Commitments and Competencies.* Minneapolis: Allina Health System.
————. 2004a. *A Guide to Making Values-Based Decisions.* Minneapolis: Allina Health System.
————. 2004b. *Allina's Good to Great Journey: 2004 Strategy Overview.* Minneapolis: Allina Health System.
Balik, Barbara, Lori Peterson, and Nancy Watson. 2004. *Just Culture Principles.* Minneapolis: Allina Health System, pp. i–5.
Lerner, Maura. 2005. "When Words Help to Heal a Medical Error." *The Star Tribune,* January 23. <http://www.startribune.com/stories/1556/5199521.html>. [January 30, 2005].

CHAPTER 10

Ethical Practice in a Labor Union: The UAW Case

LINDA EWING
United Auto Workers

Within the labor movement, discussions of ethical practice invariably return to the idea of union leadership as a "sacred trust." There are good reasons for that. The individuals whom union leaders report to aren't anonymous, as a corporation's shareholders generally are. They—the union members—aren't called brothers and sisters lightly. They have names and faces; they work hard, in jobs the union's leaders know very well; they share certain core values and life experiences. When members entrust their dues to the union, moreover, those dollars carry hopes and expectations very different from those of investors purchasing shares of company stock. Investors expect honest financial statements, while hoping for a decent return on their investments. They don't (generally) hope for that investment to transform their lives—much less the world.

The growth of industrial unions, in contrast, arose from a movement that had as its aim nothing less than the transformation of workers' lives and of the society in which they lived them. Those aims continue to shape the hopes and expectations of union members today. Members expect their representatives to advocate for them in the workplace. They also expect opportunities to voice opinions, set the union's priorities, and shape their own future. They hope for a rising standard of living and for better working conditions. In many cases, they also draw satisfaction and inspiration from being part of something—a movement—bigger than themselves.

These basic distinctions shape the way unions approach ethics, and they create unique issues and institutional dilemmas. In part, they simply raise the ethical bar. As Walter Reuther, the UAW's much-revered late president, once remarked, conduct accepted as perfectly proper for a business executive—say, using personal connections to "make a fast million dollars"—qualifies as corruption in a labor leader (Reuther 1957:66). Historically, the UAW has responded by creating clear ethical standards, with an emphasis on bright lines that must not be crossed. The goal is to preclude (drawing again on Reuther's perceptive words) the "process of little compromises that lead to big compromises . . . cutting corners here and cutting corners there until finally the values are so confused that people are going down the wrong road" (1957·66).

But the difference between the union and business contexts is not just a matter of a higher ethical bar. As institutions that are also part of a social movement, unions face unique ethical dilemmas. What happens, for instance, when the imperative to build a different, more just set of economic institutions runs up against ethical principles developed within the context of existing, flawed institutions? That is, in effect, the dilemma unions face when they seek to build economic justice by intervening more directly in corporate governance—not only at the bargaining table but in the board room and at the shareholders' meeting. Where traditional approaches to ethics emphasize bright lines, advancing the movement in a changed economic and social environment may well call for new—and more complicated—forms of engagement.

Though this dilemma arises out of the unique position and concerns of the labor movement, the way in which it is addressed may well offer broader lessons for other institutions, including the business community.

This chapter opens with an overview of the UAW's approach to ethics, beginning in the 1950s (when the ethical shortcomings of some U.S. unions were headline news, much as corporate scandals are today—leading, then as now, to congressional action) and culminating in the adoption of the union's Ethical Practices Codes in 1970. I then use the example of former UAW president Doug Fraser's service on the board of directors of the Chrysler Corporation to explore how traditional approaches—with their emphasis on arm's length relationships and avoidance of outside business and financial entanglements—translated into practice in a new era, as the UAW confronted a radically different political and economic landscape and new ethical dilemmas. The discussion then circles back to the 1950s, to what was arguably the most important ethical innovation in the UAW's history: the creation of the union's Public Review Board. I argue that the significance of the board lies less in its role as enforcer of the UAW's Ethical Practices Codes than in the democratic safeguards it provides members at all levels of the union. While written codes of ethical behavior are important for the tone they set, democracy and transparency are ultimately the best guarantors of ethical conduct within a labor union—or, for that matter, any other institution.

Setting the Stage: Origins of the UAW's Ethical Practices Codes

At the time of the UAW's 16th Constitutional Convention, held in Atlantic City in 1957, the U.S. labor movement was at a high-water mark. The rival American Federation of Labor (AFL) and Congress of

Industrial Organizations (CIO) had recently merged to become the AFL-CIO. Union density in U.S. industry stood at 26% of the wage and salary workforce, just under its historical peak. The UAW itself had 1.3 million dues-paying members. When retirees, strikers, and workers on layoff were factored in, the proud banner at the front of the convention hall that proclaimed the UAW to be "1-1/2 Million Strong" was no idle boast.

But if the mid-1950s were a high-water mark of sorts, they were also a time of increased scrutiny that was putting unions on the defensive. For a decade, the Taft-Hartley Act had allowed individual states to adopt "right to work" laws, an option that many conservative legislatures were pursuing with alacrity. In the U.S. Senate, a select committee chaired by Arkansas Democrat John McClellan was making headlines with its revelations about union corruption and labor racketeering.

Such was the backdrop to the UAW's 1957 gathering. Delegates who glanced at the Sunday *New York Times* before hurrying to the convention's opening session on the morning of April 7 would have seen both aspects of their time play out across the paper's pages. On the one hand, attesting to the importance of the labor movement's role in postwar economy and society, the convention itself was front-page news. On the other hand, large sections of the business community had never reconciled themselves to collective bargaining, and they seized on every tool at their disposal to avoid it. And so *Times* readers that morning were informed of the disastrous impact that revelations about union corruption were having on union organizing efforts, particularly in the right-to-work South.[1]

If this was troubling for rank-and-file members, it was doubly so for those in leadership roles. The leaders of the UAW and other industrial unions began as revolutionaries, and they continued to view the groups they had helped to build as movements for social change; still, by the 1950s, those unions had become significant economic institutions in their own right. Some union leaders, including the UAW's Walter Reuther, responded to this development with a heightened attention to ethical issues. It was increasingly clear that the manner in which an insurgent social movement approached ethics—with a not-unreasonable faith that anyone who was willing to put his or her life on the line for a cause was not after personal gain—no longer sufficed. There was, accordingly, a growing emphasis among CIO unions on formal codes of ethical behavior.

Ethical concerns had, in fact, been a stumbling block on the way to the CIO's merger with the AFL. CIO leaders including Reuther drew an unflattering contrast between the CIO's tough response to its "Communist problem" and the AFL's failure to take on corruption within its ranks. Reuther and other CIO leaders called for the united body not only to declare its ethical principles but also to establish internal mechanisms to enforce them—leading to the creation of a Committee on Ethical Practices for the new federation.

In light of this history, it's not surprising that the need for unions to uphold the highest ethical standards was a recurring topic over the six days of the 1957 UAW convention. To provide a sense of the time, it's worth quoting from the proceedings at length. Reuther himself set the tone in his keynote address:

> American labor had better roll up its sleeves, it had better get the stiffest broom and brush it can find and the strongest soap and disinfectant, and it had better take on the job of cleaning its own house from top to bottom and drive out every crook and gangster and racketeer it finds, because if we don't clean our own house, then the reactionaries will clean it for us, but they won't use a broom, they'll use an axe and they'll try to destroy the labor movement in the process (UAW 1957:13).

Other speakers elaborated on Reuther's challenge. As Monsignor George Higgins cautioned the assembled UAW delegates on the second morning of the convention,

> The labor movement at the present moment is confronted with a very serious crisis—perhaps the most serious crisis in its entire history. It is basically a moral and spiritual crisis and one which has its roots within the labor movement itself. Generally speaking, in the past the labor movement could, with a certain amount of justification, blame its troubles on real or alleged enemies outside its own ranks—unfriendly legislators, anti-union employers, or a biased and prejudiced press. At the present time, however, it must be said in all candor that labor's principal enemies are dues-paying members and elected officers of its own affiliated organizations (UAW 1957:77).

The internal enemies to which Higgins alluded weren't only, or even primarily, racketeers like those identified by the McClellan Committee. Higgins's critique went beyond these flamboyant examples—people who could and hopefully would be caught, convicted, and brought to justice—and led him to counsel the delegates against resting complacently on the UAW's reputation as a clean union. The "moral and spiritual crisis" of which he warned went beyond a handful of corrupt individuals. He saw traces of it in the movement's defensive mentality, in self-imposed limits on debate and criticism, and above all in members' apathy.

While past conventions had also acknowledged the importance of ethical practices, the theme of a crisis in union ethics—partly real, partly perceived, partly a pressing moral issue, partly a weapon in the hands of labor's enemies—permeated the 1957 gathering. The ethics resolution passed by the assembled delegates differed from past resolutions not only in its length (it runs five dense pages in the convention's printed proceedings) but also in its tone. In the place of ritual celebration of the UAW as a "clean" union and of easy applause for leadership initiatives, the 1957 resolution takes a rambling tour through U.S. history, juxtaposes examples of union corruption against corruption within the business and political worlds, and looks critically at its own movement. It is at once introspective and defensive; in its unevenness of tone, it demonstrates the uncomfortable position of the convention delegates—and the labor movement as a whole—at a time when the ethical failings of some union leaders were front-page news. How much self criticism can a movement afford when it is surrounded by enemies all too eager to magnify its flaws? Should it first demand a balanced accounting? Or should it accept revelations of its own shortcomings, the better to correct them?

In the end, the resolution unanimously adopted by convention delegates came down on the side of open and honest criticism. Even as they decried the biased reporting that damned "labor racketeers" but left corrupt management off the hook, delegates acknowledged that it was appropriate to set a higher ethical bar for the labor movement. As the resolution put it, "We restate our belief that it is not sufficient to require officers of unions merely to act within the law. Labor leaders must reject the 'business ethic' which justifies the use of position and influence for self-enrichment. Like Caesar's wife, the labor leader must be above suspicion; his [sic] standards of morality and ethics must be higher than the average in our society" (UAW 1957:95).[2]

Despite the spotlight on ethical practices, the 1957 gathering did not adopt specific rules for ethical conduct; the most important ethical initiative to come out of that convention—the creation of a Public Review Board to act as an independent watchdog over the union—is discussed later in this chapter. Instead of adopting an ethics code of its own, the UAW relied on statements adopted, at its urging, first by the CIO and later by the merged AFL-CIO. While these general statements of principle were no doubt taken more seriously by some affiliated unions than by others—and enforcement was largely left to individual affiliates—they did, for a time, provide the UAW with a set of ethical guidelines (UAW 1955, 1957).

After the UAW's 1968 break with the AFL-CIO, however, the newly independent union chose to adopt its own code of ethics, and to do so in a way that raised the profile of ethical issues within the institution. Accordingly, delegates to the union's next constitutional convention approved new Ethical Practices Codes to stand alongside (and with the same weight as) the union's governing constitution. Although the initial action was presented as a technical matter of housekeeping following the UAW's disaffiliation from the AFL-CIO, the resulting document has become an enduring point of institutional pride (UAW 1970:187).

The UAW's Ethical Practices Codes are actually four codes, covering democratic practices; internal financial practices; the special issues posed by health, welfare and retirement funds; and the business and financial activities of union officials. (The full text can be found in the appendix to this chapter.) The code begins not with a list of prohibited practices or a discussion of conflicts of interest but with what amounts to a bill of rights for members. Freedom of speech, due process, freedom from discrimination, and democratic procedures are spelled out first, before the code addresses what are more commonly viewed as ethical practices—maintaining integrity and transparency in the union's financial dealings, avoiding real or apparent conflicts of interest by officers and representatives, and, of course, not using union positions for personal gain. The codes apply to all levels of the union, from its international executive board to headquarters and regional staff to individual locals.

To a considerable extent, the UAW's Ethical Practices Codes echo the legal requirements of the Landrum-Griffin Act. That statute's "bill of rights of members of labor organizations" also guarantees free speech, due process, and the right to participate in democratic decision-making, in terms similar to those used in the UAW code on democratic practices. While there are areas in which the UAW code goes further—the right to due process, for example, includes not only adequate notice of charges and the right to a fair hearing but also opportunities to appeal an initial finding—its real significance is its role in the institution's internal governance. Guaranteeing the democratic rights of UAW members in an internal document has value both symbolic (including them in the union's constitution means that they are widely known and understood) and practical (creating additional avenues of enforcement).

The same applies to the UAW codes' treatment of conflicts of interest and financial malfeasance. The UAW codes' treatment of conflicts of interest and outright financial malfeasance also overlaps with Landrum-Griffin in many ways, while going beyond it in others—by, for example, banning the outside use of union mailing lists. As with the codes' guarantees of democracy and due process, the existence of an institution-specific code of conduct—even one that largely parallels statutory requirements—provides both an additional touchstone for ethical behavior and an additional enforcement mechanism.

Subsequent administrative letters—communications from the UAW president to local unions on internal policy matters—have restated, clarified, and, on occasion, strengthened the codes' basic provisions. In recent years, such letters have stressed the need for arm's length relationships with outside vendors, both those with which the union itself does business as well as those that provide (or would like to provide) goods and services to members. Officers and representatives at every level of the union are strictly prohibited from accepting meals, tickets, and other items of value from either type of vendor, nor may they endorse outside businesses. Vendors doing business with the UAW may not make contributions to the union or offer it special discounts not available to other purchasers (UAW 2003a, 2003b).

Across the decades, one enduring theme in the UAW's approach to ethics has been an insistence on keeping a proper distance from outside commercial interests. "Caesar's wife"[2]—cited more than once by speakers during the debate at the 1957 convention—remains the model. By avoiding outside financial entanglements, entering into business transactions at arm's length, and generally steering clear of any activity that could create the appearance of a conflict of interest, the union's representatives, too, can remain above any suspicion of impropriety.

When "Caesar's Wife" Steps Out

Sometimes practices that served an institution well under one set of circumstances become dysfunctional under another. Are the ethical principles articulated earlier in the UAW's history adequate today? Or do new times call for a rethinking of union ethics, as old concerns fade and new ones arise? What happens when Caesar's wife leaves the confines of home and engages with an imperfect world?

Certainly, the circumstances of the U.S. labor movement differ vastly today from the 1950s, '60s, and '70s. Union membership as a proportion of the wage and salary workforce has fallen from more than 25% in the 1950s to under 13% in 2003. The UAW no longer has wall-to-wall coverage in the U.S. auto industry, and its membership in other key industrial sectors—agricultural and construction equipment, aerospace—has shrunk dramatically. Employers, emboldened by a favorable political climate, are on the offensive.

Like other unions, the UAW has responded by seeking out new strategies to advance the interests of its members and further the cause of economic justice. Some of these new strategies approach capital markets—and the leverage provided by the labor movement's collective investments—as a way to influence employer behavior. This represents a departure from traditional approaches to financial matters. The UAW's Ethical Practices Codes, with its focus on conflicts of interest held by individual union representatives, is essentially silent on the topic of the *union's* investments. Is it proper for the union to invest its institutional resources in the stock of companies with which it bargains? How should those investments be managed? What are the ethical guideposts on this new terrain?

There are precedents for such departures from arm's length relationships. Few things could represent more of a departure, in fact, than a union official's service on a corporate board of directors. Although former UAW president Doug Fraser's presence on Chrysler's board did not prove the harbinger of a new era in U.S. corporate governance, as some speculated it might, the history of that presence does illustrate both the limits and the enduring value of the UAW's ethical code under changing circumstances.

The context for Fraser's board service was, of course, Chrysler's near-bankruptcy. In 1979—a bargaining year for the UAW and the Big Three automakers—Chrysler Corporation faced a projected loss of $1 billion. That was, at the time, the largest loss ever faced by a U.S. company. Any hope of help from a generally skeptical Congress hinged on cuts by both the company and the union. In order to preserve jobs, UAW members made concessions that, for the first time in the history of their bargaining with the major automakers, meant that autoworkers at one company would not have the same wage increases and cost of living protection as workers at others.

In exchange, the union sought and won a larger role in nontraditional areas—from decisions about pension fund investments to, most dramatically, a seat for workers on the company's board of directors. In May 1980, by previous agreement, Chrysler chairman Lee Iacocca nominated then–UAW president Doug Fraser to serve on the Chrysler board. It was the first time in U.S. history that a union leader would serve on the board of a major corporation with which the union had a collective bargaining relationship.

Although taking a seat on the board was unprecedented, pursuing one was not. The UAW had long called for a greater voice for workers in the kinds of decisions that, in the U.S. industrial relations system, are typically made in board rooms, not at the bargaining table. In its previous round of auto negotiations, in 1976, the union had specifically pushed for board representation at Chrysler. The company, which had itself made such a proposal to unions in the United Kingdom, resisted its application on the other side of the Atlantic. It took the extraordinary event of Chrysler's near-collapse to bring the idea to fruition.

In public statements, the UAW portrayed its Chrysler board seat as an advance for industrial democracy and a natural extension of the union's advocacy for its members. The announced closure of Chrysler's historic Dodge Main plant became a rallying point. As Fraser put it in an address to UAW political activists shortly after the Chrysler deal was finalized, "Where the Chrysler Corporation, just with a stroke of a pen wipes out a plant . . . when they can do that and let you know a half-hour before the announcement's made, you have to ask yourself why does the labor movement have to be in a position where they can only challenge the positions of the corporation, why can't they have a voice when these decisions are made" (Fraser, 1980a). As a board member, Fraser pledged, he would fight against plant closings and fight for product quality, better health and safety practices, and a more democratic workplace. "Being on the board," he told delegates to the UAW's 1980 convention, "means we have one more front on which to fight" (Fraser, 1980b:18).

But while board membership did open up an additional front, it was not an entirely natural extension of the union's customary role. The act of putting a union leader on a corporate board raises thorny questions for any union, particularly one with the UAW's ethical traditions. What does it mean to be a director of an employer with whom one also bargains? Can membership on a board compromise a union in its dealings with the employer in question (or, alternatively, with competing employers—a concern that was voiced by Ford and General Motors at the time)? Are there some discussions from which a union representative should abstain? And if avoiding a conflict of interest entails silence on key issues, does board representation still further the cause of industrial democracy, or is it merely window dressing? Worse, does it implicate the union in a flawed system, in which the interests of shareholders will invariably take precedence over the interest of workers and communities?

These are not questions that the UAW's Ethical Practices Codes address explicitly. Its focus, as noted earlier, is on individual rather than institutional conflicts of interest. And so, while it is clear that it would be unethical for a UAW leader to benefit financially from board service, guidance beyond that is limited. The irony is that concerns about personal gain would be relatively easy to address even in the absence of a formal code of ethics. In the case of Fraser's service on the Chrysler board, he addressed such concerns before he assumed his seat by committing to donate any money he received for his board service to labor causes and announcing that he would not purchase any stock in the corporation (although stock contributions to UAW-represented Chrysler employees were part of Chrysler's financial rescue package).

On other ethical issues, lacking clear precedents or established guidelines, the union improvised. Fraser and his UAW colleagues distinguished between issues that posed a direct conflict of interest between his union and his board roles, such as Chrysler's collective bargaining strategy, and other issues in which the union held a direct stake. Where conflicts existed, Fraser promised to abstain from voting, or even to leave the room when the relevant issues arose. On other issues, including such topics as plant closings and Chrysler's overseas investments, he vowed to press the union's case. Despite the corporation's insistence that Fraser was being nominated as an individual, he made it clear that he would be serving as a representative of the union and its members.

To what extent were ethical concerns addressed any more clearly— or, for that matter, raised at all—in the broader public discussion of Fraser's history-making board nomination? Critics fell into two camps. Within the UAW and the broader labor movement, critics generally downplayed the significance of the board seat (and thus, implicitly, of any attendant ethical conflicts). While some grumbled that the board seat was a payoff to the union's leadership for delivering a concessionary agreement, few took that argument very far—probably because Fraser had made it quite clear up front that he would not gain financially from his board service. Instead, the critics argued that Fraser would be a "minority of one," unable to exert a meaningful influence on the company's direction. The union, in this view, had settled for symbolism while the company pocketed substantive concessions. For the critics on the political left, it was a perceived lack of militancy by UAW leadership— evidenced by the concessions made to Chrysler and then, a few years later, to Ford and General Motors—that was at issue, not the ethics of union membership on a corporate board per se.[3]

Critics in the business community and on the political right did use the language of ethics to attack Fraser's seat on the Chrysler board. They were not particularly concerned with the ethics of union leadership, but they were extremely concerned (in this instance, at least) with the ethical obligation of a corporate director toward corporate shareholders. How, they demanded, could Fraser put workers first and still represent the interests of shareholders? Executives at Ford and General Motors voiced particular reservations about the propriety of Fraser's dual role as union leader and as director of one of their competitors.[4]

Fraser served on the Chrysler board until 1984.[5] To answer those who charged that the union's board seat was merely symbolic, Fraser could point to his role in the creation of a special board committee formed to study the social costs of plant closings. On the plant closing issue, more than any other, Fraser's considerable persuasive powers had an impact on other Chrysler directors; one result was a reprieve for the company's Detroit glass plant.

The thorniest ethical dilemma faced by the union during Fraser's tenure on the board came in 1982, when the UAW and Chrysler entered into a new round of negotiations. Though the UAW settled with Chrysler in the United States, UAW members in Canada struck the company's Canadian affiliate. Fraser thus found himself on the board of a corporation that was the target of a UAW strike. While insisting that there was no real danger of a conflict of interest, Fraser acknowledged that his board seat could lead to the appearance of one (*BusinessWeek* 1984). To avoid any such appearance, he opted to suspend his board service for two months, resuming it after the strike was settled.

Despite the radical departure from traditional arm's length approaches that Fraser's service on Chrysler's board represented, it did not result in an alternative set of ethical guideposts. Instead, Fraser and the UAW improvised—successfully, by general agreement—to apply traditional ethical standards to nontraditional forms of engagement and struggle. One possible gauge of that success: in the years since, other union representatives have served on corporate boards in a variety of industries, with little of the controversy that surrounded Fraser's 1980 election at Chrysler.

Now as then, labor representation on corporate boards arises out of extreme circumstances, when a company on the ropes agrees to board representation as part of a turnaround plan that also typically involves contract concessions and an ownership stake for employees. In that sense, Fraser's board service at Chrysler did not usher in a new era of co-management, or even mark a sea change in union tactics. Over the past decade, however, the UAW and other unions have also become more involved in corporate governance as a day-to-day concern. Historically, "labor's capital"—the investments held by unions directly, or by union-administered health and welfare funds—was passive. As unions have joined forces with other institutional investors and shareholder activists to press for reform measures (and, on occasion, to seek leverage in contract and organizing campaigns), the old arm's length approach has evolved into a much more active engagement with the world of capital markets.

This shift has generated very little ethical controversy. Within the labor movement, discussions have revolved around the effectiveness of the approach, not its propriety. Outside the labor movement, whatever controversy has attended union-backed shareholder proposals and other initiatives has been on their merits, not on the ethics of a union acting within a shareholders' forum. While the labor movement's agenda may well be at odds with a short-term stock market focus, unions have argued forcefully—much as the UAW did at the time of Fraser's service on the Chrysler board—that opening corporations to the voices of other stakeholders is entirely compatible with increased shareholder value over the long term.

Ethics, Democracy, and Transparency

As the Chrysler board experience demonstrates, there are limits inherent to any attempt to codify ethical behavior. Spell out dos and don'ts in exhaustive detail and you risk a code of ethics frozen in time: well suited to today's quandaries, not so well suited to issues that may arise tomorrow. Take the opposite approach, emphasizing broad principles over hard guidelines, and you risk a code too general to carry real weight. But while no code of ethics can address every situation now and in the future, institutional practices and structures *can* encourage ethical behavior, even in changing circumstances. That has been the real lesson of the UAW's efforts to uphold ethical standards over the years.

The delegates to the UAW's 1957 convention, facing a platform heralding the union's membership of "1-1/2 million strong," could hardly have anticipated the challenges the union would face decades later or the new strategies those challenges would call for. However, they could—and did—recognize that ethical dilemmas are best addressed in an environment of democracy and openness. The most enduring legacy of the 1957 convention wasn't the passage of a resolution on ethics, however strongly or eloquently worded. It was the creation of a new body, the Public Review Board, to safeguard the democratic rights of UAW members while also keeping watch over the union's conduct.

The idea of an oversight body composed of distinguished outsiders had been pioneered by the small Upholsterers' Union, and it was considered by UAW leadership for several years before being presented to convention delegates as an amendment to the union's constitution. Reuther made the case for the new body in both his written report to delegates and his keynote address to the convention. In his words,

> *More and more the leadership of the labor movement must be prepared to have their stewardship and conduct of the affairs of the Union under their leadership subject to public review.* The leadership of the UAW is prepared to have its stewardship reviewed, and we are proposing the creation of a Public Review Board for this purpose and to further strengthen and

refine the internal machinery of our Union to insure that the justice which comes from the Union's internal appeal procedures, meets the standards of fairness and honesty consistent with public standards in a free society (Reuther 1957:70, emphasis in original).

In addition to providing members an additional avenue of appeal, the new board would have special authority to monitor and enforce ethical behavior. Where possible violations of ethical practices were concerned, Reuther and his fellow leaders proposed that the Public Review Board have the authority to undertake investigations, hold hearings, and make findings, even in the absence of a formal appeal.

When the proposal to create the Public Review Board was floated in advance of the 1957 gathering, it was not universally well received. One anti-labor columnist, writing in *Newsweek,* mocked the proposed watchdog body as a "private, handpicked court" created only to further the political ambitions of the "unctuous" Walter Reuther (Moley 1957). To convention delegates, Reuther made precisely the opposite point: this was to be a watchdog with teeth, with the authority to modify or reverse decisions of the union's elected leadership. The Public Review Board's decisions, Reuther stressed, would be final and binding, with "no ifs, ands, buts or loopholes" (UAW 1957:96).

The response from delegates was not universally positive either. Minutes before the proposal to create the Public Review Board was presented, the strongly worded resolution on ethical practices had passed without debate. In contrast, the constitutional amendment to create the Public Review Board faced opposition from a vocal minority. One speaker bristled at the thought of non-members "laying down laws and saying that we have to do this or that." Another fretted that creating a public panel would amount to an admission that the union was "rotten" and unable to police itself. Still others cited the expense of maintaining such a panel (UAW 1957:104–8). Though voiced by a small minority (in the end, the creation of the Public Review Board passed overwhelmingly), these views highlight the difficulty of moving from general statements of ethical principle to concrete changes in organizational structures.

In its nearly 50-year history, the Public Review Board has functioned more or less as Reuther and his contemporaries originally envisioned it. Its members—a total of 25 individuals have served on the seven-member panel since its inception[6]—have included law professors, judges, industrial relations scholars, academicians from other fields, and religious figures. The board's written decisions are published, and a summary report detailing the disposition of each case is provided to the union's membership. Often these decisions have upheld actions taken by the International Executive Board (some of which, it should be noted, themselves overturned the actions of UAW locals or other bodies). Less often—though not infrequently—they have reversed them.

The composition of the nearly 1,500 cases decided by the Public Review Board over the years is noteworthy. While a full categorization is difficult, not only because of the sheer number of cases but also because of the complexity of many of them, relatively few deal explicitly with financial misconduct, conflicts of interest, or personal enrichment. When such cases *have* arisen, the Public Review Board has moved aggressively. That was the case in the mid-1980s, when the UAW was shaken by a financial scandal in one of its regions. Asked by the union's executive board to investigate the allegations, respond to any wrongdoing, and propose remedial measures, the Public Review Board spearheaded a multi-year investigation that untangled a web of loosely monitored funds, used over a period of years for the personal benefit of the region's leadership. While many of the individual transactions were almost laughably petty (a motor for the director's boat, veterinary bills for his mother's dog, football tickets), they added up to thousands of dollars, and the violation of trust underlying them was major indeed. The Public Review Board responded by recommending specific sanctions against individual wrongdoers and proposing a list of reforms—from the adoption institutionwide of more rigorous accounting and record-keeping standards to the restructuring of Region 4's education center and various special funds to new guidelines on the employment of family members—that were, with a few minor adjustments, promptly adopted by the International Executive Board (UAW Public Review Board, case 640).

The Region 4 case remains the most extensive in the history of the Public Review Board. Most of the cases before the body are not nearly so weighty—except to the individual members they involve. That, of course, is the point. The great majority of board cases, now and in the past, arise from the basic stuff of union democracy: disputed elections, allegations of unfair or discriminatory treatment, grievances arbitrarily withdrawn. Its first several decisions, for example, upheld the political rights of a number of left-wing UAW members who had refused to "name names" when subpoenaed by the U.S. Senate Subcommittee on Internal Security. Other early actions dealt with an administratorship, following allegations of local union election irregularities; a bitter dispute between a member and her local leadership; and a local president's right to resume office at the conclusion of a leave of absence (UAW Public Review Board cases 12, 13, 19). More recently, the Public Review Board has weighed in on wide-ranging matters: a local union's withdrawal of a member's grievance (affirmed), a dispute over payment of travel expenses for alternate delegates to the union's convention (in which the action of the local union to deny payment, previously sustained by the International Union's internal appeals process, was overturned), a charge that a local union health and safety representative was removed from her position for political reasons. In the last case, the Public Review Board sharply rebuked the International Union for its previous handling of the matter, and it remanded the case back for a more thorough investigation (UAW Public Review Board cases 1468, 1469, 1476).

While the Public Review Board's jurisdiction does not extend to the union's collective bargaining policies, virtually every other aspect of the union's operation falls within its purview. It is precisely this close involvement in the vital, everyday business of the union that makes the board an important ethical institution. The Public Review Board safeguards the two things—democracy and transparency—that make a code of ethics more than words on paper. The genius of the Public Review Board, in short, is to foster an ethical environment by holding all levels of the union to its democratic principles.

Lessons from the UAW's Experience

The UAW's approach to ethics was forged in the 1950s, against the same backdrop of headline-making scandals that led Congress to pass the Landrum-Griffin Act in 1959. Landrum-Griffin established new reporting and disclosure requirements for labor organizations, as well as safeguards for the democratic rights of union members. That dual focus on transparency and democracy mirrored the approach taken by the UAW in its own internal initiatives. Did it also render those initiatives superfluous?

In the wake of Congress's action, some unions answered in the affirmative. For a time—fortunately, past—the AFL-CIO took a similar stance and allowed its Committee on Ethical Practices to wither, on the grounds that the committee's watchdog and enforcement functions had been taken over by the federal government (Bureau of National Affairs 1981).

Obviously, the UAW reacted differently. It not only maintained but, over the years, strengthened its internal ethics policies. The significance of that choice lies less in the content of the UAW's internal policies (which, though stricter and more specific in some areas, substantially overlap the legal requirements established by Congress) than in the institutional culture they furthered. The existence of an internal code of ethics—particularly one with constitutional weight—raised the visibility of ethical issues within the institution and provided internal enforcement mechanisms to police unethical behavior. Those effects in and of themselves were a meaningful advance beyond simple compliance with federal law. The UAW went a step further, though, by maintaining an independent watchdog—the Public Review Board—with the power to enforce ethical behavior, even to the extent of overruling decisions by the union's executive board.

As corporate executives, citizens, and policymakers wrestle with a succession of scandals in the business world, what lessons might be drawn from the UAW's experience? Increasingly, the direction of public policy in business ethics is to require increased transparency; that, for example, is the thrust of much of Sarbanes-Oxley. The UAW's experience would imply that this is not enough. Financial malfeasance can be proscribed, conflicts of interest identified and regulated, and more disclosure required in an attempt to increase transparency. Violations can be prosecuted and legal penalties imposed. However, effective enforcement, the kind that creates a truly ethical culture, depends heavily on the existence of democratic procedures to give shareholders (as well as more broadly defined stakeholders) the means to hold institutions accountable. Unfortunately, legislative efforts to make corporations more transparent have not been accompanied by efforts to make them more democratic.

Democracy, transparency, and the means to enforce both—along with, but not limited to, a strong written code of ethics—are entwined at the heart of the UAW experience. It's worth noting that in decades past, the union challenged corporate America to follow its lead by establishing independent watchdog bodies similar to the Public Review Board.[7] There were no takers at the time. Perhaps, in light of the corporate scandals of the last few years, it's time to revive that call.

Appendix:
UAW Ethical Practices Codes

Democratic Practices

The UAW is proud of its democratic heritage. Its Constitution is carefully designed to insure each member her/his full democratic right, both as an individual and through her/his elected representatives, to express her/himself freely and to participate at all levels in the decisions governing the Union. Moreover, individual rights as a UAW member are protected against infringement and abuse, for a member may appeal complaints concerning the administration of the Union, to the Local Union, the International Executive Board and the Constitutional Convention; and has the right to submit her/his appeal to the UAW Public

Review Board, comprised of citizens with national reputations outside the labor movement, whose decisions are final and binding.

The democratic principles which have always governed the International Union, UAW, and its Local Unions are:

1. Each member shall be entitled to a full share in Union self-government. Each member shall have full freedom of speech and the right to participate in the democratic decisions of the Union. Subject to reasonable rules and regulations, each member shall have the right to run for office, to nominate and to vote in free, fair and honest elections. In a democratic union, as in a democratic society, every member has certain rights but s/he must also accept certain corresponding obligations. Each member shall have the right freely to criticize the policies and personalities of Union officials; however, this does not include the right to undermine the Union as an institution; to vilify other members of the Union and its elected officials or to carry on activities with complete disregard of the rights of other members and the interests of the Union; to subvert the Union in collective bargaining or to advocate or engage in dual unionism.

2. Membership meetings shall be held regularly, with proper notice of time and place and shall be conducted in an atmosphere of fairness.

3. All Union rules and laws must be fairly and uniformly applied and disciplinary procedures, including adequate notice, full rights of the accused and the right to appeal, shall be fair and afford full due process to each member.

4. Each Local Union shall maintain adequate safeguards so that all of its operations shall be conducted in a democratic and fair manner. No corruption, discrimination or anti-democratic procedure shall ever be permitted under any circumstances.

Financial Practices

Union funds are held in sacred trust for the benefit of the membership. The membership is entitled to assurance that Union funds are not dissipated and are spent for proper purposes. The membership is also entitled to be reasonably informed as to how Union funds are invested or used.

1. The International Union and its Local Unions shall conduct their proprietary functions, including all contracts for purchase or sale or for rendering housekeeping services in accordance with the practice of well-run institutions, including the securing of competitive bids for major contracts.

2. The International Union and its Local Unions shall not permit any of their funds to be invested in a manner which results in the personal profit or advantage of any officer or representative of the Union.

3. There shall be no contracts of purchase or sale or for rendering services which will result in the personal profit or advantage of any officer or representative of the Union. Nor shall any officer, representative or employee of the International Union or any Local Union accept personal profit or special advantage from a business with which the Union bargains collectively.

4. Neither the International Union nor any of its Local Unions shall make loans to its officers, representatives, employees or members, or members of their families, for the purpose of financing the private business of such persons.

Health, Welfare and Retirement Funds

1. No official, representative or employee of the International Union or a Local Union shall receive fees or salaries of any kind from a fund established for the provision of health, welfare or retirement benefits, except for reasonable reimbursement provided for in a collective bargaining agreement and expressly approved by the International Executive Board.

2. No official, employee or other person acting as agent or representative of the International Union or a Local Union, who exercises responsibilities or influence in the administration of health, welfare and retirement programs or the place of insurance contracts, shall have any compromising personal ties, direct or indirect, with outside agencies such as insurance carriers, brokers, or consultants doing business with the health, welfare and retirement plans.

3. Complete records of the financial operations of all UAW health, welfare and retirement funds and programs shall be maintained in accordance with the best accounting practice. Each such fund shall be audited regularly.

4. All such audit reports shall be available to the members of the Union covered by the fund.

5. The trustees or administrators of such funds shall make a full disclosure and report to the members covered by the fund at least once each year.

Business and Financial Activities of Union Officials

Any person who represents the UAW and its members, whether elected or appointed, has a sacred trust to serve the best interests of the members and their families. Therefore, every officer and representative must avoid any outside transaction which even gives the appearance of a conflict of interest. The special fiduciary nature of Union office requires the highest loyalty to the duties of the office.

1. The mailing lists of the Union are valuable assets. In order to protect the interests of our entire membership, Union officers and representatives shall not, under any circumstances, turn over a Union mailing list to an outsider for use in the promotion or sale of any goods or services that benefit

an individual or a private concern. Mailing lists are to be used only to promote the necessary legitimate functions of the Local Union and for no other purpose. It is improper for any official or representative of either the International Union or Local Union to permit the use of any mailing list by any third party to promote the sale of furniture, appliances, automobiles, insurance, eyeglasses or any other item, or to enable professionals to solicit the membership.

2. No officer or representative shall have a personal financial interest which conflicts with her/his Union duties.

3. No officer or representative shall have any substantial financial interest (even in the publicly-traded, widely-held stock of a corporation except for stock-purchase plans, profit sharing or nominal amounts of such stock), in any business with which the UAW bargains. An officer or representative shall not have any substantial interest in a business with which the UAW bargains collectively.

4. No officer or representative shall accept "kickbacks," under-the-table payments, valuable gifts, lavish entertainment or any personal payment of any kind, other than regular pay and benefits for work performed as an employee from an employer with which the Union bargains or from a business or professional enterprise with which the Union does business.

5. The principles of this Code, of course, apply to investments and activities of third parties, where they amount to a subterfuge to conceal the financial interests of such officials or representatives.

Notes

[1] Being "clean" does not immunize a union from corruption charges, of course. The UAW under Walter Reuther had charges of racketeering hurled against it by the Kohler Company during a long and bitter strike (Kohler 1957). Similar charges remain a staple of union opponents, as any number of websites developed by anti-union committees will attest.

[2] References to "Caesar's wife" abounded at the 1957 convention, and she is still invoked by UAW leaders. The specific reference is to Julius Caesar's second wife, Pompeia, whom he divorced at the merest suspicion of scandal. Her actual guilt or innocence was immaterial since, as he is traditionally held to have declared, "Caesar's wife must be above suspicion."

[3] For Fraser's thoughts on his board service and those who criticized it, see Fraser (1982). For the view of his critics, see the special report on Chrysler in *Labor Notes* (1979).

[4] For a sampling of typical reactions from business leaders and conservative commentators, see Hayes (1979); *Wall Street Journal* (1979); *BusinessWeek* (1980); and Raskin (1980). For a statement of General Motors's views, as expressed by then-chairman Thomas Murphy, see Hadden (1979).

[5] Chrysler always insisted that the board seat was Fraser's, based on his personal qualifications, and not the UAW's as an institution. In 1982 negotiations, the company rejected a union proposal to recast Fraser's seat as a UAW seat, much less to increase labor's representation to four board seats. As Fraser's retirement approached, he and Chrysler's Lee Iacocca wrangled over whether Fraser's successor as UAW president, Owen Bieber, would be nominated for Fraser's board seat. In the end, Fraser stayed on the board, on what was understood to be a transitional basis, for a year after his retirement from UAW office. In 1984, Owen Bieber was nominated to succeed him and served until 1991. After a lapse of seven years, the UAW's governance role resumed in a different context when Chrysler merged with Daimler-Benz and then-UAW president Stephen P. Yokich assumed a seat on the supervisory board of the new German-headquartered company.

[6] There was one vacancy as of October 2004, following the death of Professor Marilyn Yarbrough.

[7] See, for example, the resolution on corporate responsibility passed by delegates to the UAW's 1970 convention (UAW 1970:250–3).

References

Bureau of National Affairs. 1981. "UAW President Says Indicted Union Officials Should Step Down Until Cleared of Charges." *Daily Labor Report* 103, May 29, pp. A7–8.

BusinessWeek. 1980. "The Risk in Putting a Union Chief on the Board." May 19, pp. 149–50.

_____. 1984. "Labor's Voice on Corporate Boards: Good or Bad." May 7, pp. 151–3.

Fraser, Douglas. 1980a. Keynote address to 1980 UAW National Community Action Program Conference. Text provided in UAW press release, January 13.

_____. 1980b. *President's Report to 26th Constitutional Convention, Part One: UAW in Action.* Detroit: UAW.

_____. 1982. "Worker Participation in Corporate Government: The UAW-Chrysler Experience." Kenneth M. Piper Lecture, Illinois Institute of Technology. Reprinted in *Chicago Kent Law Review,* Vol. 58, No. 4.

Hadden, Jeffrey. 1979. "Murphy Sees Problems with Fraser-Chrysler Ties." *Detroit News,* November 8, p. 14d.

Hayes, Thomas. 1979. "Fraser Board Role Riles Critics, Raises Questions." *New York Times,* November 26, p. D1.

Kohler, Herbert. 1957. "Can a Free Economy Tolerate Union Violence? The Menace of UAW-CIO Coercion." Address to Detroit Economic Club, delivered February 25. Reprinted in Kohler Company pamphlet.

Labor Notes. 1979. "Labor Notes Special Report: Substandard Chrysler Contract Ratified," November 20, pp. 6–7.

Moley, Raymond. 1957. "The Ultimate Wrong," *Newsweek,* April 8, p. 120.

Raskin, A.H. 1980. "The Labor Leader as Company Director," *New York Times,* April 27, p. F1.

Reuther, Walter. 1957. *President's Report to 16th Constitutional Convention, United Automobile, Aircraft and Agricultural Implement Workers of America.* Detroit: UAW.

UAW, International Union. 1955. *Proceedings, 15th Constitutional Convention, United Automobile, Aircraft and Agricultural Implement Workers of America,* Cleveland, OH, March 27–April 1.

_____. 1957. *Proceedings, 16th Constitutional Convention, United Automobile, Aircraft and Agricultural Implement Workers of America,* Atlantic City, NJ, April 7–12.

_____. 1970. *Proceedings, 22nd Constitutional Convention, International Union, United Automobile, Aerospace and Agricultural Implement Workers of America,* April 20–24.

_____. 2003a. "Ethical Conduct in Dealing with Vendors, Suppliers and Other Providers of Service." Administrative Letter, Vol. 49, No. 1 (February 14).

_____. 2003b. "UAW Policy Against Endorsement of Outside Businesses." Administrative Letter, Vol. 51, No. 2 (November 11).

UAW Public Review Board. *Digest of Public Review Board Decisions.* Multiple volumes, covering 1957–2002 (case numbers 1–1421). Individual decisions, including those not yet compiled in summary volumes, are available free of charge to UAW members directly from the Public Review Board.

Wall Street Journal. 1979. "Plan to Elect UAW's Chief to Chrysler's Board Raises Issues," October 26, p. 3.

Chapter 11

The Critical Failure of Workplace Ethics

Gordon Lafer
University of Oregon

Power concedes nothing without a demand.
—Frederick Douglass

It is unsurprising that, in an era of high profile corporate scandals, business ethics has again become a popular topic. Whenever household-name companies start showing up in stories about graft, corruption, and securities fraud, we can expect to hear pundits wondering where things went wrong and calling for more ethics classes in the nation's business schools. While such jeremiads have typically focused on the defrauding of consumers or shareholders, it is understandable that recent debate has included a greater focus on workplace ethics. We are living through an economy that is relentlessly downsizing. Notions of job security and employee loyalty, or corporate commitment to a living wage and afford-able health care, have been torn asunder. Moreover, the logic of down-sizing—layoffs, subcontracting, contingent labor, slashed benefits—has crept slowly up the occupational ladder, coming to affect a growing share of white-collar and professional jobs. In this context, it is unsurprising that increased attention is being paid to the ethics of employment relations.

But does the category of "ethics" really add much to our understanding of employment relations? And is there really any way that scholarship or education on this topic can lead to improvements in the actual behavior of employers?

The body of scholarship that falls under the heading of "workplace ethics" can be roughly divided into two groups. The issue that divides these groups is the question of whether ethical education—in business schools or in the workplace—can be effective. In one group are critics such as Roy Adams (2001), Lance Compa (2000), and others, who critique business practices from an outsider's viewpoint. While such works voice ethical criticisms of employers, they do not consider the unethical treatment of employees an aberration but rather the inevitable logic of capitalist employment. Thus, these scholars' conclusions tend to call for higher ethical standards being forcibly imposed on employers, generally through either government regulation or collective bargaining. These scholars are not trying to convince business managers to get in touch with a softer side of their souls. Instead, their real audiences are those interested in taking up the work of making such regulations politically feasible. This group is the minority.

Scholars in the second broad class approach workplace ethics in much the same way as we might approach the ethics of friendship or marriage, treating the behavior of employers as the outcome of a series of individual choices that are ultimately shaped by the personal morality of managers. While it is rarely stated explicitly, these scholars' field as a whole is built on the assumption that providing ethical education to managers will lead them to change their behavior and ultimately to adopt more ethical corporate policies. Proponents may disagree as to whether virtue, care, duty, or utility is the best foundation for ethics, but they implicitly agree on something much more profound. By focusing on a managerial audience, all of these arguments implicitly advocate a common ontological view of the world: that the best way to create a more ethical workplace is by appealing to the ethical proclivities of business managers. It is this literature—which dominates the field of HR ethics—that I will focus on for the remainder of this essay. To state my conclusion up front, I believe that this sort of HR ethics is bankrupt, that it has failed and will continue to fail to meaningfully improve the real governance of actual workplaces, and that it functions more as a legitimizing diversion than a genuine field of social scientific inquiry.

Human Resource Ethics: The State of the Field

If you go by shelf space, the field of human resource (HR) ethics is not doing too well. Virtually every bookstore has a large section of business readings, but only a few of the larger stores contain even small sections on business ethics, within which may be an even smaller subsection devoted to HR ethics. Similarly, while many large corporations have a designated "ethics officer," the higher-ups don't seem to take this role very seriously. In a recent Conference Board (2004) survey of corporate HR officers, more than two thirds reported that their board of directors had never taken part in an ethics compliance training. It's not that there aren't any ethical issues to be concerned about; for instance, two thirds of those surveyed believe that senior executive compensation is "out of control." The problem is that even clear ethical violations are not particularly punished, especially if the culprit has been a good performer in terms of the bottom line. A strong majority of HR officers reported that, even when an executive is forced to resign due to a violation of ethics codes, he or she is rewarded with a compensating severance package. Nor are HR officers optimistic about the power of ethics training to reverse such trends. In 2003, a majority of those surveyed believed that even if Enron managers had undergone ethics training, it would have made "little or no difference" in the actions that led to that company's demise and the liquidation of its employees' retirement funds (Conference Board 2004).

The view from academia is similarly discouraging. While there is much debate over the correct philosophical approach to HR ethics, the one thing that most scholars share is the knowledge that their work is largely ignored by business managers. Winstanley and Woodall, for instance, introduce their comprehensive review of the field by noting that "on the whole, ethical issues have been of marginal significance to the unfolding academic debates around HRM [human resource management]" (2000:4). In the papers that follow, authors repeatedly outline a theoretical case for ethical behavior, only to acknowledge the unlikelihood of its being put into practice in real firms. Liff and Dickens, for instance, note that stakeholder ethics could be put into practice if only individual managers were rewarded "on the basis of their contribution to furthering equality . . . in addition to more traditional business performance measures" but concede with a graceful understatement that "currently this is rare" (2000:96).

Indeed, there is a curious disconnect at the heart of what should be the vital field of workplace ethics. On the one hand, most adults spend most of their waking hours as employees, and in the normal course of work they confront a host of questions about ethics and fairness: Are promotions really based on merit, or on favoritism? What can I do about a sexist boss? Should I put myself at risk by helping someone who's falling behind and in danger of getting fired? Is it fair that the boss makes so much and they're raising our health insurance premiums? For those interested in morality and fairness, the workplace is a forum that might be termed a "target-rich environment," rife with moral issues that are concretely acted out in our everyday lives. The curiosity is that, for all the relevance these topics would seem to hold, the academic field of workplace ethics seems to attract few readers and little enthusiasm.

Why is a field that should have so much to offer to so many instead confined to the margins of relevance? I believe it is because its scholars are talking to the wrong audience. Overwhelmingly, the assumed audience for the literature of workplace ethics is management rather than workers. Furthermore, in addressing current or prospective HR officers—a set of people who are simultaneously managers and employees—the literature overwhelmingly addresses them in their capacity as managers rather than as employees. Because the singular purpose of business is to generate shareholder returns, the role of business managers is to shape all their policies to maximize profits. Even for upstanding citizens (who may conduct noble volunteer work in other parts of their lives), the role of business manager allows little room for ethical considerations—particularly when ethics conflicts with profit maximization. By focusing on managers as their audience, HR scholars have set up the field of ethics to be permanently marginal. Moreover, the scholarship itself becomes distorted by the assumption that ethical arguments must be framed in terms that appeal to people whose roles make them structurally disinterested in ethics. In seeking to craft ethical arguments that might be palatable to private sector managers, scholars have produced a host of tracts that are convoluted and dreamy. The field is characterized by tepid and speculative theories that rarely offer critical prescriptions for the real world of work, and that therefore have failed to engage much of a readership among either management or workers.

What Is Ethics?

To say anything clear about HR ethics, it's critical to start with an understanding of what ethics is and is not in this context. Much of the literature focuses on compliance with legal regulation; thus, a review of business ethics textbooks found that the single most commonly discussed HR issue was employment discrimination (Ciulla 1999:271). But obeying the law is not the same thing as acting ethically: both ethical and unethical firms presumably obey the law not out of conscience but out of fear of the consequences of disobedience.

So, too, perhaps the single most common argument about HR ethics—heard from both the left and the right—is that treating employees ethically actually serves the long-term interests of shareholders. I will address later the accuracy of this claim. But for now, what's critical to point out is that, to the extent that this view is true, it makes ethics irrelevant. If acting "ethically"—whatever that may mean—is acting in the long-term interests of shareholders, then the category of "ethics" is useless, because it adds nothing to our understanding of the business world. We already know that smart businesses act in order to maximize long-term shareholder return; noting that those exact same actions may also be deemed ethical gives us no new insight into business management. Things that are in the selfish interest of shareholders will be pursued by smart managers no matter what their ethical leanings. If it's true that paying employees well, for instance, leads to improved customer service, increased sales, and ultimately increased returns to shareholders, you don't need ethics to tell you to do it. And if an ethically concerned management acts exactly the same as an ethically unconcerned management, then the discussion of ethics is a waste of time.

For business ethics to mean anything, it must at least sometimes lead managers to do something that cuts against their otherwise dominant drive to maximize profits. Only in this way will "ethics" designate something that has any independent reality to it. If HR ethics never lead managers to insist on some ethical behavior that flies in the face of the profit motive, it is meaningless. And unfortunately, precious little in the literature on HR ethics—much less in the practice of actual HR managers—stands up to this test.

Is It in Business's Interest to Be Ethical?

Since so much of HR ethics focuses on the overlap between ethics and the profit motive, it is critical to examine whether, or to what extent, these two things really do overlap. Does the pursuit of profit lead managers, for selfish reasons, to adopt ethical practices? In some ways it seems difficult to even debate this proposition with a straight face. To anyone who looks around at the economy, to anyone who has experienced the labor market, to anyone who as a child was told to "share" or "be nice" and then grew up to learn how the adult world functions, the suggestion that the market inherently encourages morality may seem absurd on its face.

But to walk through the theoretical basis for this intuitive perception, it is worth examining the two most common foundations of business ethics: utilitarianism and deontology. The first principle of utilitarianism, as developed by Bentham ([1789] 1996) and Mill ([1868] 2002), is that policies must be based on what will produce "the greatest good for the greatest number." One look at any normal business, which—without any illegal behavior, but simply in the normal course of doing what it is supposed to do—seeks to maximize the wealth of its owners and upper management while paying as little as needed to everyone else, shows that no business in America can pass this most basic test of utilitarian ethics.

Any number of hypotheticals immediately clarify the impossibility of applying utilitarianism to business practice. Imagine that the employees who manufacture Nike sneakers asked to be paid the retail value of at least one pair of sneakers per day—a rate that would still leave the company comfortably profitable but would vastly increase wages. Alternatively, think of any of the decisions that employees might make in a worker-owned company, where they are dedicated to the business's financial viability but are otherwise interested in sharing the wealth. Suppose, for example, that employees in a privately held company proposed that all profits be divided in four, with equal quarters going to the owners, community organizations, consumer rebates, and a fund for increased vacation time so employees can spend more time with their families. This would unquestionably be a superior choice in terms of utilitarian ethics. And it would unquestionably be rejected out of hand by every company in America—most likely with whomever suggested it being tagged a troublemaker and marked for increased surveillance, if not immediate termination. No business in America can meet the most simple test of utilitarianism. It is no wonder, then, that the authors of a recent compendium on HR ethics concede that "these [utilitarian] approaches have been less useful in HRM" (Winstanley and Woodall 2000:12).

The second most commonly articulated basis for ethics is deontology, or ethics that springs from one's duty to treat others correctly. Whether articulated by Kant, Rawls, or Jesus, deontological ethics boils down to the Golden Rule of treating others as one would choose to be treated. It is immediately obvious that business fails to meet this standard. By and large, few employees would choose to be treated as they are. Everyone would prefer a bigger share of the profits and greater control over the work process (hence the ubiquitous late-night infomercials hawking the allure of self-employment). And virtually no managers would choose to be treated the same as those working under them; on the contrary, the purpose of moving up to management is, in part, to escape the condition of being bossed around and underpaid. If we consider the Kantian version of deontological ethics, Kant's "categorical imperative" requires that we treat others as ends rather than means, in part by appealing to them on the basis of reason rather than coercion. As MacIntyre explains, "in offering [another person] reasons I offer him an impersonal consideration for him to evaluate. . . . By contrast an attempt at non-rational persuasion embodies an attempt to make the agent a mere instrument of my will, without any regard for his rationality" (1984:46). But no business functions this way. At the heart of every capitalist employment relationship is the employer's coercive power to fire, demote, or discipline employees. Whatever carrots may also be offered, no employer operates without this stick. Thus, again, there is no American business that can meet this first, most basic test of Kantian ethics.

At the broadest level, the ethical nature of business seems painfully simple to grasp. Is there anyone who believes that if Jesus, Buddha, Mohammed, or Moses returned to earth and saw Safeway CEO Steve Burd making $5 million in stock options in the same year he forced healthcare cuts on tens of thousands of employees—or saw the richest 1% of Americans growing dramatically richer over the past decade while the number of uninsured, pensionless, and contingent workers reached record heights—that he would say, "Yes, this is how I intended it to be" (California Congressman Challenges Safeway's Claims, 2003)? If our society is judged by how we treat the least among us, can anyone think corporate America would be judged positively? Reasonable people may debate ad infinitum whether the capitalist employment system is necessary for material progress. But even being necessary does not make something ethical.

It is, of course, difficult to translate broad religious or philosophical principles into concrete policies for the modern workplace—particularly since Plato and Aristotle, the Bible and the Talmud all contain multiple and conflicting edicts. But without getting too sophisticated about things, we might focus on just the simplest of principles that may be assumed to derive from these sources. Most ethicists, for instance, believe that it is obligatory to pay employees justly. It is difficult to settle on a specific definition of "just pay." However, it is not that hard to identify a minimal standard. Conservative Christian ethicist Larry Burkett deems that "a Christian employer has a responsibility to meet the minimum needs of the employees" (1998:160). How does one calculate such a standard? Burkett reasonably explains that "one of the most helpful ways I have found to determine other people's minimum needs is simply to put myself in their position and see if I could live on what they are earning" (1998:161). He then concedes that "if employers would do this with their employees (and be honest about it), most would have to admit they aren't paying a fair wage" (1998:161). As economists across the country have used a version of this same methodology to calculate "living wage" levels, it has become painfully clear just how right Burkett is. Furthermore, not only do many businesses fail to meet this minimal standard of workplace ethics, but much of the business community has lined up to lobby *against* the adoption of living wage standards. The U.S. Chamber of Commerce, for instance, has worked to oppose the living wage movement ("U.S. Chamber Challenges 'Living Wage' Law" 2002). Thus, again, even at the most basic level, business appears to fail the test of the Golden Rule. It seems self-evident that, whatever else it may be, business is not an enterprise driven by ethical principles. Business exists to make money—hopefully within the confines of the law but otherwise unrestricted by any outside philosophy.

It is critical to note that, if business is an "ethics-free zone," it is not due to the moral failings of individual managers. The same people who fire union activists and raid employee pension funds to enrich already-wealthy shareholders may be model ethical actors in other areas of their lives. But their noble acts as parents, neighbors, or soup-kitchen volunteers do not carry over into their roles as managers, precisely because in the volunteer realm they are acting as individuals and in the work realm they are embedded in a coercive corporate organization in which thinking for yourself can get you fired. The absence of ethics in HR practice is not a personal failure; it is a systemic failure. This is why ethical appeals to individual managers have no traction; they are based on a fundamental misunderstanding regarding what kind of problem this is.

"Contested Exchange": Why Employment Ethics Remains Marginal to Business

Why is business such an ethics-unfriendly environment? The most obvious barrier to ethical behavior in business is simply the drive to maximize profits in the hands of shareholders. Since many of the most important ethical edicts involve a more equal sharing of the wealth, there is a simple conflict of interest between this ethical impulse and the imperative for shareholder return. But beyond the straightforward financial conflict, there is still a wide range of employment practices that might be conducted in a more ethical manner. Even if the division of wages, salaries, and profits was to remain as is, management could make the workplace less authoritarian and more inclusive. Why do pleas for movement in this direction so often fall on deaf ears?

To answer this question we must understand the very thing that euphemistic talk about "associates" and "teams" serves to obscure: the fundamentally coercive power relations that lie at the heart of capitalist employment. As discussed by Bowles and Gintis (1990), the fact of human consciousness makes labor unlike any other factor of production. If a steel mill buys 100 tons of ore, it gets exactly what it paid for. But if the same mill hires a worker to work for 100 hours, it's not clear exactly what it has bought. Employees may work faster or slower, seeking to maximize production or maximize rest time. They may take the initiative to point out defects or may let them slide, may encourage co-workers to speed up or slow down, may be friendly or surly, may solidify support for management or foster rebellion against the boss. In the neoclassical model of economic behavior, rational actors always seek to maximize their personal utility. To the extent that this is accurate, employees can be expected to generally work the minimum amount necessary to keep their jobs, preserving as much as possible of their health, strength, energy, and time for more freely chosen pursuits.

This fundamental conflict of interest is what makes employment relations into what Bowles and Gintis (1990) term a "contested exchange." Obviously, it is the threat of firing that ultimately undergirds managerial control. Termination is to the firm what imprisonment is to the state: the ultimate enforcement mechanism, rarely invoked, but without which the whole system crumbles. But the threat of termination is not enough by itself. If fast-food servers are to project friendliness, if telephone support staff are to promote upgrades, and if production workers are to reach their quotas, management must have a sophisticated system of surveillance and control. In early industrial production, Taylorism sought to solve this problem by prescribing the exact physical movements required of workers. For most of the current economy, this solution no longer works. Particularly in the service sector, maximum production requires controlling what is in employees' hearts and minds as well as what they do with their hands. As Edwards notes, the highest and most ambitious form of management control is fostering the "internalization of the enterprise's goals and values"—so that workers become self-driven and self-policing (1976:58). The variety of employee participation schemes that stem from this goal may look like ethical practices, and they may even be described in those terms by upper management. However, scholars who take such pronouncements at face value and seek to extend this logic to broader forms of power sharing or workplace democracy find their fantasies quickly crushed. Because no matter what elevated language may be used to describe employee participation programs, they remain first and foremost mechanisms of control (Slaughter and Parker 1994). As Claydon notes, even in "high performance" organizations, "the fact that management needs to be able to control and dispose of labor as if it were a commodified object while at the same time requiring the active cooperation of workers as willing subjects creates a contradiction at the heart of the employment relationship" (2000:208).

In this context, it is not surprising to discover that even those firms celebrated for one or another supposedly progressive HR practice are elsewhere revealed to be callously impoverishing their employees. Among the companies trumpeted as models in *The War for Talent* (Michaels, Handfield-Jones, and Axelrod 2001:49), for instance, is Enron, whose commitment to hiring and retaining the best apparently did not prevent it from knowingly destroying their retirement savings while a handful of top managers made out like bandits. IBM, a firm often touted as a model employer, similarly engaged in a wholesale raid on the pension holdings of its most loyal and veteran employees ("Sanders Hails Federal Court Ruling" 2003). So too is Jack Welch— whose penchant for mass layoffs earned him the nickname "Neutron Jack" hailed in *The HR Scorecard* (Becker, Huselid, and Ulrich 2001:175) as a visionary proponent of strategic HR. Finally, even Wal-Mart, a company notorious for, among other things, sex and race discrimination, stealing employees' overtime wages, and vicious anti-unionism, apparently treats some of its professional staff well enough to land it more than once, most recently in 2002, on *Fortune Magazine*'s list of The 100 Best Companies to Work For (Great Place to Work Institute 2002).

Wishfully thinking HR ethicists may focus on the one corporate policy that appears to be driven by ethical concerns and then find themselves confused by what seems to be contradictory behavior. In fact, there is no contradiction, because even the "model" policies should not be read as evidence of a general orientation toward ethical treatment of workers; they are simply a sign that in that one particular function, management has found it effective to adopt this practice as a means of motivating workers. From a management point of view, there is no contradiction between, for example, holding participatory "town meetings" and firing union supporters. Again, this is not a critique of particularly unscrupulous managers. This is what *normal* managers are *supposed* to do in the course of running a normal business. Thus the oft-repeated call to "banish fear from the workplace" (see, among others, Clark and Lattal 1993:106) is literally impossible; it would collapse the capitalist firm.

The Distorted Ethics of Management-Friendly HR

Because this literature is implicitly restricted to practices that are consonant with maximizing profits, "HR ethics" has become distorted, producing a host of analyses that seem eccentrically one-sided. From a disinterested viewpoint, for instance, one might think that a discussion of whistleblowing would revolve around how strong the guarantees need to be to enable employees to notify government regulators about corporate misdeeds. Instead, the literature assumes that whistleblowing must be limited to protect damage to the corporation and then probes the circumstances under which it should be allowed. Thus, in a review of HR textbooks, Ciulla (1999:271) finds that eight of the nine texts that address the ethics of whistleblowing do so under the category of "loyalty." Lewis similarly frames a chapter around the question "Is whistleblowing ethical?" (2000:268). He notes that the "conventional" view sees whistleblowers as "troublemakers who deserve to be punished for disloyalty" (Lewis 2000:269) and stresses the importance of complaints being raised internally to one's supervisors rather than shared with the outside public. Ultimately, he breaks with the conventional view but only for cases in which whistleblowing may actually serve the company's long-term interests by leading management to address mistakes early and avoid messier problems down the road.

Similarly, Taylor and Jones's (2000) concept of an "employee charter" plays off an analogy with political citizenship, but it fundamentally distorts the analogy to make the proposal fit with a management perspective. "The stakeholder concept," they explain, "aims to describe and emphasize the reciprocal set of rights and responsibilities that exists between individuals and society. Individuals earn and deserve rights by recognizing their personal responsibility to make appropriate contributions to society" (2000:251). Here, the authors seek to legitimize business practices by suggesting that they are the same as those of any human "society." But in actual political society, "rights" are not earned. The rights of a citizen—to complain, protest, bring suit, and have a say in electing one's rulers—are not a reward for good behavior but are "endowed by the creator" and inalienable. This fundamental basis of democracy is twisted in order to legitimize the functioning of actual HR regimes. Both these cases point to an endemic problem in the literature: an eccentrically pro-management orientation has come to dominate ethics discussions to the point of deforming basic ethical concepts in order to avoid challenging the profit motive.

Anachronistic Ethics

In part, ethicists legitimize business mores by drawing on moral categories that predate industrial capitalism. In many cases, scholars promote biblical, Greek, or other ancient sources for lessons about how people should treat each other in personal relationships, then seek to apply these lessons to 21st-century workplaces. While there are many realms of life in which ancient wisdom has much to teach us, it is simply anachronistic to apply economic ideas from that time to ours. As Polanyi (1947, 1968) has shown, while trade, employment, and exploitation have existed for thousands of years, the specific form of capitalist firms—with monopoly control of the means of production and a ceaseless quest for ever-growing profits—is qualitatively different from what came before it. In this sense, it is ironic that MacIntyre's work (1984) is so often invoked as the foundation for a form of HR ethics ("virtue ethics"). MacIntyre's own argument was not that Aristotelian ethics should be applied to contemporary life but the contrary: that virtues are meaningful only in the context of the social order that created them. To pick an assortment of virtues from other times and cultures and apply them in our own is to create an incoherent and unsustainable code of conduct.

This, ultimately, is one of the reasons why the field of "HR ethics" is so marginal and lifeless: it offers an imagined terrain that is systematically disconnected from the reality of workplace relations. Thus, Lewis, for example, invokes "the common law implied duty of fidelity"

(2000:270) as grounds for limiting whistleblower protections. But common law fidelity sprang from the economy of feudalism, in which lord and serf were each bound by a set of reciprocal, if highly unequal, obligations. All of this is changed in a system where the means of production are monopolized by a few and in which firms recognize no obligation whatsoever to employees except for employing them to the extent that they contribute to profit maximization. In the context of capitalist employment it is anachronistic—and nonsensical—to talk of a virtue of "fidelity."

On the other side, Winstanley and Woodall complain that the potential for communitarian or partnership ethics in the workplace may be limited by "greedy employers" (2000:15). Again, while it may have made sense to characterize an Athenian merchant as "greedy," it makes no sense in the contemporary context. In capitalist economies, greed is not an ethical failure. Greedy is what companies are *supposed* to be, and greed is what management is supposed to pursue.

Ethics of Free Individuals Versus Ethics Under Coercion

The single most important anachronism in the literature of HR ethics is the assumption that workplace relations can be modeled on relationships between two free and independent actors. As Duska notes, American HR theorists predominantly view employment as "a contractual relationship of two self-sufficient individuals, agreeing to engage in commerce with one another" (1999:262). Indeed, this view fits with the classic articulation of neoclassical economics, which treats all acts of economic exchange as originating in the free choice of independent individuals (see, for example, Menger, 1981:175–90). While many ethicists doubtless recognize that the workplace involves an imbalance of power relations, much of ethical theory is nevertheless implicitly premised on the assumption that employment is a freely chosen exchange.

Take as one example Dubinsky's explanation for the function of workplace rules:

> Every group of human beings sets rules for how its members ought to behave. . . . Individuals are expected to learn what is required of them . . . and to bring their own conduct into line with these minimum expectations. The setting of conduct rules by groups occurs in families, communities, civic organizations, social clubs, schools, and, of course, business organizations (1999:386).

By grouping the workplace with a host of organic or voluntary organizations, this analysis sets up the "ethical" discussion as "What should happen to people who don't follow the rules?" While this may be appropriate for children or for freely chosen social clubs, the same question becomes divorced from reality when applied to a workplace where rules are not chosen but imposed, and where the central dynamic holding the organization together is not love or affiliation but coercion and threat of impoverishment. On this distorted basis, Dubinsky goes on to articulate an obnoxious psychologization of worker resistance, explaining that "just as groups feel a need to set rules . . . so do some individuals feel a need to rebel against those rules. . . . There will always be rule followers, rule breakers, and those who delight in testing the limits" (1999:386). By taking ethics that may be appropriate for voluntary organizations and misapplying them to a fundamentally different setting, the author renders them nonsensical.

Burkett (1998:135–6) likewise stresses the importance of workers' honoring authority, obeying orders, and maintaining loyalty to the firm; he recommends that employees be financially rewarded for loyalty (a form of favoritism that others might view as ethically suspect) and fired for disobedience. Indeed, he goes so far as to call for discipline or termination as a response to "subtle disobedience" such as that illustrated by a troublemaking secretary described by one employer:

> When any disciplinary action was taken against any hourly employee for tardiness or absence, this secretary would immediately go to console the person and fill him or her in on what she perceived to be management's blatant violation of the Fair Labor Standards Act governing hourly employees. I found myself defending my decisions at staff meetings for nonexistent abuses (1998:135).

What Burkett has described is the equivalent of a union steward. That such behavior is deemed intolerable by some ethicists reflects the extent to which the field is embedded in a managerial perspective that assumes employment is freely chosen. But in less extreme forms, this problem plagues the field of HR ethics as a whole. Virtually all ethics proposed for the workplace—whether deontological or utilitarian, stakeholder or virtue, discourse or caring—look very different if we assume that the workplace is not a freely chosen relationship between independent individuals but a coercive relationship between those who control the means of production and those who must sell their labor in order to survive.

HR Managers: An Ethically Unfree Audience

Why does the field of HR ethics focus so disproportionately on maxims that fit with profit maximization? I believe that, ultimately, this reflects the reality of HR managers' own position within corporate organizations. Because the HR literature largely speaks to current or prospective HR managers, it must be cast in terms that are realistic to their work environments. And at the core of their reality is the fact that, like all other employees, HR managers will be fired if they act in ways that conflict with the firm's goal of maximizing profits. There is a wide array of ethical choices that HR managers confront at work that fall outside the bounds of profit-maximizing behavior. Ethically sensitive HR managers might, for instance, feel that it is wrong to facilitate strikebreaking or to write memos justifying high executive compensation when rank-and-file health care is being cut. But managers with such beliefs who choose to follow their consciences will soon find themselves on the street. Thus, there is a logical self-censorship at the heart of the HR "ethics" literature, based on understanding the real-world constraints that HR departments operate under. The field known as "HR ethics" can more appropriately be understood as "the ethics of HR management, assuming that HR managers are prohibited from doing anything other than helping management maximize profits."

This reality points to an even more fundamental problem with the field of HR ethics. The literature focuses on ethical choices, but the subjects are people who are not free to make their own ethical choices. But if the system as a whole is corrupt, what is the point or function of writing articles, publishing books, and holding conferences about HR ethics? We would not, presumably, encourage academics to devote energy to the field of the "ethics of dictatorial rule," even though much of the world is ruled by undemocratic regimes. The suggestion that we take seriously the dilemmas of how to ethically dispense justice or levy taxes in a dictatorial state seems oxymoronic at best. At worst, it seems like an attempt to mask the offensiveness of the state structure by focusing on marginal decisions and imbuing the bureaucrats of repression with the air of deep moral thinkers.

New Ethics for a Coerced Workforce

If the field of HR ethics were not artificially bounded by the need to get along with upper management, it would confront much more lively and critical issues. To begin with, we would consider the definition of ethical behavior for employees from a much broader perspective than the themes of loyalty, hard work, and cooperation that dominate management-based ethics. Consider, for instance, the following description of how one group of employees balanced their own goals against those of their employer:

While working as a coil winder in a big transformer factory, we workers faced the dehumanizing "science" known as Minutes Times Motion, which is where a computer estimates how long it should take to complete a task such as building a transformer. Every day, we would check the number and type of transformers built, and at the end of the week we would get a computer-generated analysis of our efficiency rate. If we "beat the clock," we would get a happy face on our evaluation report. A frown face would mean that we were just not up to par, as far as our computer was concerned.

To get a grip on this bad situation, especially in a non-union plant, we required a total conspiracy amongst workers. Starting with the guy I knew the best, we each agreed to slow down production on one of the transformer types. We each handed in approximately the same number of units as our co-workers. After a few frowning faces on our monthly reports and a talking-to by the supervisor, the management had to readjust their computer time accordingly. It makes management look bad to have a product constantly come in under production goals. Adjusting to our new time made them come out around 100 percent again. This victory encouraged other assemblers to do the same, with equally good results.

As we became faster at winding, we would overproduce and thus we would have to store some units in our lockers. We soon saw the wisdom of having a bank of units, in case we didn't want to work as hard one day, or a friend needed one because they messed one up. We earned more free time at work, and were still working at 100 percent, as far as management was concerned (Sprouse 1992:112).

Is this behavior ethical? It certainly violates a number of principles frequently articulated by business ethics theorists. From an alternative viewpoint, however, it is arguable that these employees are doing the morally correct thing. They are conserving their own energy, strength, and safety. They are enriching their lives by winning themselves more free time. And they have created a system of solidarity, where one worker can help out another who may fall behind due to error, illness, or fatigue. They are clearly misleading their superiors, although the evidence suggests that the company remained profitable. Yet in the context of understanding capitalist employment as a coerced exchange—particularly in the context of a Taylorized speedup—it's not clear that these workers "owe" their employer any more than they've given. My point here is not to prove that this behavior is ethically correct—that's a subject that may be open to prolonged debate—but rather to point out that such debate is almost entirely missing from the existing literature on workplace ethics, because it has confined itself to what is acceptable to upper management.

An Irrational Commitment to a Win-Win View of the World

Despite the seemingly clear-cut divide between ethics and the profit motive, the literature on HR ethics remains preoccupied with arguments about how the two coincide. Thus, Sillanpaa and Jackson's review of The Body Shop—one of the foremost champions of progressive employment relations—concludes that

> companies which are run with a view to the long-term inter-
> ests of their key stakeholders are more likely to prosper
> than those which take a short-term "shareholder first"
> approach. . . . Put simply, companies need to listen, to
> process and to respond constructively to the values and
> needs of their stakeholders, most especially their employ-
> ees, customers and investors. Failure to do this will reduce
> long-term commercial viability and increase the risk of cor-
> porate demise (2000:227).

On the other end of the political spectrum, conservative corporate advocate Elaine Sternberg voices a nearly identical argument:

> The business that treats its customers contemptuously, or its
> staff unjustly, or its suppliers dishonestly, will often find
> them hard to retain. In a free market, the most productive
> staff, the finest suppliers and the cheapest and most flexible
> sources of finance can do better than to stay with a business
> that cheats or treats them unfairly. . . . In the long run,
> unethical business is less likely to succeed (2000:19).

It is striking that authors who disagree so broadly on the role of ethics in business nevertheless share this central conviction: that the drive to maximize long-term profits naturally overlaps with the impera-tive to treat employees justly. It is, in fact, more than striking. It is a fact that begs for explanation, because the shared conviction is so palpably at odds with actual evidence from the business world.

For anyone who has lived a little, who has seen a little of tragedy or injustice, the theory seems preposterous. Who can believe that this is the way the world works: that the pursuit of selfish power and gain leads automatically to ethical treatment of others, while those who exploit employees and customers are inevitably driven out of business? Have these ethicists never read the biblical book of Job, a man who bitterly rebukes God for creating a world in which

the wicked live, reach old age, and grow mighty in power. . . .
Their houses are safe from fear. . . . Their bull breeds without
fail; their cow calves. . . . [The wicked man] dies in full prosperity, being wholly at ease and secure, his body full of fat and
the marrow of his bones moist (Job 21:7–24).

Is it really possible that learned scholars believe that someplace in
the world exists a mechanism that naturally aligns greed with good? For
that matter, to take Sternberg's conclusion, do serious students of industrial capitalism really believe that the natural function of a laissez-faire
market is to drive out unethical businesses? Should we expect that the
maquiladoras employing 16-year-old girls kept on a regimen of barbitu-
rates and birth-control pills will be driven out of business by those who
employ higher-wage adults and observe stricter environmental standards? Should we consider it a temporary market irregularity that Wal-
Mart—a company whose employees have filed class-action suits in more
than 30 states charging sex discrimination and theft of overtime wages—
tops the Fortune 500? Or that garment and toy manufacturers who rely
on sweated and child labor around the world are turning handsome profits? One wonders how to explain why, after 150 years of a market economy, exploitation still appears so common.

In reality, the area of overlap between the profit motive and the ethical treatment of employees seems extremely limited. To begin with,
much of the literature really applies only to professional and managerial
employees. Tracts such as Harvard Business School's *The War for Talent*
(Michaels, Handfield-Jones, and Axelrod 2001), warning of the competitive imperative to retain valued employees, are not much concerned with
the two thirds of Americans in jobs that do not require a college degree.
Indeed, there is great evidence that even white-collar professionals,
rather than being wooed with perks and participation, are seeing their
benefits cut and hours increased, on the assumption that they have no
choice but to run faster to stay in place (see, for example, Fraser 2002).
But to whatever extent the logic of profit maximization leads to careful
treatment of professional employees, this logic is largely absent for those
further down the food chain. It is not hard to imagine, for instance, that
Nike could be a great place to work for Portland-area marketing professionals and a hellish place to work for Malaysian production staff.

It is doubtless true that, even for nonprofessional employees, there
are certain occupations in which owners' interests are served by treating
employees well. But the dominant trend in the country is in the opposite
direction—toward lower real wages, continuing cuts in benefits, and a
weaker voice for workers on the job. And when hard work can be
extracted through fear, discipline, Taylorization, or surveillance, there is

no economic need for ethics. Thus the theory put forth by so many business ethicists is not utterly false, but it describes only a small slice of the business world.

The True Focus of HR Ethicists: Convincing Managers That Ethical Actions Will Prove Profitable

If so-called ethical actions are in the long-term selfish interest of shareholders, they will be carried out by any smart business, without need for ethical ruminations. What, then, is the relevant project of HR ethicists? What, in business-speak, is their value added? It appears that the actual goal of most HR ethicists is to *convince* business managers that ethical behaviors may serve their profit motive in ways they have not yet realized. This is the central thrust of article after article: that business executives need a broader and more sophisticated understanding of their self-interest and that business ethicists are the ones to enlighten them.

There are at least two problems with this view. First, it relies on the assumption that academics and consultants know better than CEOs what will maximize long-term profit. While it is certainly true that business owners may be short-sighted or myopic, a general theory of how a free market operates must assume that, for the most part, business managers are correct in their assumptions about which labor practices will yield the greatest profit. The actual record of business successes and failures seems to support this view. Union-busting manufacturers, produce growers exploiting undocumented immigrants, and "all-temp" supermarkets may practice sleazy labor relations, but empirical data suggest that management has correctly identified these as effective profit-maximizing strategies. At the same time, managers are also correct in perceiving that ethical innovations such as guaranteeing a living wage, providing employees with the same quality health insurance as the CEO, and granting employees more power over their conditions of work will limit the return to shareholders. To focus primary attention on the notion that academics understand long-term profit better than business managers is to orient a field of study around the exception rather than the rule. It's a poor framework with which to analyze employment relations.

The second problem with this focus on convincing management of the utility of ethical behavior is that it restricts "HR ethics" to an exceedingly narrow terrain. If we start out viewing all of employment relations as a potential subject for ethical debate, and then constrict our focus to those parts of HR in which ethical behavior overlaps with profit motives, and then narrow our vision even further to those cases in which these two truly do overlap but management doesn't yet realize it, we're left with a tiny slice of the work world for our subject of analysis. Yet this is exactly how many scholars identify their task: as *advocates* to managers, pitching the notion that the scope of profitable ethics is slightly broader than management may perceive.

The limitations to this project are evident in surveys of corporate managers themselves. Both scholars and practitioners of HR generally start from the acknowledgment that HR is of marginal concern to most senior managers. Recently, a number of scholars have attempted to concretize the contribution of HR practices to the bottom line, in hope of transforming HR from an administrative to a strategic function. If ethics truly adds to profitability, this is where we would expect its impact to be revealed. Yet it is striking that, when scholars have calculated the monetary value of HR practices, they have not identified ethical practices as a significant source of untapped profit. One of the most ambitious of such projects is *The HR Scorecard* (Becker, Huselid, Ulrich 2001), which is dedicated to making HR more relevant by identifying measurable "HR deliverables" that impact the return to shareholders. The study is based on a 10-year survey now covering the 3,000 largest publicly traded corporations. Though the authors developed an extensive list of relevant HR strategies, ethics per se is notably absent. Instead, the key practices identified are items such as the number of hours of training for new employees or the share of workers whose pay is tied to performance (2001:16–17). Nowhere in the list is there a single item that explicitly concerns ethical treatment of workers. On the contrary, the share of workers who represent themselves in collective bargaining—from Kant's viewpoint an ethical good—is identified as a negative factor to be avoided by firms bent on establishing "high performance work systems" (2001:18). Upon reflection, one of the striking things about the Becker book is how obvious and commonsense it is. *Of course* it is practices such as recruitment and retention of professionals that matter rather than anything overtly ethical. *Of course* profit-maximizing companies want to deny their employees the leverage that comes from unionization. None of this is surprising. But it points once again to the pervasive marginality of ethical concerns, even among those who champion the importance of HR to overall corporate strategy.

Merely Useless, or Actually Harmful? "Ethics" as a Disguise for Power

Because the field of HR ethics has largely confined itself to the consideration of management-approved practices, it has produced a large volume of vague, convoluted theories that have little grounding in reality. To a large degree, scholars of HR ethics lay out complicated theories but pull back from either endorsing or condemning any particular path of practice. Winstanley and Woodall thus conclude their comprehensive review of the field by noting that "there is no consensus either about what constitutes an appropriate ethical framework or about the possibility for ethical intervention" (2000:278). But if a set of leading scholars in the field can't even agree as to whether ethical intervention is possible, this suggests the field has little relevance to the lived reality of the work world.

For the most part, then, the field of HR ethics seems useless but harmless. In some ways, however, the field may actually prove damaging to the very interests of workers that it purports to safeguard. As I have discussed, the general structure of capitalist employment and the actual practice of most firms are built on a fundamentally coercive relationship. Management's goal is to operate this coercive system without triggering a rebellion from the employees, who vastly outnumber their higher-ups. But from the workers' point of view, some sort of rebellion is exactly what's needed. Even focusing solely on incremental reforms such as more equal sharing of profits and increased worker control over the labor process, these changes are unlikely to come about without collective pressure from angry workers. To the extent that the discourse of "ethics" helps forestall such pressure by defusing workers' anger or organization, it serves to undermine the long-term well-being of the workforce. Claydon (2000) raises the question of why the field of "ethics" has taken on increased prominence in the past decade and concludes that it is in direct proportion to the increase in work intensification and aggressive management. In other words, the world of "ethics" serves as a sort of political cover for more exploitative management.

Indeed, many employee participation schemes represent nothing so much as the co-opting strategies of anti-union consultants described by Levitt (1993) and Slaughter and Parker (1994). For instance, Taylor and Jones trumpet the creation of "employee charters," defined in part by "a notion of partnership and mutuality" that "highlights the shared responsibility the individual and the employer have to the achievement of the organization's aims," along with "a series of rights and responsibilities" that apply to each individual employee (2000:252–4). All of this is worked out in a process of "consultation" that gives everyone the right to speak up but leaves senior management with a free hand to make whatever decisions it chooses. The outcome of such ventures is unsurprising. The authors celebrate one hospital's charter that includes the principles that "staff have the responsibility to adopt an attitude of positive cooperation" as well as "the responsibility to work flexibly" (2000:256). It is telling, of course, that what management seeks is a unilaterally authored "charter" rather than a collectively bargained "contract." In the language of ethics, using community and responsibility as a gloss for increased management control is a bastardization of what the field is supposed to represent. And it's a use of "ethics" that sets workers back rather than advancing their cause.

The Path to a More Ethical Workplace: Advocacy or Agitation?

Beyond the potential use of "ethics" to inappropriately gloss over management control strategies, there is a broader sense in which the discourse may prove harmful. Because so many ethicists have been reduced to seeking to convince business managers that ethical practice serves their long-term interests, they have developed an allegiance to this strategy for workplace improvement, to the exclusion of others. This is the ontological assumption I discussed earlier, which undergirds so much of this field and which implicitly frames the choice of strategies one looks to for reforming current business practice.

I believe the weight of historical evidence is overwhelming that business practice changes not by executives being convinced to voluntarily adopt altruistic policies but only by the collective action of workers and their allies forcing business leaders to change, against their will. This—and not appeals to enlightened self-interest—is how we got the eight-hour day, the minimum wage, and the end of child labor. No amount of clever convincing would have won those gains without tens of thousands of workers engaging in workplace and political agitation.

In this sense, Sternberg's heartless analysis is refreshingly candid. In the preface to her book, she decries the

> oxymoronic view [which] holds that being ethical in business means replacing the pursuit of owner value with the pursuit of some other end—social welfare, environmental protection or stakeholder interests, for example. Since, however, the essence of business is maximizing owner value by selling goods or services, this view of business ethics is literally absurd: it makes refraining from business the condition of being ethical in business (2000:x).

Here Sternberg is almost right, but her analysis needs to be stood on its head. "Business ethics" is oxymoronic because—since the telos of business is, indeed, to maximize owners' return—there's no way for it to be "ethical" according to any moral criteria other than its own will to power. If workplace conditions are to be improved, workers must be clear that these changes will come only from their own actions and not through the enlightenment of a benevolent employer. To focus on the project of convincing management to be more moral is to mistake the nature of the firm and to encourage workers to place false hope in a process that we know cannot deliver.

Yet this is exactly what numerous scholars are up to. For many, the goal of getting management to "talk ethics" is an end in itself. "The language of management has illegitimized even the mention of words such as ethics and morality in the cult of business," declare Winstanley and Woodall, "and we hope to get these words at least acknowledged as worthy of debate and inclusion in the management vocabulary" (2000:19). They conceive of the project of workplace ethics at its core as one of advocacy to management. When presented with arguments suggesting that there's little room for truly ethical behavior in profit-maximizing companies, they insist that this view must be rejected because it leaves no room for advocacy. "The problem with this argument," they assert, "is that such pessimism leads to fatalism—the scope for ethical advocacy is limited and nothing can be done anyway. Taken to its logical conclusion it ultimately implies that the practice and the study of HRM *is* a waste of time" (2000:279). In fact, the study of HR ethics is largely a waste of time. But the fact that ethical advocacy is a futile project does not mean that "nothing can be done." What can be done is what has always been done—employees organizing workplace and/or political power in order to enact their vision of ethics. This is how we got the right to organize, restrictions on sex and race discrimination, health and safety protections, and the weekend. To conclude that the only way forward must be through appealing to the good intentions of private managers is to ignore the history of almost every advance won by American workers.

In its worst form, the advocacy of "ethics" is promoted specifically as an alternative to political or workplace pressure. Thus, for instance, Liff and Dickens (2000) warn against attempting to force changes on business—whether through governmental regulations or union contracts—because this reinforces the old, supposedly false, dichotomies between ethical behavior and selfish interest. "Consumer boycotts, or ethical investment, and trade union action" are a concern, they warn, because "if they operate in an environment where a social justice/business split in motivations for action is the dominant discourse they risk reinforcing such thinking rather than challenging it" (2000:96).

Winstanley and Woodall similarly conclude that seeking to change business practice through legislation is dangerous since "by itself the law does not change attitudes and does not always promote awareness" (2000:282). But this is putting the cart before the horse. The ultimate goal is to change not employers' attitudes but their behavior. Here, these scholars are actively arguing against pressure tactics. Instead of being confrontational and assuming business must be forced to change, they urge employees to restrict their efforts to the cooperative and educational, hoping to convince management to see workers' interests as part of their own full measure. I believe this argument is based on a naïve and dangerous view of business management. The history of employment reforms over the past 150 years of industrial capitalism offers very little hope for management "education" outside the context of external pressures. On the contrary, it appears that it is only after union struggles are won, or after progressive legislation is passed, that management attitudes come around to accept the new logic. The lesson of history is the opposite of that put forth by ethicists: nothing educates a boss like a strike or a lawsuit.

There is no need for workplace ethics to be a marginal and lifeless field of inquiry. But to make it realistic and compelling, scholars must speak less to managers and more to workers, and they must be willing to counsel resistance as well as cooperation. Of course, there is a long tradition of critical theorists, Marxists, and IR scholars who have approached workplace ethics in just such terms, but these voices have been in the minority. I believe it is now time for the majority to take up this framework. If workplace ethics are to be relevant to the real world, they must break out of the constraints of profit maximization and be willing to challenge the prerogatives of upper management. And if ethicists are to truly support the workers whose welfare they seek to safeguard, they must be willing to promote rebellion and confrontation for all the places where education and advocacy fall short.

References

Adams, Roy J. 2001. "Choice or Voice? Rethinking American Labor Policy in Light of the International Human Rights Consensus." *Employee Rights and Employment Policy Journal*, Vol. 5, no. 2, pp. 521–48.

Becker, Brian E., Mark A. Huselid, and Dave Ulrich. 2001. *The HR Scorecard*. Cambridge, MA: Harvard Business School Press.

Bentham, Jeremy. [1789]. 1996. *An Introduction to the Principles of Morals and Legislation*. Oxford: Oxford University Press.

Bowles, Samuel, and Herbert Gintis. 1990. "Contested Exchange: New Microfoundations for the Political Economy of Capitalism." *Politics and Society*, Vol. 18, no. 2, pp. 165–222.

Burkett, Larry. 1998. *Business by The Book: The Complete Guide of Biblical Principles for the Workplace*. Nashville: Thomas Nelson.

"California Congressman Challenges Safeway's Claims on Health Care." 2003. Press release, United Food and Commercial Workers, December 4. <www.ufcw.org/workplace_connections/retail/industry_news/burd_stocksale.cfm> [March 12, 2005.]

Ciulla, Joanne B. 1999. "Business Ethics and Work: Questions for the Twenty-First Century." In Robert E. Frederick, ed., *A Companion to Business Ethics*. Malden, MA: Blackwell, pp. 269–79.

Clark, Ralph W., and Alice Darnell Lattal. 1993. *Workplace Ethics: Winning the Integrity Revolution.* Savage, MD: Rowman & Littlefield.

Claydon, Tim. 2000. "Employee Participation and Involvement." In Diana Winstanley and Jean Woodall, eds., *Ethical Issues in Contemporary Human Resource Management.* New York: Palgrave Macmillan, pp. 208–23.

Compa, Lance. 2000. *Unfair Advantage: Workers' Freedom of Association in the United States Under International Human Rights Standards.* New York: Human Rights Watch.

Conference Board. 2004. "Comparison Data: The Conference Board Business Ethics Conference, 2002 and 2003." The Conference Board Ethical Leadership Group. <www.conference-board.org.> [May 10, 2004.]

Dubinsky, Joan Elise. 1999. "Investigations and Due Process." In Robert E. Frederick, ed., *A Companion to Business Ethics.* Malden, MA: Blackwell, pp. 386–98.

Duska, Ronald. 1999. "Employee Rights." In Robert E. Frederick, ed., *A Companion to Business Ethics.* Malden, MA: Blackwell, pp. 257–68.

Edwards, Richard C. 1976. "Individual Traits and Organizational Incentives: What Makes a 'Good' Worker?" *Journal of Human Resources,* Vol. 11, no. 1, pp. 51–68.

Fraser, Jill Andresky. 2002. *White Collar Sweatshop: The Deterioration of Work and Its Reward in Corporate America.* New York: Norton.

Great Place to Work Institute. 2002. *100 Best Companies to Work for in America.* <www.greatplacetowork.com>. [May 10, 2004.]

Levitt, Martin Jay. 1993. *Confessions of a Union Buster.* New York: Crown.

Lewis, David. 2000. "Whistleblowing." In Diana Winstanley and Jean Woodall, eds., *Ethical Issues in Contemporary Human Resource Management.* New York: Palgrave Macmillan, pp. 267–77.

Liff, Sonia, and Linda Dickens. 2000. "Ethics and Equality: Reconciling False Dilemmas." In Diana Winstanley and Jean Woodall, eds., *Ethical Issues in Contemporary Human Resource Management.* New York: Palgrave Macmillan, pp. 85–101.

MacIntyre, Alasdair. 1984. *After Virtue: A Study in Moral Theory,* 2nd ed. South Bend, IN: University of Notre Dame Press.

Menger, Carl. 1981. *Principles of Economics,* New York: New York University Press.

Michaels, Ed, Helen Handfield-Jones, and Beth Axelrod. 2001. *The War for Talent.* Boston: Harvard Business School Press.

Mill, John Stuart. [1868]. 2002. *Utilitarianism.* New York: Hackett.

Polanyi, Karl. 1947. *The Great Transformation: The Political and Economic Origins of Our Time.* Boston: Beacon Press.

_____. 1968. *Primitive, Archaic, and Modern Economies.* Boston: Beacon Press.

"Sanders Hails Federal Court Ruling that IBM Cash Balance Plan Is Age Discriminatory." 2003. Press release, Office of Congressman Bernie Sanders, July 31. <bernie.house.gov/documents/releases/20030731180235.asp> [May 10, 2004.]

Sillanpaa, Maria, and Charles Jackson. 2000. "Conducting a Social Audit: Lessons from The Body Shop Experience." In Diana Winstanley and Jean Woodall, eds., *Ethical Issues in Contemporary Human Resource Management.* New York: Palgrave Macmillan, pp. 227–49.

Slaughter, Jane, and Mike Parker. 1994. *Working Smart: A Union Guide to Participation Programs and Reengineering.* Detroit: Labor Notes.

Sprouse, Martin, ed. 1992. *Sabotage in the American Workplace: Anecdotes of Dissatisfaction, Mischief and Revenge.* San Francisco: Pressure Drop Press.

Sternberg, Elaine. 2000. *Just Business: Business Ethics in Action,* 2nd ed. New York: Oxford University Press.

Taylor, Paul, and Peter Jones. 2000. "Staff Charters: a Framework for Employers and Their Staff." In Diana Winstanley and Jean Woodall, eds., *Ethical Issues in Contemporary Human Resource Management*. New York, Palgrave Macmillan, pp. 250–66.

"U.S. Chamber Challenges 'Living Wage' Law Amicus Brief Filed in New Orleans." 2002. Press release, U.S. Chamber of Commerce, April 25 <www.uschamber.com/press/releases/2002/april/02-80.htm>. [May 10, 2004.]

Winstanley, Diana, and Jean Woodall, eds. 2000. *Ethical Issues in Contemporary Human Resource Management*. New York: Palgrave Macmillan.

ABOUT THE CONTRIBUTORS

Jonathan E. Booth is a Ph.D. candidate in human resources and industrial relations at the Industrial Relations Center in the University of Minnesota's Carlson School of Management. His research interests are in the areas of labor relations and organizational behavior. Prior to pursuing his Ph.D., he was for several years a consultant in information technology, customer relationship management, change management, and training development with firms such as AT&T, Halliburton, Ingersoll-Rand, Intel, Marriott International, and webMethods. He has a B.S. in business administration from Georgetown University.

Norman E. Bowie is the Elmer Andersen Chair in Corporate Responsibility at the University of Minnesota. He has published 15 books and more than 75 articles. His most recent book is *Management Ethics*. His co-edited text *Ethical Theory and Business* is in the seventh edition. He has held an endowed chair at the London Business School and has been a fellow at Harvard's Program in Ethics and the Professions. He is past president of the Society for Business Ethics and the American Society for Value Inquiry and is past executive director of the American Philosophical Association. He is currently a member of the Business Roundtable Institute for Corporate Ethics.

John W. Budd is a professor in the Industrial Relations Center at the University of Minnesota's Carlson School of Management, where he holds an Industrial Relations Landgrant Professorship. He is the author of *Employment with a Human Face: Balancing Efficiency, Equity, and Voice* (Cornell University Press, 2004) and *Labor Relations: Striking a Balance* (McGraw-Hill/Irwin, 2005). He has received Excellence in Education and Outstanding Young Scholar awards from the Industrial Relations Research Association. He is also director of graduate studies for the University of Minnesota's M.A. and Ph.D. programs in human resources and industrial relations.

John T. Delaney is associate dean for MBA programs and professor of management in the Eli Broad College of Business at Michigan State University. He has also been a faculty member at the University of Iowa and Columbia University. He received a B.S. degree from LeMoyne College and A.M. and Ph.D. degrees from the University of Illinois. He has written extensively about labor relations, negotiation, dispute resolution,

299

and ethical issues in the private and public sectors. He was co-editor (with Paul Clark and Ann Frost) of the 2002 IRRA research volume, *Collective Bargaining in the Private Sector.*

Linda Ewing is the research director of the UAW. She and the research staff provide technical support for collective bargaining as well as industry and policy analysis intended to help build the union and improve the lives of working people.

Ronald S. Heinz is vice president, compensation and benefits, at Allina Hospitals and Clinics, a healthcare system of 22,000 employees operating in Minnesota and western Wisconsin, and is responsible for all compensation and benefit program design. He holds a B.A. in psychology from the University of Minnesota-Duluth and an M.A. in industrial relations from the University of Minnesota. Prior to joining Allina in 2000, he worked for Honeywell for 25 years in a wide variety of businesses and human resources leadership positions.

Michael W. Howe is executive vice president of human resources and chief talent officer at Allina Hospitals and Clinics, a healthcare system of 22,000 employees operating in Minnesota and western Wisconsin. Since 1981, he has served as an officer at Allina and its predecessor organizations. His human resources career began in employee assistance at Xcel Energy, and prior to that he was an assistant professor at the University of Minnesota. He earned a bachelor's degree in psychology from Mankato State College and an A.M. and Ph.D. from the University of Chicago.

Bruce E. Kaufman is professor of economics in the Andrew Young School of Policy Studies and senior associate of the W. T. Beebe Institute of Personnel and Employment Relations at Georgia State University. He is editor or co-editor of three previous LERA (IRRA) research volumes—*Employee Representation: Alternatives and Future Directions* (1993); *Government Regulation of the Employment Relationship* (1997); and *Theoretical Perspectives on Work and the Employment Relationship* (2004). His most recent book is *The Global Evolution of Industrial Relations: Events, Ideas and the IIRA* (2004).

Gordon Lafer is an associate professor at the University of Oregon's Labor Education and Research Center and is author of *The Job Training Charade* (Cornell University Press, 2002). He has served as an employment policy advisor in the New York City mayor's office and as a strategic consultant to a wide range of labor unions.

John J. Lawler is a professor of labor and industrial relations at the University of Illinois at Urbana-Champaign. His research interests in recent years have focused on human resource management policies and practices, particularly in companies operating in East and Southeast Asia. He has recent publications in the *Academy of Management Journal*, *Industrial Relations*, the *Journal of Applied Psychology*, and the *International Journal of Human Resource Management* dealing with international HR and IR topics. He has had several teaching assignments in Asia and serves on the editorial board of the *International Journal of Human Resource Management*.

Richard S. Rosenberg is a professor emeritus in the Department of Computer Science at the University of British Columbia. His research interests are the social impact of computers and artificial intelligence (AI). He has written many papers on computational linguistics, intellectual property rights, freedom of expression and speech, ethics, and privacy issues and has appeared before federal parliamentary and provincial legislative committees. His most recent book is *The Social Impact of Computers* (Elsevier, 2004). He is also a vice president of Electric Frontier Canada and on the Board of the British Columbia Freedom of Information and Privacy Association.

Elizabeth D. Scott is an associate professor at Eastern Connecticut State University. Her research focuses on dishonesty, moral values, and prejudice. She has more than 10 years of professional HR experience with various Georgia state agencies, an undergraduate degree from Brown University, an MBA in industrial relations from Georgia State, and a Ph.D. from the Wharton School at the University of Pennsylvania. She previously was an assistant professor at Penn State in the Department of Labor Studies, where she developed a course on ethical HR.

James G. Scoville is professor of human resources and industrial relations at the University of Minnesota. He received an A.B. from Oberlin College and A.M. and Ph.D. degrees from Harvard University, all in economics. He is the author of numerous articles and books on subjects ranging from job design to the economics of caste, from child labor to the theory of the labor movement. He was president of the international section of the IRRA in 1999–2000.

Hoyt N. Wheeler is professor of management and Business Partnership Foundation Fellow, Moore School of Business, University of South Carolina. He holds the degrees of B.A. *cum laude* from Marshall University, J.D. from the University of Virginia, and Ph.D. from the University of Wisconsin (industrial relations). He has taught at the University of Wyoming; the University of Minnesota; the University of Paris I, Sorbonne; and the University of Paris II, Panthéon-Assas. His publications include *The Future of the American Labor Movement* (Cambridge

University Press, 2002) and *Workplace Justice Without Unions* (co-author; W. E. Upjohn Institute for Employment Research, 2004).

Xiang Yi is an assistant professor at Western Illinois University. She earned a bachelor's degree in economics from Peking University in China and a Ph.D. in human resources from the Institute of Labor and Industrial Relations at the University of Illinois at Urbana-Champaign, in 2002. Her research interests include cross-cultural analyses of human resource practices, leadership, organizational socialization, change management, organizations in transition economies, and creativity.

INDEX